VENICE
La Laguna
TORCELLO
BURANO
MURANO
S.ERASMO
Canal Grande
S.G.dei GRECI
S.MARCO
ARSENAL
CASTLE
Porto di Lido
Canal della Giudecca
GIUDECCA

CANDIA
M.t IDA
RUINS OF KNOSSOS
S.DIMITRO
ARSENAL
OLD TOWN
S.PEDRO
Moat

Vienna
Buda
Pest
HUNGARY
Drava R.
Mohács
CROATIA
TRANSYLVANIA
MOLDAVIA
Sucevita
CARPATHIANS
WALLACHIA
Danube
CRIMEA
CAUCASUS
BLACK SEA
Trapezunt
OTTOMAN EMPIRE
Belgrade
Smederevo
Morava
Manasya
SERBIA
Studenica
Niš
BALKAN RA.
DINARIC ALPS
DALMATIA
Spalato
Milesevo
Sopoćani
Peć
Gracanica
Decani
Sophia
BULGARIA
Adrianople
Constantinople
Nicaea
Brussa
Angora
Kayseri
Erjias
Tel Keuy
to Ani 150 mi.
to L.Van & Achtamar 100 mi.
Euphrates
Ragusa
Scutari
Andrejas
Neresi
Ochrid
L.Ochrid
L.Prespa
Kurbinovo
Florina
Kastoria
Verria
Siatista
Scupi
Vardar
MACEDONIA
Rila
RHODOPE M.TS
Athos
Thessalonika
Troy
ADRIATIC SEA
GREECE
PINDUS
Corfu
(to Venice)
Lepanto
Athens
Mycaene
Sparta
Mistra
Cephalonia
Cythera
Smyrna
Konya
TAURUS
St.Simeon
Aleppo
Antioch
RHODES
CYPRUS
Krak de Chevaliers
Beirut
Damascus
LEBANON
Khania
CANDIA
CRETE
(to Venice)
Ionian Sea
Ramla
Jerusalem
Dead Sea
Cyrene
CYRENAICA
Alexandria
EGYPT
Cairo
Suez
Fayum
Nile
M.t Sinai
Aswan is 400 miles up the Nile
Ragusa
Messina
15°
20°
25°
30°
35°
40°
45°
50°

EL GRECO REVISITED

CANDIA · VENICE · TOLEDO

BOOKS by PÁL KELEMEN

BATTLEFIELD OF THE GODS
Aspects of Mexican History, Art and Exploration
1937, 1939

MEDIEVAL AMERICAN ART
A Survey in Two Volumes
1943, 1944, 1946

BAROQUE AND ROCOCO IN LATIN AMERICA
1951

MEDIEVAL AMERICAN ART
Masterpieces of the New World, One-Volume Edition
1956

EL GRECO REVISITED

CANDIA · VENICE · TOLEDO

PÁL KELEMEN

THE MACMILLAN COMPANY

NEW YORK 1961

The Macmillan Company, New York
Brett-Macmillan Ltd., Galt, Ontario

Illustrations printed in Italy
Text printed in the United States of America

Library of Congress catalog card number: 61-13343

TO MY WIFE

PREFACE

In the first decade of our century, Europe appeared a civilized continent. In most of the world there was peace, and it seemed as if it would be a lasting condition. Exchanges between countries in science and the humanities were lively. No travel passport was necessary except for Spain and Russia. This was the period in which the idea of this book came first to my mind. Perhaps here some personal history might be in place.

Years before I graduated from Latin School, Impressionist painting had gained a wide following in my native Budapest; also, a considerable number of works by El Greco were accessible. El Greco fascinated and puzzled me. I was drawn to his unconventional color combinations, his unusual composition, and was puzzled by a strange tenseness in his painting. I could not fit him entirely into either the Venetian or the Spanish school. Somewhat later, when I studied the beginnings of Christian art and got away from the routine chapters of art history, my perplexity gradually gave place to understanding. At that time I was writing and translating poetry and had published essays on music, literature, and the arts. One of my favorite pastimes was visiting the Magyar National Museum of Fine Arts, which was then barely a few years old and not only utilized modern exhibition techniques but even was equipped with a type of air conditioning. Though I had my favorite paintings, I made it a habit to walk slowly through the halls of Byzantine and Gothic art and so work my way up to the Italians. I liked to stand before an early panel and look beyond, into another room where the Venetian canvases glowed. I tried to identify them by learning their characteristics through my eye. The guards knew me and let me lean close to observe details. I still recall vividly some of those pictures, their composition and tonality, and I remember too the patterned or plain wall coverings in rooms where I sat long. Going home on the sunny side of a broad avenue, I had the feeling of coming from a banquet.

Scholarly interest and connoisseurship were oriented nearly exclusively toward Western art. The great civilizations of Asia, Africa, and America were little appreciated. Even that vast world, the Levant, where Christ was born and his teaching gained the first followers, was neglected. The biblical lands had belonged for centuries to the Ottoman Empire. They were not easily penetrated, and when explorers were able to visit one or another region they found the Christian monuments in ruins, mosaics and murals damaged or erased. The records of their voyages are mostly without clear illustrations.

PREFACE

The Hungarians do not belong either racially or linguistically to the great European families. The Latin saying *Ex oriente lux* (Light comes from the East) has not lost for them its deeper meaning, while in other countries of the Western world scholarship has overemphasized the arts of Italy and France and isolated itself from those inventive, vigorous, and sophisticated civilizations which gave Europe nearly all its humanistic values. Most of Western Europe has created a history for its self-justification and self-glorification. Faulty to a high degree, it shows now a tarnished glory, and the consequences of its philosophy are erupting in many parts of the globe. If an analogy can be offered, the spreading tree of the humanities has not received perceptive and balanced attention; no honest tree surgeon would treat, even pamper, a few upper branches of an oak without examining the trunk, the roots, and the soil upon which it feeds. Hungarians, being descendants of Mongol tribes, their relatives long submerged in the flood of Asian migration, had a curiosity and a will to understand the cultures of the Levant and even those that lay East of the broad belt of Mohammedanism.

World War I, which many in the Western world had believed impossible, commenced, and by August 1914 I was in uniform and beyond the Carpathian Mountains. There, where the fertile Polish plain meets the foliaged valleys of Moldavia, I saw wooden churches in archaic design, with graceful open towers on their peaked gables. The ominous tolling of their bells started a panic of flight, and people with sleepless eyes—in carriages and peasant carts piled high with bedding, packages, sewing machines, perambulators, bird cages—stared at us who rode in the opposite direction.

Later, under an arbor of shells flying across the Lower Danube, we floated one night in a broad barge to the Serbian shore near the fortress Semendria, built to defend Christianity against the Turks. The sky streaked with flame, the heaving stream, the angular outline of the citadel would have been inspiring to a colorist painter, except that the lethal yellow will-o'-the-wisp flames leaping up, now here, now there on the other shore, meant that villages were burning and that the spectacle was war. The next day we began a long ride south in the valley of the Morava River, where fragrant fruit trees offered their harvest. The onion-domed small churches became familiar—another region of the Orthodox world. Built of carefully laid stones, their sturdy proportions gave them a winning aspect. The few narrow windows kept in perpetual dusk the painted interiors. From the heartland of Macedonia to the Bocche di Cattaro and Dalmatia was a stimulating change. Here the somber modulations of the Slavic hinterland were replaced by the smiling architecture of Italianate cities opening on the Adriatic Sea. Sturdiness was exchanged for subtlety of craftsmanship. The earthen terraces supported by stone walls, built up and repaired through generations, bespoke men who knew how to defend the handfuls of soil perched on the mountainsides not only against the torrential rains but also against the weapons of their enemies. Finally Friaul and the Veneto offered a vast open-air museum of Western art from pagan Roman remains to Rococo villas, their gardens bursting with the impact of spring.

By the end of the year 1918 it became evident that the Golden Age was an illusion—it was the twilight of an irretrievable epoch. Hate, revenge, and ignorance carved up Europe, creating the vacuum into which first Hitler and later Stalin marched. But my lucky star, which had brought me through more than four years of war, was still over me. I could go on studying and traveling. I even visited Spain—then anything but fashionable—more than ten years before their civil war began. With an excitement as for no other journey, I prepared myself. I read everything I could put my hands on about Spanish art, especially El Greco. I learned the language. In manifold ways the Spanish experience was unsurpassed. The king still sat on his throne. In Madrid one Sunday afternoon I stood all alone on the vast square of the Puerta del Sol. It looked as if the city had suddenly died. But it was only a great day for the bullfight. Even all the streetcars were at the arena, out of town. In the sunny city of Seville, beside the splendors of art, we tasted a variety of wines nightly in the bodegas, where cask rested beside cask, decorated with labels that read like romantic poetry. The Granada Palace Hotel in its unsurpassable location was nearly empty; in the mezzanine the faded green tables stood abandoned, and the roulette wheels with which unfortunate Alfonso XIII tried to lure moneyed tourists to the country were still and dusty. Córdoba's more than uncomfortable hotel drove me out into the streets. I found a compensation in the cool interior of the cathedral, once the grand mosque. There I witnessed a great musical High Mass in all its pomp. I was dazzled by the velvets, laces and silks, the silver, gold, and jewels among which the priests moved, somnambulant, unreal as oversized wax effigies. In the streets was dismal poverty and in the houses utter squalor.

Not much later, in the Dolomites, on a trip which was planned to bring me once more to Venice, I met an American girl living in Europe with her parents to study music. We were married in Florence and took up residence there—a fitting vantage point from which to observe how from Byzantine, Romanesque, and regional elements, Western Europe created—late—its national styles. Here I began writing a study of El Greco that had been occupying me for some time. However, a number of other books were to precede it.

In October 1932 we came to the United States for what was planned to be a six months' visit. After weeks spent in the museums and libraries in New York, we rented an apartment in Boston where I continued my work, in the Fine Arts Museum. In their transplanted murals of a Catalan chapel I felt an indeterminable relationship to El Greco. While visiting across the Charles River, one late autumn Sunday, I saw the art of America before Columbus exhibited on several floors in the Peabody Museum. The pieces lay on gray-painted bare shelves in more than Puritanical presentation which was not conducive to bringing out their strange, powerful beauty. Nevertheless it was for me the opening of a fascinating chapter in the history of art, about which little was known either here or abroad. The next day I went around again, this time with the director of the museum. I urged my host to have a comprehensive illustrated survey written of the architecture, sculpture, weaving, metalwork, and other accomplishments of this sunken world; and I was persuaded to carry out myself the project that I had proposed for an American scholar. In April 1933 we were in Yucatan and later in Mexico. What I saw there strengthened my conviction of the unique importance of pre-Columbian art. In a short interlude, having just visited Maya temples, I returned for a time to El Greco—to the magnificent exhibition of the Cretan's work gathered by the Art Institute of Chicago for the World's Fair of 1933. In subsequent travels from Mexico to Bolivia, the Baroque and Rococo of Latin America unfolded another splendid subject which clamored for publicity and more understanding. Long before all this, the initially reluctant visitor had become of his own choice a contented citizen.

Nearly twenty-five years passed before I returned to my project on El Greco. Lecturing and other assignments took me to Europe repeatedly, and from Spain to Turkey I could follow at leisure the path of my interest.

Byzantine art, long misrepresented, if not ignored, in Roman Catholic and Protestant countries as an example of degenerate Christianity, shines each year more radiant through the reexamination made possible partly by a more enlightened attitude and partly by better facilities for travel and photography. From the fairy-tale naïveté of Ethiopian religious panels to the complexity of Russian icons with their tight-lipped saints, from the domed basilicas of Constantinople, with modern traffic swirling round them, to the inspiring, peaceful monasteries of Sinai, Athos, and their sister houses, not only a religious expression but also a spiritual experience can be drawn. But the enrichment comes all too belatedly for the Western world to benefit from it fully, because of the deluge of different religions and philosophies of the peoples of Asia and Africa, in which all white nations and the entire Christian community are in danger of becoming a muffled minority.

I hope that no harm came to my book because of my delay in concluding it. Wherever I traveled, I encountered numberless expatriates, exiles, immigrants, émigrés, refugees who for one reason or another had left their native lands and had to make a living among strangers whose language was different from their mother tongues and whose customs were alien to their upbringing. In 1909, when I stood before my first El Greco, the movement of peoples by the tens of thousands was highly unusual and their behavior—one may say their psychology—little observed. Fifty years later, many a reader has merely to look across his corridor or his lawn to see a human being who was born and reared thousands of miles away. Fifty years added maturity to me and wider knowledge to my subject. The answers to some of the questions that I posed in my youth came to me in the intervening years.

This book, originally the dream of a very young man, is then the result of a long period of gestation. For me a book is still much what it was fifty years ago when I began to browse in bookstores. Many such stores had a hushed, devotional atmosphere, where something of a communion took place with great authors who knew their craft and honored it. The printed page carried the dignity and prestige of a responsible human being and bespoke the spark that was divine.

It was in itself a visual and spiritual enrichment to be able to visit so many places—some repeatedly—that are mentioned and reproduced here, and to exchange ideas with scholars, connoisseurs, and just people. Alas, some of them are no longer among us: Bernard Berenson, whose interest in my work and hospitality I enjoyed from the time that I was myself a resident of Florence; Hans and Erica Tietze—although for years in America, their generous human comprehension remained in the best Austrian tradition; Nicholas G. Lély, Greek diplomat, witty conversationalist, first civilian governor of the community of Mount Athos; Gregorio Marañón, enthusiastic and erudite Spanish historian of Toledo and El Greco.

Because space does not permit individual mention of all the officials of various governments, universities, museums, and libraries, as well as the many ecclesiastics, archivists, photographers, and connoisseurs in many countries who facilitated my work, I express my gratitude to them in summary.

There is another group whose assistance was of such measure that individual credit is due them: in England I benefited from the supreme knowledge of Arab art and architecture of K. A. C. Creswell (formerly of the Egyptian University, Cairo) who furnished also some rare photographs. Geoffrey Webb (Royal Commission on Historical Monuments), authority on Romanesque and Gothic architecture, clarified problems in this field. With Jocelyn Toynbee (Cambridge University), expert in biblical archaeology, I discussed the entirely inconclusive findings of the excavations under the Basilica of St. Peter in Rome. Natalie Jiménez Cossío (Oxford), daughter of the author whose monograph first brought El Greco into the right focus, offered pertinent information from her late father's unpublished notes and her own valuable observations.

In Istanbul: Clio Papadopulo and Mazhar Sevket Ipsiroglu (National University) provided, respectively, the Greek and the Turkish historical backgrounds of that unique city. Paul A. Underwood, E. J. W. Hawkins, Carroll Wales, and Laurence Majewski, all of the Byzantine Institute, accorded us admission during the restoration of Kariye Cami and have been generous in furnishing data.

In Athens: Demetrios Sicilianos (former Ambassador to the United States), a discerning connoisseur, shared some of his experiences with us and facilitated our work in closed private collections. Manolis Chatzidakis (Benaki Museum) and Anne Hadjinicolaou (Byzantine Museum) were helpful in many ways in their important institutions. To Helen Stathatos and A. D. Loverdos my thanks for permitting us to work and photograph in their exquisite collections, and to Angelo G. Procopiou (Polytechnic Institute) my gratitude for valuable assistance.

In Crete: Konstantinos D. Kalokyris (Archaeological Museum, Heraklion) reviewed the whole field of restoration of murals on the island and gave us all relevant publications. Nicholas Stavrinidis (Municipal Library) shared with us his vast knowledge of Venetian, Turkish, and Cretan archives, often far beyond his official hours, during our two weeks' stay. In Macedonia: Stylianos Pelekanidis (Department of Byzantine Monuments) with devoted and indefatigable energy guided and advised us. Michael Papamanzaris (Mayor of Kastoria) opened the city and its history to us. Eleanor and Henry Hope Reed (American Farm School) were gracious hosts and offered the use of their jeep and an expert guide to the Peninsula of Athos. Joyce Loch, benefactress of the village of Prosforion on the confines of the Holy Mountain, provided comfort and wise council.

For a number of years Helly Hohenemser, Rome; Hanna Schramm, Paris; and Rudolf Bedö, Budapest, assisted us with dependable research material. Helen Pandelakis, New York, besides, acted as our interpreter in Crete and Macedonia. Gratitude is due staff members of the United States State Department and Information Service in various cities abroad, especially Maro Holeva, Cultural Assistant, who was constantly in touch with us from Athens. Fern Rusk Shapley (the National Gallery of Art) and Marvin Ross (Dumbarton Oaks, Washington) have shown helpful interest in the preparation of this volume. In New York, personnel of the Library and Photographic Divisions of the Metropolitan Museum of Art, the Frick Reference Library, The Hispanic Society of America, and particularly the staff of the Arts and Prints Departments of the New York Public Library, were most accommodating.

Various authorities kindly consented to look over different parts of the manuscript. Chapter I was read by David Talbot Rice (University of Edinburgh), widely known Byzantologist and coauthor of a book that appeared decades ago, pointing to the locale of the birth of Western painting; Chapter II, by Pandelis Prévélakis (Superior College of Fine Arts, Athens), inspired poet of his native Crete and author of two books on his famous sixteenth century compatriot; Chapter III, by A. Hyatt Mayor (the Metropolitan Museum of Art), whose vast knowledge of various periods of art is imparted, whether in word or writing, always with grace; Chapter IV, by Beatrice Gilman Proske (the Hispanic Society of America), expert on the plastic arts and general cultural values of the Hispanic world. The second part of the book was read by the following: Chapter V, James A. Notopoulos (Trinity College, Hartford), distinguished teacher of the classics and recorder of the oral tradition of his ancestral land; Chapters VI and VIII,

Elizabeth du Gué Trapier (the Hispanic Society of America), a renowned lifelong scholar of Spanish painting, with several outstanding contributions also on El Greco; Chapter VII, Julius M. Moravcsik (University of Michigan), promising third-generation representative of a family of biblical and Byzantine scholars. Although many of their suggestions were gratefully followed, the responsibility for the text of this work rests entirely with the author.

David Rogers made the artistic layout of the illustrations. Florence M. Morrow, with painstaking attention, carried out the typing of the complex manuscript, and Helen B. Hartman, for the third occasion, has compiled my Bibliography and Index and given editorial help.

There is still one person whose unfailing help and cooperation throughout the decades has made this work possible. Her name appears on a separate page of this book.

PÁL KELEMEN

Norfolk, Connecticut
August, 1961

CONTENTS

·I·

BYZANTIUM WAS A WORLD

Two continents on two tongues of land face each other across the Bosporus, where the Sea of Marmara and the Black Sea form a narrows. Six centuries before Christ, Greek colonists settled there under a leader named Byzaz and called the place Byzantion—now more familiar as Byzantium. It developed into an important harbor for the shipment of wheat from the Black Sea to Athens and beyond. In A.D. 330 the Emperor Constantine removed his capital there from Rome, and created a city which for more than a thousand years stood as a center not only of commerce but also of Christian culture.

Constantine was born in the Balkans. As a general of the Roman Empire, he fought in Gaul and Britain. In a military campaign in the spring of 312, Constantine had a vision. The Chi Rho, the Greek monogram of Christ, appeared in the sky, accompanied by the admonition in Greek, "By this conquer." Thereafter he favored the Christian religion, and the sign became his personal device.

To Constantine, the site of Byzantium, surrounded by the lands of early Christianity, may well have seemed more propitious for his capital than Rome, where the pagan gods had still a large following. In Constantinople the Hellenic heritage that was preserved in Syria and Egypt came to flower. The Greeks have always been a nation of mariners. Greek was the common tongue of the Mediterranean world, though Latin remained for some time the official language of the administration. Many colonies of pagan Rome whence valued trade flowed lay in the eastern Mediterranean and never spoke Latin. At least up to the end of the second century of the Christian era, the inscriptions in the catacombs even of Rome—pagan or Christian, and those of the large Jewish colony there—were largely in Greek. When Christianity began to spread, the Gospel was translated from the original Aramaic, a Jewish dialect, into Greek. Thus language was a major factor in disseminating the teachings of Christ through the known world, while at the same time Greek philosophy aided in formulating the new religion.

The emperor gathered at Constantinople all talent to make the new capital supreme. In Constantinople the great engineering and architectural achievements of the fabulous East were utilized. The city set the patterns of taste also in jewelry, ivory- and enamel-work, and other crafts. Manuscripts of ancient and modern authors were carefully copied and multiplied. Constantinople was known as "the City" not only throughout the empire but also throughout the medieval world. Istanbul, as the Turks renamed it, means also "the City." And when Greeks today use the word "polis," they mean Constantinople.

The western part of the ancient Roman Empire—from Britannia to Dacia, from Germania to Hispania—weakened through the disintegration of a centralized administration, staggered under the various waves of barbarian invasion. In the Byzantine Empire, since the time that Constantine established his capital up to its fall to the Turks, uninterrupted contact was maintained with those lands beyond the eastern borders of Christianity, already famed as fabulous, sophisticated in more than one way. In the Byzantine Empire, Christianity achieved body and character. The expression "Dark Ages," if justified at all, applies only to the westward lands of Europe.

The Byzantine emperors embodied the supreme authority of both state and church. Approval of appointments to the rank of patriarch (bishop) depended upon the emperor—including the choice of the Bishop of Rome. From this early power date the "apostolic rights" of later sovereigns, of which more will be said later. From Byzantium also stems the custom of bestowing medals on those who had proved themselves especially worthy of commendation. These were usually crosses of silver, with the head of Christ on one side and an expression of the appreciation of the emperor on the other; distributed at religious festivals, they are forerunners of the Victoria Cross, the Leopold Cross, and many others.

The bishops or patriarchs at the head of the council represented Alexandria, Jerusalem, Antioch, Constantinople, and Rome. When voting in council among the ecclesiastics, the Bishop of Rome cast the first vote. This privilege became a prerogative, and in later centuries, when schism developed, it was a ground for claims. At the start of the controversy, the Orthodox part of the Christian world was the larger in territory, more numerous in believers, and more influential. Not only the geographical situation of the four bishops residing in the East but also the different mentality represented made the Bishop of Rome the rallying point of opposition.

Meanwhile, from the Arabian Peninsula, the standard-bearers of another religion and another civilization rode forward victoriously. The rise of the Mohammedan Arabs in the seventh century also shook the Byzantine Empire, which lost Syria, Palestine, and Egypt. Under a centralized rule, the Arabs developed impressive knowledge in mathematics, astronomy, physics, and medicine. They absorbed much of classical Greek and Jewish culture; Moslem and later Byzantine profited mutually from each other's architectural achievements. All this the Arabs were to transmit directly into Spain, Portugal, Sicily, in succeeding centuries, and indirectly into France and more northern lands—reviving the interest of Western Europe in the almost forgotten civilization of the Greeks.

Though the Byzantine Empire did not suffer so much as Europe from the migration of the peoples, it had to wage long wars to maintain its position. The emperors came to depend for their armies on the feudal lords, who grew into a powerful caste. At the same time the Orthodox monasteries, in possession of "miraculous" icons (from *eikon*, image) that drew masses of pilgrims, extended their influence over the common people and gained immense power which could be turned against the emperor. Beginning with the early eighth century, for more than a hundred years iconoclastic edicts forbade the worship of images and decreed their destruction, in an attempt to deprive the religious authorities of their most effective means of propaganda. In the end, however, the position of the monasteries may have been strengthened by the resistance centered in them. The popes of this time never accepted iconoclastic decrees, and always defended the cult of images, thus increasing the incentives of schism. Continually growing differences between the Orthodox and Roman denominations over matters of dogma harassed the once "Universal Church."

When Charlemagne (ca. 742–814) established his empire in Western Europe, though he greatly increased the authority of the Roman Church, the relationship between Eastern and Western empires remained on the whole amicable. Contact with Constantinople contributed greatly to the revival of arts and letters in his realm. Gold-, ivory-, and metal-work, as well as book illumination, achieved a high standard. The Palatine Chapel at Aachen (Aix-la-Chapelle) was adorned with columns and bronzes, Byzantine in style, looted from Rome and Ravenna during Charlemagne's campaigns in Italy.

Between mid-ninth and mid-eleventh centuries, the Byzantine Empire reached another of its several cultural peaks. The Bulgars and Moravian Slavs were evangelized; Kiev attained metropolitan brilliance. In Constantinople the arts came to a new flowering upon the revocation of iconoclasm. New buildings went up. The university, founded in the fifth century, was reconstituted. Trade throve. Special quarters were assigned to various foreign commercial groups—the Syrians, Arabs, Armenians, Russians, Bulgarians, and the representatives of Italian cities such as Amalfi, Pisa, Venice, and Genoa. From them, the influences of Byzantine art radiated throughout East and West.

Nations balanced precariously between the two powerful spheres of influence tried to keep on good terms with both. The youthful Kingdom of Hungary, recently Christianized, was important because of its dominating position in the Danubian Valley. Pope Sylvester (reigned 999–1003) sent a crown to its first ruler, St. Stephan of Hungary. A second crown came from Constantinople as a gift from the Byzantine Emperor Michael VII, who ruled from 1071–1078. The Hungarians, conscious of their need for the friendship of both powers, blended the gift into a single crown which has as its solid lower half the piece from Constantinople, upon which as a second tier the peaked elements of the papal gift are soldered. Important is the fact that both the pope's gift and that of the emperor are so similar in spirit that experts were long puzzled in solving which part came from where. For the West had not yet found its own style.[36]

Pilgrims from all parts of the world had sought the Holy Land, since St. Helena, mother of Constantine the Great, went in search of the sacred relics in 321. By mid-seventh century, Jerusalem was in Moslem hands, but for some centuries, through negotiations, pilgrims were let in. Then, in a new surge of Moslem power, the Temple of the Holy Sepulcher was destroyed. Clamor arose throughout the Christian world, and in the late eleventh century the First Crusade began its cumbersome course. The participants wore a cross as badge on their helmets, armor, shirts, sometimes even on their horse trappings—and from the Latin *crux, crucis,* the word "crusade" was coined.

Constantinople was the rallying point. Many thought the occasion propitious for the healing of the schism between the two branches of Christianity. It was also the first time that masses of people coming from Western and Central Europe stood face to face with the wonders of Byzantium.

While the motive of the crusades was noble, economic interest and human rivalry all too soon became predominant. The establishment of the Latin Kingdom of Jerusalem in 1100 marked a turning point in the balance of power in the Mediterranean. The Franks now controlled the heartland of Mediterranean trade as well as the Holy City. The various religious orders—best known among them the Templars and the Hospitalers—who backed the crusades, had to finance armies and navies. They came to possess banks, land, and finally grew into commercial companies.

The great centers of Levantine trade were Acre in Galilee (now in Israel) and Famagusta on the island of Cyprus. From there the spices, sugar, oils, fruits, silks, rugs, and velvets poured into Venice, Pisa, and Genoa, on Italian ships, by-passing the controls of Constantinople, to be dispersed throughout Europe. One of the most frequented trade routes led from Venice over the Brenner Pass, down the Rhine as far as Bruges; and prosperous cities still mark this route.

Rivalries arose among the participating nations; newcomers were unwelcome, as the feudal lords jockeyed for power. Christians confessing the same faith fought one another in the foreign land, sometimes causing more casualties in the Christian camp than the Moslems. The situation was further complicated by the fact that Constantinople looked upon the liberated territory as part of her lost empire and its European lords as her vassals.

At this time the Seljuk Turks, possessing great military skill, had brought a new energy and vigor to the Moslem world and had begun to penetrate into Asia Minor. They defeated the Byzantines decisively in 1071 and recaptured Jerusalem in 1197. Two new crusades were unsuccessful in liberating it.

A fourth crusade was organized to proceed from Venice against the Moslems in Egypt, attacking Jerusalem from the south. Although the pope hoped to direct the struggle again into spiritual channels, the feudal leaders prevailed and the force of the crusading armies was diverted against Constantinople, which by that time had shown too plainly its disdain of the West. The city was captured in 1204 and mercilessly plundered of its treasure. A northerner, Baldwin of Flanders, became the first Latin emperor of that Orthodox Greek world. Venice had its reward when the Venetian Morosini became the patriarch, with allegiance to Rome. It is as if a Protestant bishop had been placed in the chair of the cardinal at Notre Dame (for the Roman Church regards the Orthodox as schismatic, but the Orthodox looks upon the Roman as heretical). The Doge of Venice added a salient part of the Byzantine Empire to his domain, including the island of Crete.

In art and architecture, much that Europe now takes for granted as its own originated in the Near East. After fifteen hundred years certain buildings are still extant to bear testimony. In Persia, Egypt, and Syria, where working in brick and stone had ancestral tradition, the arch had early taken on a pointed form. Pointed arches constructed in mud brick occur in buildings in Egypt as early as mid-fourth century after Christ. Brick was easier to handle than stone, and many daring forms could be created with the aid of wooden supports that were removed when the mass had solidified. By the eighth century, cities such as Baghdad, Palmyra, Samarra, Ankara, all had buildings with pointed arches.[3] Similarly, the transverse vault is found in a fourth century building, and the ribbed ogival vault was not uncommon by the ninth.[42]

To keep the historical continuity, the illustrations will be discussed later in this chapter.

Byzantine architecture itself borrowed from a number of styles of the Near East. By the end of the sixth century it had achieved a highly individual blend of Greek and oriental elements. In the regions of the Byzantine Empire, basilicas (from the Greek *basilic,* kingly) rose, rectangular buildings divided into nave with side aisles. Other typical Byzantine ground plans were based on the dome. Though the Romans—after thorough contact with the Near East—constructed domes, they were never successful in placing a dome on a square or polygonal base.

This must be declared a Syrian invention.[3] The expanse of the Byzantine dome on pendentives, with its many windows to lighten the structure and illuminate the interior, has never been duplicated.

The greatest of the Byzantine domes, that of the church of St. Sophia in Constantinople, which will be discussed somewhat later in detail, was consecrated in its present form in 561. The church of St. Sophia in Thessaloniki, built probably in early seventh century (the mosaics were put up in mid-ninth), was one of the earliest buildings to use pendentives in the construction of a dome at the crossing. St. Mark's in Venice, begun in 1063, was modeled strictly on Byzantine precepts, and exerted a great influence on the architecture of Western Europe. The much-eulogized dome of the cathedral of Florence, commenced by Brunelleschi, was not completed until 1431 and not furnished with its lantern until 1471 after the first cupola had collapsed in building; at that, it is not a true dome but a vast octagonal cloistered vault.

It was a Syrian-Arabian custom to inscribe a building with the names of the architect and those who contributed to its erection, as well as with the date. The great freedom in the treatment of moldings, the trifoil and the cinquefoil derive from the brick and stucco which the Levantines used with virtuosity. The style we know as "Venetian Gothic" was first practiced in buildings of the Arabic Near East.

The Romanesque style was developing in Europe when throughout the Byzantine Empire—from Cairo to Damascus, from Constantinople to Thessaloniki, and even in some Italian towns—splendid buildings stood, tall and crowned with shining domes. Influences from Byzantium helped the West greatly to ennoble its cumbersome architecture. It was the ambitious and technically advanced Romanesque which prepared the ground for the next epoch. Such characteristics of the Gothic as the ribbed vault, the groined vault, can be found in Romanesque architecture; even the flying buttress was present in those centuries, though kept neatly under the roof.

Charlemagne's builders at Aachen drew on the Lombard skill, which in turn learned much from Constantinople and the Byzantine of Ravenna, at one time in close touch with "the City." St. Mark's in Venice has a ground plan derived from the church of the Holy Apostles in Constantinople. Also, in France, Saint-Front at Périgueux follows the same five-domed plan. Over an even greater distance, the eleventh century west front of Lincoln Cathedral in England, with its entrance portals recessed in three tall archways, appears to have been modeled on the contemporary façade of St. Mark, just then in building, which in turn is closely connected with the Koimesis church in Nicaea [2]—destroyed in the Greco-Turkish War about 1922.

Little attention has been paid to the influence of that area of North Italy where the long fingers of the lakes reach from Lombardy into the French, Swiss, Austrian, and Slavic-speaking lands. The cathederal of Como, for instance, is a stunning document in stone of the various changes in architecture from Romanesque to Gothic to early Renaissance, and contains elements that came from the Byzantine and went by way of Venice to the West. The three-aisled church of Sant' Abbondio, also in Como, manifests still more the great but little-publicized contribution which this region made in transmitting styles.

The early religious orders in Europe employed master masons, frequently laymen, who by mid-eleventh century were constructing imposing buildings. The *maestri comacini,* the master masons of Como, learned their craft in colleges and corporations, and their work can be traced as early as mid-seventh century. They were itinerant masons, and through their journeying carried the high achievements of their homeland in a broad swath from France to the Balkans—so powerful that the Lombard style is often identified as *comacine*. Their activities continue into the Gothic epoch when other regions also began to exert powerful influences.[63]

Even less known than Como are its neighbors—Morcote, Lugano, Locarno, and across the Alpine valleys—for their role in handing on the achievements of these artists and craftsmen into Central and Western Europe. An amazing wealth of architecture, sculpture, and mural painting can be seen behind the remnants tucked away in local museums, which a handful of dedicated persons have rescued in bits or caught in pictures from the wholesale destruction of nineteenth century "advance." This was no provincial school or cultural backwater, but a firmly established center, which on the channels of growing commerce could and did spread far into transalpine lands.[60] The tradition is preserved in various later examples. A great figure of Christ in Majesty, the Pantocrator, fills the apse ceiling of a number of churches, as in the Byzantine world.

The crusaders came to the Levant in full force in late eleventh century, when Near Eastern technical achievements had become architectural tradition and were applied more generally over the vast area than appears today. With the crusading armies came their military engineers, their armorers, as well as scribes and draftsmen who recorded in word and picture what was of interest and value to Western Europeans.

To separate clinically one epoch of architecture from what existed before and came into being afterwards is a sterile pastime. People built, not to express spiritually lofty ideas but because they needed bigger and better buildings. The development of an architectural style is a slow process—of outside influences, of experimentation, adaptation, and of change.

In the Gothic, the structural solidity of former periods was relieved through a more highly developed use of the pointed arch and through ribbed vaulting. The flying buttress, placed outside the building to counterbalance stress, served to relieve the walls of weight and permitted better illumination—a practical constructional element which the nineteenth century sentimentalized with all other particulars of the style.

While the Romanesque was in considerable part spread through the work of the Benedictines, in a number of countries the Cistercian order is closely related to the development of the Gothic.[17] This order, which was not founded until mid-twelfth century, gathered power from the prosperity of its agricultural enterprises, its animal husbandry. The order spread into various lands, coinciding with the maturing of the Gothic style. But this architectural development could become a reality only by benefiting from all that went before.

Abbot Suger of Saint-Denis in France (ca. 1081–1151) has left an account of the rebuilding and enlargement of the church in his care and its treasures. It is a eulogy to his own great feats. In circles where the cult of the French Gothic still reigns unabated, Abbot Suger is given disproportionate importance in the history of this style. It is characteristic, however, that an Italian Roman Catholic encyclopedia mentions him only as a cleric who *scrisse qualche opera e molte lettere*—wrote some works and many letters. . . .[1] An objective reading of Suger's paragraphs will reveal that he inquired repeatedly of travelers who came from Constantinople whether his church was as beautiful as, and whether his treasures compared with, those of the Eastern metropolis.[10] The mere idea shows baffling provinciality—that his one building could compete with the vast complex of churches and the immeasurable riches of the Byzantine capital. By early twelfth century the Near East had become a meeting place of Western European nations who sent home their wounded and sick; contact went on for decades through reinforcements which contained also numerous civilian observers. Whatever this abbot gathered in the twenty-nine years or so of his rule was infinitesimal compared to the splendor of the imperial city, where two-thirds of the world's wealth was concentrated.[25] Long before any of the crusades, a treasure-trove was amassed in Constantinople which could be plundered by fellow Christians for centuries and each time still yield further riches. Considering that the coming and going of the crusaders was continuous, at Abbot Suger's time the exchange was more than a century under way to the abundant profit of the hesitant art and architecture of Western Europe.

One of the rare surviving architectural manuals—alleged by some to be the only one before the fifteenth century—is the sketchbook of Villard de Honnecourt dated between 1225 and 1250. Even this appears to be fragmentary. It consists of random pages, 6¼ by 10½ inches, containing sketches of figures, religious scenes, architectural details, studies of persons in movement. Villard seems to have been present at the construction or enlargement of various French churches. Among the drawings there are also details which do not refer to France—for example, the picture of a round window of a church in Lausanne. Further, to one of his sketches he adds: "Once I was in Hungary, where I remained for a long time; I saw the paving of a church made with this design." His trip to Hungary must have been a matter of importance because a different hand added to the sketchbook in the fifteenth century, "This is the man who was in Hungary." [14]

At that time Hungary was a great kingdom, not only militarily powerful but also leading in the arts and humanities. The first reconstruction of the metropolitan church of Cambrai in France, important in the history of French Gothic, was made possible by a donation from St. Elisabeth of Hungary. She belonged to the Árpád dynasty, founders of that kingdom which stretched from the Polish plains to the Dalmatian shores on the Adriatic. Elisabeth was most religious, and after her marriage to a Landgrave of Thuringia in Germany, she spent much of their fortune on good deeds. Both her father and her husband participated in crusades. Here again is a direct connection with the Near East—by way of Hungary and Germany, to France.

Modern investigation is bringing about a revaluation in the history of art, as in other humanistic disciplines. The civilizations of the Near and Far East are only now beginning to come into focus, and the nineteenth century misunderstanding of the Gothic is in process of being cleared up. The word Gothic is derived from the Goths, barbarians from the North, and up to mid-nineteenth century it implied something uncouth, in bad taste. Travel books from eighteenth and early nineteenth centuries use the word exclusively in a deprecatory sense. In the Italian language it has that meaning even today. Around 1860 the many early French churches were full of additions from the Renaissance, Baroque, Neoclassic, and early Victorian periods, presenting living documents of centuries through which the buildings had stood—witnesses to the variety of taste. Under the influence of a group of powerful nationalistic architects and critics, seeking in the intellectual past of their nation compensation for military defeat, the "restoration" of these cathedrals began. Most of what was created in the intermediate four hundred years was ripped from the interiors—side altars, pulpits, organ screens, confessionals; and similarly the exteriors were "restored" according to what Viollet-le-Duc and his group thought a thirteenth century Gothic cathedral ought to look like. Although opposition arose, and many dignified writers and personalities, among them Anatole France, protested against this falsification, the work went on. It is now slowly being realized that those "reconstructed" buildings show a style which is synthetic and unreal.

In 1261, when Constantinople was retaken from the Franks by the Byzantines, it was evident that between the two religious denominations an almost unhealable rift existed. The Greek Church had remained throughout the Middle Ages true to its ancient character. When the Orthodox faith became established in various Slavic and other countries, the language of the service remained Greek for a time only, and then the texts were translated into the respective tongues. Thus the Russian, Macedonian, Serbian, Romanian—to mention only a few—could follow the liturgy better than the illiterate French or Bavarian peasant who understood no Latin. In the West, as early as the thirteenth century, the peasantry in various countries showed signs of restlessness. The corruption of the feudal masters—whether baron or bishop—produced such movements as the Waldensian and the Hussite long before the Reformation.

In the face of Moslem advance, now spurred by the virile and aggressive Ottoman Turks, various attempts were made toward a rapprochement and mutual defense. Between the years 1369 and 1439, three Byzantine emperors visited the West. In 1439 the Council of Florence was convened, attended by both Orthodox and Roman plenipotentiaries. The Byzantine emperor John VII Palaeologos came with a large group of important personages, including the Patriarch of Constantinople. But the discussions did not serve the Christian cause; the Orthodox patriarchs refused to ratify the concessions demanded by the West in return for a united crusade. The most valuable record of this heated bargaining is the murals painted by Benozzo Gozzoli in the Palazzo Medici-Riccardi of Florence some twenty years later. Here, in the guise of the visit of the Magi to the Christ Child, the conclave of the emperor, the patriarch, and young Lorenzo de' Medici is portrayed with jewel-like clarity and unique storytelling charm.

The history of the arts of Western civilization still works with opinions that were formed when the Byzantine Empire was under Turkish rule and when research in Near and Far East could not be more than sporadic and sketchy. Most historians, informed by overwhelming West-oriented sources, speak with deprecation of a decaying Byzantine Empire. An empire which, despite having to fight enemies from all sides, including their own Christian brothers, remained a military power to be reckoned with until its fall, and nevertheless enriched the Western world for more than a thousand years with its spiritual, intellectual, and artistic achievements, providing the spark for the Renaissance—what "decadence," what "stagnation and decay"!

While the Romanesque and Gothic were evolving in the West, great developments were also taking place in the Byzantine world. The brilliant wall mosaics (such as at Hosios Lukas, Chios, Daphni, Thessaloniki, and Constantinople), the murals, ivories, enamels, and metalwork, and the book illumination—all testify to the vitality of the arts of this period. But the two worlds were drifting apart. The schism of the churches, the acrimonious rivalries in trade put up increasing barriers. The West became less familiar with the East, and after the Turkish conquest memories died, so that by the eighteenth century, when Gibbon wrote his *Decline and Fall of the Roman Empire,* the picture he gave of the Byzantine world was essentially a false one.[44]

The Turks in their masterly campaign had by-passed the massive bastions of Constantinople, crossed the Bosporus, and subjugated the Balkan lands, thus separating the East from the West in Christendom. Finally, they dared the conquest of Constantinople itself, and after a protracted siege the city fell to Mohammed II in 1453. With the fabulous capital in the hands of the Turks, the Byzantine Empire as a political unit went down to its end. The Turkish rulers have sometimes shown a more humane attitude toward the Christian population than vice versa. Smaller places of Christian worship, where no crowds could gather to conspire against the ruling power, and the chapels in fields and on hillsides could be used. The large churches were expropriated by the Turks, and many received an addition of the minaret, that slender, gracefully joined tower from which the muezzin calls the faithful to prayer. As the Moslem religion prohibits all figurative art, the mosaics and murals were whitewashed or broken down, the religious paraphernalia disposed of—if not already hidden away by the Orthodox population. The monumental complex of the imperial residence fell into ruins. Buildings, terraces, and stairways were used as quarries. One of the marvels of the world, the church of St. Sophia, was transformed into a gigantic mosque. The city's tactical position offered a springboard for the military and commercial advance of the Ottomans into the Western world.

The century which brought the downfall of Byzantium had not yet ended, when a boy was born, allegedly of Christian Armenian-Greek parentage, who was brought up as a Turkish janissary. Sinan, as he was called, became the unequaled master of Moslem architecture and related arts in the brilliant epoch of the Osmanli sultans. He no doubt studied the St. Sophia of Constantinople; but he also saw much of Near Eastern architecture and he created a style of which the unity, elegance, and grandeur only now—when travel and photography make it possible to study his work as a whole—are beginning to be widely appreciated. Under Suleiman the Magnificent, called Lawgiver by the Turks, a thorough rebuilding of Istanbul began. And soon new mosques, not less in size or grace than churches of the Byzantine epoch, decorated the horizon of that majestic city, with their delicate tilework and their domes vibrating in the hazy sunshine. Sinan was also a remarkable military engineer.[6] He participated at the siege of Rhodes in 1522 and later in the victorious campaign when the Danube was forced. He directed the earthworks in the battle at Mohács in Hungary, when the road to Vienna was laid open (1526). The Hungarian king Lajos (Louis II), who perished in that battle, was married to a sister of the Habsburg Charles V; thus the Turkish menace thrust at the heart of the Holy Roman Empire. It was Suleiman's ambition to complete the subjugation of Central Europe, but he died during the campaign. The Turks did not penetrate beyond eastern Austria, but halted to consolidate their overextended line of supplies.

The Greeks who remained in Istanbul after the conquest withdrew to the shore quarter and the hills on the southern edge of the Golden Horn. Here they formed a tightly woven community, known as Phanar, which received many privileges from the first. The Moslem conquest and the vicissitudes of Frankish rule had long engulfed the patriarchates of Alexandria, Antioch, and Jerusalem. The patriarch of Constantinople became the sole head of the Byzantine Church, the administrator of all Orthodox Christians under Turkish rule.

The collection of tithes in distant provinces was in the hands of Greeks from Phanar, and seemingly they handled their office so efficiently that the Turkish administration had them collect the taxes as well. In Romania, even after it became an independent kingdom in the last century, the collection of taxes was still entrusted to the descendants of Phanariot Greeks. The successful management of the various tax moneys might explain the presence, even in recent years, of very wealthy Greek bankers and shippers in Cairo, Damascus, Smyrna, Sophia, Bucharest.

Even if the Orthodox patriarchs had acceded to the demands of Rome and the West had joined in full force against Ottoman might, it is doubtful whether a final victory over the Turks could have been achieved. The terrific momentum of the Moslem onslaught probably could not have been stemmed. And the Orthodox world, having bargained away its individual culture and spiritual unity, would have foundered in the aggressiveness of the West.

Although as a political unit the Byzantine Empire became a memory, its influence was by that time profoundly established in Greece, Russia, Bulgaria, Serbia, Romania, and beyond, as well as in the Near East. In the occupied Hellenic lands patriotism and religion, fused into a spiritual flame, kept language, literature, and art alive until—within the past century—freedom was regained.

The fortifications of Constantinople underwent one major enlargement and many repairs in the course of the centuries. But certain sections still present much the same appearance as when Emperor Theodosius II, in mid-fifth century, enlarged the city and consequently strengthened the fortifications (*Pl. 1A*). The bulwarks were massive enough to repulse attacks by Huns, Avars, Persians, Arabs, Bulgars, and Russians successively, and even held back the Turks for a long time. There were two walls, some thirty-six feet high. The inner one was built of cut stone and brick, five or so courses of each alternating. As reinforcement in each were ninety-six towers, spaced some 165 feet apart, those in one wall alternating with those in the other. Then came a moat between high escarpments. This massive construction had ten gates, the grandest of which was called the Golden Gate. Legend says that it was walled up after the Turks took the city because of a prophecy that through this gate would enter the reconqueror. But from the stonework it appears that it was filled in in preparation for the crusaders' attack in 1204. The vast network of fortifications stands today in melancholy ruin; but the gates still have power enough to strike back at truck fenders when careless drivers come too near to them.

The church of St. Sophia—Holy Wisdom—in Constantinople was erected by the Emperor Justinian to replace an earlier basilica, and was dedicated in 537. Its plan is daring and original. Over the central square, a dome one hundred feet in diameter rests upon huge arches with pendentives at the corners. It took a little over five years to complete the church, which was for centuries the largest in the world. The Byzantine system of construction, alternating courses of brick with mortar almost as thick, was not suited to such rapid work.[45] The mortar dried unevenly and some of the arches buckled. An earthquake in 553 may have damaged the structure; another, four years later, caused the dome to fall. When it was rebuilt, it rose 180 feet above the ground. The church was justly called the newest "wonder of the world." Its delicately proportioned walls are one of the glories of architecture.

This superlative building did not stand alone. Between 527 and 536, the church of SS. Sergius and Bacchus was erected, as well as the churches of St. Eirene and the Holy Apostles, each representing an exquisite variation in the development of Byzantine architecture and art. The five-domed plan of the Holy Apostles was copied in St. Mark at Venice.

St. Sophia today (*Pl. 1C*), despite the minarets and Turkish buildings that surround it, stands apart through its supple construction. The incredibly flat dome, its drum pierced by forty openings, appears bubble-light. The vast space of the interior is enclosed with the least possible sense of confinement, producing an atmosphere warm and colorful and at the same time uplifting. The many windows give the interior an even and noble illumination. Throughout the Romanesque and Gothic this goal was striven for, but it took the West seven hundred years more to achieve it.

Among the various impressive architectural remnants of the Near East, a few examples have been chosen to illustrate the early dates of the edifices and the skill of workmanship.

The Egyptians were among the earliest followers of Christ's teaching. The converts, known as

Copts, were in communion with the neighboring Ethiopians, likewise Christianized in very early times. Murals and manuscripts of the latter land preserve a strong touch of the Coptic manner, and some Abyssinian churches were hewn out of living rock, probably influenced by Egyptian technique from pre-Christian times. In the Sudan, south of Egypt, where mighty monuments of the Pharaohs are now endangered by the building of the Aswan Dam, the figures of Christian saints are found on the walls of pagan temples among the gods of the earlier religion. In the ruins of a Coptic monastery near Aswan (*Pl. 2A*), founded in the fourth century, the powerful arches, the remnants of tunnel vaulting, and the carved decorations give an idea of the regional type of construction in clay and stone.

At Til Keuy, thirty miles southwest of the city of Kayseri, which was once the capital of Cappadocia, in Central Turkey, lie the ruins of the church dedicated to St. Andrew, built in the sixth century (*Pl. 2B*). The large, well-dressed stones make possible a wide span. It was a two-aisled mortuary church with some twenty tombs under the floor of the north aisle. Originally it seems to have been a basilica with columns and a flat roof; a painted inscription survives from this earliest structure.[32] The region was a prosperous province under Byzantine rule. It is tragic that such influential accomplishment must be judged from such fragments.

The monastery church of St. Simeon the Stylite (*Pl. 2D*), some thirty miles northwest of Aleppo, Syria, was erected on the site where the hermit saint died in 459. The stonework of the basilica shows assurance, even elegance, achieved with fine metal tools; highly feared sword blades were fashioned in nearby Damascus. The massivity of the construction is lightened by the use of free-standing columns in the archway, and by the grace of the cornices, moldings, and other sculptural decoration. It is a building of unusual plan, with four basilica-like bodies radiating from a center, where the column stood on which the saint had spent much of his contemplative life. While some authorities date the building from early seventh century, others would have it more than a hundred years older. It stood near a road that was important from a military point of view since Hittite times and that Arabs, Egyptians, and crusaders used as a battleground. By the end of the tenth century, it fell victim to the continuous strife that raged about it.

The population of the large area known as Syria and Palestine before World War II—comprising the biblical territories of Galilee, Samaria, and Judea—was among the first to convert to Christianity. By the early years of our epoch, Syrian culture had developed to a height and originality that affected the entire Mediterranean world. Even their earliest buildings for Christian worship show considerable deviation from the classic style. The Omayad Mosque, the "Great Mosque," in Damascus (*Pl. 2C*) was originally the church of St. John the Baptist, begun by Theodosius I in 375 on the site of a Roman temple and apparently making use of its classical columns. It was considerably rebuilt in the eighth century to turn it into a mosque. Here was venerated as a relic the alleged head of John the Baptist, which disappeared after the crusaders ransacked the area. Now two French churches, Soissons and Amiens, claim its possession.

Looking back through the perspective of history, it may appear that while the Moslem benefited from the intellectual and practical achievements of the "infidel," he also gave much. Ramla or Ramle, in Israel today, is an Arab foundation dating from the early eighth century. The name is derived from the Arabic *raml,* meaning sand. Situated on the way between Jerusalem and the ancient port of Jaffa, it was a city of great importance even after the advent of the crusaders at the end of the eleventh century. An Arab historian describes it as "well-built, its water good and plentiful, its fruit abundant, commerce prosperous, its bread . . . the best and the whitest."

Among its historical monuments, the hospice was a Byzantine foundation, the great mosque from the twelfth century was originally a crusaders' church, and the tower from the fourteenth is Moslem.

The cistern of Ramla (*Pl. 4C*), built under the Caliph Harun-al-Rashid in 789, is a subterranean structure with strong retaining walls and a well-preserved pavement. It was laid out into six aisles, covered by tunnel vaults which spring from low lateral pointed arches and are reinforced by higher transverse arches.[3] Each vaulted bay was pierced by an opening some two feet square, so that twenty-four people could draw water at the same time. A staircase led down to the bottom of the cistern. In this case posterity showed appreciation, in surrounding the structure with a public garden.

Alone in Syria, eight other well-preserved examples of such cisterns can be found. In Constantinople, where an adequate water supply was paramount in case of siege or drought, every reign built new cisterns, some open, some covered, whether for palace, mansion, monastery, or church. Over thirty of them exist today, showing great variety of construction. Many of the bricks used in the cisterns were stamped in mid-fifth century, others in the time of Justinian, and the upper courses show the monograms of Byzantine stonemasons.[45]

Another clear forerunner of the Gothic is the Nilometer in Egypt (*Pl. 4B*), datable through its inscription at 861–862. Travelers from various lands remark that the rise or fall of the water level was the object of daily concern, and served as the usual opening of conversation in Egypt.[22] The Nilometer, on Roda Island near Cairo, was a gauge. It consisted of a tall graduated column rising from a stone-lined pit. The waters of the Nile flowed in through three tunnels, making possible continuous observation of the level. The four sides of the stone pit are strengthened by arched recesses, their pointed arched vaults resting on a pair of engaged colonnettes. Careful measurements reveal that the arches have been struck from two centers one-third of the span apart; thus they comprise what Gothic architects called, much later, "tiers points." [3]

Although relatively near the heartland of the Byzantine Empire, the Kingdom of Armenia cannot be considered a mere offshoot of the civilization that centered in Constantinople. The racial history of the Armenians is different; the pre-Christian centuries brought them in touch with other cultures. When a national church was established there, as early as 303, the Greek language was replaced by Armenian, a national alphabet introduced, and the Bible translated. Much fighting occurred with the Arabs' rise in the Near East, and early in the eighth century the Armenian *katholikos,* or supreme head of the church, intervened for peace between the Armenian princes and the Arab caliph. Late in the following century, the country freed itself entirely and for nearly two hundred years enjoyed unusual prosperity, although it was divided into various kingdoms. Throughout Greater Armenia the ruins of innumerable monuments, irrigation works, churches, and palaces still stand as tokens of the native virtuosity in construction.

The church of Achthamar (*Pl. 3A*) was built in 915–921, on a small island in Lake Van. The plan is a square with four buttressing niches projecting from it and so forming a cross. One of them constitutes the apse, and the others, tiny side chapels. Adequate lighting is achieved by windows in a high octagonal drum that houses the cupola. These features are later encountered in the Balkans also. Especial interest lies in the fine handling of the stone and in the sculptured reliefs that adorn the whole of the exterior. Stylistically these sculptures embody the influence of Sassanian Persia. Three encircling friezes of animals, hunters, grapevines and pomegranates stand out as if formed with a cooky mold. The story of Jonah (*Pl. 3C*) gives a clear idea of the storytelling charm of this work. In the medallions, local saints and heroes appear, as well as evangelists and biblical characters.[37]

Armenian painting can best be studied today through the numerous book illustrations, which show influences varying between the Byzantine-Greek, the Persian, and the work of neighboring Syria—such as the Rabula Gospels from the sixth century (see *Pl. 62A*). Remnants of wall paintings are extant at Achthamar and even in some forerunners from as early as the seventh century. Besides apostles and church fathers (*Pl. 3B*) here are also faded remnants of scenes representing the Visitation, the Nativity, the Entry into Jerusalem, among others, rendered with an immediacy that is close in style to the carving. From this plate it can be seen that the church structure, with its semicircular niches, suave domes, and pleasant transitional members, was far more subtle than the exterior shell would indicate. Though the interior of the church at Achthamar was apparently covered with wall paintings, the vicissitudes of nearly a thousand years have taken a heavy toll of them. Perhaps even this much survives only because the building stands upon a lonely island, completely deserted. The adjacent royal palace is just a pile of stone. Dangerously near the Russo-Turkish border, it sees visitors very seldom. It is an abode only to the sea birds that nest there undisturbed.

The cathedral at Ani occupies a still more striking place in the highly advanced architecture of Armenia (*Pl. 4A*). Ani lies north of Achthamar, indeed about halfway from Lake Van to Georgian Tiflis. Built between the years 989 and 1001, it is a cruciform domed church, constructed entirely of fine dressed stone. The side aisles are roofed with barrel vaulting. Although not of monumental size, its interior is imposing because of the harmony of proportion. Pointed and stepped arches rise from powerful clustered piers, supporting a dome on pendentives. Recessed pilasters are placed against the north and south walls. Small semicircular niches enliven the apse. The same elements as seen here were used in other contemporary churches of the region. Arches and cross ribs to bear the weight of the stone web were common.[37] The small double-arched windows (even triple sometimes) familiar from the later Venetian Gothic are found in Armenia constructed in stone.[18] One is strongly reminded of the early Gothic of Western Europe, with the difference that these forms appear here much earlier. When Achthamar and Ani were in construction, the Cistercian order did not exist.

It is recorded that, when the dome of St. Sophia in Constantinople was damaged by earthquake in the late tenth century, the architect of Ani was called in to make the repairs.

Besides the possession of the Holy Sepulcher and control of trade routes, the Holy Land offered highly attractive and desirable property for the crusaders to occupy. To consolidate their position, well-defended bases were necessary, where men and war materials could stand at call. Such fortresses were garrisoned by their feudal lords—a practice that tended to strengthen local units and weaken the central power. Krak des Chevaliers (*Pl. 5A*), a fortress begun in the early thirteenth century, belonged to the Knights of the Order of the Hospital of St. John of Jerusalem, better known as the Hospitalers. This order of lay brothers was originally formed as a sort of medical corps to serve the sick and wounded of the crusades. Their hospital at Jerusalem could accommodate two thousand patients, and was remarkably modern in its friendly service, excellent diet, and individual care. Their success brought tremendous wealth. They owned banks, land, trading houses, and exercised sovereign rights as a feudal entity that extended far beyond the frontiers of the Holy Land.

The great fortress housed about two thousand men. It stands on a height in North Syria near the Lebanese border, dominating the important inland road from Aleppo to Damascus, and seems impregnable with its double row of massive walls, one peering above the other, divided by a moat. Just as in Guatemala the Maya Indian and in Peru the Incas' descendants constructed churches and palaces for their Spanish masters, here also thousands of local laborers must have been impressed to erect this fortress with the necessary speed. It duplicates in line and construction methods a number of Arab fortresses in the area. Clearly visible is the device known as machicolation that can be traced to Arab architecture. The machicolation is a corbeled parapet at the top of a building, with openings in the floor through which the defenders can see the foot of the structure and drop various unpleasant objects on the heads of attackers. The device, apparently derived from the projecting latrines of Syrian tower-houses, does not appear in Western Europe before the end of the twelfth century. Examples at Norwich and Winchester in England date from 1186–1193 and somewhat later in the town halls (*signorie*) of Florence and Siena.[8]

To local stonecutters and masons—masters of their craft—must be attributed also the graceful yet thoroughly sound "Gothic" arched passageway (*Pl. 5B*). The fortress of Krak des Chevaliers was taken in 1271 by the troops of the Sultan of Egypt. Driven from the mainland, the Hospitalers moved to Cyprus, then to Rhodes, and later withdrew to Crete. Finally Charles V, Emperor of the Holy Roman Empire, granted them the island of Malta (1530); hence they are known today as the Knights of Malta.

Of all the centers of architecture, culture, and thought in the Near East, Constantinople, the Byzantine capital, was the most important. The churches that were built there were of all periods, and extremely numerous. Some, such as St. Sophia, were constructed within the time span of a few years and have kept their character for almost a millennium and a half; others have undergone many changes across the centuries. An example is the church known today as Kariye Cami, St. Saviour in Chora (*Pl. 1B*), meaning "in the fields" or "outside the walls." Thus the first structure here must have antedated the period in which the land walls of Theodosius (see *Pl. 1A*) were constructed. Ruined in its earliest form by an earthquake, it is believed to have been rebuilt by Justinian, only to be destroyed by another temblor in the mid-sixth century. It was again rebuilt a century later, and a number of important personalities were buried there. During the iconoclastic period the monastery attached to it was suppressed, and the church must have suffered. Restored in the ninth century, it had again fallen to ruin by the twelfth; then, in its fifth version, it was rebuilt more or less on the plan visible today. Although damaged during the Frankish domination, the church and monastery buildings were brought back into condition by Theodoros Metochites, then chief treasurer of the empire and confidant of the Emperor Andronicus II of whom we shall hear again. Theodoros built an aisle across the north side as a mortuary chapel (at the right) and had it decorated with the wall paintings which are of special interest to us. Brilliant and lively mosaics depicting the lives of Jesus and the Virgin cover the walls of the two narthices. According to a Greek chronicler, the work was finished before 1321. Later, Theodoros fell into disgrace and died there as a monk in 1331.[50]

The murals of Kariye Cami are thought to have been executed by the same anonymous master who designed the mosaics of the narthices. The theme is the Triumph over Death. Christ in Limbo is represented in the apse (*Pl. 75A*), a figure of superlative power, lifting Adam and Eve out of the kingdom of Hades. The delineation of Christ's figure—expression, pose, and his garments—was by this time firmly established, and characterizes him in Byzantine art through the centuries. The text above, *Anastasis*, signifies the Resurrection, embodying also the sense of the Redemption of Mankind.

The Turkish official under whose jurisdiction the buildings fell after the conquest may have had some appreciation of their beauty and artistic merit. At any rate he did not have the decorations torn away; instead they were covered with thick coats of whitewash, so that recent careful restoration has revealed them almost in their pristine hues. With its immediacy, storytelling power, and fine colors, the mural demolishes the oft-repeated assertion of the dull, conventionalized character of Late Byzantine art. It gains importance when we consider that Kariye Cami's mosaics and wall paintings were set up in the very years of Giotto's mature output.

The capture and pillage of Constantinople by the crusaders in 1204 was a blow from which the Byzantine Empire never fully recovered. Although by 1261 the Greeks could reenter their capital, the Peloponnesus was divided among the Franks, with some Greek lords holding out against them and Venice in firm possession of strategic harbors. In an effort to consolidate their holdings, the Franks established a string of three fortresses on three heights across the peninsula. One of these is the site of the present Mistra (*Pl. 12A*). But the power of Byzantium was again on the rise, and the emperor finally won command over the heartland of the Peloponnesus.

It is recorded that an old town of Mistra, some two miles southwest of Sparta, was important in the twelfth century for its production of silken webs "finer than the spider's"—largely the work of a Jewish colony there. Reestablished on a sharply sloping hill, enlarged and embellished by the Palaeologos family some 150 years later, Mistra became known as "the wonder of Morea." Constantine XI Palaeologos, the last Emperor of Byzantium, was brought up there and ruled for six years before he left to be crowned at Constantinople and to die fighting the Turks on the ramparts of his capital. The region around Mistra survived the holocaust until 1460. Then the Turks garrisoned a fortress on the summit, and the cosmopolitan little city sank into neglect and ruin.

One climbs steep and narrow paths, passing buildings that are sometimes no more than piles of stones. Through glassless windows, broken roofs, and fissured walls, animals crawl and birds fly in and out. Yet in at least seven churches the great performance of Late Byzantine mural painting can be observed.[33]

The church of Peribleptos, the Conspicuous, perched at the edge of a bluff, dates from the second half of the fourteenth century (*Pl. 12C*). Its interior is frescoed from ceiling to floor, and glows like a jewel box. In the apse, the Virgin in the aspect of the Mother Church is seated with the youthful King on her knee, on the typical throne of a Byzantine sovereign (*Pl. 12B*). At each side the tasseled ends of the "imperial purple" (that is, crimson) cushion are clearly to be seen. Angels flank the scene. Plate 13 shows the left side of the apse, where different compositions are separated by a narrow dark-red band with white edging. Nearest the eye is the scene of the Supper at Emmaus. The table is covered with a tasseled and embroidered cloth. The toylike architecture is draped with a curtain to indicate an interior, as is traditional in Byzantine iconography. Above this scene, Mary, surrounded by the apostles and flanked by two archangels, witnesses the Ascension. Despite what the building went through, the colors are warm and well differentiated. The trees, conventionalized and far from realistic, make one think of the work of Fra Angelico and Benozzo Gozzoli in Italy nearly a century later. In the arch of the apse, Christ in a circular aureole is carried upward by four magnificent angels in shining colors; a rosy red and a vibrant yellow shading to orange stand out. The subject matter and, to a great extent, the sequences of the murals are all established elements of Late Byzantine painting, and occur nearly unchanged—even in icons, or portable holy paintings—into the nineteenth century.

"Conservation and restoration" were done here before modern methods could be applied. In the last years the murals are getting more attention, as their outstanding importance is being realized.

The call to spend one's life in contemplation, celibate and solitary, is as old as mankind's striving to fathom the mystery of divinity. Long before Christ, highly organized monasticism existed in India and other parts of Asia. Buddhistic religious practices are in many ways forerunners of the Christian, such as the tonsure of monks and priests, the adoption of uniform garb, the establishment of monasteries on mountaintops, or in remote valleys. The service in the temple as communion with God, the chanting, the accompaniment of music, the use of the prayer wheel and of bells and incense, pilgrimages, the veneration of relics and holy images, are all pre-Christian. Even the rosary is found in the Buddhist religion. From the *om mani padme hum* to the Pater Noster is not a long way.

In the arts, also, Christianity took over much from the great previous religions. The glory or halo of light about the head of a holy personage, the aureole or the almond-shaped *mandorla* enveloping the whole figure occur in ancient depictions. Particular colors are reserved for a particular occasion or saint. Heaven and hell, demons and furies, miracles, are all represented in pictures and in carving before Christianity. Angels, as heavenly guardians or winged ministers of good, appear in Buddhist art several centuries before Christ. In a scene of unusual poetic feeling, on a sculptured stele, the young Buddha is shown leaving his home at dawn; four winged angels uphold the legs of his horse so that he can depart without awakening his parents.

Christianity went through its formative phase in the Near East. Christian monasticism stems from Egypt, where it first took the form of retirement into solitude. The wilderness around Mount Sinai was a favorite place for hermits. An ancient caravan road crossed the wedge-shaped Sinaitic Peninsula, trodden by countless multitudes between Palestine and Egypt. This region had the reputation of sanctity since antiquity. It is recorded that the heathen Arabs celebrated a moon feast there to "Sin," who was a moon god also in Babylonian times. The mountain itself figures as setting for Elijah's ascent, for Moses' vision of the Burning Bush, and for the delivery of the Ten Commandments into his hands.

Once, the peninsula was better wooded, and numerous Christian hermits lived in its many caves. Later they gathered into communal groups under austere rules, which were first laid down by St. Basil the Great in the fourth century. Soon the necessity arose to erect quarters to protect the monks from harassment by the Arabs and to accommodate pilgrims to the holy mountain. The Byzantine Emperor Justinian built the first monastery and church in the mid-sixth century, surrounding the place with a fortification. When, some three hundred years later, the bones of the martyred St. Catherine of Alexandria were deposited there, the monastery took on her name.

Besides its Judaeo-Christian associations, the place was venerated also by the Moslems. According to tradition, a monk at Mount Sinai wrote down the Koran at the dictation of Mohammed the Prophet, who was unlettered; and Mohammed, who always evinced admiration and respect for cultural accomplishments, granted a charter to the monks in gratitude, assuring them the safety of their lives and property from his followers. From Mount Sinai, Mohammed is believed by some Moslems to have been carried aloft to Heaven on the back of a great camel which left its footprint on the peak.

As the schism between the two Christian denominations became marked, in the mid-eleventh century, and amidst the engulfing conquest of the Moslems, the monastery of St. Catherine at Mount Sinai served as the link between the biblical lands—at that time no longer in Christian hands—and the rising civilization of Western Europe. Up to the fifteenth century the Roman Catholic hierarchy accepted the popularity of the Coptic saint, and the pilgrims of that faith going to the Holy Land stopped there also as at an important shrine. A sketch from that time shows on the mountain a Saracen mosque, the church of Elijah, a church "where the Law was given to Moses," the church of the "garden of the Blessed Catherine" with its well of miraculous water, and the monastery dedicated to her. In 1483 Felix Fabri, a Swiss monk from the Dominican monastery in Ulm, Württemberg, made the pilgrimage, and in his old age described his visit to Mount Sinai. Although he had been taught to regard the monks of St. Basil as without virtue in the eyes of God, he was deeply moved by the holiness of the spot.[43] We realize from his pages what chasms of bitter resentment, petty grudge, and unrelenting suspicion separated the two denominations of Christianity.

The monks of Mount Sinai received income from local sources, especially in the form of offerings from the pilgrims, and could count on subvention from various daughter houses, notably communities on Rhodes, Cyprus, Crete, and Corfu, even after all but the last had fallen to the Turks. The charter "sealed by the hand" of the Prophet was renewed in the early sixteenth century by the Ottoman sultan and, although not always honored, was nevertheless important in preserving, in a number of lands, branches and dependencies dedicated to St. Catherine of Sinai.

The monastery at Mount Sinai has a tremendous religious radiation, even after one and a half millenniums of existence in an Arabic country. And the most important monasteries in Greece, those at Mount Athos and Meteora, looked toward it for orientation, as the keeper of the oldest Christian tradition.

As at Mount Sinai, caves and other natural shelters attracted hermits to the small peninsula of Mount Athos in eastern Macedonia. There, on a tongue of land some thirty miles long and eight miles at its widest point, twenty monasteries with their appended hermitages are functioning even today—a unique agglomeration of religious bodies. The Holy Mountain—*Aghion Oros* in Greek—rises nearly seven thousand feet at the end of the peninsula. Its associations reach back into legendary times. It is a "weather breeder" of fierce, sudden thunderstorms and incalculable winds, which defeated Xerxes' navy in 491 B.C. The Christian legend has it that the ship on which the Virgin sailed with St. John for Cyprus was blown out of its course to Athos, then the abode of ancient gods. When she stepped ashore, the idols shattered. Before leaving, she blessed the place and called it her garden, devoted to contemplation. Since then, entrance is forbidden to any other woman; not even female animals may cross the boundary.

Here, in the protection of idyllic forests, surrounded by the changing green-blue depths of the Aegean Sea, those religious men found peace as early as the fourth century. By the tenth century they had grown so numerous that Athanasius organized for them the first monastery—or "community," as it is called, reflected in its Greek name Lavra—the nucleus of what became a republic of monasteries. In the eleventh century the Byzantine emperor gave further privileges and donations, and the Holy Mountain became a fountainhead of spiritual power and religious art. At its highest period it had forty monasteries, with a multitude of inmates. Today, with only half the religious establishments, their numbers are constantly shrinking.

The monasteries fall into two classes, the cenobites, who live in communities under strict rules administered by a single head, and the idiorrhythms with an elected leader, whose lives are freer and whose discipline is less severe. Besides these, there are the hermits whose abodes are scattered throughout the peninsula; they are free to follow the dictates of their "inner rule."

When Thessaloniki fell to the Turks (1430), Mount Athos saw its first Moslem officials. But these left the holy men in peace and respected their privileges. Isolated from the suffering and death which war brought to wide areas, libraries could be gathered, with works both copied and composed there. Many of the finest murals at Mount Athos were executed in the second half of the sixteenth century, when the Greek mainland and the rest of the Balkans had long been under Turkish rule. However, the uprising of the Greeks for a national independence (1821) brought the monks also into the conflict, and they gave shelter to Christian fugitives. A Turkish army of three thousand men occupied the peninsula and housed in the monasteries for nine years. Four-fifths of the monks fled; the old buildings began to decay. Many art pieces and books were hidden or taken away, but the murals continued to deteriorate. The cultivated lands, olive groves, and gardens began to revert to wilderness. At Chilandari, once one of the wealthiest monasteries in art and worldly goods, only three monks remained as caretakers. One can imagine what they availed in the vast complex, in which soldiers and their women were living, cooking, washing, and disregarding—even perhaps trying to desecrate—the painted images of the "infidels." In the last quarter of the nineteenth century an economic upswing, the result of independence achieved in a number of Balkan countries, and lavish gifts from Russia contributed to a wave of restoration. But by that time much of the original medieval character of the monasteries had already been lost. Even skillful and trained restorers—rare indeed at that time—could not have saved many of the details.

Thus the monasteries at Mount Athos saw the flowering of Byzantine mural painting, and contributed toward it considerably. But they also saw their treasures pillaged and soiled. Now, in the present day, with a sparse and ignorant younger generation which cannot carry on the great tradition, the future looks far from bright.[31]

The east side of the peninsula has a mildly rising terrain, and the establishments reach down on even ground to the water's edge. Since shipping and fishing were important, we often see service buildings near the shore, where boats could be sheltered when the fierce wind blew the waves to a perilous height. As were all monasteries of the Middle Ages, those on Mount Athos were provided with fortifications against pirates and other raiders attracted by the treasures accumulated there. One of the earliest establishments, Vatopedi (*Pl. 6A*), still displays its sturdy bleak citadel-like walls. Expanding in later centuries when life was more friendly, it made use of the outer walls as foundations for further construction. The upper stories were frail, usually built of wood, and fell prey to frequent fires. The large court (*Pl. 7A*) has an extended pavement, trodden smooth by the feet of monks and pilgrims through many centuries. The lead-covered domes of the churches have the outline of St. Mark's in Venice. Fountains of pure water welcome the traveler.

The *katholikon,* or main church (*Pl. 7C*), placed as usual in the center of the courtyard, offers a display of taste ranging from inspiring manuscripts and finely chased enamels of the thirteenth century to factory-made chandeliers of the nineteenth. The gifts of powerful donors had to be exhibited; this is why so many lamps in so many styles hang in so many churches. Note the magnificent candelabrum at the right, resting on crouching lions, so characteristic of Eastern Christianity. The lion was known from life by the early Christians of Africa and Asia Minor, and was realistically rendered, while the West long represented it rather as a dog with a human face. As a backdrop to the scene stands the elaborate iconostasis, hung with icons and curtained in velvet, which screens the altar from public view. In the tall, narrow, domed stand at the left center, that particular icon is exhibited which has bearing on the day or season. Flowers, blessed by use in the service, are strewn on the floor after special ceremonies.

The *trapeza*, or refectory (*Pl. 6B*), has plain stone slabs as tables, but the walls are richly painted with religious subjects. Life-size figures of the Virgin and the Angel of the Annunciation occupy the two niches, separated by the masonry bay. In the upper left is the Feast of Abraham, at the right the Last Supper. In the large curvature of the bay Mother and Child sit enthroned, surrounded by apostles and saints. The wall paintings were periodically "refreshed"—sometimes all too effectively—and dating and authorship are thus rendered uncertain. For other illustrations from Vatopedi, see *Pls. 66C* and *88B*.

Lavra, the earliest and largest of the foundations, also went through many changes. The passageway to the church, now enclosed in nineteenth century glass of dubious taste, displays a mural of the Last Judgment (*Pl. 9A*). The monstrous maw of Hell swallowing the wicked is frequently encountered in Late Byzantine painting. The categorical divisions with their explanatory text, the harsh coloring, and the folkloristic flowered frieze running the length of the benches show how benevolent but crude "reconstruction" can eradicate vestiges of earlier centuries. (See also *Pl. 65B* and *C*.)

Also on the east side of the peninsula stands Iviron (*Pl. 10A*), another of the larger and more important monasteries. It was founded in 980, traditionally with the approval of Athanasius.[31] It was in its harbor that the Virgin's boat is said to have found refuge from the roaring storm. The hills, thickly wooded even today, that rise behind the complex, offer a wide view of the Holy Mountain, which is often wreathed in clouds. Since wood was the only material at hand for cooking and heating and even for much of the building, fire has done much damage here, as among most of the monasteries on Mount Athos. But the great gate tower stands in medieval massivity.

Lord Curzon who visited Iviron in 1831 judged the monastery to be even larger than Lavra or Vatopedi at that time, and called it a fortified town.[22] (See also *Pl. 24B.*) Curzon spent some time in the library, and noted an octavo manuscript of Sophocles and a Coptic psalter with Arabic translation, as well as superb specimens of Greek manuscripts from the eleventh and twelfth centuries, the works of SS. Chrysostom and Basil, and a large folio New Testament executed in magnificent calligraphy, its red velvet binding an art piece in itself. His rather cursory statistics mention some 5,000 printed books, 2,000 manuscripts on paper, 1,000 manuscripts on vellum—many of them immensely thick quartos, as much as 18 inches square and 6 inches through. Considering the destruction of time and the diminishing number of monks, it is reassuring that the Greek Ministry of Religion and Education, through its Archaeological Service, has classified and inventoried the Iviron Library as one of the most important on Mount Athos today.[20] There are still close to 1,400 manuscripts and 15,000 printed books on hand, many of them first editions; the overwhelming majority of them are in Greek, but Russian and other Slavic languages, Latin and West European tongues are also represented.

The most imposing position on the west coast is held by the monastery of Simopetra (*Pl. 8A*). It stands on fortress-like abutments on an isolated rock, its height greatly accentuated by the steep cliffs that fall away below it. Since its foundation around the mid-fourteenth century, it has been several times laid waste by fire, and little could be saved from earlier days. Even its katholikon is without wall painting. Altogether some two dozen monks live in this romantic but forsaken abode, mostly Greeks, some from Asia Minor.

The monastery of Grigoriou (*Pl. 9C*) was founded in the late thirteenth century by Gregory, a monk from Mount Sinai. The present building, constructed with donations from a Moldavian prince (Romania), is of late eighteenth century, and its frescoes date from about the same time, with recent "refreshings." [31] Its compact outline is more like that of a palace than of a fortress; modern cement piers like elegant columns support the superstructure. The painstakingly constructed terraces grew vegetables, olives and other fruits for the use of the monks. (Many of the monks never tasted meat, and allowed themselves fish only on special feast days.) Beyond, stretch the rocky bluffs of the west coast, heavily wooded in patches and, owing to the absence of grazing animals, luxuriant with the rare wildflowers of the seasons.

The monastery of Panteleimon (*Pl. 8B*), or Russiko, as it is popularly known, is built on a gentle slope and is one of the largest establishments on the peninsula. It was founded by Russian monks, as the name implies. Walking its streets, one has the impression of being transported to a nineteenth century Russian town as described by Gogol and Turgenev. The gilded sheen has faded from the onion domes. Exteriors and interiors show the melancholy marks of decay. But they are still reminders of the great attraction that this place had for the Russians before World War I. At one time Russian monks outnumbered the Greeks on the peninsula.[20] The refectory, enlarged at the end of the nineteenth century to seat eight hundred monks, was not sufficient to accommodate all the religious at one serving.

Several four- and five-story modern buildings line the shore, where the numerous Russian pilgrims who came by boat on the way to or from the Holy Land could lodge. The Athos monks in their free time carved crosses and other religious objects of wood with an admirable delicacy, in a special style; what is sold today is less than a shadow of the craft. The visitor is received in a vast, once-magnificent audience hall, the walls hung with the dusty portraits of Russian and Balkan rulers. As the amenities of welcome are being offered, one can notice that the velvet of one's armchair is split and that the lace doily on the table falls to shreds at a touch. The monumental dining hall once catering to the pilgrims is now locked, and sea birds flying in and out of the broken windows bring the only life to it. The pier is in dire need of repair, and the frail old gatekeeper merely waves one goodbye, lying pale on his sagging divan.

The monastery of Dionysiou, founded in mid-fourteenth century by Dionysius of Kastoria, has the patina of ages upon it, as one of the very few that for centuries has had no destructive fires within its walls. A steep stone-paved walk leads upward from the sea to its one gate, which could have served a medieval castle. From the narrow dilapidated balconies, supported by aged struts, an inspiring panorama opens across the water toward the west, where Mount Olympus stands (*Pl. 10B*). In the refectory (*Pl. 10C* and *D*) the monks sit before rigorously scrubbed wooden tables on benches without backs. The crude cabinet under the pulpit shows the simple taste of the last generation. In strong contrast is the golden Rococo pulpit with its perforated pattern of vines. On the lectern, shaped like an eagle with spread wings, lies the book which is read aloud during the meal. The monastery is said to possess unrestored murals by the Cretan painter Zorzi from the mid-sixteenth century.[31] Among more frequently encountered subjects (*Pl. 10C*), the Ladder of St. John Climacos depicts, with a light touch and vivacious detail, the progress of the monastic soul toward final salvation. Climacos, born in Palestine in the late sixth century, was a monk at Mount Sinai and for a while a hermit in the Arabian Desert. He wrote a classic work on ascetic philosophy called *The Climax or Ladder of Perfection,* hence his nickname.

As a special favor the abbot conducted us down into the foundations to see a chapel in the earliest part of the structure. After descending several flights of very narrow stairs, in pitch darkness, by a wavering candle flame, we found ourselves in a tiny room with a simple wooden iconostasis half empty of icons—and whatever wall painting was visible was shockingly bright and new.

We arrived in late afternoon at Dochiariou, the last of the monasteries visited. Luckily the big gate was still open, but we had to wait for the evening service to come to an end. The mellow voices of the monks had an overtone of lament; the *a cappella* singing gave the traditional melodies an eerie timbre as they floated out over the courtyard where we sat on a bench. The katholikon is a tall, majestic church, said to be the largest on Athos. We were admitted as the candles were being extinguished; smoke floated in the air mixed with the musky aroma of incense. The bearded old monks were leaving, some of them in whispered conversation. The vast interior with its rich iconostasis is painted throughout—walls and ceiling—said to be the work of Cretan painters from the second half of the sixteenth century.

Today, the most authentic paintings can be found high in a dome or a gallery, preserved by the protected position and out of easy reach of a restoring brush. The awe-inspiring Pantocrator, Christ in Judgment, in the dome (*Pl. 9B*), is placed with great skill so as to show no distortion from any point. The colorful folds of the garments contrast with the expressive, majestic face. Under Him, the heavenly hierarchy form a circle, and their proportions and color harmonies make His figure seem still more elevated above the church floor where we stand. As the parting sun strikes into the lofty lantern, the cupola glows with golden warmth and color. One understands the constant inspiration, the pride of belonging there that emanates from the abbot. As he speaks of historians who previously visited the monastery, his eye scans lovingly the seascape and the dark mountains iridescent in the sunset.

Before the peninsula joins the mainland, it narrows to a strip of land something over a mile wide, across which the Persian king Xerxes undertook to drive a canal. A low stone wall closes off the celibatic retreat of the monks from the outside world; and just beyond it, on the western shore, a village of some ninety small houses, called Prosfori, lies, clustered around a medieval building which gives the popular name Pyrgos (the tower) to the place. Once this was an outpost of the monastery Vatopedi, and it is still the last point where women and female animals may go (*Pl. 7B*). In its present form the tower was built by Andronicus II (1260–1332), but it has been suggested that it stands on an earlier foundation. It served as living quarters for the wife of the Byzantine emperor while he was doing penance on the Holy Mountain. Sunshine falls through long cracks in the masonry. The tower has an inner structure of wood, probably not much younger than the stonework. Through its open windows vistas are framed into idyllic landscapes. Below, the sea reveals in emerald clarity pebbles, fish, and the crumbled walls of a submerged settlement several yards below the surface. Today again a noble lady is hostess there, benefactress of the whole village. Spartan-furnished rooms, with a candle set beside the rough bedstead, await those who return from that unique experience—a visit to Mount Athos.

In 1839 a French glass painter and art collector, A. N. Didron, while staying at Mount Athos noted that although the dates of the many murals extended through centuries, certain religious scenes were repeated almost exactly. Frescoes were being painted at the time of his visit. One monk spread fresh plaster on the wall; the master—without the use of a cartoon or model—sketched the composition. A pupil filled in the outline with colors, while another gilded the halos or lettered the inscriptions and still another executed the ornamentation. Beginners were set to grinding and mixing colors. If any question arose, the solution was sought in their "Primer of Painting," a much-thumbed manuscript which they said was three hundred years old. The manuscript was credited to one Dionysius, or Denys, monk of Fourna, who in turn credited his master for the knowledge. Try as he would, Didron could not acquire the painter's vade mecum, which the monk called "his eyes and hands." So he chose what appeared the oldest and best edition and had it copied at the monastery. It was published in Paris in 1845.[24]

It must be pointed out that the Byzantine artistic canon was held to be as much the revelation of truth as was the Holy Writ, and therefore all repetitions and multiplications had to adhere to tradition. It was not the aim to entertain or delight, but to instruct and edify. Naturalism was irrelevant. In Byzantine art a scene was not presented from a single visual angle; one section might be looked at from above, another from below—with the purpose of obtaining emphasis and guiding the eye. The often repeated gestures stem from the language of hands which came down from ancient Greek drama.[40] Denys's "Primer" is based on the ruling of the Council of Nicaea that the structure of the painting is not the invention of the painter, but must preserve the statutory rules and traditions of the Universal Church. The first section of his manuscript gives technical directions on how to prepare the materials. The second describes the scenes to be represented, giving their protagonists and the symbols which identify them. The third section instructs the painter what scenes should be assigned to what part of a building; and the last lays down details for the depiction of Jesus, the Trinity, Mary, and the saints, their expressions, gestures, garments, and the proper colors for various occasions. Thus it is clear that the painters of Mount Athos, though rarely innovators, were the guardians of the Byzantine iconographical tradition. Since traveling students came to them and Athonite painters journeyed far and wide, this artistic tradition was long upheld, and spread throughout much of the Orthodox world.

Three death scenes (*Pl. 11*) demonstrate that while following the vade mecum of Orthodox painting, the personality of the painter nevertheless comes through. Athanasius the Athonite, founder of Lavra, was born in Trebizond (ca. 920–1003). When he died, he was abbot general of sixty communities of hermits and monks, all on Mount Athos. It is only natural that his life as a paragon should be painted again and again. The Death of St. Athanasius (*Pl. 11A*), attributed to a painter of the Cretan School from the early sixteenth century, follows the strict principles which ruled Byzantine painting at the time. The saint is seen lying in state within the walls of his monastery, surrounded by his followers who are crowded into a tight arc of figures. In the background, scenes of his early life are depicted—the study of holy books in a hermit's cave, consultation with an ancient stylite saint on his column who is being fed by means of a basket pulled up by a rope. In the upper left corner an angel carries Athanasius' soul in the form of an infant to Paradise. In the center a sixteenth century church is represented —not, as would be historically correct, one from the tenth century. Other paintings from Lavra are shown on *Pls. 60C, 62C, 65B.*

Very similar in composition is the Death of St. Ephraim, at Dochiariou (*Pl. 11B*). This popular hermit saint, who died about 370, was a native of Mesopotamia, the head of a school, and later a monk who devoted his days to writing. His work, written in Syrian, was translated early into Armenian, Greek, Coptic, Arabic, and Ethiopic. In the mural, which was executed in 1568 by a painter of the Cretan school, Ephraim lies in the open. The semicircular mounds indicate hills. An icon is laid on his breast, as with Athanasius. Tall candles burn at his head, and a priest swings a censer while a fellow monk leans down to catch his last words.

A mural by an Athonite painter showing the same subject (*Pl. 11C*) extends along the exterior wall of the church of Paraskevi (Holy Friday) in Siatista in western Macedonia, on the important trade route that leads into the Danubian Valley. It is dated 1611. The scene follows established rules, but a certain loosening of the composition is noticeable. Monks, light- and dark-cowled, flock to pay their respects. An aged man is carried in on a ladder. Note the figure on a mule and the old man with a bundle over his shoulder (right) that appear also in the earlier composition. As in other versions, his soul is carried to Heaven in the form of an infant. Here some fifteen feet of wall are given to concentrated storytelling. Many details are not clearly separated, and blend into a tapestry-like composition; the "message" seems somewhat subordinated to the decorative effect. Colors are monotone—white, brick-red, brown, and black. The row of saints in the lower section, carefully differentiated in type and labeled, are medallion-like in appearance because of their great halos. A red strip edged in white separates the two subjects, a method encountered in other parts of Macedonia, as well as on the island of Crete. Another section of these murals can be seen on *Pl. 97A*.

This arrangement in death and burial scenes remained popular, and occurs even on small icons in many lands into the nineteenth century. The prototype is the composition prescribed for the Dormition of the Virgin (see *Pls. 15C* and *19A*).

An idea may have been gained by now of the high standard of painting in places of great importance and culture and in the isolation of monasteries, where the art could be preserved. But the simple folk of the villages also cared much that their places of worship should be worthy of their religion. In unknown, unimportant, and seldom visited regions, icons and murals are preserved which testify to this ideal.

Macedonia, a land with a long and great historical past, gave birth to such different personalities as Alexander the Great and Mustafa Kemal. To draw its borders would be difficult, because in various periods the demarcations differed. The Macedonians—with territory now divided between Bulgaria, Greece, and Yugoslavia—had enough historical, national, and religious identity to force Belgrade to acknowledge a separate Macedonian Orthodox Church, which has an archbishopric at the ancient town of Ohrid although recognizing the Serbian patriarch in the capital. The region was trodden by numberless folk driven away from their birthplaces. Although separated on the north by mountain ranges, it was not far from the Danubian Valley, the source and goal of much of its commerce. It shows the impact of Roman, Orthodox, and finally Turkish influences that met on its ground. It took over many cultural traits from Greece, but even today Greek Macedonia is regarded as "foreign" territory by the Athenians.

While the Roman visits either of Peter or of Paul are far from clarified, Paul's presence in Greece, Macedonia, and Crete is documented in some detail in the Bible. The Apostle to the Gentiles preached in Thessaloniki in the winter of 49–50 of our era. He founded a church in

Thessaloniki for which he had a predilection, and in his Epistle to the Thessalonians there is a special reference to the women of the city. He spoke in Greek, spreading the Gospel in the common language of the eastern Mediterranean.

Most of Macedonia came under Turkish rule in 1371 and by 1407 was irretrievably lost. Large tracts of land were bestowed upon Ottoman chiefs, and they in return furnished soldiers for the Moslem forces, drawn from the population on their properties. The Orthodox religion was kept up stanchly by the peasants, aided by the local priest. His life differed little from that of his farming neighbors. By Orthodox rules he should marry and have children (only the monks are celibate). And just because he lived like the villagers, in his little whitewashed house with its roofed porch, looking out upon the everyday life of the community, he grew intimate with the joys and sorrows of his parishioners. The Christian religion was generally tolerated as long as it was not conducive to visible national demonstrations against the Turkish overlords. As few larger cities existed, there were few places where the population was dense. For the Christian believers, small clan chapels or village churches sufficed. Much feuding went on between the pashas and the Porte, and the surveillance of the population was sometimes lax, sometimes eased with bribes. By the eighteenth century the local governors had become practically independent—which meant on occasion still less rigidity in keeping the established rules.

The manors of the well-to-do were enclosed within walls, and comprised barns, sheds, various outhouses, as well as dwellings. It was not difficult to disguise the family chapel that had nestled among these, often so small that it could hold no more than ten or twenty. A porch might be placed around it, over which the old roof was skillfully extended, or a lattice before it, reaching to the eaves. Some twenty such concealed churches can be found in the town of Verroia alone (the biblical Beroea). Ayios Christos, one of the earliest, contains frescoes signed Kalergis and dated 1315—among them two kneeling angels which, through the weightlessness of their bodies and the grace of their design, compare with those of the fifteenth century Baldovinetti (see also *Pl. 23*). Other churches date from the sixteenth century, while some murals seem to be from the mid-seventeenth and were refurbished as late as 1804 and even 1858—witnesses to the persistence of these people.

West of Verroia lies Siatista, somewhat off the present road, on an elevated incline of a hill that leads to a mountain pass, still used by pack trains of mules. Sections of the exterior mural of the church of St. Paraskevi are reproduced on *Pls. 11C* and *97A*. The interior shows the pride which the wealthy community took in its place of worship. The elaborate woodwork was once heavily gilded, as were the backgrounds and halos in the murals. It seems that after an uprising against the Turks, the Christians, in fear of losing the pride of their town, smeared the church interior with charcoal dust—available in abundance here, where charcoal is burned. Only spots of the gold of a halo and a few glimpses of lively coloring glint through the smoky layer, awaiting expert hands to reveal the beauty of the decoration.

Where the borders of Greece, Albania, and Yugoslavia meet, there are little-disturbed river valleys with sheep grazing along the shores, delightful lakes framed by rugged mountain ranges. At a distance, the town of Kastoria, on a hilly peninsula, shimmers like a mirage across its lake. On entering the place, one sees immediately the lively tempo of an energetic mountain people. Owing to its geographical position, Kastoria has been a flourishing commercial center since pre-Roman times. The town takes its name from the Greek *kastor*, beaver, which abounded in the region. The tradition of working fur remains a main source of wealth and craftsmanship today. The prosperous merchants built opulent houses, sometimes three stories high, and spent much on their decoration. Typical are the deep bay windows, richly carpeted and strewn with velvet and embroidered cushions, the lace-like wood carving, the flower-painted paneling, and the patterns in colored glass. The use of gilding and white lacquer shows that the mode of the Baroque and Rococo was known here also.

Altogether more than sixty painted churches and chapels are found in and around Kastoria. The steep hillside is dotted with small stone buildings commanding a magnificent view (*Pl. 14A*), and only the initiate will recognize them as chapels by the tiny shell-like apses. They date from the tenth and eleventh centuries to the seventeenth and even later.[41] Many can be approached only up rough footpaths or mulepaths. Unfortunately, few of the population are aware what national and art-historical significance such edifices have. This writer called on the Metropolitan of Kastoria. After the customary courtesies—the offering of a fruit conserve, the ouzo (native brandy), the tiny cup of Turkish-style coffee—I mentioned the damage to murals and icons from the careless placing of tapers and candles. The tall, bearded bishop, erect in his high chair, leaning on his silver-topped staff, fingering a jeweled cross on his breast, answered in deep-toned indignation that he could not accept criticism of the way his flock chose to worship. Icons often suffer also from a yearly washing by the devout with rosewater, wine, or a mixture of water and vinegar. While the cleaning might brighten the colors for a time, in the long run it dulls the picture.

The church of Anargyri is one of the largest in the town, a three-aisled basilica, dedicated to the mendicant "healing" saints—best known of whom are Cosmos, Damian, and Panteleimon (*Pl. 14B*). Dating from the tenth and eleventh centuries, it is constructed mostly of brick, with some stone and heavy mortar in between, laid in a decorative pattern. The narthex, or vestibule, is like a separate wing across the front of the building, behind which rises the high clerestory that lights the nave. Remnants of frescoes can still be discerned on the exterior walls. Inside, covering walls and ceiling, the entire Orthodox repertory of saints and scenes is on display. Because of its somewhat remote situation, the paintings have suffered little and are now being cleaned by a new method which does minimum damage to the original lines and colors. For details of the murals see *Pls. 22B, 23C, 82B, 95C*.

The former monastery and pilgrim shrine of Mavriotissa is idyllically situated at the tip of the peninsula, under enormous plane trees (*Pl. 15A*), about half an hour's walk along the shore from the center of the town. Two chapels were joined here; the larger and taller, with an apse (right), dates from the eleventh century, the smaller from the sixteenth. Traces of exterior murals remain (*Pl. 14C*). The door at the left leads into a large bare narthex, with a mural of the Last Judgment (*Pl. 15B*). Worn and faded though it is, it has not been defaced or glaringly repainted. The Saviour sits enthroned as judge, flanked by the Virgin Mary and the Baptist as intercessors and surrounded by the company of apostles and the blessed. Below Him are the Cross, the Dove, and the Book, symbols of the Godhead, likewise enthroned and guarded by archangels. Two figures kneel at the foot—some say the donors, others Adam and Eve as symbols of redeemed mankind. A river of fire descends from the foot of the Throne, and archangels with long spears are thrusting the wicked into the curling flames. A comparison with the vast mosaic of this same subject at Torcello near Venice shows revealing similarities (*Pl. 15D*). The dates of these two Judgments are close to each other: the mural is assigned to the end of the twelfth, the mosaic to early thirteenth century. The former shows in various decorative details the tradition and feeling of mosaicwork. Both seem to have been drawn from an Orthodox prototype.

The inside of this same wall is occupied by murals of the Crucifixion and the Dormition of the Virgin. The latter scene (*Pl. 15C*) follows the traditional arrangement which served as model for death and burial scenes of other saintly personages in Byzantine art. One sees the apostles gathered about the bier—Peter, with a censer, at the head, Paul at the foot. Another figure leans down to catch the last words—legend has it that she spoke again after expiring. Christ himself takes up her soul as a white-clad infant whom angels reach down to receive. The inclusion of the two figures in front of the bier—the importunate Jew and the punishing angel from a late legend—places the painting as not before the end of the fourteenth century.

Not only in Macedonia but in other Balkan lands, frescoes, whitewashed for generations, are now being uncovered, revealing how generally and how well the craft was practiced even after the fall of Constantinople.

While in the wide areas of the Orthodox faith, the religious service was conducted in the language of the country, paintings used a visual language that was understood everywhere. Slowly each country developed preferences in its manner of painting, but greater differences can be observed in the architecture.

Bulgaria, a neighbor to Byzantium, fell in 1396 to the Turkish power and remained under it until 1878. After the first century or so, the occupation lost much of its rigor. As elsewhere, the Turkish administration was lenient in matters of religion, so long as it did not become ostentatious. The church in Bulgaria was placed by the Turks under the patriarch of Constantinople. A remarkable example of the persistence of tradition is the monastery of Rila, Bulgaria (*Pl. 16B*), which is situated in a picturesque gorge surrounded by forest-clad mountains that rise to some eight thousand feet. The largest and wealthiest of Bulgarian monasteries, Rila, was founded in the mid-fourteenth century—the square tower is datable at 1335—and remained an active center whence religious stimulus and artistic influence could be dispersed throughout the land.[29] It is known that connections were kept up with the Athonite monasteries, some of which were sustained by contributions from the Bulgarian people. Indeed, today Chilandari has more Bulgarian than Serbian monks.

This complex shows well how monastic architecture, leaning on the tradition of Mount Athos, has been adapted in the hands of regional craftsmen. Like neighboring Balkan monasteries, it is built of stone, with some brick, rubble, and mortar, smoothed over with plaster, and whitewashed. Since the monastic principle was that of seclusion, the attractive face of the establishment looks onto the star-shaped court (*Pl. 16C*). A great fire destroyed most of the complex in 1833. The Turkish authorities permitted rebuilding under the stipulation that the old dimensions be kept. Today it is impossible to judge whether this dictum was strictly adhered to—but what now stands (the picture was taken in 1932) is certainly imposing. In the foreground is the brown- and white-striped church, typically Byzantine in line, with a number of little domes sheathed in metal. The interior (*Pl. 16D*), finished around 1847, displays exquisite carving and sumptuous gilding. Where there is no woodwork, the walls are bright with murals.

The sometimes skeptical visitor is nearly always assured that everything in these old buildings is unchanged, but the sight of a monk repainting a section of the church atrium (*Pl. 16A*) contradicts the statement. Damaged and faded sections were all too often freshened by persons who lacked the understanding of how to conserve without changing. The familiar subject of the Last Judgment, so obviously "restored" (*Pl. 17A*), loses nearly completely the medieval concept in its modern garb. (Compare *Pl. 15B* and *D.*)

On the northeastern slopes of the Carpathian Mountains lies Moldavia, a former principality. The monastery of Sucevita, founded at the end of the sixteenth century, is the largest of thirteen monasteries there with churches painted outside and inside (*Pl. 17C*). Its square ground plan still recalls a medieval fortress. The massive block of the living quarters has little architectural refinement. The style of the church itself harks back to wooden prototypes, which preceded masonry construction in the timber-rich region. The tendency was to keep all religious buildings modest, and often chapels or churches were sunk a half-story into the ground.

Religious establishments received not only subsidy from their patrons but gifts such as jewelry, illuminated manuscripts and, later, printed books. The imagination of the regional painter was fertilized by these and later by woodcuts which were produced in the land throughout the Turkish occupation. The painters were often monks, but the names of itinerant lay craftsmen are also recorded, some of them said to have come from Macedonia.

The outside apse of the church at Sucevita shows an extended shingle roof, reminder of the tradition of the wooden churches (*Pl. 17B*). Painted panels in the arched surface alternate with those placed on the wide pilasters, giving through the different levels a play of sun and shade. Represented on the exterior are: the Heavenly Host, the Child Emmanuel, the Virgin, bishops, martyrs, and hermits. Such wall paintings also commemorate historical events, including the fall of Constantinople.

Extremely effective is the representation of the Spiritual Ladder of St. John Climacos, painted in 1582 (*Pl. 17D*). Angels nudge the monks forward in their upward climb, the wedge-shaped wings give the composition rhythmic emphasis. Each rung of the Ladder represents a virtue, and the humans who reach the top are received by the Lord at what looks like the open trapdoor of a hayloft. The paintings were retouched in 1882 in a "barbarous way";[30] again only the upper sections, difficult to reach, preserve in patches their older flavor.

Besides murals, the painters also furnished icons on wood and, from the eighteenth century on, holy pictures on glass. These, hanging in a peasant house, with their vivid colors gave a religious touch to the room and at the same time were a declaration of Orthodox faith. Talented hands carved benches and other church furniture. Unavoidably, oriental and Turkish motifs were mixed in, lending the work strong folkloristic flavor.

Across the border toward the east lay the vast territory under Russian dominance. This country also was converted to Christianity from Constantinople. Its twelfth and thirteenth century art and architecture, as much as remains, show strong Byzantine influence. But, as the country's power grew and the Gospel was spread in the language, the Russian arts and crafts took on more and more national characteristics. While the general plan of a church or the composition of a holy painting reveals the common ancestry with other Orthodox lands, from the fifteenth or sixteenth century onward Russian art wrote its own history.

Serbia, an old kingdom, is the nucleus of present-day Yugoslavia which comprises also Slovenia, Croatia, Bosnia, Hercegovina, Dalmatia, Montenegro, and a part of southern Hungary. Belgrade, the capital, stands at the great bend of the Danube, where the river turns at right angles and flows eastward. The history of the Serbians is perhaps the most turbulent of all the

Balkan States. Always excellent and courageous fighters, with Slavic fanaticism for what they thought was right, they had to struggle for independence under cruel pressure, on one side from Venice and Hungary serving Rome, and on the other side from the Byzantine Empire representing the Greek Church. By the mid-twelfth century Serbia was a unified nation and had established a dynasty that reigned for nearly two hundred years, a continuity rare in those times. By the thirteenth and fourteenth centuries, their Orthodox monasteries and churches show national spirit and style.

From the first onslaught of the Turks in the mid-fourteenth century, the Serbs allied with the Hungarians to stem the advance. But the constant squabbles and scheming among Christians weakened the Serbian position, and in 1371, on the field by the Maritsa River, the first decisive defeat was delivered by the Turks. A few years later the disaster at Kossovo took the flower of Serbian aristocracy and military leadership. Nevertheless, for seventy years, by paying tribute to the sultan, Serbia was able to maintain a government under its own rulers. A number of alliances with Western powers were tried unsuccessfully, and in 1459 the country was fully occupied by a large Turkish army. Some two decades later Turkish dominance of the Balkans was complete. The only fragments of land to retain independence were the city republic of Ragusa, today Dubrovnik (see *Pls. 34B, 35A*), and the tiny mountain principality of Montenegro. Under Suleiman I, the Turks resumed their relentless forward march north along the Danubian plain. After the battle of Mohács, Hungary's power was also broken. Between 1550 and 1648, when the West was fighting its wars of religion, the Ottoman Empire extended its power from the northwest Carpathian mountain range of Hungary to the Adriatic shores of Hercegovina with a gigantic hinterland through Asia Minor and along the coast of North Africa.

Although the land was submerged in a Moslem sea, the Serbian Orthodox Church kept the national spirit alive. In 1557 the Grand Vizier, Mehmed Sokolovic, a native of Hercegovina, revived the patriarchate of Pec (Ipek); and while the nation's literature virtually ceased to exist, Serbian was spoken by the local beys and pashas during the sixteenth century and freely used in correspondence between the Porte and Ragusa and some Hungarian princes in the north.

The church at Sopocani (*Pl. 18A*) began as a burial chapel for the Serbian King Uros I, who died as the monk Simeon at the monastery of Chilandari, Mount Athos, in the mid-thirteenth century. It was first a simple single-nave church; later a chapel was added, surmounted by a small cupola. The semicircular apse is characteristic of buildings in Byzantine style. Greatly damaged by the Turks, the church and the monastery attached to it were deserted for a time, but its frescoes are now well restored and are considered by many the finest example of Serbian art of that period.[49]

The Dormition of the Virgin (*Pl. 19A*) shows the typical Byzantine composition. Christ stands at Mary's bier, holding her soul as an infant in His arms, amid the grieving apostles. Above, in accord with Byzantine practice which combines various episodes of a story within one picture, the apostles are seen being transported by angels in cloud boats to her bedside. Christ is seen again in a mandorla in Heaven. The grouping has rhythmic grace; the colors are characteristically mild and harmonious. Ocher, green, and violet predominate, and parts of the background were once gilded. The coloring brings out the variety in the folds of the garments. The postures and gestures, as well as facial expression, communicate sorrow.

On the curving wall of the apse, a touching array of saintly witnesses attends the Mass (*Pls. 18B* and *19B*). The text on their scrolls is in Cyrillic lettering.

Pec was the seat of the Orthodox patriarchate, and its first metropolitan church was built in the early thirteenth century, dedicated to the Holy Apostles. Within a few decades churches were added to left and right, thus achieving more breadth than length in the complex (*Pl. 20C*). Each of the additions is different enough in detail to be noticed, but together they form a harmonious unit. The low apses have a friendly curve, as do the roofs, giving the whole a look of joviality.

The frescoes, originally from the mid-thirteenth century, have been restored and are darkened again by the smudge of tapers, candles, and incense. Even so, the archangel and the warrior saint represented here (*Pl. 20A*) convey the sense of energy and readiness. Their weapons record mid-thirteenth century armature. Note in the figure on the right the bow, the mace, and round target shield slung over a shoulder. In a parallel representation, in the church of Peribleptos in Ohrid, the painter has put his own name and the date on the arc of a bared sword: Master Michael, 1295. The presence of fierce warriors inside the church is not to be wondered at, when we know that Pec was chosen for the patriarchate after an earlier site had to be abandoned as too close to enemy territory.

In the courtyard of the convent of Studenica, founded at the end of the eleventh century, King Milutin had a little church built in 1314 which was named for him: the King's Church (*Pl. 20B*).[49] It has pleasant proportions, and its relationship to the space in the court and conventual buildings is worked out delightfully.

With the church of Gracanica (*Pl. 21A*) a more advanced ground plan comes to the fore. Erected in the first half of the fourteenth century on the cross-in-square plan, it has a central cupola with pendentives and four lower domed structures at the corners. Narthex and exonarthex (left) were added some years later. The outside walls are a colorful combination of stone and brick, while for the interior arches only brick was used. Although much ravaged, its elegant lines could be restored to good advantage, and it stands today as a masterpiece of Byzanto-Serbian architecture.

The monastery-church of Mileseva is set among pine forest and pasture land. Founded about the first third of the thirteenth century, the church was restored in the sixteenth century, when its narthex and lateral chapels were added (*Pl. 21B*). The triple apse is unusual in form. The murals, dating from about 1237, are remarkable even among the fine harvest which this century produced in the country. In this rare instance the names of the painters are preserved—but only as Dimitri and Christophorus. In Italy, where Duccio, Giotto, and their contemporaries are heralded as precursors of the Renaissance, little can be found more expressive or better painted than the radiant and eloquent angel at the tomb of Christ (*Pl. 21C*).

Ohrid, on a lake of the same name, is near the border where the Greek and Serbian sectors of Macedonia meet Albania. The church of San Jovan Kaneo is the pride of the small fishing community that lives on the shore (*Pl. 22A*). It was built at the end of the thirteenth century on the cross-in-square plan, with an octagonal cupola, and amazing decorative skill is apparent in its brickwork. One is reminded of some of the small churches at nearby Kastoria in Greece —curiously enough, also a lake region. Another, much larger and more important, church, St. Sophia, stands in Ohrid, where besides numerous objects of fine Byzantine craftsmanship, outstanding murals of the eleventh century have been restored, which will be discussed shortly.

Approaching Manasija, which was built in the early fifteenth century (*Pl. 24A*), one is struck by the similarity of the massive walls and towers to some of the Athos monasteries, especially Iviron (see *Pls. 10A* and *24B*). In the Athos prototype, living quarters were added on top of the original walls and windows opened in the medieval masonry. But at Manasija, the walls were left in their forbidding plainness, surrounded by a moat and closing in the compound as originally planned. The church with its smooth stonework presents a contrast to the somber aspect of the citadel—"a delicate nut in a powerful shell." [49]

Among the murals within this church, the warrior saints (*Pl. 25B*) are especially well known —and with right. Full-panoplied, with lances, arrows, and swords, they are on the point of going into action. For some, there may be an echo of mosaic tradition in the variety of decorative detail.

The fifteenth century Mercurius from Karyes, Mount Athos (*Pl. 25C*), is related to the warriors on the Serbian wall. Here again costume and armament are delineated with much attention to detail. This work was recently ascribed to the legendary Manuel Panselinos and placed a century earlier. In the fresco of Pippo Spano (*Pl. 25A*) by the Florentine painter Andrea del Castagno, we have a Western version of the warrior of the mid-fifteenth century, and some elements in this figure, such as the curved sword and the fringes of the shirt, show similarity. But in the spirit there is a marked contrast. The truculence and swashbucklering of the mercenary are here individualized, while in the Byzantine renditions the individual has been elevated to the hero-saint.

In *Pl. 22B* and *C* two scenes of the Ascension are compared. The latter, in St. Sophia of Ohrid in Serbian Macedonia, is said to have been painted before 1056. Here seven rainbow colors form the circular glory which is embraced by four angels. The majesty of Christ's figure, the ingenious arrangement of the rich folds of His garb, and the weightlessness of the whole composition command respect in such an early work. The angels seem to cleave to the outer circle; their draperies are floating in space, as if wafting them upward. The same theme was rendered in Greek Macedonia about the same time (*Pl. 22B*). The glory here is the almond-shaped mandorla, in four colors. Very recent discoveries in Byzantine murals in widely distant places prove that the stars were part of the original composition, often glimmering with gold. The folds of Christ's garments are exquisitely drawn. Here the angels are loosened away from the geometric contours of the mandorla, giving the feeling more of upholding than of floating, and the wings are designed to stand away from the central figure.

A cloud boat (*Pl. 22D*) from the Dormition of the Virgin at Sopocani is shown here in detail (see also *Pl. 19A*). There is an interesting differentiation of the two figures, the intellectual apostle and the celestially sweet angel. The wings are not arranged "realistically" but for decorative necessity. The cloud boat is drop-shaped, rounding toward the earth; its scalloped upper section emphasizes the heads and wings.

The wings of the kneeling angel at Ohrid again are adjusted to the design (*Pl. 23A*) and made especially impressive through fortunate coloring—from white to blue to gold. Note the live movement of the figure, in his sweeping obeisance.

Both standing angels (*Pl. 23B* and *C*) carry long thin staves; they are attending Mother and Child who are pictured in the apse. The angel on the left comes from a church built in the mid-twelfth century, in Kurbinovo, near Lake Prespa, Yugoslavia. He has a nervous, fluttering quality and Byzantine attenuation. The swirling folds and wings strengthen the impression of hovering above the earth. The other angel, like as he is, in the apse at Anargyri, Kastoria, is more stable in effect. The undulating garments and the delicacy of the gesturing arms make the figure seem to sway like a lily.

These examples from a little-known area of Christian art, demonstrate amply, in their variety of detail, the spontaneity, coloristic appeal, and storytelling power of Late Byzantine art.

The world of the Orthodox faith, once larger than that of the Roman Church, was ravaged by centuries of Turkish occupation. But even harassed and persecuted, religious activities went on. For religion meant life to the nation, and where life was, there had to be also religion. An easing occurred in the Balkans when the declining Turkish power retired beyond the borders of the Austro-Hungarian monarchy. Refurbishing of old and construction of new religious establishments went hand in hand. A number of monasteries were built in Croatia alone, just across the Danube from where Serbia was still occupied by the Turks. These buildings reflect taste and techniques of the seventeenth and eighteenth century West, although the iconography adhered in general to the Byzantine tradition.

The process of Westernization can be observed in Orthodox churches in whatever part of Europe or America they may stand. The casual stroller may not even notice that he passes an Orthodox church. But within, the congregation listens still to gripping Byzantine chant and a service that harks back to the earliest years of Christianity. The church is for them an island on which they stand proudly, restating their loyalty to a civilization from which the West borrowed so much, when Byzantium was a world.

·II·

CANDIA

Homer praised it at the dawn of history—the fair rich island called Crete in the midst of the dark blue sea, washed by waves on every side, with countless men and ninety cities from the harbors of which the dark-prowed ships were borne forth by wind and wave. Islands such as Cyprus, Rhodes, and Crete, lying as they do on the waterway westward from the Levant which in turn had access to the Far East, were steppingstones for commerce and travel. Touched by ships from afar, they profited from such contacts since earliest times, yet many were able to keep their individual cultures to a high degree. Ceylon, Java, Sumatra, with their complex and stunning arts, as well as the islands in the Mediterranean, are proof of this.

Crete was more than an island; it was the cradle of a civilization. No land of Europe has an older history. When Western Europe was inhabited by primitive hunters and the people in the Danube Valley were groping with the beginnings of agriculture, Crete, from about 3000 B.C., had produced an art and architecture fascinating to archaeologists and laymen alike. From the Minoan civilization which reached its zenith some fifteen centuries before Christ, enough remained for Sir Arthur Evans in the early twentieth century to reconstruct the great palace-city of Knossos in a valley surrounded by olive groves, wheat fields, and vineyards. In their knowledge of natural history, geometry, mathematics, hygiene, the Minoans compare favorably with contemporary Babylon and Egypt. Other sites, excavated or in process of excavation, attest also to the ancient greatness of the island. Crete lay comparatively near across the waterway from the delta of the Nile and also from Haifa. Not only ships but also ideas traveled from these harbors. The Levant boasted efficient highways—unknown in Europe—with established stations for nightly rest. In this epoch the landlocked cities of the mainland were of limited importance. Although earthquake and fire destroyed Knossos some twelve to fourteen centuries before Christ, Cretan civilization did not perish. Cretan influence is evident in the Near East in the fourteenth century B.C. Colonization from the mainland began, and Aegean coins dating from the fifth century show that lively intercourse was still going on.

The fighting quality of the Cretans is praised in legend and epic. A thousand years before Christ, Cretan men were famed as masters in handling the bow. Their fractiousness was sometimes turned against one another, and clans were enmeshed in fratricidal quarrels. But at the appearance of outside enemies, all rallied for the common cause.

When in 66 B.C. Caecellius Metellus made the island a Roman province—an important station in the network of a vast empire, with Gortyna (Gortys) in the south as the capital—Crete lost its autonomy forever. Though stone was the main building material there, the abundant timber of the island was invaluable for the construction of galleys and trading ships. Through the millenniums deforestation went on, with the Venetians and Turks doing their part also, and today the vast, barren mountainsides bear witness to the robber economy of foreign powers.

One of the sources of Cretan pride is their consciousness that they were Christians long before most of Europe had even heard the Word. The island's unabated connections with Egypt, Palestine, and Syria, where Christianity gained its first foothold, furnish explanation why Cretans were converted so soon. Apples from Crete were standard items in the market of Jerusalem at the time of Christ. The ship carrying the Apostle Paul to Rome wintered at the island. A small memorial chapel near the town of Sfakion (Sfakia) marks the spot where according to legend the ship was driven ashore. The first Christian church was erected in Gortyna, and Paul's companion Titus became the first Bishop of Crete, and died there around A.D. 96. Gortyna lost its prominence in later centuries. Today it shows remnants of the ancient fortifications, the ruins of temples to Isis and Serapis, and a palace of the Roman governor; a considerable part of a large Christian basilica is still standing, dedicated to St. Titus and dating from the fourth century (*Pl. 27B*).[57] It is revealing of the vicissitudes of Cretan history that the alleged head of the saint is now preserved as a relic in the Basilica of St. Mark in Venice.

In the last years of the fourth century Crete became part of the Byzantine Empire, and stood with her. Its Christianity was nourished from Constantinople, and the traditions of the Greek Orthodox Church prevail among the population even today. Fragments of mosaics have been discovered in early basilicas at various points of the island, and marble and stone ornaments show the close connections with the Byzantine capital.

In the ninth century the Arabs occupied the island, and it became headquarters for pirates. Its position made it ideal for fast sorties into the main stream of shipping, and its small harbors were used for the hide-and-seek of pursuit. At this time the capital was again moved to the site of an ancient northern port which the Arabs named Rabt-el-Khandak, or moated fortress. In 961 the Byzantine general Nicephoros Phocas, of Cretan descent, liberated Crete, and for nearly 250 years it again belonged to the Byzantine Empire. Then, with the capture of Constantinople by the Franks, it was allotted to Venice. The capital became a principal Venetian stronghold, and its name was Italianized into Candia. With the dawn of independence in the mid-nineteenth century, the ancient name Heraklion again came into use.

Crete was for Venice a vital point in the net of her extended commerce. The maritime transport was severely controlled. But just as happened in the Latin American colonies, where Spanish and Portuguese authorities permitted the goods of other nations to slip into American harbors, Cretan merchants made many ducats through deals on which no duty was paid.

There were enough Italians among the officials, the army of occupation, sailors, merchants, agents, and professionals to mitigate the feeling of the transient Venetian of being in an alien land. Many buildings and institutions reflected the Venetian spirit and talent, especially in harbor towns. The curving breakwaters, with their heavy stone bastions and crenelations and the stone-vaulted berths for ships, resembled those in towns in the Veneto and along the Dalmatian coast, then also under Venetian control (*Pl. 26*). The city walls with their massive earthworks and impressive proud gates were rebuilt and fortified and again strengthened by military engineers in the service of the doges. Many noblemen in high posts on the island built *palazzi* with balconies, finials, and other stone decorations, displaying proud coats of arms—all as if lifted out of the ambience of the Canal Grande. From this time too come the heraldic tablets of generals, commanders, governors who were connected with Cretan history, all of whom lived the luxury life by grace of the Council of Ten of the Republic. Some Cretan churches, even in the provinces, show a late Venetian Gothic or Renaissance style. The Lion of Venice was a familiar emblem everywhere, though it is a question how welcome by the Cretans. Candia had its own two-storied loggia with graceful Renaissance arches, classical columns, elegant balustrade decorated with statues, so Venetian that it could have stood along the Piazzetta somewhere near the Basilica of St. Mark. The main square of Candia displayed an octagonal fountain with Venetian lions. Khania, developed by the Venetians as a foothold in the west of the island, is even more Venetian in character. Foreign merchants were encouraged to settle there instead of in Candia, where the Greek population was restive.

The central administration in Venice, according to the custom of the time, leased the power over Crete to Venetian nobles, and only when the situation became critical did the Senate intervene in an endeavor to bring order and justice. The commanders of the Cretan garrisons were mercenary soldiers, not always native citizens of the republic, who gave generally efficient service to the government which paid them the best. Soldiers from the Venetian-controlled mainland were preferred—Croats, Slovenes, Dalmatians, Istrians—also Bulgarians, Germans, Serbs. Being on foreign ground they had more cohesion as a military unit than the natives, whose villages and parental hearths lay just beyond the hills and who fought only when they felt the cause was just.

Greeks and Latins could and did live peaceably side by side for long periods. In some instances, Orthodox and Roman Catholic services were performed at different altars in the same church, as was the practice in certain churches in Venice at one time. After all, both services are based on the liturgy of the Mass. Differences in creed and administration did not much affect the general population except in times of stress. Unfortunately, then the clash of nationalism acerbated the religious issue. Rome, more than Venice, insisted on attempting the "conversion" of the Cretans, and it should not be forgotten that the Venetian senators several times explained to the Vatican that they had to act first of all for the welfare of the republic and then as Roman Catholics—which throws a new light on the familiar phrase *Siamo veneziani, poi cristiani.*

The Cretans were deprived of their Orthodox bishops for long periods, and Latin services were offered in their churches. To function at all, the metropolitan had to have the full approval of the Venetian authorities. The Cretans were subjected to the forced maintenance of the Roman clergy. Roman monasteries and nunneries were founded and drew income from the land. By the mid-fourteenth century Franciscan, Augustinian, Dominican, Serviti, Crociferi, and Benedictine friars and numerous nunneries were established there. All the orders tried to stay near towns as it was not safe for them in the country.

A special effort was made to lure the population into the Uniate Church, which held services in the language of the land but accepted the authority of the Roman Catholic Church, conceding the disputed points of doctrine. Highly educated Uniate priests and propagandists who spoke Greek spread through the island. They circulated books and read proclamations from the church steps, emphasizing that there was really no difference between the two factions, at the same time mocking the simple village priests as uneducated and uninformed.[56] Paradoxically, some Venetians became Hellenized and changed religious allegiance, as was also the case on the Venetian-held island of Cyprus.

The Italians marshaled all the blandishments their highly developed art could present to draw the folk into their fold—an art which had much enticing charm and was triumphant in the Western world. Statues and figural decoration were lavished on the churches the Roman Rite raised on the island. Many of the clear-toned bells that rang over Crete came from Venice. The museum in Khania has two fine examples of Italian bronze casting, dated 1589 and 1590. They bear garlands on their edges, and the surfaces are used for scenes in relief, of the Crucifixion, the Holy Mother, and figures of the saints. There was always room in the composition for the coat of arms of Venice, with the lion resting his right forepaw on the Scripture—not quite symbolizing the truth.

The Cretans expressed their resistance with the means at their command. Many left their children unbaptized until an Orthodox priest could be found to perform the ceremony. Their art, the murals especially, became a demonstration of nationality and faith. Everything Italian was looked upon with suspicion, as born of the passion for material beauty, redolent of a realism entirely alien to the Orthodox faith. Especially after the Council of Florence, the Cretans reacted vigorously against the agitators who were misinterpreting the issues involved. One of the chief points of division between the two denominations is the disagreement over a phrase of the creed: whether the Holy Spirit proceeds from the Father (as held by the Orthodox) or from the Father and the Son. The Cretans asserted their faith in numerous murals that present the Trinity in strictly Orthodox interpretation.[55] Although, as we shall see, the icons were more open to trends from the West, it is worth noting that Italian influence appears in Cretan wall painting as a reverberation, after Venetian occupation had ended and the Turks took over as rulers of the island.

Another declaration of loyalty can be found in the signature labels, the painted cartouches still visible in various churches. Disregarding the fact that the island had already been for centuries under Venetian rule, one tablet is inscribed: "renovated during the reign of Andronicus the Palaeologos, by . . . [name], living in sin, unworthy bungler. . . ." Another, dated 1446, reads: "renovated and recorded during the reign of our most pious king John Palaeologos Emperor of the Romans. . . ." Sometimes the name of the wife or the mother of the Byzantine emperor is included on the painted tablet. The sponsor is more often chronicled than the artist, and sometimes an entire family is mentioned as having contributed for the construction of some chapel.[56] The dates sometimes run beyond the fifth millennium before Christ, as many are reckoned from the hypothetical age of Abraham.

Venice had risen to her zenith and was with right called the Queen of the Adriatic. She had the power to engage in a successful struggle with her Christian rivals, such as Genoa and Milan, and she had amassed riches and consolidated connections upon which she flourished until the mid-sixteenth century. It was in this epoch that Venice began to attract a gay and easy-living society. Gambling houses and bordellos multiplied. Some of the courtesans became public figures and attained considerable political influence—so much so that the Council of Ten decided to expel them from the city. Many then settled in Candia, augmenting there the mundane atmosphere of luxury and leisure. But their stay was not long. The Venetian authorities realized that with the courtesans gone, vice was growing more uncontrolled. So they were recalled, the favorites received back their palaces, and other restitutions were granted. The

Venetian archives of 1580 reveal more than eleven thousand courtesans as officially licensed.

Though sections of Candia presented to anyone who knew Venice many reminiscences of that city, beyond lay the Cretan town, where the Candiotes, in spite of restrictions, preserved their own life, spoke their own language, and worshiped in their own Greek Orthodox churches. The churches were unostentatious; services were held before the iconostasis on which painted panels were mounted, presenting episodes from the lives of Christ and the Virgin and the saints. Otherwise the buildings had little furniture and no statuary.

Throughout the centuries that Venice was in control in Candia, riots, rebellions, and subversive activities made the life of the Venetian administration uneasy. Usually the leader of the trouble disappeared into the mountains or across the water. The Venetians tried at first to be on good terms with the aristocratic families of Crete, but following an insurrection in the early years of occupation privileges were curtailed and some estates were confiscated. Shortly afterward, the Duke of Candia and a number of Venetian nobles perished in a revolt which within three years had spread over the entire island. In 1341 another rebellion arose, instigated, as often, from Constantinople, and the authorities required seven years to restore a semblance of order. The second half of the fourteenth century was no less full of disquiet. Twelve thousand men were sent in to quench the smoldering revolt. Throughout the fifteenth century similar disturbances attest to the intransigence of the Cretans. On one occasion, when the Venetian administration applied too much pressure on the Cretan youth for military service, more than five hundred families, among them many of the nobility, left the cities for the mountains, thus slipping beyond reach. Messengers for the Venetian authorities passing through the Cretan hinterland carried a white flag to declare their peaceful intentions; and officials very often made use of the same device to assure their safe passage from one region to another. The Italian phrase *una vera guerra di Candia* (a real war of Candia) was the expression, into the nineteenth century, for any endless, acrimonious feud.

Cretan troops fought so valiantly in defense of Constantinople (1453) that at the capitulation the conqueror permitted them to leave with their armor and their flags—an honor seldom accorded the defeated. The Turkish grip now extended over the Levant and into nearly all the harbors of the eastern Mediterranean; soon the Greek mainland also was occupied. From then on, Crete gained importance. New refugee families arrived, bringing not only capital and new commercial connections but also the high standards of metropolitan culture. Venice invested much in strengthening the island, and the following period was a very prosperous one, though still marked by unrest.

The Sfakiotes were a special breed, even among the Cretans who called themselves "the best of the best Greeks." They were a mountain folk who wore their beards and hair long and otherwise were distinguished by their carriage, their costume, and their weapons. Their fierce independence was promoted by their isolation at the southern end of the island behind a nearly impassable mountain range. The name derives from the Greek *sphakia,* implying a region of ravines or gorges. At the nucleus of nearly every rebellion were the Sfakiotes—and the villages beyond the mountain range offered ready shelter for those who had to stay in hiding. From here a movement originated that Crete should be governed by Cretan natives. Though for a time the Venetians were forced to accept the conditions, they bided their time to change the situation. In 1570 the son of one of the most powerful Sfakiote families fell in love with the daughter of a Venetian citizen whose property was near Khania. Three hundred and fifty men and a hundred women came down from their mountain fastness to celebrate the wedding. At the end of the feast they were set upon and made prisoners by a Venetian force of seventeen hundred men with a hundred and fifty riders; the captives were divided into four groups, taken into four separate townships, and hanged there. The Venetian commander then arrested a number of the remaining best Greek families of the region and burned their property. The twelve most respected of the men were hanged, while four women who were with child were cut open before the assembled population, as a warning that thus would those be rooted out who defied the Republic of Venice. It was decreed that any outlawed Cretan would receive amnesty if he appeared before the authorities with the head of his father, brother, cousin, or nephew; it was not asked that a father deliver his own son.[53] Barbarous as this seems, it should be remembered that the massacre of St. Bartholomew's Day occurred even later (1572), and in France. It also was planned on the occasion of a wedding, and it has been estimated that in the subsequent six weeks some fifty thousand people were killed.

Rhodes fell to the Turks in 1522. The pirates of the Algerian corsair Barbarossa, who was at the same time a Turkish admiral, were harrying Mediterranean shipping and repeatedly raiding Crete. Chios fell in 1556 and Cyprus, also a Venetian colony, in 1571. The same year the Turks attacked Crete from Suda Bay, burning Rethymnon and ravaging the wheat fields of Khania. With the Turks standing near Vienna also, the pressure of Ottoman power was for the Venetians no longer a distant threat but a colossal conflagration, burning in their direct neighborhood. The salient points of Crete were refortified. New vaulted berths were built to hold the galleys, and casemates were constructed for the storage of gunpowder and arms. The city of Candia received additional stone ramparts and the walls and bastions were strengthened and heightened.

A large part of the able-bodied population of young men were impressed into service in the Venetian galleys, and the peasants were commandeered to forced labor on the earthworks. The guarding of the fortifications of the "Kingdom of Crete" was intrusted to the so-called militia, professional soldiers amounting to 3,000 to 3,500 men, who were stationed in eight forts on the island. By the end of the sixteenth century, however, the militia had become dismayingly demoralized. An attempt to recruit Cretans to form a reserve army remained largely an edict on paper. It is understandable that they did not rally with enthusiasm to the Venetian flag, even at the approach of the grand Turkish assault on their own island, and that the saying became current, "Rather the turban of the sultan than the tiara of the pope."

Political conditions continued to deteriorate, and in the last decades of the century emigration of Cretans to Istanbul and other Turkish-held territory reduced the island's population from 270,000 to 190,000. After all, they were going to Hellenic cities, with large Greek-speaking populations, where also there was a great demand for art as an expression of Greek Orthodox solidarity.

Nevertheless, Crete held out longer against the Moslems than any other outpost of Venice, indeed until 1669. When the Turks were finally established on the island, the Orthodox faith became again the leading Christian denomination there. What was unheard of under the Venetians, some of the privileges of the metropolitan were reinstated; he was even permitted to ride a horse again as a civic as well as religious leader. The island remained a Turkish possession until 1898, when it was granted autonomy of a sort. In 1913 it joined Greece.

With the passage of time, the changes in trade routes, and the achievements of modern transportation, Crete might seem out of the way and of little importance today. But its continued strategic value was made evident in the last war, when Nazi German parachutists descended upon the western end near Khania in 1941. It is estimated that 80 per cent of the German shock troops were lost, owing to the fierce defense in which the civilian population took a valiant part. But the occupation forces stayed until the general situation of the war forced their evacuation early in 1945.

A visitor to Crete today can see clearly the scars of age-long struggles and the marks of the immense vitality and individuality of its people. Khania's harbor still has strong Venetian echoes. In a main position on the quay stands a vast Turkish mosque, only recently transformed into a museum. Rethymnon retains some minarets and large mosques. In the last war the jagged mountain range no longer protected Sfakion, that nest of continuous rebellion. On the promontory above the little harbor, the houses stand shattered, roofless and windowless, from the heavy fighting in World War II when the British forces were literally pushed into the sea before the Nazi German armies. The Sfakiotes made the enemy pay so dearly that they returned in force with tanks, and "pacified" the countryside in twenty-five days of pillage and murder. Nevertheless the war memorial to the German parachutists, a brazen eagle with extended talons, has been left standing on the road to Khania. As Cretans told us: Monuments make one remember.

Everywhere is evidence that for Crete her religion during the centuries of occupation was the flag of her soul, the anchor of her intellectual balance in a storm in which she was tossed from one owner to another, from one nation to another, always strangers, never benevolent. For Crete, religion became the repository also of the language—the language in which the nation's soul lives. The Cretans, inheritors of the earliest form of Christianity, became, after the fall of Constantinople, the guardians of the Hellenic tradition. Popular literature flourished on their island from the tenth century, and chivalresque poetry can be traced back to the fourteenth. Didactic poems, satirical tales, historical epics, and love songs were written in the language of the great Classical Age; drama, both comedy and tragedy, was created and produced in the tradition and idiom of Euripides. Such Orthodox literature as the Acts of the Martyrs and the lives of the saints led directly into the religious novel. The continuous literary production was not confined to the written and later printed page. The custom of recitation transmitted the Homeric epic until the present day. Men of the island still improvise ballads, treating the legends of the Middle Ages, into which they have woven references to the cruelty of Venetian and Turkish overlords, to the struggle for independence, and lately even to the air-borne invasion of Crete by the Germans.

An exact count has never been attempted of the number of churches and chapels with murals in Crete. A count in the early twentieth century estimated about 800.[52] Since World War II wrought its havoc, some 580 have recently been declared worthy of preservation and study. The earliest date found on a Cretan mural is 1225, and the last 1523—possibly 1550. After Turkish occupation no new murals (increasingly rare) or restorations were signed or dated.[56] These buildings never had mosaic decorations. Mosaic, which in earlier centuries added so much luster to Byzantine architecture, became rare by the fourteenth century. Prerequisite were expert craftsmen, much time, and great affluence. With the imperial treasury and other sources of patronage at low ebb, mural painting came to the fore.

The Cretan murals take on special importance after the fall of Constantinople and the occupation of the Greek mainland. Crete, the largest island free of Turkish occupation, became a workshop for Late Byzantine art that would continue for two hundred more years. Many Greek refugees who fled there for safety were well educated, with high spiritual standards and artistic training. There was a constant replenishment of inspiration from manuscripts and books. To the end of the fifteenth century, signs of contact with Constantinople continue and even become intensified.

Cretan mural painters were active not only on the island but elsewhere, especially in the monasteries of Sinai, Athos, and Meteora. Their journeying produced a new "acme" in those establishments, many of which were enlarged and refurbished at this time. Notable is the work of Theofanis the Cretan, a monk, who with his father and brother painted murals at Meteora around 1528, at Lavra and elsewhere on Mount Athos between 1536 and 1564.[47] Their influence is met in other Balkan lands and in Russia.

The Cretans' loyalty to their artistic tradition helped them preserve their national character. Religion was fortified through art and art through religion. In their places of worship were continuously affirmed the greatness and exquisite provenience of their nation. During the entire period that Crete was occupied—over 450 years by the Venetians and nearly 250 by the Turks—they clung to the tradition of their ancestors. It is significant that in spite of unremitting pressure, not a single Uniate is today in Crete. When Crete was liberated and the Turkish troops were evacuated, the last of the Roman Catholic clergy left the island. The population worships as a body in the One, Holy, Catholic and Apostolic Orthodox Church.

As on the Greek mainland, in Crete the countryside is dotted with tiny stone chapels put up by family groups and farm communities in the wheat fields, at the edges of olive groves and vineyards (*Pl. 27A*). The Turks disapproved large buildings where the population could gather in numbers and foment unrest. Tradition has it that the small chapels where only one family could be accommodated were preferred by the menfolk, who did not want their women in the proximity of the males of other clans. Often no larger than a spacious room, all these buildings have their little apse and barrel vaulting. The earliest preserve remnants of an iconostasis or altar screen of masonry; later, wood was used, but many of these disappeared for firewood in World War II. Today few of the chapels are locked—and there are no signs of recent vandalism, no names or dates scratched on the walls, no painted features defaced. The worst cracks have been filled in with plaster and the earthen floors are swept clean.

Generally the interior of these structures—walls and vaulting—was covered with murals. Often the exterior also was painted. Even in the early twentieth century the buildings on other Greek islands also are reported to have been bright with exterior murals.

Monks, priests, and itinerant craftsmen were the painters. They were not expected to create, but to repeat—to preserve the established pictorial tradition, which was laid down in such painters' handbooks as the manual of Denys of Fourna. Stencils were sometimes used to guide the performance. But in many cases the painter must have worked freehand—in the murals we have seen we have never found an exact replica. Through rigorous training and much repetition of the same subject, he was able to enlarge or reduce a composition according to the wall surface at his disposal and render the features of Christ and the saints so that they were always recognizable. The posture of the body and the gesture of the hands also spoke a universal language.

Sometimes even a small chapel followed a more pretentious design, as that of the Twelve Apostles just outside Sfakion on a hill looking toward Africa (*Pl. 32A*). Gables at the two ends of the nave suggest a peaked roof. But the inside shows barrel vaulting, buttressed by the thick side walls. The windowless dome-on-square is supported by half-domes over the tiny low side chapels and the apse. Our tiring journey there was undertaken because we had heard that the building was painted throughout exterior and interior. Alas, to cover serious war damage the population had whitewashed it all.

Better fortune was encountered in the shrine of St. John at Komitades not far away (*Pl. 32C*). One of the earliest still standing, it is built of stone and rubble, roofed with large rough tiles with the remnants of a stone "roof comb" which was once decorative as well as utilitarian. Colorful majolica bowls in the "pediment," which have lost long ago their luster, still proclaim the tradition of the Levant. The small narthex has fallen in, but the only entrance to the chapel with its sturdy stone uprights and lintel stands firm. The entire vaulted interior, including the ribs, is painted (*Pl. 32B*). On the entrance wall, the Crucifixion is depicted with mourning figures gathered under the Cross; on the ceiling, well preserved, Demetrios on his white horse. Toward the apse (upper section) episodes from the life of John the Evangelist are still discernible, and a kingly figure, his jeweled robes and crown picked out with white dots reminiscent of mosaicwork. By the door a painted cartouche declares the murals to be the work of John Pagomenos in the year 1313. It is not known whether Pagomenos was a native Cretan, but his name occurs on various signature tablets from 1313 to 1347. His work is individual, characterized by free gestures and a "curly" line.

Similarly in a forsaken situation, and almost beyond repair, is the tiny chapel at Drakona in western Crete, dedicated to St. Stephen the First Martyr. Here, in a mural near the entrance door, Anne and Joachim are seen bringing the Virgin to the Temple (*Pl. 31B*). Mary stands among the group of maidens beneath a vase-shaped lamp typical of the fourteenth century, while the bearded and haloed high priest with his crescent-moon headgear can be seen at the upper right. As in the mural just discussed, buildings, furniture, and drapery are depicted in some detail. Unquestionably the finest work is preserved in the figure of Anne as she stands beside her husband. The rosy-red of her garb retains the mildness of shading and translucency of tone associated with painting in tempera. Her expression is tender and immediate. One leaves regretful that the brutal cracks in the wall will soon put an end to this hidden treasure.

Each village had at least one church, usually a more pretentious rectangular structure built entirely of stone with a round apse at the east end and a barrel vault over the nave. When more space was needed, a second rectangle might be placed beside the first—with its own apse and nave and frequently its own name—and openings broken through the adjoining walls (*Pl. 30C*).

Examples survive where even a third church was joined to these, as in the monastery church of the Dormition, less than a mile north of the village of Kritsá (*Pl. 29A*), where the north nave is dedicated to St. Anthony Abbot and the south, to St. Anne. The good-sized dome on pendentives—a cautious structure without openings—is probably a later addition.[51] To support this and the three stone vaults, all built at different times during the fourteenth century, thick buttresses have been thrown against the outer walls and a minimum of windows constructed. As is general in such edifices, the murals can be viewed only by the sunlight reflected across the floor from the doors and filtering through the slits in the apse.

Except for a few square feet rubbed off by the shoulders of those who sat on the masonry benches along the walls, the murals are in good condition, having been recently expertly cleaned. They present perhaps the most complete repertory of biblical scenes and favorite saints in present-day Crete. In each of the apses stand the four Church Fathers of Orthodox rite, always recognizable, though each group shows the hand of a different painter. The four archangels of the Ascension are depicted in the dome; the tympanum has the Twelve Prophets dressed in dark tones. It is notable that the garments are painted in one color, such as red, and shaded in another—dark blue—a typical Byzantine practice.

The detail of the Ascension shown here (*Pl. 29B*) is from the left wall of the central nave. At the left stands an archangel in admonishing pose, his expression full of solemnity. Of the six apostles, Peter and the youthful John are especially well preserved, while the four others show the damage of the centuries. Even so, the first named tell the whole drama—the older man looking up in awe and also in sorrow, his left hand on the scabbard of his sword, his right extended far heavenward as if he would try to follow the miracle. John is portrayed in the classical tradition as a serene, beardless youth. The irregular overlapping circles of the halos are unconventional in placement and heighten the feeling of tension and excitement. Compare the more hieratic presentation at Mistra (*Pl. 13*).

The wall paintings of Kritsá are dated 1354–1355, but some work in the church comes from a century later, and recent cleaning has revealed signs of previous frescowork in a different style. There are two painted tablets, giving the names of the donors—man, wife, and children, and the year (partly effaced), in one case even the nickname of a son—and the information that they are "confirmed" Orthodox. Burials in the church are inscribed from the end of the sixteenth and early seventeenth centuries.[56]

About the time of our stay on Crete, a French moving-picture company came to the island to make a film which was shown in the United States as *He Who Must Die.* It was based on *The Greek Passion* by Nikos Kazantzakis, himself a Cretan, and since it is a tale of Turkish persecution, soldiers and extras were needed to wear the uniform with fez. But even for short hours and in a play, no Cretan was willing to masquerade as a Turk. Finally Americans from the nearby air base helped out. During filming, the Turkish flag had to fly over the simulated mansion of the Turkish commander. Each day, when the "shooting" was finished, the villagers turned out to make sure that it was hauled down.

Even the monasteries in Crete were generally unpretentious, accommodating only a handful of monks—not the massive stone complexes of the West, overlooking their large domains like feudal castles. Monasteries of small dimensions are extant in Potamies in eastern Crete, Valsamonero, Vrontissi, and Kritsá among others. Gouvernotissa (the Ruling One, the Queen), for instance, at Potamies accommodated probably less than a dozen monks and had a courtyard not broader than that of a normal farmhouse (*Pl. 30A*). Its small church has a ground plan in the shape of the Greek cross and was once adorned with murals both outside and inside. The cupola with its graceful blind arcade is a superior achievement. Within, the dome is not shallow, as appears from the exterior, but springs from the base and is greatly lightened by the eight tall windows that reach almost to its apex. Note the quatrefoil above the door. The narrow vertical slit illuminating the apse might have been closed with a thin slab of alabaster or other translucent stone; since glass was rare and expensive, oiled animal skin, spanned tightly, was also sometimes used. Over the arch to the sanctuary the words are inscribed, *Lávete, fáyete* (take, eat), a reference to the Sacrament. Again the procession of church fathers approaches the altar from two sides, dignified attendants at the service. Represented here (*Pl. 30B*) are Gregory and Cyril. The elongation of the figures and also the decorative spotted outlines hark back to mosaic tradition. As the buildings became higher, the figures were made taller, taking advantage of the available space. Although recorded as of the fourteenth century, the murals appear to have been retouched at a later date.

The monastery of Gonia stands on a promontory overlooking the picturesque Kolimbari Bay in the western part of Crete (*Pl. 31C*). Founded in the early part of the seventeenth century—late in Venetian rule—it shows larger dimensions than earlier establishments. Here a large panel, curved to fit a bay in the refectory, represents the Miracle of the Loaves and Fishes—an appropriate subject for monks who live mainly on bread, fish, and oil (*Pl. 31A*). It is inscribed: the work of Konstantin Paleopapas in the year 1643. It still has remnants of the gilded background traditional in icons—probably a harking back to the mosaic. On the other hand, the general composition shows considerable familiarity with Western art. The scene has characteristics of later Cretan painting which is better known to us through the hagiographers of Venice. Christ's figure is dominant; in the distance the disciples are seen distributing the victuals. All the figures use their hands in eloquent gesticulation. There is uniformity in the rendition of the feet. Paleopapas also signed a large Crucifixion in the monastery church.

When we remarked on the choice collection of icons in the church, we were told that in 1821, during the war for independence, the icons were carried to Trieste for safekeeping, and remained there for eighty years. When World War II endangered the shores, they were taken to Pola, and had been brought back only shortly before our visit.

The portrayal of important saints keeps to Orthodox tradition through centuries. Michael is the leader among the archangels. His name means "like unto God" in Hebrew, and he is described as the Captain General of the Host of Heaven. He is depicted as young and handsome, his clothing dazzling in richness and color. Resplendent wings rise from his shoulders. He carries a flaming sword, a shield, and often a pair of balances, for it is he who is supposed to weigh the souls of men at the Saviour's command on the Day of Judgment.

Three favorite saints of the Byzantine world appear in the damaged mural at Platanias, Crete (*Pl. 33A*). Michael stands on the dragon of evil and holds a scroll and a medallion of the young Christ. St. George, venerated in East and West as the model of knighthood, rides a brown charger at the left. Demetrios, after him the most famous military martyr of the East, is mounted on a white horse and holds a slender lance. Compare the warrior saints on *Pls. 20A* and *25*. The steeds may look rather like carousel animals to us, but the rich trappings and carefully groomed manes and tails, together with the riders' highly dignified bearing, make a full and decorative effect. The line which separates the one figure from the others, cutting into the raised hoof of the white horse, shows how careless and damaging repainting can be.

From the heavy hair to the elaborate battle dress and the menacingly upright sword, the figure from the distant Macedonian heartland of Kastoria, Greece (*Pl. 33D*), is easily recognized as Michael also. In this sixteenth century version, his wings are like epaulets and he carries the scales in his left hand. Here he is placed in a semicircular arch—a challenge to the painter's command of spacing and proportion. A better known example from Formis, South Italy (*Pl. 33C*), was executed in the eleventh century for a Benedictine monastery in which finely painted murals are preserved. This figure also is placed in a lunette with great skill, the gracefully curving wings filling the entire space. The authorship of these murals was disputed for a long time by those who would like to disparage Byzantine art and minimize its influence in Western lands. But the discovery of an inscription referring to the painter, in clear Greek cursive script, has finally settled the dispute.[26] Here the archangel carries a lance—a mark of the work's early date. From his left hand curls a scroll bearing his motto.

Again placed in a semicircular space, in a church in Athens (*Pl. 33B*), is a figure similar in many details, such as the stern expression, the thin line of the nose, the small tight mouth, as well as the heavy crown of hair. The wings are spread to imposing effect, and the folds of the garments have much variety, enlivening the whole picture. But here there is no weapon. The hands are exquisitely drawn; the right is raised in the gesture of blessing. This is Christ Himself, identified by the letters in the aureole—the *omicron omega nu* (I am that I am), which was spoken out of the Burning Bush to Moses on Mount Sinai. The inscription reads "The Angel of the Most High," and just below is the monogram of Jesus. This mural came recently to light when, at the excavations of the Agora (the market place) in Athens, the ancient church was restored by American archaeologists.

The last date found on murals in Crete has been deciphered as 1523, possibly 1550. Slowly, wall painting was discontinued. But the development of icon painting went on. The icon was movable, while the mosaic and the mural were fixed. Fragments remain to indicate that early churches had masonry iconostases that served the mural painter as an outlet. With the introduction of wooden altar screens, the painter's work was transferred more and more to transportable panels. An icon could be ordered in a particular size and subject at a studio or monastery; when carried to the village its reception sometimes amounted to a religious procession. Symbols of faith in those times of increasing vicissitude, icons could travel, they could be hidden, and, as all small objects, they had a personal nature. The mural painter was under constant control and had little inspiration to deviate from the standard tradition. The icons were broadly marketable, and it was natural that they were more prone to influences from wider fields. Within the small space, a complicated story could still be told; thus the icon and the page of the illuminated manuscript are related. With the decline of hand-illuminated codices, after the invention of book printing, the miniature painter often turned his talent to the icon. Indeed, in the sixteenth century icons began to influence the mural painters, and details from icons executed at Mount Athos and Meteora have been found on church walls in Crete.

A striking blend of the Byzantine and Western influences is seen in the icon of Haralambos, a saint popular in the Orthodox Church (*Pl. 28C*). Haralambos was martyred in Anatolia toward the end of the second century, when that part of Asia Minor was a Roman province. Various incidents of his death and apotheosis are represented on the panel. The crowned ruler sits on a gilded throne within the walled city. The saint's last moments are comforted by angels who bring him the wreath of martyrdom. At the edge of Eternity, where a cluster of cumulus clouds forms a kind of threshold, his soul—again represented as an infant—flanked by two angels, is received by Christ. The Holy Ghost hovers above and, in commanding position over all, God the Father sits alone. Various choirs of angels surround him, and fine-lined gilded rays radiate downward from his figure. The compartmentalization of the scenes, the gold background, and the rose-colored depths of Heaven are Byzantine, while the landscape in the foreground, the richly detailed costumes, and the architecture show Western, strongly bookish, influence. The icon hangs in the old Cathedral (Little St. Minas) in Heraklion. It is dated 1758, and the painter is named as George Kastrophylax—whose work is found at Mount Sinai as well as in Crete.[47] The same saint is depicted on a large votary icon in the former monastery dedicated to St. Catherine of Sinai in the Greek quarter at Istanbul (*Pl. 112C*). Beyond the large figure of the saint we see his coronation as a martyr. The work is signed: "Hand of Dorotheus, monk of Peloponnese," and on the scroll is written "Prayer (or offering) of the servant of God, Constantine the monk"—evidently the donor. The date is 1736. While both Byzantine and Western influences can be detected, the exquisitely patterned textiles might even be of Turkish inspiration.

Heraklion today—Candia in the sixteenth century—is framed by the remnants of monolithic bastions and gigantic walls, rising from moats filled with the drift of centuries (*Pl. 26*). The west gate is entirely Venetian. Ruins of the first belt of fortifications are extant, but were superseded as the city grew. Inside the town many vestiges of recent Turkish occupation remain, but the resplendence Venice encouraged has been effaced by time and indifference. When Crete gained her independence, the Roman Catholic Church withdrew entirely. The church of St. Mark with which the Venetian colonists thought to honor their patron, today serves a very different purpose. Begun in 1239, destroyed by the earthquake of 1303, again rebuilt—elegant with loggia, five arcades, and campanile—it was transformed into a mosque by the Turks. Today the companile's stones have been carried away and the building has become a moving-picture theater. Other Roman churches are barracks, depots, offices, garages. The site of the Franciscan monastery was found ideal for the new Archaeological Museum. As one walks through the ancient city, stones of different provenience, sometimes with marble surfaces, used heterogeneously in recent masonry, are reminders of ancient magnificence.

There are indications that certain Orthodox monasteries on Crete nurtured generations of especially able mural and icon painters. To call them "schools," in the sense of groups whose performance can be sharply defined stylistically, is somewhat forced—especially today, when few murals remain in their original state. The itinerant painters and the icons themselves carried the prototypes of various modes over a wide territory.

Valsamonero, with fine murals dated 1431, was a center of painting, also Kritsá and Vrontissi in rural communities. In Candia, theology and painting were among the subjects taught at the monastery of St. Catherine, a dependent of the See of Mount Sinai. In the Byzantine world it was not necessary to belong to the feudal higher class or to the clergy, or to be subvened by them, to receive an education. If a youth had ambition and talent, he could advance himself in a number of fields, in the democratic tradition of classical Greece.

The monastery of St. Catherine was destroyed by the Turks. The present church of St. Matthew is the repository of that Orthodox tradition which St. Catherine once represented. There is no longer a school of painting there, but the establishment preserves a variety of icons, a number of them portraying the saintly patroness. The iconostasis (*Pl. 28B*) contains large panels, bordered by smaller ones of the Twelve Feasts of the Church. Dragons at the foot of the Crucifix symbolize the defeat of the Apocalyptic beasts through the Redemption. Even in the capital, the churches, except for the New Cathedral, are of small size, and one is not lost in them, intentionally dwarfed by the tremendous mass of architecture. In such a church a special intimacy is established with Divinity, and one feels strongly the archaic power of the religion.

The old Metropolitan Church does not hold more than some three hundred persons. Christ is depicted on a large icon in central position on the iconostasis (*Pl. 28A*), wearing the crown of Heaven. The Baptism, the Raising of Lazarus, the Crucifixion, and the Descent into Limbo—or, in the Orthodox concept, the Resurrection—can be recognized on the small panels. The fifth frame, at the right, is empty. Here belonged the Transfiguration. In search of this panel we visited an old icon painter who had taken it to his workshop for repair. Luckily this old man still had reverence for the ancient art and was spending hours in study and contemplation before touching it; but what will happen in a generation or so, when another cleaning and restoration are necessary, one would rather not think. Especially noteworthy is the fine gilded woodwork of the altar screen, as frame; the entwined eucharistic grapes and the flying angels over the door are carved with Baroque freedom. A markedly narrow rectangular panel above the opening represents the Lamentation over the Body of the Dead Christ, a favorite subject, always placed on an important point of the iconostasis.

Only one row of wooden benches runs around the walls of the old church. The community stands during services, even those that last for hours. While we were photographing the icons, we witnessed a baptism. One bearded priest filled the chalice-shaped font with warm water and poured in warm oil, testing the temperature expertly with fatherly concern. A second priest, wearing an apron-like mantle, his lace-bordered sleeves turned back, held the naked child over the font, as mother and godparents stood by with lighted candles. The service was chanted throughout, and the velvety young voices of the priests filled the stone vault with music full of majesty and love. After the baby was immersed and the baptismal blessing given, it was dressed in new clothing and carried in a procession around the font, while the chanting resolved into a joyful melody. Standing in the semidarkness of a corner, one thought that this same ceremony might have taken place more than four hundred years ago, the infant receiving the name Kyriakos—Domenikos.

For out of this cultural and religious background, filled with fierce national pride that was based not only on the classic past but also on his Hellenic education, emerges the elusive shadow of a young man who later, as El Greco, became one of the most enigmatic figures in the history of art. The young Candiote, born in 1541, grew up when the oppression of the occupying power threatened his people and perhaps himself with bodily harm. At the same time, increasing appreciation of Cretan painters in the Mediterranean world might have spurred him to try his fortune beyond his native island. It is known that he went to Venice. His ship followed the route of ancient mariners and, barely underway, he could already see how various nations were adjusting to the turbulent times.

As the boat left the Sea of Crete, the ancient island of Cythera came into sight, legendary seat of Aphrodite. Then the island of Zante or Zakintos, once a favorite place of the emperors of Constantinople and since 1482 a Venetian possession. Though the town life bore the strong imprint of Venice, on the land the ancestral Orthodox faith persisted. Nearly all the population spoke Greek as well as Italian and were patrons of Greek literature and music. On the nearby slopes of Mount Skopos stood the old convent of Panagia Skopotissa. There was a colony of skillful hagiographers on the island.

At the northernmost end of the Ionian Sea, where the Italian boot and the shoulder of the Greek mainland form a narrows, the Strait of Otranto, lies Kerkyra, Italianized into Corfu, praised by poets for fabulous beauty. It was probably on Corfu that the legendary meeting took place between Nausicaa and the most romantic of all wanderers, Ulysses. South of the town of Corfu, beyond its classical ruins, an inlet forms a veritable lake, and a breakwater leads across to the convent of Vlacherna (*Pl. 34A*). The nearby island of Ponticonissi, also called Mouse Island for its small size, completes a landscape over which sentimental travelers have raved through the ages. The Venetian fortress with its double ramparts still encloses a labyrinth of whitewashed houses. Although repeatedly attacked by the Turks, the town remained in Venetian hands and served as a refuge for Greek scholars.

There were a few good harbors on the rugged shores of Albania, but the Turks had ruled there for a century. Therefore the captain of the ship probably steered toward the Bocche di Cattaro, where beyond the narrow gate of bluffs a lovely sheltered bay awaited. While in deep winter snow lies on the highest peaks, the landscape along the shores is dotted with dignified villas surrounded by semitropical gardens. Here the Greek language was still understood, but among themselves the natives spoke either the Venetian dialect or Serbo-Croatian. A number of churches along the coast served the Roman Rite, not so much honoring the power of religion as the religion of the power; in the mountains where the Slavs lived, the Orthodox faith was dominant.

Farther north lay the coastal Republic of Ragusa (Dubrovnik now, from the Slavic for oak tree), where the Slavs kept a small independent city-state flourishing, even after Serbia beyond the mountains was overwhelmed by the Turks. Ragusa was governed by patricians, burghers, merchants, and shipowners, who elected a rector as their head for a limited period. Ragusa was able to free herself from Venetian protection as early as the fourteenth century. Slavery was abolished in 1417, on the grounds that it was "disgraceful, wicked, and abominable." Though Ragusa was within the powerful area of the Roman Rite, the Inquisition never made greater inroads than the burning of three books. The ruling class was ready to discover and reinterpret for its own use the humanistic culture of Venice. The mansion of the rector (*Pl. 34B*), built at the end of the fifteenth century, is strongly Venetian in its feeling. The leaders were fluent in Italian, but their wives, servants, and the peasants spoke only Serbo-Croatian. Thus the city was anchored in a patriotic and healthy ground. It also harbored a large colony of Greek refugees. Ragusa, with its repeatedly strengthened fortifications (*Pl. 35A*), was one of the great medieval centers for the distribution of merchandise from the Levant. It issued its own currency, which the Venetian Republic honored. It is one of the few states which refused to be disheartened by the opening of the ocean routes to India and the Americas, and it continued to send out its "argosies" (that is, ships from Ragusa) until, in an unwise alliance with Spain, its last squadron was lost with the Armada.

The next large port on this unique coastland was Spalato (now Split). It had the best harbor on the rocky coast, and a number of commercial roads led to it from the hinterland. It was raided by the Avars, Goths, and Huns, and at different times was a vassal of Hungary, Venice, Bosnia. In the early fifteenth century the Duke of Spalato was a Greek who had a Serbian hymnbook written for him in Cyrillic characters. In 1420 the place was ceded to Venice and was thereafter managed as a colonial town, though the population contained the strains of various nationalities.

The site was originally the palace of Diocletian (245–313), and its ground plan is that of a Roman camp, almost square, with four gates, and four streets meeting in the center of the town. Diocletian was himself a Dalmatian, and built the place for his retirement. He brought in Anatolian and Syrian craftsmen who blended fantasy and grace of line with the precision of Roman design. The floor level of the main church was once the vestibule of the palace. The inner court or peristyle (*Pl. 35C*) is today a piazza where café tables stand. An unusual picturesque record was made by Robert Adam, architect (1728–1792), father of a Neoclassic style in England. The young Scotsman journeyed to Italy to study classical architecture but was disappointed by the little that remained. The stones had been carried away for recent structures and for roads. Half-ruins were being used as mass quarters. Then he heard about a building still extant in Spalato in Dalmatia that covered more ground than the Escorial in Spain and had the added importance of having been built as a private palace. He sailed across the Adriatic, and although at first arrested as a spy he managed in five weeks, with the help of three other draftsmen, to accumulate sufficient measurements and sketches to produce a work of lasting value. It was published in London in 1763, an exquisitely produced album from which the illustration is taken (*Pl. 35B*). The engraving has detail and romance enough to satisfy any armchair traveler.[16]

In the old days unfavorable winds, danger of corsairs, or the news of pestilence raging in the next port might cause a boat to veer west and seek Ravenna, whose harbor once could accommodate 250 ships. A dozen churches in Byzantine style stood in Ravenna to remind the traveler of the past glories of the place. Honorius, retreating from the Visigoths, transferred the imperial court there in 404. His sister Galla Placidia, who was regent from 425 to 450, built a church there in fulfillment of a religious vow, after a voyage to Constantinople. Ravenna was residence of the Goth Theodoric, and was restored to the Byzantine Empire under Justinian. The church of San Apollinare in Classe (*Pl. 36D*), some three miles from the city, dates from that period and gives evidence of the dominant Byzantine influence which spread to many parts of Europe. At Ravenna, Greek *mosaicisti* blended the style of early Constantinople with regional influences. The majestic mosaic in the apse shows a highly symbolic representation of the Transfiguration. Below it stands St. Apollinare, the first Bishop of Ravenna, in prayer, with upraised arms and open palms, in the typical *theomeni* attitude of the Orthodox Rite, known in the West as *orans*. The sheep represent the apostles. Later, Ravenna's harbor silted up. The city lost its importance. Life became stagnant, and thus the place remains the most Byzantine of Italian towns.

But if the ship's course had been uneventful, the obvious harbor to land in was Parenzo (Porec), on the Istrian Peninsula. In the upper corner of the Adriatic, coastwise traffic becomes heavier, hauling cargoes that range from stone and timber to wine and olive oil. Even recently each boat sailed under the special protection of the patron saint of its home port, whose image it carried on its lofty lateen sail. The figure was sometimes fifteen feet tall; George or Demetrios was portrayed in full upon his rearing charger. Like Venice, Parenzo was built up as a place of refuge when the wave of migrating peoples swept down upon northern Italy. In the fourteenth century it had a population of some three thousand, but at the end of the sixteenth century it was devastated by pestilence and reduced to a mere three hundred. With the passing of the epidemic, the city was repopulated by refugee Albanians, Dalmatians, and Greek-speaking people, especially from Crete, who kept up their Orthodox religion. Here stood a spacious basilica (*Pl. 36A*) built also in the sixth century by the same architectural team that was active at Ravenna, with which it has much in common. The exterior mosaics are today in fragments. A mosaic of the Virgin and Child, attended by white-robed saints and angels, fills the vast shell of the apse (*Pl. 36C*). Above the arch, Christ sits in judgment, flanked by the apostles. Parenzo suffered more than Ravenna, as its Byzantine monuments reveal. The walls of the basilica are covered with canvases of a late period and doubtful value. The once-elaborate mosaic pavement was replaced with dull stone slabs, as also in Ravenna. Superior craftsmanship went to Venice, where there was affluence enough to keep up Byzantine perfection, even in the pavement (*Pl. 36B*).

The last lap of the long voyage entailed the least danger. When all was readied, the anchor could be lifted and the harbor left behind. The wind bit into the sails of the ship, and a new pilot stood on deck to guide it among the shoals of the Lido into wondrous Venice.

·III·

VENICE

From the air Venice looks like an inundated city. Colored patches of sea grass wave beneath the shallow water of the lagoon. The irregular clusters of houses on their hundred islands seem afloat. The white stone bridges form a broken pattern over the murky waters of the innumerable canals. On the piazzas paved with bleached stone slabs, carved wellheads gape black, that once supplied water for the city's needs. The various greens of the vegetation mingle with the gray and white of stone and the mellowed rose color of brickwork.

The fascinating mixture of land and water long attracted book illustrators and map makers to show the city from above. Jacopo de' Barbari's magnificent woodcut, made in 1500 and measuring over four feet by nine, remains one of the most important views as well as the most effective of the city (*Pl. 37*). Even at that time, the commercial value of such a story-telling document was grasped, and a German merchant living in Venice at once purchased a four-year copyright for its publication. The city spreads out like a flattened hand with fingers extending toward the east, where a long sandbar guards it from the open waters of the Adriatic. The Canal Grande traces its familiar S. The population at that time, estimated at somewhat over 150,000, did not overcrowd the city as it does today with more than two and a half times that number. Many garden patches are visible. The low-lying sandbanks are empty, with an occasional boat drawn up upon them. Yet many of the monuments that make Venice what it is today stood there in 1500. The buildings facing the Canal Grande already display the Byzantine, Venetian-Gothic, and Renaissance styles side by side, which later accommodated also the Palladian and the Baroque in splendid harmony. The only bridge that spans the main artery of the town is of wood, with a center section that can be lifted for the passage of ships (visible in the lower left on *Pl. 37A*). For the magnificent Rialto Bridge of stone was not built until nearly a century later. Many of the big churches, each with its campanile, or bell tower, can be recognized among blocks of dwelling houses. While full attention was paid by the draftsman to the island of San Pietro at the entrance to the arsenal, to the Giudecca on the south, and the Isola di San Giorgio Maggiore at the entrance to the Canal Grande, the focus is on the Ducal Palace and the Basilica of San Marco. In the foreground, heavy masted vessels clog the harbor, with an empty space along the quay at the end of the Piazzetta where gondolas ride. A gigantic Neptune is mounted on a monster dolphin. His left hand holds a chain to harness the animal, and his right, a banner proclaiming the port to be his residence.

From the woodcut to a detail painted by Titian sixty-six years later no change can be observed (*Pl. 39B*), and today we see practically the same view. The Piazza di San Marco, elegant open-air reception room, flanked by the Procuratie, is easily traversed in imagination. On the map there is an inconspicuous church at the west end, where Napoleon had the Procuratie Nuove built to close the space with homogeneous architecture. And one misses the church of Santa Maria della Salute with its opulent scrolled decoration so typical of the high Baroque in mid-seventeenth century Venice.

The city's arsenal was her fiery heart of power—at once an armory and a fortress which protected her from the side of the open sea. Its battlemented walls, strengthened by fourteen towers, had a circumference of some two miles. The three official keepers of the arsenal had to live in the houses provided for them nearby throughout their term of something less than three years. Each magistrate was on duty for fifteen days, during which time he was responsible with his head for the safety of the establishment. He slept inside the fortification and guarded the keys of the arsenal in his room. Only one passage led out of the compound, an impressive Gothic portal framing a massive iron gate.

In the arsenal were manufactured weapons, cannon, and munitions, and here were the depots for army and navy. It had facilities to take care of a fleet of 45 heavy warships and their accompanying smaller craft, in a large square water-bay with hangar-like sheds that could be closed (visible in the upper left on *Pl. 38A*). Here also were the shipyards, the dry docks, ropewalks, model rooms, and warehouses. The weekday scene was one of roaring forges, billowing smoke, and the clangor of toil. The workmen, the *arsenalotti*, had their own guild, and considerable privileges were accorded them. Sixteen thousand men were employed as shipbuilders, and 36,000 seamen manned the various craft. There were as many as 11,000 of the military gathered when the fleet was in port. The surrounding area had peaceful open spaces where vegetables were raised.

Sometimes 10,000 logs of walnut were floating in the basin. With the Dalmatian mountains and the Alps near the Veneto under the control of the republic, vast wood-producing areas were at their disposal. The Julian Alps and the Croatian Karst also were heavily forested at that time. The demand for wood was insatiable. As well as for the repair and construction of ships for commerce and for battle, wood was needed for docks, sheds, and warehouses, for the numberless bridges and drawbridges, even for the piles which, driven into the mushy ground, sustained the splendid buildings of the city. Trees were felled in ruthless disregard of future devastation.

Near the arsenal, a sort of "garage" was provided where public gondolas were berthed. Here also rested the Bucintoro, official barge of the doge—a monumental showboat, gilded, upholstered in red velvet, and adorned with polychrome statues. Its deck was of ebony, and its eighty-four oars, touched with gold and inlaid with mother-of-pearl, flashed as it sped out into the lagoon to meet the vessel of some visiting sovereign. It paraded in the yearly celebration when the doge dropped a ring into the water to symbolize the mystic marriage of the city with the sea. Alas, the more resplendent the Bucintoro became as time went by, the more curtailed was the power of Venice over the seas, and in the end the performance was not much more than an excuse for a *festa*.

Venice grew into a town in the fifth century as the coastal population found refuge there from Attila's invasion of northern Italy. In later centuries, Venice herself was to become the conqueror of vast territories—not as the Mongolian horsemen with swift and head-on attack, but by devious and shrewd diplomacy, with recourse to foreign mercenaries and *condottieri.* At the height of her glory, at the end of the fourteenth and the beginning of the fifteenth centuries, she could boast a commercial fleet of three hundred large ships and three thousand smaller vessels. She was dominant not only on the Adriatic and the Aegean but also as far as the Marmara and the Black seas. Venetian warehouses were established in Egypt and on the Levantine coast, at Thessaloniki and Constantinople, and even in harbors of the Black Sea. Rhodes, Cyprus, Crete were under her power, and Apulia and Sicily in the south served her interests. The commerce of Venice provided all that Europe desired: cloves, cinnamon, mace, ginger, and nutmeg from the East Indies; ebony from Indo-China; ambergris from Madagascar and musk from Tibet; pearls, rubies, lapis lazuli from Ceylon and India; muslins, silks, and brocades from India and China; sugar from Egypt; perfumes and rugs from Arabia. From the nearer Mediterranean slopes came fruits and wines, and the city itself was famed for its textiles and glass. All business transactions were supervised by an official of the republic. The weights and measures used in trade were regularly checked, and duty was exacted on merchandise both entering and leaving the city.

The highest section of the island group, the Rialto (Rivo Alto), was the first area inhabited, and it remained the nucleus of the vigorous sprawling city (*Pl. 38B*). The merchants of various nations were assigned quarters where their goods were gathered and expedited and where each group could find safe and congenial lodging.

The Germans had a mercantile establishment, or *fondaco,* there as early as the twelfth century. This substantial building lay directly on the shore of the Canal Grande, just across from the Rialto, at the foot of the connecting bridge. Merchandise was stored on the ground floor at the quayside, and above, even in that early version, over fifty bedchambers accommodated the merchants and travelers. The foreigners were under the strict rule of their own chief officers. At the "third bell" the place was locked up for the night and could not be opened except for a new arrival. From various Germanic lands and the Low Countries, printers, shoemakers, bakers, weavers, wood carvers, lutemakers, goldsmiths, and armorers were resident in Venice. They had their own churches. Their inns, restaurants, and other places of entertainment were off limits for Venetians.

In 1505 the Fondaco de' Tedeschi was rebuilt on a still grander scale following a devastating fire. As the use of marble, mosaic pictures, and statuary was restricted by law to the façades of special buildings, the Germans employed Giorgione, who with his assistant Titian painted the exterior with noble allegories in lavish color. Though the centuries have obliterated these murals, sketches still survive. Such decoration was by no means exclusively Italian; Rubens painted the outside of his house at Antwerp with mythological scenes and allegories.

Private ships were not permitted to trade in ports to which Venice sent her fleet. Vessels were built and equipped by the republic, then auctioned off to the merchants. These still had to be licensed before taking on cargo, and they sailed under state regulations in command of a Venetian. A respectable share of the profits fell to the state. Goods destined for the North had to be carried on barges to the mainland, reloaded on pack trains for the arduous journey across the Alps. Nevertheless the traffic was so profitable at the time of Dürer's visit in the early sixteenth century that a weekly post was kept up with German lands.

Fondachi were maintained by various Italian cities, and some Eastern nations, such as the Armenians, also had establishments there. The Riva degli Schiavoni at the east end of the city was the quay of the Slovenes and Dalmatians, where foodstuffs, wine, fruit, wood, and other articles from the Adriatic Coast were traded.

The Ottoman Empire also had its representatives in Venice at that time. In 1621 the elegant palace of the Duke of Ferrara, overlooking the Canal Grande, was purchased by the republic and put at the disposal of the Turkish merchant guild. Since then the marble-veneered building, with ten open arches and decorative finials, was known as the Fondaco de' Turchi. The Venetian merchants in Constantinople had to pay for their ground privileges, and the Signoria of the republic charged 130 gold ducats' daily rent to the Turks. As the Turks were infidels, the windows had to be walled up, and the rooms were lighted only from the courts. A Venetian warden locked the doors at sunset. No women or children were permitted, and no Moslem was allowed to lodge elsewhere.

At the turn of the seventeenth century Venice started into an eclipse from which she never emerged. America was open, and her riches were pouring into Portugal and Spain. Though reduced by English, Dutch, and French corsairs, the goods, even as loot, reached European markets. Arabian sea raiders, running out of North African bases, took a heavy toll of Mediterranean shipping. Improved navigation to Africa and Asia had changed the map of world trade.

Meanwhile, the century-old enemy, the Moslems, were still gaining ground. To stem their advances, Venice, Genoa, the Papal States, and Spain allied for a campaign, gathering over three hundred ships. The supreme command was put in the hands of John of Austria (1545–1578), who was the natural son of the Holy Roman Emperor Charles V by the daughter of a wealthy citizen of Regensburg. A Turkish fleet of about equal strength encountered the allies off Lepanto (in Greek, Navpaktos) and was forced to retire with great losses (1571). Europe was jubilant. The triumphant admirals and captains, returning from the battle, were lionized. *Te Deums* were offered, mass amnesties were granted, and bonfires were lighted. Each ally claimed it as his special victory.

But the price was costly. The Turks had lost a navy, but the Christian powers lost island after island, foothold after foothold in the Levant. The sultan had just secured Cyprus, which was held until the twentieth century and even today is the object of contention. Dynastic jealousies in Spain and corroding suspicion among the allies broke the Holy League again into rival factions, and they were unable to consolidate their advantages. In 1573 Venice purchased a separate peace from the Turks, trebling the indemnity for the Ionian island of Zante, her lifeline to the East, which was called "fior di Levante."

For a period in the sixteenth century the sultan formed an alliance with France and permitted only the French to sail under their own colors in his waters. Other great powers were forced to fly the French flag at a price, and even the proud Venetian lion was hauled down from mastheads. Then came a respite and better times for the republic. The sultan Murad III (who ruled 1574–1595) took a Venetian known as Sultana Safie as his only wife. She furnished him with beautiful slave girls, accepted bribes, and influenced relations favorably at the Porte with her native city.

When in 1204 Venice had deliberately diverted the might of the Fourth Crusade against Constantinople, she may have believed that she was reducing her greatest competitor. But the Eastern outpost of all Christianity was fatally weakened thereby. While frantic effort was made to stem the Turks when they already stood well in Europe, the valiant tradition of the great *condottieri,* such as Gattamelata and Colleoni, had been squandered, and there was not much left of the spirit that had brought the republic to her zenith.

Venice was one of the earliest republics of the modern world, governed by a chief magistrate with the title of Doge or Duke, assisted by a Cabinet, the Council of Ten, and a Senate. At first the doge was elected for life by popular vote; after the early sixteenth century he was selected from among the city's patricians by the two councils for a two-year term, to discourage dynastic ambitions. Similarly, democratic principles forbade wealthy families on the occasion of a baptism to invite patricians or high officials as witnesses, because it was feared that the families would become too powerful if closely allied. A part of the marriage ceremony between important families had to be held in the Ducal Palace, to assure publicity and enable the Senate to have full knowledge of the new connection; the religious rite became quite a secondary matter.[69]

The Ducal Palace, with its pink and white façade resting on two rows of lacy Gothic arcades, looks in two directions. Its southern face surveys the lagoon and the quay. Its western façade looks into the Piazzetta, where the Council of Ten could observe the movements of the citizens. The roof was laid out in a garden, with trees and perfumed shrubbery.[43] The luxurious palace, of which only a few rooms were the private domain of the doge, has gone through frequent additions and alterations since the eleventh century. It remains a lasting testimonial to the glory of Venetian architecture, sculpture, and painting.

Adjacent and connected with the Ducal Palace is the Basilica of San Marco, which constituted the doge's private chapel. Its beginnings go back to a period before exact historical data is available. After a great fire, reconstruction and enlargement were begun in the eleventh century. Designed by a Greek architect in the shape of a Greek cross, it is said to have been modeled largely upon the church of the Holy Apostles in Constantinople, with a great central dome and equal arms, each crowned by a dome. The addition of a narthex across the main front and a vestibule on the north side brought the ground plan to form a square. The bubble shapes of the domes, sheathed in metal, were once heavily plated with shining gold, as was the custom in Constantinople (*Pl. 39A*).

The Orthodox warrior saints Theodore and George were the early protectors of the city. The figure of the former, now standing on a column on the Piazzetta, was originally a pagan statue, a piece of booty, recarved to represent the patron of the fisherfolk in Venice. These two were relegated to second-class rank upon the arrival of the relics of the Evangelist St. Mark, which—the story has it—were whisked out of Alexandria by three enterprising Venetians in a tub of pickled pork, a meat repulsive to the Moslems.

The brick structure of the basilica was faced with marble plundered from Byzantium, alabaster from Arabia, porphyry from Egypt, and embellished with columns, capitals, and statuary from Greece and her ancient colonies. Later additions of Venetian Gothic and Renaissance ornaments do not dilute the Byzantine-Romanesque aspect of the building but only enhance its unique individuality.

The four bronze horses closely identified with the main portal of St. Mark were once gilded and stood in the Hippodrome of Constantinople when the city was sacked in the Fourth Crusade. Some sources say that they were not original even to the Hippodrome, but were of classic provenience, brought from Greece. Whatever the truth, they did not come to rest in Venice. Napoleon—greatest looter of modern history before Hitler—had them placed on top a small triumphal arch beside the Louvre to honor his own victory. Much Napoleonic treasure (Stendhal was one of the plunderers) had been sent to the provinces and made to disappear—which accounts for some masterpieces in French provincial museums today. When the Congress of Vienna ordered France to restore the artistic loot, deceptive tactics did not enable the French government to retain the four bronze horses. The French made the excuse that they had no craftsmen skillful enough to dismantle them without damage, but Italian experts went to Paris and brought back the horses intact.

At the time the bronze horses were taken from Constantinople, a colossal bronze equestrian statue of a Byzantine emperor (see *Pl. 66A*) stood nearby which remained there even after the Turks took the city. Nearly a century later, about 1530, a traveler reports seeing the broken pieces carted away to a foundry to be melted down into cannon. It is interesting to speculate why the Venetians left such a masterpiece unmoved. One reason may have been its monumental size, which made it too difficult to dismantle and transport; another, the ingrained aversion of the Venetians to the cult of personality. They made no exception even for one of their own heroes, Bartolommeo Colleoni (d. 1475). When the great *condottiere* bequeathed Venice ample funds to erect a statue to himself "on the Piazza San Marco," the Council of Ten cleverly circumvented his wish by allocating space for Verrocchio's magnificent monument in the Campo San Marco, a small square some distance from the heart of the city.

Few of today's visitors to the Basilica of St. Mark are aware of the immense Byzantine heritage accumulated there, upon which the art and culture of Venice drew. Church plate, jewelry, rare textiles, illuminated manuscripts, and early printed books lie unphotographed, uninvestigated. There are no less than thirty-two chalices in the Treasury, all datable in the tenth and eleventh centuries, all loot from the sack of Constantinople, some of silver, some of onyx, adorned with jewels and enamel medallions of the saints (*Pl. 41*C).[45] Many Byzantine objects were placed in Gothic or Renaissance mountings, thus obfuscating their true origin.

The main altar of St. Mark is free-standing, as was customary in the early church. Behind it, the Pala d'Oro, or golden altar screen, glitters with Byzantine enamelwork, in silver gilt with plaques of gold encrusted with precious stones and pearls (*Pl. 41A*). Eighty-five panels arranged in horizontal rows present scenes from the Scriptures and figures of saints. The lower section, with the Pantocrator (Christ in Majesty) and the Evangelists (*Pl. 41B*), was ordered from Constantinople in 1105 by the ruling doge. The upper section was plundered from the Byzantine capital in 1204, probably from the church of the Pantocrator. Gothic frames and decorations of Venetian workmanship were added in mid-fourteenth century.

Brilliant mosaic compositions adorn the exterior of the basilica, and within, the entire ceiling —domes and vaulting—is tapestried with them (*Pl. 40*). The art of the mosaic comes also from the East. Examples survive from Mesopotamia and from Egypt as early as 3500 B.C. The technique began with the placing together of bits of marble, glass, bone, and other suitable material to form a design. The Greeks, who adopted all manners of art, improved the technique, so that it could be used on a large scale. By the mid-sixth century of our era new vibrancy and elegance were gained by the use of gold leaf, compressed between two layers of glass. In the Greek manner, the colorful pieces were tilted at irregular angles, bringing out high lights and subtleties of shading, and eliminating glare. The Italians, adapting the Roman manner of laying mosaic floors, set each row flush with the next, producing an even surface, often with marked sheen. In Byzantium, mosaic decoration is associated with imperial privilege and wealth; little evidence has been found up to now of mosaics in small or provincial places.

The mosaics of St. Mark in Venice show both traditional and later styles. The work, executed by Greek *mosaicisti*, is known to have begun as early as the tenth century; fragments from the ninth exist, but most of the panels date from the twelfth and thirteenth centuries. Repairs and additions continued all through the Renaissance. As late as 1836 mosaics were still being put up. Great Venetian masters, such as Tintoretto and Veronese, furnished designs for St. Mark's mosaics, and these have a three-dimensionality and a painterly effect not previously encountered. It is known that Titian went to the basilica to study the early mosaics when contemplating a new composition.[71]

In the mid-sixteenth century St. Mark's square was paved with bricks set on edge in a herringbone pattern and was bordered by booths selling glassware, lace, beads, and religious articles. The market also was held in the piazza, with meat, fish, poultry, and fruit in abundance, as well as sausages and herbs. Jugglers and mountebanks had their stands there. The residences of the nine procurators, who with the doge made up the presiding Council of Ten, were erected on the two longer sides during the sixteenth century and were called from their occupants the Procuratie. Ample colonnades sheltered senators, patricians, and merchants from bad weather as they made their daily promenade. A vast relief map of the world as it was then known was on display, showing the many ports touched by the ships of Venice. There congregated bankers, brokers, manufacturers, and the agents of foreign houses who had their counters nearby. An early traveler reported that St. Mark's lofty bell tower was showing signs of weakness, but actually it did not fall until 1902.

Venice was one of the first cities to have communal lighting. In the twelfth century oil tapers were placed on poles where the *traghetti,* or ferries, functioned. Their flickering light was multiplied on the vibrating water. Lamps were set at dark corners of the narrow passageways, where an image of the Virgin or a saint, often with some flowers before it, served to distinguish the different quarters. Night watchmen were employed at least a century before such service was introduced into any other European city.

An additional factor in the growth of the power of Venice is often overlooked. As its commercial enterprise expanded, the whole community became increasingly interested in distant lands. Not in vain was it the Venetian Marco Polo (1254–1323) who went to explore an easier trade route to the Far East. The printing of maps and the publishing of books, many of which enlarged geographical knowledge, became an early profession in Venice. The interest with which Venetians took part in the events of the expanding world is indicated by the fact that two years after Seville had published a letter of Cortés on his conquest of Mexico, Venice had a translation in print.

Books were printed from woodblocks before the end of the first millennium in Japan, China, and Korea. Movable type appeared in China in the mid-eleventh century. In Europe in the mid-fourteenth century, image prints and playing cards were produced from blocks. Indulgences, printed on single sheets from type cast in a mold, bear the date 1454. The unscrupulous sale of such mass-produced letters of pardon was one of the abuses against which Luther remonstrated.

Two Germans set up a press in Venice in 1469, and soon the city became an important center of printing. By the year 1500, printers to the number of 155 were established in the city, among them craftsmen from Scandinavia and Germany, employing engravers to decorate and illustrate their books. From that early date on, Venetian books became collectors' items.

In 1484 a Greek printing press began activity in Venice, joined by three other Greek establishments by the end of the century. The number of Greek presses grew rapidly, with additional craftsmen coming from Crete. Editions of most of the Greek classics were brought out in Venice. The famous press of Aldus Manutius functioned there from 1495. He originated the italic lowercase letter type, to which italic capitals were added later. Roman capital letters were taken from the abundant Roman monuments in Italy. Greek was the language of Manutius' household. To promote Greek studies he founded an Academy of Hellenists which spoke Greek and had Greek rules. His descendants continued the firm and also became dealers in rare books. The Aldine Press brought out the first Greek Bible in 1518. The last Greek book printed in Venice on a religious subject bears a medallion of St. George and the date 1850.

Other cities also were active in publishing works in various languages. The first psalter in Greek and Latin was printed in Milan in 1481. What few would expect—a psalter in Ethiopic appeared in Rome in 1513 and a New Testament in Syriac in Vienna in 1555. In 1498 the Venetian Senate granted Ottaviano Petrucci the privilege of printing music for twenty years, for which time the city enjoyed the monopoly of that very important craft.

Book production required paper which sometimes came from afar. As the reams were voluminous and heavy, they were moved more easily by ship than overland. Similarly, for the ready product, transport by ship was preferable.

Even before Venice became a city of printers, the Senate had in its possession a number of rare and handwritten illuminated books—notably the manuscript library of the poet Petrarch and the legacy of Basilius Bessarion (1395–1472). Once titular Patriarch of Constantinople and an illustrious scholar of Greek letters, Bessarion had accompanied John VII Palaeologos to Italy in the hope of bringing about a union between the Greek and Roman Churches; he was persuaded to remain there, where the pope invested him with the rank of cardinal. In a new land and in the service of a new master, Bessarion remained to the end of his life a renowned disseminator of Greek culture and, nineteen years after the fall of Constantinople, he died at Ravenna—that most Byzantine of the Byzantine towns in Italy. In 1518 the Venetian Senate created a Chair of Greek, stating that instruction in Greek would be necessary to complete the education of all Venetian youth, whether patrician or plebian. Eighteen years later they instructed one of their favorite architects, Jacopo Sansovino, to design a library to stand opposite the Palace of the Doges. The building was in construction when young El Greco wandered about Venice; today it is known as the Libreria Vecchia or the Biblioteca Marciana, and houses a unique choice of manuscripts and early printed books.

Like various other European powers, the Republic of Venice was sovereign—*città apostolica e santa*. Its church was a national church and its patriarch was the heir of St. Mark—for the Venetians he was peer to that other bishop who sat on the throne of St. Peter. At the head of the administration stood the doge, equal with the cardinal or archbishop. In Europe at that time apostolic rights were wielded by the rulers of the Holy Roman Empire, Hungary, Poland, France, and Spain, to mention the most powerful. This meant that their persons were holy, sacred, inviolable, and any affront against them brought death as punishment. They stood like gods above the people, and their wish was command. Where the ruler was holy and apostolic, no decree of the Vatican was valid until the sovereign had approved it. In smaller matters this was of little consequence; but in affairs of higher policy and personality the royal veto effectively crossed the pope's intentions. In witholding acknowledgments, bargaining for benefits, the holy and apostolic ruler could make the pope wait on royal approval to the end of the life of one or the other. This acted as counterbalance to the assertiveness of the Vatican; the idea of papal infallibility (decreed in 1869) would have met an energetic demur.

Nowadays it is difficult to visualize such authoritarian power, since with the exception of the King of the Belgians all Roman Catholic rulers, from Portugal to Austria, have been swept from their thrones. One of the last and most striking demonstrations of autocratic influence occurred in the case of Cardinal Rampolla (1843–1912). When Rudolf of Habsburg, son of the Emperor Franz Josef, killed his mistress and himself in Mayerling, Rampolla, then secretary of state to the Vatican, denied him full religious honors at the funeral. Franz Joseph refused to accept the ruling, and his son was laid to rest with pomp in the Habsburg family crypt. Years later, when the pope died, Cardinal Rampolla was the favorite candidate as his successor. But the emperor, using his ancient prerogative the veto, instructed the three cardinals of his monarchy to blackball Rampolla. Although only one obeyed, Rampolla lost the election.[1]

While the Republic of Venice had no royal line, the Council of Ten adopted for themselves the prerogatives of the holy apostolic despots. The *Parrochia Primaria,* seat of the highest ecclesiastical dignitary of the republic, the church of San Pietro di Castello, was situated on an island near the arsenal, separated from the town by a broad canal (*Pl. 42C*). As mentioned before, the spectacular Basilica of St. Mark was the personal chapel of the doge; and only after Napoleon conquered North Italy and reorganized the administration did it become the seat of the cardinal.

The republic surrendered to no one her ancient rights and privileges. The Council of Ten inspected the religious houses in Venice, and no "foreigner"—that is, outsider—was admitted to the hierarchy. The superiors of convents and monasteries had to be natives of Venice. Oppression and favoritism were equally frowned upon. Parish priests were elected by the parishioners and their names sent to Rome to be confirmed. The republic refused to send its nominee for the patriarchy to the Vatican for examination, and he received the symbols of his office from the hand of the doge. Ecclesiastics were not permitted to hold state office. The Council of Ten tried all criminals, even clerics, and if any official or ecclesiastic sided against the republic he was expelled and his property confiscated. Whenever a pope interfered in some dispute, the Council refused permission to make his edict public. When the pope excommunicated the doge, the councilors, and all the citizenry of Venice, the republic sent its officers to tear down the proclamations that were posted on the churches. The religious personnel in the city continued to offer Masses and to perform services until peace was declared.

Many phases of Venetian life were developed on Byzantine customs, and perhaps the Hellenic tradition was responsible in part for the republic's independence when in council with other European nations. One of the points on which Venice laid herself open to outside criticism was her tolerance of various nationalities and faiths within the city. An English traveler in the sixteenth century noted that no one bothered in Venice "if a man be a Turk, a Jew, Gospeller, a Papist, or a believer in the Devil, nor does anyone challenge whether you are married and whether you eat flesh or fish in your home." The doge and his council were regarded by many in Europe as the greatest protagonists of natural liberty against the political meddling of the Vatican. This naturally brought the accusation of a leaning toward the Reformation, to which the doge replied, "We are as good Christians as the pope, and Christians we will die."

Jealous of its independence, the republic would not allow the Jesuits or other religious organizations to maintain educational institutions either in Venice or in Padua. On the other hand, a very high level of secular education was achieved there, almost unique in that period. The city sustained a college for young men aspiring to civil service; there were a number of private schools and state grammer schools, one in each precinct. For, as in the Hellenic world, the republic never considered learning the prerogative of ecclesiastics.[67]

The Dominicans were unpopular in Venice and, though the Inquisition was permitted to function there from 1542, it was under the supervision of three Venetian patricians. Their task was to protect the citizens from arbitrary action, and they could change any judgment, even when it concerned a priest. The Holy Office was not granted a separate building—like those menacing massive palaces in Spain and the Spanish colonies—but met in rooms accorded to it in the Ducal Palace. Any ordinance it wished to publish had to be submitted first to the Council of Ten. Its prison and police were under state supervision, and inquisitors and chancellors were required to be Venetian subjects. As accusations of witchcraft and blasphemy were tried by the Council of Ten, a large group of offenses was taken away from the jurisdiction of the Inquisition. The stake was never lighted in a Venetian piazza.

While the fondaco served the commercial interests of Venice, another institution, the *scuola* —one of the most original facets of Venetian life—was concerned with social welfare. The scuola embraced the functions of a lodge, a guild, a trade union. Within its semireligious organization, it dispensed charity, arranged insurance, banked savings for its members, binding them into a proud and responsible community group. On occasion, the scuola even provided money and ships for the aid of the republic.

There were six *scuole grande* in Venice up to the mid-sixteenth century. Among these confraternities the Scuola de San Rocco is most notable today, not so much for the distinction of its members as because of the paintings preserved there, mainly from the brush of Tintoretto. These gigantic canvases were in a deplorable state when Ruskin saw them in the last century, but they and the whole building were restored for the Tintoretto exhibition in 1937 and constitute since then one of the prides of the city.

When the guild of San Rocco had completed its new Renaissance building (1553), they were honored, as they recorded, "to have the excellent painter Maestro Tiziano of Cadore leave a record of his incomparable skill in our School." Titian delivered a large picture for the assembly hall but never went beyond this token. Some years later the guild decided on a competition, and a number of painters, Tintoretto among them, were invited to submit drawings dealing with the glorification of the patron saint. In less than three weeks, Tintoretto appeared, not with a sketch, but with a full-size canvas which he put into place as a gift to the guild, with the assurance that if it was accepted he would add all the finishing touches. It was vibrant, true in proportion, and sufficiently finished to be judged by the committee. Fifty-one votes were cast in favor and twenty-one against. For seventeen years more, Tintoretto worked on the decoration of the guild hall. His gigantic feat must have been quite a sensation in the city of sensations, when young El Greco lived there.

During the sixteenth century the number of minor scuole in Venice increased immensely, until more than two-thirds of the population belonged to one or another. Some embraced members of various crafts, some honored a patron saint. Among the foreign population the organization of the scuole was advantageous both for the members and for the republic. While some foreign communities were permitted to reside near the center of the city, others were allotted space on more outlying islands. The Armenians, early refugees, had, besides a church in the city, a monastery on the island of San Lazzaro, once a leper colony. Its library contains many illuminated manuscripts and early books; its printing shop functioned through the centuries and even today is one of the main sources of Armenian religious literature. In 1516 the Jewish population, who had been living scattered throughout the city, were concentrated behind walls on another island, and gates were locked upon them at midnight. A cannon factory was established there—*gietto* in Italian. Some believe that the word "ghetto" may derive from this. Later, Jews were permitted to settle in the district of the kitchen gardens. The most notable of the five surviving synagogues was built by the architect of Santa Maria della Salute, for the refugee Spanish and Portuguese Jews. A confraternity known as the Scuola Spagnola belonged to the establishment.

In the eastern part of the town, almost exactly between the arsenal and Riva degli Schiavoni, stands the Scuola degli Schiavoni, the lay foundation of Slovene, Serb, and Dalmatian residents, dating from the mid-fifteenth century. For the small upper room they occupied at that time, Carpaccio (from 1502 to 1511) painted the stories of St. Jerome and St. George. Some forty years later a more spacious building, designed by Sansovino, was erected, and the Carpaccio paintings were transferred to their present site. Nearby is the Ponte della Paglia (straw) where the barges laden with hay and straw used to unload—at that time horses and mules had a place in Venetian life.

The Greek quarter lay still nearer the palace of the doge, only two city blocks east of the Piazza di San Marco, but separated from the "inner city" by gates which were locked at night to safeguard the homes of the procurators, senators, and patricians. Walking past the Parrochia San Zaccaria, in a narrow of the way, one can still see the stone uprights and lintel, with the empty iron hinges embedded in the masonry.

The Greek colony in Venice goes back into medieval times. Countless Greek merchants and mariners made a good living there. Greeks set the mosaics of San Marco and other churches. They were skilled in the glass industry, another craft that came from the Levant. They were employed as panel and miniature painters, as engravers on copper and wood, as illuminators and copyists of books. The community was constantly increased by refugees adept in various professions, fleeing from the Turkish advance in the East. Other Greek craftsmen included gold- and silver-smiths, workers in enamel, the decorators of signs, flags, and coats of arms, the embellishers of military shields. Some made playing cards, masks for carnival; they gilded and colored leather panels widely used in interior decoration; they bound books and fashioned furniture.

Toward the end of the fifteenth century, the Greek colony, hitherto permitted to practice their Orthodox rites in some eight churches of Venice and also to harbor Greek monks, were restricted to the use of a side chapel in a church dedicated to San Biagio.[73] The structure stands on the quay of Schiavoni where boats arrived with their Greek sailors and travelers; today it serves the military and marine personnel as well as the population clustered around the arsenal. Even now traces of its Byzantine atmosphere remain: a miraculous icon of the Madonna with Greek text, probably brought from the sack of Constantinople, and a painting of St. Catherine of Sinai, another immediate link with that fountainhead of Orthodox religion. In addition, some of the lamps are characteristic of the Near East.

On the threshold of the sixteenth century, permission was granted for the establishment of a Greek scuola, which at that time had 250 members and was dedicated to St. Nicholas, patron of seamen. In 1511 a petition was submitted to the Venetian authorities to erect a church exclusively for the practice of the Orthodox Rite. In the application, the Greeks in Venice pointed with pride to their service to the republic: they not only had taken a responsible part in the industry and commerce of the city but had furnished light cavalry troops under the command of a Venetian nobleman; they listed a number of Greek, notably Cretan, heroes. Thirteen years later the permission was granted them.[66] First a small building went up in which services could be held. By 1539 the first stone for a large edifice was laid, erected by Sante Lombardo from designs by Sansovino, and so notable in execution that Banister Fletcher includes it in his *History of Architecture* as "a marvel of marble work, both within and without." On *Pl. 38A*, it is the church with bell tower nearer the center, on the left edge.

The exterior of the church of San Giorgio dei Greci (St. George of the Greeks) does not differ much from other contemporary churches of Venice. It has a well-proportioned dome and a slender separate campanile (*Pl. 44A*). Its graceful Renaissance façade of stone is adorned with mosaic medallions and three pediments over the entrances. The church is surrounded by a wide paved yard, onto which other parish buildings open. Before it passes one of the innumerable canals of Venice, the Rio dei Greci, overlooked by a high wall with a stone coping and elaborate iron grillework. The interior is more unusual in Venice, as it adheres closely to Byzantine prototype. There are no benches in the aisleless inner space which is covered with a central dome, but a row of finely carved stalls encircles the walls. The building has the Orthodox sanctuary with three apses closed off by an imposing iconostasis (*Pl. 45B*). Richly embroidered gold brocade curtains the three gates of the altar screen, and the icons are encrusted with silver ornaments and darkened by the smoke of tapers, candles, and incense. Even now the church is illuminated only by candles. In the vault of the apse, a gigantic mosaic of the Pantocrator seems to lean outward, obliterating the limits of its frame.

The imposing edifice was dedicated in 1561, although it was not yet fully ready. In this decade El Greco is believed to have arrived in Venice. Another ten years were required before the dome was finished. In connection with it, a Messer Andrea is mentioned, who some would like to think denotes Palladio. A Giovanni di Cipro (from Cyprus) decorated the cupola. Some of the interior was painted by the Cretan Michele Damaskinos, renowned as a painter both in his homeland and in Venice. Tintoretto's name is on record as consultant in various matters. The slim campanile was begun toward the end of the century by a builder recorded as Bernardino Angarin, apparently not an Italian; the words *angaro* and *angary* both are of Greek origin, the former referring to pyrotechnics, signaling with fire, the latter to one in charge of requisitioning means of transport, including ships.

The Greek colony then numbered some four thousand souls, among whom fourteen hundred were fully literate. A Council of Forty regulated their affairs. Manousos Theotokopoulos, possibly the brother of El Greco, was twice nominated for this body but never was successful in election. A superior magistrate, the *kastaldo*, who held office for seven years, headed this group. He was responsible to the Venetian administration for the moral, social, and financial life of the colony, and was ex-officio procurator of the church.[114]

The religious personnel were under the jurisdiction of the Patriarch of Constantinople. Near the side door of the church is the tomb of Gabriele Seviros, who as first bishop presided for thirty years over the Greek colony (*Pl. 45A*). He is said to have been a friend of Manousos Theotokopoulos. Besides the bishop, the vigorous colony supported two archimandrites and a deacon. The choir with two cantors was so famous that foreign visitors were advised to attend a service in order to hear them. The Greek community sustained a school, their own hospital, and for a time even a convent. Many of the schoolteachers were refugees. Emphasis was laid on the study of Greek and Latin classical literature and the preservation of the tenets of the Orthodox faith. The list of illustrious professors extends into the eighteenth century; some were invited to Western universities. One Tommaso Flanghinis, a lawyer from Corfu, and president of the confraternity, planned a college for the Greek community, which began functioning in 1665 and ceased only with the arrival of the Napoleonic armies in 1797. Graduates often went on to the University of Padua; some took positions as priests in the Greek-speaking world. Many teachers were priests, and a number of these were trained as well in painting—since this was regarded as a pious act—working in the tradition of the monasteries of Mount Sinai and Mount Athos. Numerous professional painters who were not clerics lived in Venice, coming mainly from Cyprus, Crete, Zante, and Corfu (*Pl. 44B*).

The hagiographers, or saint portrayers, were not restricted in their activities to the Greek community. Their products were spread out for exhibit on the Rialto Bridge and in the nearby streets, center of busy commercial life, together with those of the Italian *madonneri*, hack painters of Madonna pictures. The work may not have shown much individuality, but it satisfied popular taste at a small price. Sailors—and the Greeks were notably sailors since prehistoric times—were among the best purchasers of icons. Thus the Byzantine prototypes traveled far. Greek merchants could buy a souvenir of their Venetian stay in traditional style. And many a Venetian patrician, contemporary of Titian, preferred in his private chambers icon-like panels with gilded background, tapers burning before them.

Certain characteristics were traditional: the figure of Christ or the saint represented was placed in the foreground and was usually larger than any other in the composition. The human figure was always fully clothed in ample garments, never emphasizing the body underneath. Especially for Christ and the Virgin, the coloring was prescribed; frequently a contrasting color was used for shading. Gold backgrounds were favored. Gold high lights were often applied to the folds of drapery, and radiating gilded lines made up the halos or emanated from the figures (see *Pl. 61B*). Mountains were indicated by chestnut-colored rocks piled in parallel layers and highlighted in white. Clouds were small conventionalized interwoven balls. Curling, spiraling waves represented the sea. Buildings and trees were stylized as for a theatrical décor. The storytelling was often delightfully straightforward and simple. For a long time, the compartmentalization of various scenes on one panel betrayed the Byzantine origin of a painting even when other details followed contemporary Western style.

By that time engravings and woodcuts were circulating throughout Europe. Naturally, the Orthodox painter, especially in Venice, was stimulated by these—for selectivism was part of the age. He had also mastered the technique of painting in oil, although icons were chiefly executed in tempera on panel. The many-sided interest of the Byzanto-Venetian painter is evident in the case of Thomas Battas of Corfu, resident of Venice, who bequeathed to his pupil Emmanuel Tzanfournaris a collection of etchings and engravings as well as icons and triptychs (1599).[47]

The best known of the Cretan painters in the Venice of that period was Michele Damaskinos, whose activity falls between 1570 and 1591. His icons were in great demand. He also executed murals in the church of San Giorgio dei Greci, and it is recorded that the community contemplated having him decorate their entire building. In 1581 he sold his collection of prints and engravings, which included some by Parmigiano.[59] Apparently he returned to Crete, where he died a few years later. Of Damaskinos too it is said that he was willing to work according to the wishes of his patron, in strict Byzantine style, or in the contemporary Italian manner, or in a blend of both.[47] About this time, painters began to sign their panels—partly perhaps because they had become export articles and the prestige of a "name" brought a higher price. Damaskinos always signed in Greek, frequently adding "the Cretan" and the words "creation" or "poem." His icons can be found in Corfu, Zante, and Mount Sinai, as well as in Venice and Crete.

Cretans were in majority among the Greek residents of Venice and probably also among the hagiographers who worked there. The Cretan Joannis Vlastos, besides painting icons, executed some of the mosaics in San Giorgio dei Greci in the early seventeenth century. Eight "portraits" of Byzantine emperors by George Klontzas (active between 1590 and 1609) are now in the Marciana Library of Venice; his work shows the influence of Western engravings. The Lambardos family, originating in Rethymnon, brought forth three excellent painters, of whom Emmanuel (datable 1598–1632) is the best known (see *Pl. 97B*). Another artist family were the Moskos, of whom Elie went from Crete to Venice and in 1645 to Zante. A Joannis Moscos signed a panel with the date 1711.

Emmanuel Zane (1610–1690), born in Rethymnon and coming to Venice by way of Corfu, was a priest at the church of San Giorgio dei Greci and a composer of hymns and psalms, as well as a painter. His icons (see *Pl. 87B*) often bear the names of the donors who commissioned them. A painter brother, Konstantinos, is also documented. The panels of Zane and his circle, painted in a blend of styles, are of the type that have been confused with the early work of El Greco.

Theodoros Poulakis, from Khania, seemingly was especially proud of his origin, and to the signature of his icons (dated 1666–1692) he sometimes added "from the famous island of Crete." At that late date he painted only in tempera, using golden backgrounds and golden gleams in costumes and halos. In his later years he went to the Ionian islands and died in Corfu.

From Cyprus came Joannis Cyprios, a priest at San Giorgio dei Greci at the end of the sixteenth century. The Tzanfournaris family were from Corfu—the best known of whom was Emmanuel, mentioned above, also a priest at San Giorgio. Some of his icons traveled as far as Mount Sinai. He painted a Death of Ephraim, today in the Vatican Gallery, which retains the Byzantine compartmentalization, as seen on *Pl. 11B* and *C*, although it is otherwise executed in a more Italianate manner. It was not infrequent for a priest to sign only his first name. One instance is "Priest Victor" whose activity falls in the second half of the seventeenth century and who is said to have signed in several languages; more will be said of him in the chapter on El Greco's paintings (see *Pl. 111A*).

After the fall of Crete, Zante and Corfu gained importance as outposts of icon painting. Their output shows the increasing influence of the Italian and Western manner, lacking the Orthodox cohesion and the fierce spirit of Crete. By the end of the seventeenth century, some of the painters of the Ionian islands had oriented themselves definitely toward the West. In the churches of Zante icons in a wide variety of styles were preserved until a recent earthquake destroyed nearly all the collection. A book published in 1935 lists 258 names of Byzantine painters who were active after the fall of Constantinople, still working in the traditional style.[47] The last date found on such an icon in Crete is 1796. This writer photographed a panel in the Loverdos collection in Athens signed and dated in Greek letters 1834. In Venice the latest Greek text and date on such a painting is 1866.[65]

By the nineteenth century the Greek colony in Venice had shrunk, and with it the output of Byzantine panels. In 1834 the community counted about four hundred members and employed two priests. The Greek government contributed a small subvention, but the colonists were unable to keep up their hospital, the college, or the printing plant. In the early 1930's the Greek colony consisted of some 120 souls, mostly old and invalid. No regular services had been held in San Giorgio dei Greci for years; for important occasions a visiting priest was called in. In the chapter house the stairwell and the big assembly hall, with its stalls of fine wood, were full of paintings hanging amid cobwebs and layers of dust. But the forlorn financial situation did not permit employment of more than a sexton who was at the same time janitor, and the interest of the frail old man in the pictures was understandably small. Grime and neglect marked the archive, the library, and the adjacent storeroom, as we tried to find traces of earlier activity. Many windows, once laid in an elegant pattern of leaded frames, were cracked or lacking altogether, and through the openings pigeons came and went to pester the tourists on the Piazza di San Marco. Pigeon droppings produced grotesque streaks and false high lights all down the Renaissance façade. It is admitted that the once-rich library was nearly completely reduced. After the occupation of the Napoleonic army, the confraternity was impoverished. Treasures disappeared, and what came in later as replacement was not near the previous standards. Considerable change may have occurred in the collection of icons at the same time.

Very few families of the small colony had clung to their icons, and many panels had been deposited in the Scuola. In 1947–1948 an inventory was published which lists 231 paintings in the possession of San Giorgio dei Greci.[65] From the material at hand can be traced how the hagiographers adopted more and more the manner of the Venetian popular painters, although with a certain time lag. Thus their paintings from the seventeenth century are strongly reminiscent of the output of the studios of Tintoretto and still more of the Bassano family, of whom three generations painted biblical scenes in an ingratiating style.

By the mid-1950's the Greeks numbered less than fifty and, though some income from rents on property was still forthcoming, the community could not have survived had not one wealthy family from the outside strongly subvened the church. In recent years a Hellenic Institute of Byzantine and Post-Byzantine Studies was begun, with measures for the cataloguing and preservation of the paintings, producing a marked betterment in the general conditions.

The guilds in Venice maintained a magisterial register in which all historical events were reported. The Scuola degli Schiavoni still proudly displays its "Mariegola," the constitution or mother-rules, in exquisite binding decorated with precious stones. In it the moral obligations of the confraternity are set down, the communal Masses to be attended, and the charitable works to be undertaken, as well as the amount of dues exacted from each member. The Scuola dei Greci also has such a register, and while it contains thirty pages referring to the period 1560–1570, El Greco's name has not been found.

Except in one or two cases, the dates on icons in the Scuola dei Greci begin in the last two decades of the sixteenth century; the majority of the paintings date from the seventeenth century, extending into the eighteenth. Up to the end of the sixteenth century any dates referring to the Greek community are scarce. Among icons and archival material great gaps exist. The best-known near contemporary of El Greco in Venice is Michele Damaskinos whose records in that city fall between 1577 and 1586. As the first document that refers to El Greco is a letter dated 1570, when he was already in Rome, and in 1577 he signed a contract for work in Spain, it would appear that he came and left Venice too early to be included in the records of the reorganized Greek community. Earlier records might have been lost in the move to the new, splendid establishment. But most losses—especially among the early documents—probably occurred in later centuries as the colony deteriorated.

Byzanto-Venetian icons were in continuous demand, and favorite scenes were painted again and again. A number of such pictures could be mistaken for early work of El Greco, especially when the subject has been somewhat retouched and a doubtful signature in Greek redrawn. If then an "expertise" is included, we have an explanation for the many "early El Grecos" of questionable artistic merit now appearing on the market. On the other hand, museums such as those in Vienna and Paris, basing their conclusions on recent research, have put new labels on paintings which were attributed to El Greco thirty years ago, ascribing them now to followers of the sixteenth century Venetian school.

Venice harbored deep into modern times a center of medieval Byzantine tradition, yet the city was also most advanced in oil painting and in a style that was the forerunner of Impressionism. On the threshold of the Renaissance, Western Europe had made a unique contribution to the technique of painting, mixing oil with the pigments and applying it to canvas spanned on a stretcher. In countries where the climate does not vary much between the humid and the dry, wooden panels lasted a long time. But in Venice, where snow lies for days in winter and the sea water rises into the churches, while in summer burning heat bakes the buildings, paintings on wood and walls deteriorated rapidly. Oil paint applied to stretched canvas proved the ideal medium for Venice's climate, while in Florence and elsewhere in Italy, panel and canvas, tempera and oil, were employed side by side for decades longer.

Venice produced through five centuries a unique roster of masters—inventive, individual, and brilliant—a sequence unequaled anywhere else in the world. When her power was declining, her art and architecture came to fullest flower. In the spirit of the Renaissance, secular paintings were created for decorative effect and the enjoyment of the eye. Classical fables, the adulation of heroes—local as well as legendary—were fashionable. The nude favored in Venetian painting became generally acceptable.

For many, Titian is the most Venetian of all painters, the painters' painter. His life (1477–1576) was the life of Venice, spanning nearly a century of its most brilliant epoch. Nevertheless, though all possible sources have been investigated, no biographical data has been found concerning him up to his thirtieth year. Here a parallel to El Greco can be drawn, who was twenty-nine when the first trace of his activity appears. By the time Titian reached forty, his name was known in the courts of Europe. Charles V was his patron and he was made a Count Palatine and Knight of the Golden Spur. In 1531 Titian settled in a fashionable district called Birri Grande. From his window he could see the rugged Dolomites where he had roamed as a boy. His garden stretched along the water's edge, and in the evenings the lagoon was filled with boats, pulsing with music and song. As Titian grew older, his wisdom and kindliness were well known. A contemporary visitor describes an evening with him, with artists, scholars, and wits gathered about him; a banquet was laid, and beautiful women drifted by in their gondolas. When Titian died of the plague, the property fell on bad days. Today the Fondamente Nuove is a drab section of the town, with workers' flats, and the great painter's house is preserved only in an eighteenth century engraving (*Pl. 42A*).

Titian was a culmination of the Renaissance. Tintoretto (1518–1594) was the fulminant expression of the Baroque. When Henry III, King of France, paid a visit to Venice (1574), Tintoretto, an established master, painted a triumphal arch for the occasion.[70] He dressed himself as one of the doge's bodyguards and made sketches when the royal guest boarded the state barge, the Bucintoro. Then he presented the visiting monarch with a ready portrait but refused the knighthood offered to him—he was born a Venetian, and no foreign decoration could add to his status. In 1574 Tintoretto with his family moved to the Fondamente dei Mori, where he worked until he died some twenty years later. This house also is today in a rundown district of Venice (*Pl. 42B*), but at least one can stand before it, trying to visualize the great master as he delivered his huge canvases to the nearby church of Madonna dell' Orto, where he was later laid to rest.

From Titian, El Greco may have learned a virtuoso colorism and technique; from Tintoretto, a certain dithyrambic quality. Some of his early work shows a certain resemblance to the canvases of the Bassano family. They were favorite Venetian painters and repeated their religious genre subjects, such as the Annunciation, the Adoration of the Magi, the Flight into Egypt, over and over again. It is in these subjects that El Greco in his Italian manner comes near to them. Several paintings in the retrospective Bassano exhibition, held in Venice in 1957, were at one time attributed to El Greco. However, on closer inspection, the Venetian painters show a different concept of three-dimensionality, a more practiced and subtle hand in composition.

Ruskin says that the source of Venice's glory should not be sought in the power of her arsenal or in the pageantry of her palaces but at the altar of Torcello's basilica. Nine hundred years ago Torcello was a thriving community. The residence of the first doge was established there. Then life gradually ebbed away, and Venice herself came to ascendancy. Santa Maria Assunta, the main church (*Pl. 43*), was founded in the seventh century, rebuilt in the ninth and eleventh centuries. It is long and narrow, like the early basilicas we have seen in the Omayad of Damascus, in Parenzo, and Ravenna (see *Pls. 2C, 36C* and *D*). The episcopal throne is set against the apse wall facing the congregation, as the judge sat in the law court that served as model for early Christian churches. A mosaic of the Virgin and the twelve apostles overhead (*Pl. 43C*) probably dates from the first decades of the thirteenth century. On the west wall, a vast mosaic from about the same time, now restored and in parts renewed, presents the Last Judgment with archaic symbolism and involuntary humor (*Pl. 43B*). In iconography it is very close to the mural in Mavriotissa, Kastoria, which is dated a little earlier (see *Pl. 15B*). The base of the iconostasis consists of marble panels with Byzantine peacocks and flower vases in relief. The upper section, supported by classic marble columns, is a masonry wall decorated with frescoes—another Byzantine practice, also found in Crete. The adjacent church, dedicated to Santa Fosca and dating from the eleventh century, is built entirely of brick on an octagonal ground plan. Here the roof is drawn down to cover arcades resting on marble columns—similarly in Byzantine tradition. Roman and Byzantine marble statues, capitals, objects of bronze, wood, and glass from buildings now defunct are exhibited in the former Palace of the Council. Torcello has been called "the mother of Venice." Today it is a shadow town, scarcely populated —a melancholy enchanted spot, with its lonely cypresses reaching into the cloud-streaked sky.

The sixteenth century traveler from the North to Rome passed through the city's massive wall by way of the Porta del Popolo, the People's Gate. Inside it lay the Piazza del Popolo, a great unpaved space, framed by the food kitchens, the inns, and other buildings of trade folk catering to travelers (*Pl. 46B*). The piazza was remote enough from the center of the city to be used for the execution of brigands taken in the countryside. Among nondescript houses stood the modest Renaissance church of Santa Maria del Popolo, where a young monk of the Augustinian order, named Martin Luther, offered Mass upon his safe arrival from his native Germany in 1510. Little more than a decade later, he was excommunicated, and Charles V, who had tried to avoid a religious split in his empire, also turned against him, assured of the pope's support in his struggle with Francis I of France.

The next pope, Clement VII, a Medici of illegitimate birth, was more an Italian prince than the successor to the Apostle. He had perhaps the fate of his native Florence in mind when he maneuvered between the two monarchs. But in 1527 his wavering policy brought the emperor's army to the gates of Rome. Their commander was killed in the early stages of the siege. Leaderless, unpaid for days, demoralized by the collapse of all defense, the Spanish and German mercenaries fell upon the city in an orgy of horror unprecedented even in those times. The holocaust went on until citizens and conquerors alike were decimated by pest and famine. The pope with twelve cardinals hid in the stables of the Castel Sant'Angelo, disguised as peasants. Only the Swiss mercenaries stood by them and fought until all but a handful of guards were dead. As a reward, native Swiss exclusively, wearing a picturesque sixteenth century uniform, today make up the Papal Guard.

Both pope and emperor realized that the time had come for reconciliation. The tide of the Reformation was sweeping Europe, and Turkish might had driven to the very heart of the Continent. Ransomed from captivity, the pope promised to call a general council to deal with rising Protestantism, and placed the imperial crown on the head of Charles V. But the juggling and scheming for worldly power continued. Besides the pope, such superb statesmen confronted one another as His Apostolic Majesty the Emperor of the Holy Roman Empire, Charles V and later Maximilian II; His Most Christian Majesty of France, Francis I; His Most Catholic Majesty of Spain, Philip II, after the abdication of Charles, his father—all with authoritarian rights.

In an amazingly short time after the fatal year 1527, Rome showed the work of rehabilitation. A bevy of noted architects, sculptors, painters, and craftsmen gathered in the city. Florence was fading, Venice weakened; Rome burgeoned under the new pope Paul III (ruled 1534–1549), of the powerful and notorious Farnese family. A religious and political metropolis with renewed revenues asserted its majesty before Europe. And this opulence, in ostentatious churches and pretentious palaces, is a main characteristic of Rome today—where among colossal structures little people swarm the streets in tiny cars and on motor scooters, dwarfed by the boastful stone piles of bygone centuries.

Coinciding with the rebuilding of Rome, the traditional Renaissance concept was going through a transformation. A new liveliness of line and ebullience of proportion characterize the Baroque. Certain writers like to date the Baroque from a single Roman church—Gesù, founded in 1568. But it was actually a wave of taste not restricted to one city, made possible by advanced technique of construction and by the urge of the architects to experiment with design, stimulated by such architectural handbooks as those of Vitruvius, Serlio, and Palladio, which were widely distributed through the development of printing.

Perhaps the largest-scale manifestation of this spirit was the rebuilding of the Basilica of St. Peter—a project under way for many years (*Pl. 46A*). The ancient basilica with its open colonnaded forecourt, dignified by the patina of centuries, splendid with shining gold mosaics, had to give way to the monumental scale of the age. First the builders, honoring tradition, made a plan based on the Greek cross; later it was changed to a Latin cross. As the new basilica was planned to be far larger than the old, the surrounding terrain had to be newly graded. Soil and subsoil were thoroughly disturbed. Pagan and early Christian architectural remnants disappeared or were broken up. Some of the piers necessary to support the massive walls and the vast cupola cut through a cemetery that contained, besides pagan tombs, Christian reburials from the third century. Rough and dressed stones were reused, obliterating what clues might have existed as to the identity of the burials, compounding a puzzle for modern archaeologists.[72] Pope Paul III gave the septuagenarian Michelangelo full power to pull down or alter whatever stood in his way. But neither of them lived to see the edifice near completion. From the laying of the cornerstone to the dedication of the colonnade that enhances the square, nineteen popes held office.

The grandiose building enterprise continued through a crowded and turbulent period in history. The Council of Trent (1545–1563) fell in this time. Charles V had urged it to clarify pressing matters with the papacy—to settle the religious dispute, to reform ecclesiastical abuses, and finally to inspire a new crusade. The papacy strove to proceed against Protestantism with utmost severity, while the emperor, though a devout Roman Catholic, sought means to heal the schism which was to alienate powerful Protestant German allies and tear his empire apart. In this period war broke out again between the papacy and Spain and was hurriedly mediated. The Inquisition was reconstituted in Rome, and the first black list of books was issued, banning the works of Petrarch, Ariosto, and other giants of literature; printers and publishers fled to Switzerland and Germany. At this time Jews were segregated and forced to wear yellow caps. One Medici pope arrested the nephew of his predecessor for heresy. The fulminant spirit of the Renaissance was quenched, the enthusiasm for the classical disparaged. Michelangelo's nudes in the Sistine Chapel were repainted with drapery. Meanwhile, work on the basilica went on.

Pope Gregory XIII (ruled 1572–1585) reformed the calendar. He rehired Palestrina who had been dismissed by a previous pontiff because he was married. The Polish people, divided between the Orthodox, Lutheran, and Roman faiths, were finally committed to the last, when this pope, asked to mediate the succession, chose a Roman Catholic king. The massacre of St. Bartholomew's Day was instigated in France by Catherine de' Medici, mother of the French king Charles IX. For this mass murder of Hitlerian proportions, the French queen received the congratulations of the Catholic monarchs and the pope commanded *Te Deums* to be sung, bonfires to be lighted, and had a commemorative medal issued.

Meanwhile, work on the basilica went on. It was not finished until 1629. As the expression of Roman Baroque on a colossal scale, it has an amazing, almost improbable, subtle balance. Proportions are brought to harmony, colors to polyphonic cadences; the individual elements do not reveal their gigantic size until particular attention is focused on them. The cherubs, far larger than a man, on the colored marble holy-water receptacles do not lose their lively charm and earthy appeal. This mastery of proportion comes equally into expression in Bernini's colonnade which encloses the elliptical piazza, an overwhelming display of stairs, terraces, columns, and statues. Bernini's magic worked also to create an optical illusion. The square itself is only slightly larger than the Piazza del Popolo at the other end of the city; engineers have figured out that it could hold no more than eighty thousand people—a contrast to the hundreds of thousands sometimes reported in the newspapers.

New palaces and manor houses for the leading families offered splendid projects for the architects of the period. As early as 1514, Pope Paul III began a town palace, employing at least four of the architects associated with the construction of St. Peter, among them Michelangelo. Stones of pagan Rome, brought from the Coliseum and the Theater of Marcellus, went into the structure. The rear of the palace looked toward the river Tiber from an open loggia. Although it was not completed before 1586, many rooms were in use much earlier.

Pope Paul III provided munificently for his several natural children and their offspring. A grandson, Alexander, elevated to cardinal at the age of fourteen, became a celebrated patron of the arts. Julio Clovio (1498–1578) lived in the Farnese Palace as an old man, having entered the service of the family in 1540.

Clovio was renowned as a miniaturist. Photography was unknown and the sending of large portraits was circumstantial, but a miniature could be carried about easily. Charles V, his sister Mary, Queen of Hungary, and his son Philip II, as well as the Emperor Maximilian, all owned portraits and illuminated books from Clovio's hand.

In the year 1570, the elderly miniature painter addressed a letter to Cardinal Farnese with the request that he instruct his major-domo to provide an upstairs room in the palace for the temporary accommodation of a young Candiote painter, "disciple of Titian." It can be assumed that El Greco painted Clovio's portrait at this time (*Pl. 57A*). It reveals the young Cretan as already a painter of considerable stature, and carries his full signature. A delightful detail has recently been pointed out: Clovio is depicted holding a volume of *The Offices of the Madonna* in his hand, a work executed by him for the Cardinal Farnese, which is today in the Pierpont Morgan Library.[112]

The painting had its own travels. The Farnese family became allied with the Habsburgs through marriage, and later also with the Bourbons. At the change of dynasties in Spain, a descendant (later Charles III of Spain) was named viceroy of the Two Sicilies. The Farnese Palace thus became Bourbon property—it is now seat of the French Embassy in Rome. Some of the Farnese treasures, scattered among various residences, were transferred to the viceregal palace in Naples, including the famous Titian portrait of Pope Paul III and also the portrait of Julio Clovio. After Italy was united, the Bourbon-Farnese property fell to the state and the Clovio portrait was hung in the Naples Museum. It was long considered a self-portrait of Clovio, until a Greek connoisseur identified the painter from his full signature in Greek, hitherto disregarded: *Domenikos Theotokopoulos kres epoie.*

In El Greco's time, Rome, vigorous center of diplomatic and religious activity, was expanding rapidly. New buildings went up in outlying sections as roads were improved. The street running around the base of the Pincian hill, from the Piazza del Popolo to the Piazza di Spagna, was widened in the mid-sixteenth century and a fountain erected, fed by the abundant water that flowed from the hillside. Pure water was particularly prized in the city, as the aqueducts had been brought to final ruin by the sack of Rome. On top of the fountain a statue of Silenus, son of Pan, was placed. The folk called it a monkey, "baboon," hence the name Via Babuino. In this district were the settlements of various foreign groups—as witnessed by street names referring to Lombards, Slovenes, Bretons, and Portuguese. The Piazza di Spagna (*Pl. 46C*) took its name from the palace of the Spanish ambassador. It is a section of Rome traditionally favored by foreign travelers. Once merchants, money-changers, agents for tradesmen, and students gathered here in inns and taverns and exchanged gossip. The Caffe Greco was an international meeting place where, in the nineteenth century, the American landscape painters Frederick Edwin Church and George Caleb Bingham, among others, met their European colleagues.

This district must have had a rustic atmosphere. One section was known as the Orti di

Napoli, the kitchen gardens of Naples, suggesting that there were vegetable strips cultivated by Neapolitans. The story, however, is more complicated. By the end of the fifteenth century, a large Greek refugee group had settled in southern Italy. After all, in ancient times that area was part of Magna Grecia, and even today traces of Greek dialect persist in the local idiom and in many family names. Another wave of Greeks arrived in the mid-sixteenth century. But the Viceroyalty of Naples, which also included Sicily, was then part of the Kingdom of Aragon; with the unification of the Spanish lands, persecution was increasingly meted out to all who did not belong to the faith of Spain, and many Greeks preferred to move again. The population of the Orti di Napoli in Rome was largely Greek.

The farsighted Pope Gregory XIII made a special effort toward assimilating the foreign population in his realm. In the Via Babuino, where the Greek tongue was widely spoken, a large church and seminary were established for the Uniate faith which keeps much of the Eastern Orthodox Rite but accepts the authority of the pope. The denomination is known also as Greek Catholic. The church was consecrated in 1577, and dedicated to St. Athanasius, a favorite saint of Greek Orthodoxy.

But for a considerable time there had been a spiritual home for the Uniates where Greek tradition was kept alive. Only thirteen miles from Rome, in the Alban hills, stood the monastery of Grottaferrata, founded in 1004—before the schism had come to a head—by St. Nilo from Calabria in southern Italy (*Pl. 47A*). Unfortunately the Badia Greca, or Greek Abbey, held a commanding position of great strategic value, and was harried by warring factions through the ages. It was fortified at the end of the fifteenth century, and moats were dug in front of its medieval walls (*Pl. 47B*). The church portal carries Greek inscriptions, and some sections of the apse are decorated with mosaics of purely Greek workmanship from the eleventh century.[26] On the surface of a marble baptismal font of still earlier date symbolic fish circle. Some authentic Byzantine murals survive in the interior, inadvertently preserved by a magnificent Baroque gilded coffered ceiling which Cardinal Alexander Farnese had erected over them in 1577. In the seventeenth century, Cardinal Barbarini undertook considerable alterations that further impaired the original Byzantine aspect of the church (*Pl. 47C*). Nevertheless, if this interior is compared with that of the basilica at Parenzo (Porec) (see *Pl. 36C*), a relationship can be seen.

A seminary is still functioning at Grottaferrata with a vast and famous library, containing among many other titles about a thousand Byzantine Greek manuscripts. An almost complete collection of Byzantine music from the greatest period is said to be unique.[61] Refugee youths from Turkish-occupied territory came to Grottaferrata, as well as later to the seminary of St. Athanasius in Rome, because of their most up-to-date libraries and complete corpus of Orthodox theology. When the youths were graduated, many of them disappeared, to turn up again in countries under Turkish domination—they had gone back into the service of their ancestral faith.

Even today a handful of Basilian monks live in this idyllic place. The service is still celebrated in Greek. A paleographical school, which functioned when Cardinal Bessarion was head of the monastery in the mid-fifteenth century, is still maintained, for the copying of manuscripts in ancient style. Oddly, some bilingual publications of very early works, in Greek, Latin, and Italian, are prefaced by indulgences from eighteenth and nineteenth century popes. The bearded librarian remarked with resignation that few visitors came to see their treasures.

El Greco's figure in Rome is less evanescent than in Venice, with the evidence of Clovio's letter and portrait, besides various other paintings assigned to his "Roman period." Among these, a full-length figure of an armored Knight of Malta is included, signed with El Greco's full name. The picture once carried a posthumous text, naming the subject and giving the date of his death, 1586. Recent cleaning revealed that the large Maltese cross on the cuirass—an anomaly from an armorial point of view—was also a later addition. While the portrait shows considerable talent, it lacks the maturity and assurance in that of Clovio. The Knights of Malta, originally known as the Hospitalers, were established in Venice by the thirteenth century. They soon had a church and, for a time, a hospital situated near the Riva degli Schiavoni. The order renewed a commercial treaty with the republic in 1423; much of their activity depended on the cooperation of that maritime power. In the second half of the same century, Cardinal Bessarion gave them special privileges in the granting of indulgences. A new church was erected in the early sixteenth century, described as "a miracle of marble and other magnificence." Shortly afterward the Knights published an index of prohibited books. Ranuccio Farnese and, later, Alessandro Farnese were priors of the house in Venice, a spacious and elegant establishment of great beauty, with a garden displaying rare varieties of plants and flowers. At this time the title of prior was amended to *Gran Priore,* the result—as the chronicler says—of the megalomania inspired by "Spanish ideas, which had begun to insinuate themselves everywhere." [68] Gentile Bellini's well-known depiction of the Corpus Christi Procession in the Piazza di San Marco (1496) gives a faithful cross section of the Venetian population. Germans and Turks appear, mulattoes and Arabs, in their specific costumes. Across the Piazza walks a Maltese knight, with the identifying cross on his flowing robe, followed by his page. Indeed, El Greco's portrait might have been painted just as well in Venice.

In the Rome of El Greco's time, émigrés and refugees were in goodly number. Teachers, painters, printers, copyists of manuscripts, librarians, and craftsmen found employment with the many wealthy patrons. The gatherings at the Farnese Palace were called a veritable academy of humanists. The young Cretan was not the only Greek residing there.

The palace stood near the Piazza di San Pietro, and the young El Greco doubtless observed the building activities going on there. Possibly he visited among the Greeks in the Via Babuino. He might even have made the short journey to the Badia Greca and discoursed in his mother tongue with those who were related in spirit—more conscious that they were Greek than that they were Uniate or Orthodox. Scholars, artists, and craftsmen were being attracted to distant Spain. Whatever the reasons that made El Greco decide to continue westward, he was one molecule in the wave.

·IV·

TOLEDO

On my first visit to Spain in the early 1920's, the rumbling that presaged the devastating civil war was inaudible, especially to one whose inclination was not toward politics but toward the arts. I traveled with a young man of my own age whose main interest was music. On the narrow-gauge local train to Toledo, in an old-fashioned coach with the doors to each compartment on the outside, my friend was reading Eduard Hanslick's criticism written after the premiere of *Tristan und Isolde,* chuckling at the rage with which that leading Viennese critic censured Wagner's "cacophonic unmusical score." I also smiled, because I was reading my Baedeker in its then latest edition of 1912, in which Carl Justi in his art-historical introduction devoted 167 lines to Murillo and nine to El Greco, saying: "In Toledo appeared that odd Greek Domenico Theotocopuli, or El Greco, a pupil of Titian. His Christ on Calvary in the sacristy [of the cathedral] shows a power of spirited characterization and modeling and a genius for coloring which awoke great expectations. Unfortunately he lapsed all too soon, out of his mania for originality, into that incredible affectation which . . . was pampered by the public's taste. Only in his portraits did he catch, as few, despite all his pretenses of forced genius [*Kraftgenie*], the unique individuality of the Castilian hidalgos and the Toledan beauties."

Arriving in Toledo, we stepped outside the tiny railroad station and saw the city on its granite bluff across the Tagus. The few passengers soon dispersed. Half of them were priests, who were driven away in a mule-drawn *calèche* with a fringe on top, the long ears of the dusty animals flapping through their straw hats. The stationmaster was ready to lock up the building, since no train would be moving until late evening.

As we stood there in the crisp September morning, I remembered the admonition of Baedeker that it was advisable to have a guide, as much time could be lost in the labyrinth of streets. Looking around, I noticed a sickly ten- or twelve-year-old boy standing a few steps away, his inflamed eyes fixed on us. When I spoke to him in Spanish, his thin face broke into a smile and he courteously responded that he was local-born and could take us wherever we wished. So we crossed the bridge of Alcántara, passing through its Baroque and medieval gates (*Pl. 50B*). The water below was not deep, but in the shadow of the bluff it looked unfriendly and murky. We began to climb the dusty road, overtaking some plodding donkeys laden with boxes and sacks. Amazing to us was the lack of public transportation, but then the narrow steep medieval streets often made impossible even the passage of a mule. We headed toward the cathedral.

From nowhere can the vast complex be seen in its fullness. Much that was important had crammed itself into this area since medieval times (*Pl. 50A*). The majestic interior was nearly void of people, and its melancholy muteness was gripping. Its florid Gothic revealed a glorious story. The tapestries, velvets, and laces were all there—the statues dressed in rich clothing, the rugs, the chairs, many of them veritable museum pieces. Grilles and railings shone with the gold and silver of the Americas. At the corners of certain pews, colorful processional standards and gilded lanterns were fixed.

We were the only foreigners. With a handful of Spanish visitors we went into the *tesoro* to see the brilliantly embroidered, pearl-decorated, gold-braided chasubles and dalmatics, the chalices of gold and silver, the monstrances, crosses, cruets—all masterpieces of the jeweler's art, locked behind dusty glass cases and illuminated by two dull electric bulbs. And there also was what I expected—the statue of St. Francis by Pedro de Mena. Every fold of the brown cassock, mildly falling, had its reason, and from under the hood the pale face looked into space with sublimated gaze. I had known it for years from reproductions, and now I could admire it; the emaciated, unshaven priest was patient, even benevolent. Later we wandered along the *ambulatorio,* bewildered by the richness and nobility of the architectural detail. Statuary and painting were composed into towering retables, their gold shimmering in the languid candlelight. The Gothic in other countries can be lean and cold; here it has a tropical warmth and flavor. We were amazed to see a chapel dedicated to the Mozarabic Rite, that ancient form of Christian liturgy which antedates the Latin service in Spain and to which part of the population clung even after the liberation from the Moslem, although it was held in the conqueror's language. Up to the mid-nineteenth century six parochial churches served the Mozarabic Rite. The cathedral chapel, more than a century in building, was completed with a cupola in the early seventeenth century by El Greco's son, after the painter's death. The sacristan rattled his keys. Noontime meant closing.

As we stepped out into full sunshine from the cool semidarkness, our eyes needed some seconds to adjust. Only then did we notice that our little guide was still with us, following a step behind. He took us to a modest eating place, and we gave him some money for a meal. He asked if we had foreign stamps, and we tore some off the letters in our pockets. Later, through the starched lace curtains of the dining room, we saw him sitting on the curb in the shade across the street, sorting out his stamps.

I am glad I have seen that Toledo with its century-old patina—so different from the plundered, mutilated city, bustling with tourists, to which I came again and again afterward. On that first visit the city must have looked as it had to the painter Marie Bashkirtseff forty years earlier, when that neurasthenic, tubercular Russian girl wrote in her journal: "Toledo is all on the height, like a citadel, and resembles certain improbable backgrounds of da Vinci or even Velázquez. It is a Moorish city, with the walls and doors battered . . . marvelously picturesque courts and mosques turned into churches and daubed with whitewash. What is seen when the whitewash has crumbled off—arabesques with their colors still bright. . . . Spanish churches are something that cannot be imagined. Ragged guides, velvet-robed sacristans, strangers and dogs promenade, pray, and bark, and all has a strange charm. . . . The cathedral is a prodigy of elegance, of richness, and above all lightness." [74]

It was Théophile Gautier's *Un Voyage en Espagne,* written some forty years before her visit, that caused her to come to Spain. Strange that she, a painter, did not note the paintings of El Greco whom the French romantic writer mentions twice. In connection with the Crucifixion in the cathedral of Burgos by "Domenico Theotocopuli, called El Greco," Gautier says: "an extravagant and singular painter, whose pictures might be taken for sketches by Titian, if they were not easily recognizable by certain affectations of angularity and violent negligence. . . . In order to give his paintings the appearance of being executed with great energy of touch, he occasionally throws onto the canvas splashes of incredible impetuosity and brutality, with slender steely lights gleaming through the shadows like sabre blades. All this does not prevent El Greco from being a great painter. . . . He was also an architect and a sculptor, that sublime trinity and a brilliant triangle which is often to be found in the firmament of the highest arts." Gautier praises two of El Greco's pictures in Toledo and calls him "a strange extravagant painter who is hardly known outside Spain. . . ." Incidentally, the French writer and his friend bathed in the late afternoon in the Tagus, then had to hurry "so as to arrive before the closing of the gates. . . ." [78] This was in the year 1840.

Indeed, El Greco was then unknown outside Spain. Spain itself was little known in the eighteenth and nineteenth centuries, for it was not included in the "grand tour" of the cultured traveler.

It is an unanswered question why El Greco should have chosen to settle in a city which had already lost much of its importance and from which, with the expulsion of the Jews and the persecution even of converted Moors, a well-educated and wealthy layer of the population had been dispersed. As the capital of Castile, which then became the heart of the Five Kingdoms, Toledo was predestined to become the capital of the united Spanish Kingdom. Philip II moved there from Valladolid. But the tensions between the monarch and the prince primate of the church who had his residence there caused the king to remove his seat once more, to Madrid in 1561. The new site had the advantage of lying in a more central position; since it did not have the historical pretensions of Burgos, Valladolid, or Toledo, various court factions were neutralized.

With the departure of the court, an exodus commenced which depopulated the city that already had many empty houses. Not only tradesmen dependent on court patronage—the coachbuilder, confectioner, ladies' hairdresser, the barber, the tailor, the shoemaker—but also many artists and craftsmen found their chance for a better future in the growing new capital on the shore of the Manzanares. In Toledo remained, besides the powerful and numerous ecclesiastics, a group of aristocracy and gentry who preferred the old town to new Madrid or to the stifling rigor of the Escorial which Philip was already building. A number of them belonged to the anti-Philip faction. The dramatist and poet Lope de Vega declared that if the court moved back to Toledo, he would go to Valladolid.

Of the intelligentsia, a goodly number was wearing the cloth. When El Greco settled in Toledo, to the city proper belonged the cathedral with its large retinue, twenty-five parochial districts, twenty-nine monasteries, six great churches, nine chapels and hermitages, and four religious colleges. In the vicinity stood eight basilicas, ten monasteries, hospitals, asylums for the aged, and other institutions, supported mainly by religious confraternities.[102]

Toledo represented an ancient tradition. It contained within its walls monuments from the Visigothic, Arabic, and Christian past of Spain. The powerful intellectual climate was an inheritance that had come down through the centuries. In the seven hundred years of Moorish occupation of Spain, the Hebrew and Arabian scholars, especially of Córdoba and Toledo, guarded and disseminated the cultural heritage of classical Greece and the Orient. Thus, before the Renaissance, Hellenic culture and philosophy were fed into Europe largely through Spain. Among the industries in which the ancient city excelled were those producing superior tiles, exquisite silk fabrics often decorated with threads of gold and silver, and the legendary Toledo sword blades—crafts which were introduced by the Arab conqueror and perfected during the centuries of his occupation.

Charles V of the Holy Roman Empire, with his cosmopolitan background and connoisseurship in the arts, might have been a better patron of El Greco than his son, Philip II. Charles was a foreigner to Spain, born in Ghent (1500), and educated in Belgium under the wise tutelage of his aunt, Margaret, who was vice regent there. He did not visit Spain until he was seventeen years old. By that time much of his nature and character was formed. In the tradition of European monarchs, he commanded a number of European languages, though he spoke them with an accent. His endeavor to understand his subjects in all his lands made him esteemed, even beloved throughout his vast empire. Revealing of the difference between father and son was the scene in the Hall of the Golden Fleece in Brussels, at the time of his abdication (1555). Charles was moved to tears, as were many of the assembled nobles, as he made his farewell speech to them in their own tongue, transferring the regency of the Low Countries to his son. Philip stood beside him, haughty and dour. His reply, after a few words in French, was read by a bishop in Flemish, and must have made a chilling contrast.

Philip, born in Valladolid (1527), was Spanish-educated, Spanish-oriented, and Spanish-limited, and he could not make himself sympathetic to the many nationalities in his father's realm. He had only one ambition: to be monarch of Spain. His upbringing had made him humorless, stiff, often morose, and always suspicious of anyone with whom he could not converse in Spanish, the only tongue he commanded. His domain, besides Spain and the boundless colonies in America and the Philippines, comprised the Low Countries, the Aragonese inheritance in Italy—Naples and Sicily—the Burgundian inheritance, the Franche-Comté, and the Duchy of Milan. Philip did not want to live in the Low Countries, nor had he any love for the Germanic lands, many of which by that time were solidly Protestant. From his father he inherited also conflicts with England, France, the Netherlands, and Portugal. He was deeply involved in trying to restore the power of the Roman Catholic Church where the Reformation had already gained foothold.

Despite the incalculable wealth of "the Indies" in her control and Philip's unflagging attempts to reform the administration, Spain was bankrupt by 1570. The vitality of the national economy was being exhausted through many years of grandiose enterprises that brought no financial return. A census taken in that year reveals that a quarter of the adult population of Spain was in the clergy—312,000 parish priests, 200,000 clerics of minor orders, and 400,000 friars. In the diocese of Calahorra alone, in the north near Bilbao, lived 17,000 clergy. During the forty-two years of Philip's reign, the population dropped from ten million to eight million.[85]

Fateful events abroad added to the disintegrating economic conditions in the land. The headquarters of the Spanish treasure fleet from the Americas, Seville and later Cádiz, on the Atlantic coast, were somewhat out of reach of the Turkish navy and grew into very wealthy ports of Western Europe. But on the long voyage across the Atlantic the Spanish fleet was prey to English and Dutch freebooters and miscellaneous pirates. In 1587 all the shipping in the harbor of Cádiz was burned by Francis Drake, and again, in 1596, the fleet of the Earl of Essex sacked the city and destroyed some 40 merchant vessels and 13 warships. Between these two dates falls the destruction of the Spanish Armada, one of the great debacles of naval history. The magnificent assemblage of 130 vessels with 7,000 sailors and some 17,000 soldiers was outmatched by the English-Dutch forces, inferior in number, through superior seamanship and a lucky wind (1588). And this was accomplished by English sailors wearing civilian garb; for it was not until the mid-eighteenth century that the Admiralty put officers and men into uniform.

Philip's most successful and faithful commander in chief was the Duke of Alba (1508–1583). It was this battle-scarred commander who subdued the pope's army and stood at the gates of defenseless Rome threatening another sack (1557). When Philip moved to deprive the Low Countries of their constitutional rights, to quench the subsequent rebellion he sent in Alba. The Spaniard's first action was to lure into his camp the Counts Horn and Egmont whom he took prisoner and had beheaded. After months of terror—which spread beyond the Protestant camp—he could send his king the famous boast: "All is tranquil in the Low Countries." Later he reclaimed the crown of Portugal for Philip II. No wonder Spanish history knows him as *el Gran Duque*. In the Palacio de Liria, Madrid, the present residence of the ducal family, there is a wide variety of family portraits. But none has the piquant aptness of a statuette less than two feet high. Rather a caricature than a portrait, it shows a Quixote-like tall, emaciated knight —unmistakably with the features of the Gran Duque de Alba—driving his lance into a three-headed hydra. The first head is that of the sultan with characteristic curling mustache and turban; the second is the Protestant Elizabeth of England in a white ruff with a tiny crown; and the third—to whom our host called especial attention—is the pope in his religious garb and triple tiara.

Various portraits can be drawn of Philip II—for one the conscientious, hard-working, pious, and child-loving ruler. Another would present him as an autocrat—bigoted, cruel, unforgiving, and arrogant—who would leave his accompanying courtiers without condescending a gesture or word of dismissal.

Philip's many conflicts poisoned his relations with his family. His loveless attitude toward his own son resulted in the murder of Don Carlos. He was suspicious of his blond, good-looking half-brother John of Austria, and jealous of his successes on the battlefield. He tried to keep him out of Spain as much as possible, and sent him to the Netherlands as governor after the recall of the Duke of Alba. With little support from Philip in either men or money, John of Austria administered his post with singular justice but died in Belgium in less than two years. It was his desire to be buried at the side of his imperial father in the Escorial, who also had left instructions to this effect; and Philip could grant this wish without much risk. After a funerary ceremony in Belgium, the body was cut into three sections, packed in saddlebags, and smuggled across inimical France. One wonders whether a ship could not have been spared to bring home the remains of the hero of Lepanto, so that his last trip could have been over the water which had brought him victories and fame.

In building the Escorial (*Pl. 48B*), Philip II planned a memorial for his father, Charles V. From the idea of a tomb-chapel grew that monumental, melancholy, monastic barracks which became Philip's residence. The story goes that from Madrid he watched with a telescope—"stargazing" was then the hobby of princes—the progress of building. His private chambers in the Escorial were so arranged that he could see from his bed the priest officiating at Mass in the church (*Pl. 49*), the yellow light of candles, the clouds of incense rising into the stone arches. As Philip lay dying—and it took several weeks—Masses went on unremittingly in the cathedral, and his eyes could rest on the crucifix on the high altar. When in 1804 Lady Holland, noted for her travel reminiscences, visited the Escorial, she saw two monks kneeling in the choir, and was told that ceaseless prayers for the soul of Philip II had been observed since his death, the friars being relieved every six hours day and night.[82]

The list of artists active at the Escorial shows more Italian than Spanish painters. Before the great influence of Italy on the artistic life of Spain, artists from the Low Countries set the standard. While Greeks were also employed in the library of the Escorial, as well as in a number of other Spanish learned institutions, El Greco is the only painter of Byzantine tradition in that time who left an imprint in the country.

Many cities of Spain were enjoying a lively artistic life. Murcia, Valencia, Granada, Barcelona, as well as cities of the north, had notable studios. Seville, and all Andalusia, profited greatly from the opening of the Americas. The wealthy religious orders and the aristocracy were good clients of artists and craftsmen. The captains of vessels going to the colonies of the New World took orders for paintings, statues, and sometimes entire retables, and also sold works on commission. Contracts to this effect survive with such well-known names as Ribera, Martínez, Zurbarán. The new capital Madrid attracted many artists. Murillo in the seventeenth century painted holy pictures for a pittance for the market booths at Seville before he became a celebrity.

The Spanish people, first in the long wars with the Moors and later in battle beyond their own borders, developed a high degree of individuality. Sons returned from distant campaigns in which the Spanish foot soldier was proving himself one of the best. From the New World came not only treasures but hardened and widely traveled men. The Spanish folk were perhaps not very literate but they had intelligence, experience, and personality. And they witnessed—even though perhaps disapproving—how life moved in other lands, whether among the pagan redskins of Mexico or the Protestants in the harbors of the North Sea. Vast energy and great spiritual power, characteristics of this sovereign land, were released, after centuries of Arab occupation.

The king and the highest ecclesiastical authorities had the difficult task of channeling these energies to their advantage. Feudalism was fighting to preserve its prerogatives; the Roman Catholic Church, that had faced the necessity of a radical reform too late to save its unity, had to clamp down on any action which further endangered its authority. One answer was the reconstitution of the Inquisition to stamp out any deviation of faith; and all means to this end were justified.

Although the Inquisition was to a certain degree a national institution maintained by the Dominican order in each land, the pope was nominally its head. The papal legate, or *nuncius*, had—as he has today—full diplomatic immunity and precedence over every other diplomat. His luggage, which could not be examined by any authority, thus could contain directives, information, blueprints for conspiracy, and gold in mint. The wealth of the Inquisition in Spain was enormous. Half of the total revenues of the land went to the clergy. The wealthiest of all was the Cardinal of Toledo with a yearly income of 150,000 gold ducats as Grand Inquisitor and, as "Prince of the Church," 300,000 more from the ecclesiastic chapter of Toledo [83] —at a time when a live sheep cost only a few pennies.

The Inquisition was the first totalitarian organization which, with the credo of man's salvation, acted with ruthless cruelty. Its methods call to mind those of present authoritarian powers. There is little, from physical torture to the "terror of the midnight knock," which is a new invention.

Altogether there were nine inquisitorial tribunals in Spain—Toledo, Zaragoza, Valencia, Murcia, Logroño, Granada, and Cuenca, rivaling in zeal those at Seville and Valladolid. All too soon the system began to work with informers, professional and voluntary spies who, as they were allotted a share of the spoils, would stoop to any depth. The accused was kept in solitary confinement, often in dungeons, on rotting bread and slimy water. He was subject to various tortures. He was kept in ignorance of the accusations against him and had no recourse to counsel. The trial was secret. His accuser was unnamed, and he was not allowed to confront him. Even if he should die during the trial, secretaries were at hand who acted as witnesses to his "confession." He was left in ignorance of his fate until the day of the auto-da-fé—the "act of faith" in which the sentences pronounced by the tribunal of the Inquisition were carried out. Punishments, when not death by various dread means, were the confiscation of all property, imprisonment—usually under inhuman conditions—condemnation to the galleys. Milder penalties, for foreigners, were gagging, prohibition to leave Spain, and—best of all—exile. If by some fortune the accused was acquitted, he was not allowed to speak of his experiences, for to reveal the secrets of the Holy Office was punishable by death. As it was the custom to sequester the property of an accused until the verdict, a man might emerge free, to find his goods dispersed and his family in penury.

Only four months after the liberation of Granada from the Moors, the edict was issued expelling the Jewish population whose leaders had been friends and treasurers of kings and aristocrats. There was no longer need to conciliate minorities; the oppressed became oppressors. "Pure Christian blood"—proof of the "undefiled" ancestry of any Spaniard, called *limpieza* —was a main condition for any public position. Persons who washed their hands before meals or sometimes bathed could be accused of being *Moriscos,* following Moslem customs. As late as the seventeenth century a special midwife had to be present at a birth in any family of Moorish or Jewish ancestry to see that the infant was not put through a washing which might be regarded as ritual. Cardinal Francisco de Mendoza y Bobadilla (d. 1566) was outraged when the purity of blood of his own nephew was questioned, and wrote a pamphlet known as "El Tizón," the brand mark, claiming that all the grandees and lesser aristocrats of Spain had Jewish or Moorish blood.

By the mid-sixteenth century the Lutheran "heresy" had become the main target of the Inquisition. Since the principles of the Reformation were spreading rapidly throughout Europe, in 1559 Philip II ordered all Spanish youths studying at foreign universities to return home within four months, subject to exile, the confiscation of property, and the loss of citizenship. Excepted were the universities at Rome, Bologna, Naples, and Coimbra in Portugal, where the church still had full control. As a result, the University of Alcalá is said to have had some 12,000 students, and Salamanca, 14,000 in the late sixteenth century. In 1572 it was decreed that no Frenchman could be appointed as teacher. This is the year of the massacre of St. Bartholomew's Day.

The Dominicans and Jesuits were the censors of books. Latin Bibles were in circulation, correct in text but, according to the Inquisition, with heretical commentaries. Every book printed in Spain had first to be examined by a royal council. To prevent alterations after the "imprimatur," or permission to print, was given, every page of the manuscript had to be signed by a secretary of the royal chamber. When the book was ready, two printed copies had to be returned for comparison with the checked original. In principle, every book was supposed to display not only the name of its author but also the license number, the printer, and the place of publication. In case of a new edition, the same regulations stood. Thus it came about that in Spanish archives there accumulated a backlog of valuable reports and manuscripts, some of them still "undiscovered." Six thousand condemned volumes were burned on a single occasion—this in a country where book printing was otherwise lagging. Even Philip II named an outsider as his "royal printer," Christopher Plantin in Antwerp, who brought out religious books for Spain and the colonies, the sale of which were the royal monopoly. Plantin issued the first basic botanical book of the Spanish realm (1576). There is a strong suspicion that Protestant treatises also were printed on the Plantin Press. Lutheran symbols were allegedly discovered in woodcuts of the Passion brought in from France. Though the loading of ships was strictly controlled, demijohns in which water and wine were taken on were found to be padded with Protestant literature, some of which reached the New World. Penalty of death and confiscation of property were decreed for publishing or even printing prohibited books.

The Spanish Inquisition stretched rapacious fingers far beyond the geographical borders of the kingdom. Castaway English sailors, captured near the Canary Islands, were tried as heretics. Some of these escaped burning by declaring themselves converted; others managed to flee. Even after Belgium had won autonomy, the Spanish Inquisition tried to cancel privileges of the Guild of Weavers there, but the Belgian craftsmen rose against the suppression of their rights and stood their ground successfully. Nor were the mighty exempt. The Hospitalers, retreating from the Turkish advance, left Rhodes and came, by way of Cyprus and Crete, to the island of Malta, which Charles V had ceded to them. Though the Grand Inquisitor of Spain tried to extend his authority over them, the Grand Master of the Knights of Malta (as they called themselves by that time), claiming an older sovereignty, refused to admit any agents sent by the "foreign" Holy Office.

Persons who are today venerated as saints did not escape suspicion. St. Ignatius of Loyola (1491–1556) was twice imprisoned at the beginning of his career, accused of heresy. Teresa de Cepeda, later St. Theresa of Avila (1515–1580), was accused of misconduct and several times denounced. Her work *Conceptos de Amor divino,* which today is regarded as most revealing of her sanctity, was proscribed by the Inquisition. In 1576, when El Greco may have been already in Spain, the Archbishop of Toledo himself, Bartolomé Carranza de Miranda (1503–1576), a representative at the Council of Trent, was imprisoned for heresy and condemned to perpetual seclusion instead of death, since he was dying anyhow.

Dostoevski's parable of the "Grand Inquisitor," a chapter in his *The Brothers Karamazov,* has pertinence. After visiting Rome and seeing the papal pomp contrasted with the poverty of the population, the great Russian novelist has Jesus Christ return to earth just as the Inquisitor General, a Dominican, Cardinal of Seville, is preparing to attend the burning of a hundred heretics. Jesus tries to convince the cardinal that Christianity must work with means other than the stake. But it becomes clear in the narrative that the clergy is less interested in His teaching than in the perpetuation of their own system. In the end, the Grand Inquisitor opens the door and bids Christ leave and never return.

In the history of art, the most celebrated inquisitorial case was that of Paolo Caliari Veronese who was accused of sacrilege in Venice in 1573. The painting in question was a Last Supper of monumental size. Though the central section is dominated by a dignified and ingratiating figure of Christ, the groups at the sides are profane. They contain hilarious, if not drunken, persons, dwarfs, blackamoors and, above all, soldiers in the gaudy dress of German mercenaries recalling Lutherans. Veronese argued that the large surfaces had to be filled up in some way and that in the Sistine Chapel in Rome his master Michelangelo represented Christ and other holy figures with almost no garments at all. To the lengthy theological examination, he replied, "I paint pictures as I see fit and as well as my talent permits." [8] The painter was directed to make changes, which he thought were detrimental to a work that he regarded as one of his masterpieces. On the advice of a friend versed in canonical law, and without touching brush to canvas, he changed the title to The Feast in the House of Levi. This seemingly satisfied his accusers. In 1573 El Greco was most probably still in Italy and, considering how fast gossip travels in artists' circles, he must have heard the details very soon. A somewhat similar episode occurred in his own career, as we shall see later.

Another celebrated case involving an artist was that of Pietro Torrigiani, a Florentine sculptor who studied under the patronage of Lorenzo the Magnificent. Invited to England, he executed the splendid bronze tombs for Henry VII and his Queen in Westminster Abbey (*Pl. 53B*). Later called to Spain, he carved crucifixes and statuary for the monastery of San Girolamo in Seville, among other works. A Virgin and Child from his hand was found so captivating by the Duke of Arcos that he ordered a copy of it, promising to enrich the Italian for the favor. When the work was finished, the duke, scion of an immensely wealthy Andalusian family, sent two servants laden down with coins. However, they turned out to be mere *maravedis*—coppers of such little worth that altogether they did not amount to thirty gold ducats. Enraged, Torrigiani broke the statue into pieces. In revenge the Spanish duke accused the sculptor of blasphemy, and Torrigiani was delivered to the prison of the Inquisition in Seville. Examined daily by one judge after the other, he was menaced with severest punishment. But sentence could not be carried out, for, in deepest melancholy, he ended his own life by starvation (1522).

The Inquisition was active even in the distant American colonies where hostile Indians still made life dangerous and the foundations of the Christian faith were barely laid. The Flemish painter Simon Pereyns, a native of Antwerp, worked in Portugal, then in Toledo, and finally, in 1556, attracted by Spanish promises, he went to the Mexican viceregal capital to furnish paintings for the cathedral then in building. Not two years there, he was accused of blasphemy, and suffered torture and condemnation.

Foreigners especially were under suspicion. In 1557 a sculptor recorded as Esteban Jamete was accused of ridiculing holy objects and the holy religion; he was condemned to years in prison and his property was confiscated. He was a Frenchman—in his native land, Hamet de Orléans. It was Spanish custom to Hispanize foreign names often beyond identification. The sixteenth century painter Karel van Mander of Haarlem achieved fame with his book on painting; it was translated into Spanish and circulated even in the colonies as the work of "Carlos Bexmandes, native of Hadem."

Still closer to El Greco's career in Spain is the case of Pompeo Leoni, widely acclaimed Italian sculptor. His father, Leone Leoni, was a favorite of Charles V, and executed a portrait head of Philip II (*Pl. 48A*). Envy apparently caused Pompeo to be accused before the Inquisition of voicing Lutheran opinions.[89] Although in favor with the court, he was cut off from the outside world, and when Charles V, in his last months, inquired after him, no one dared to tell him that the Italian was imprisoned. Deprived of royal intervention, Pompeo served a year's incarceration.

The Spaniard Alonso Cano, master of architecture, sculpture, and painting in seventeenth century Spain, also came before the Inquisition, accused, as head of the confraternity of artists and jewelers, of not taking part in the Holy Week procession. A fine of a hundred ducats or a prison term was imposed. Today, when the innocent tourist watches the multitudes on the Piazza di San Pietro in Rome at Eastertime—the friars, priests, nuns, school children, sodalities and confraternities brought in by special transportation—he might remember that it cost Alonso Cano a hundred golden ducats not to march in an Easter procession. The same charge was brought against the painter Luca Giordano in the mid-seventeenth century. But he, a Neopolitan, soon found a way to leave the country, although the king tried to retain him.

Francisco Goya stood before the Inquisition in 1815, accused of painting indecent figures, especially in his *Caprichos*. Only his royal patron Charles IV saved his life, though many of his works were confiscated by the Camera Secreta.[80] The institution existed until 1912. In 1958 a Spanish book appeared in which the Inquisition is interpreted as beneficial—justified because it "preserved the cultural harmony of the country."

These factors must be taken into consideration when we review the life of El Greco in Toledo. He is named as a resident of the city in various documents dating between 1577 and 1614. In a parallel period, from 1575 to 1610, the Tribunal of the Inquisition in Toledo tried 1,172 cases. Of these, forty-seven were resident foreigners, accused of Protestantism; three persons of Greek extraction were convicted of heresy. "Doubting statements of the catechism" was one of the easiest accusations to lodge against a foreigner.[75] The questions of the Tribunal were often directed in such a way as to confuse one who did not understand the Spanish language well. It is remarkable that El Greco—who was often outspoken—was able to live through his years in Toledo without being involved. The nearest he came to the Tribunal of the Inquisition was in 1582 when he acted as interpreter for a less fortunate Greek, accused of Moslem practices.

El Greco lived through the activities of eight Inquisitors General in Toledo. Brought up in fierce love of liberty and a spirit of independence, the Cretan must have felt the oppression which surrounded him. In comparison to what he saw and experienced in Toledo, the justice meted out in Venice was mild.

All Toledo must have appeared strange to El Greco after the sun-bathed flat-roofed city of Candia, washed with color. Venice in her oriental splendor was surcharged with enterprise and lust. There, as in Candia, the sea determined the rhythm of life. In contrast, Toledo was landlocked, windswept; for many weeks the sun seldom reached its dank, canyon-like alleys. The cathedral of Toledo (*Pl. 51*), with its particular brand of Gothic, was very different from the architecture El Greco was accustomed to seeing in Crete and Italy. The Orthodox image was the painted icon, purely two-dimensional, while here, entire carved structures of biblical scenes rose inside the cathedral, gilded and many-colored, a veritable religious theater (*Pl. 52B*). The side chapels with their rigid architectural tracery contained sculptured tombs like those in the chapel of Santiago (*Pl. 52C*), documents of the cult of the dead different from those that El Greco knew. To all this came the solid surge of Spanish Baroque, presaged in the wood carvings of Alonso Berruguete (*Pl. 52A*), where even in a relief, a restless three-dimensionality is manifest.

More familiar to him might have been the architecture in the Moorish and the later Mudéjar styles. The Puerta del Sol (*Pl. 54B*) had the general imprint of military architecture, and could have stood even in the Greek archipelago. The ingenious use of brickwork in the church of

Cristo de la Luz and its small size might have been reminiscent of Arab masonry in his homeland (*Pl. 54A*). The virtuosity of the Levant in creating arches in brick he could see reflected in the interior (*Pl. 55C*). Note the Arab inscription high up on the façade. Legend has it that when Toledo was reconquered by the Spaniards, a crucifix was discovered in a walled-up niche in this building, with a taper that had burned through the three and a half centuries of Arab occupation—hence the renaming of the little tenth century mosque as "the Christ of the Light."

In the Jewish quarter stood the synagogue erected in the mid-fourteenth century largely through contributions of Samuel ha-Levi who was treasurer to the Spanish king. The elaborate carved ceiling was constructed from cedar brought from Lebanon, and Hebrew texts embellished the richly stuccoed interior (*Pl. 54C*). Upon the expulsion of the Jews, it was turned over to the Knights of Calatrava, a number of whom are buried there, and was later dedicated to the Assumption of the Virgin. The parochial church of Santiago del Arrabal (*Pl. 55B*) and its thirteenth century bell tower have a Mediterranean touch. Note the ingenious adjustment to the hilly terrain. The apse with the coffered blind arcades is closely related to Byzantine monuments, whether in Sicily, the Venetian islands, or Macedonia (*Pl. 55A*). All these styles produced a mixture, autochthonous to the city.

The quarters El Greco occupied in Toledo were once also associated with Samuel ha-Levi. Sturdy pillars and exquisitely worked arches from Arabian and even Roman occupation constituted solid foundations for the later buildings. The quarter underwent many vicissitudes. El Greco moved into a usable section of the sprawling complex and lived there until his death. Soon afterward the district became a slum. The city of Toledo had reached extreme penury. The city council reported to the king that entire streets were deserted, that a number of handicrafts had died out, and that real estate had become worthless. Collections for the royal treasurer were being taken up from house to house, and collection boxes were passed in the street as in a church.[99] The situation did not improve as time went by. By the end of the nineteenth century, the section in which El Greco had lived was in such a ruinous state as to constitute a danger, and the authorities considered demolishing it. Just about that time, interest in El Greco was awakening. In 1905 the Marqués de la Vega Inclán bought some of the old houses there and had them restored to serve as the "Casa del Greco" (*Pl. 56*). Architectural embellishment was added; stairways and rooms were made passable. Period furniture, statues, paintings, draperies were collected, and soon, with the munificent contribution of Archer M. Huntington, founder of the Hispanic Society of America, further rooms were acquired for the Museo del Greco. While these apartments are not the actual ones El Greco occupied, they give an atmosphere in which one can visualize the painter amid his household.

El Greco left portraits of three cardinals, all of whom were also Inquisitors General of Toledo. That of Gaspar de Quiroga appears not to have been painted from life but perhaps from a miniature or similar likeness. It lacks the sharpness of expression that characterizes El Greco's work. Further, it is highly unusual for him to portray his sitter in profile; in all other of El Greco's portraits the face is shown at least in three-quarters view. As Inquisitor General, Quiroga had a list of prohibited books printed in Lyons, France, in 1573, one of the early Indexes of Spain.

The best-known figure of El Greco's inquisitors is that of Cardinal Fernando Niño de Guevara painted in full length as he sits in a stiff chair (*Pl. 57C*). It is a severe, unloving person who looks out with scrutinizing eyes. His left hand rests in clawlike tension on the chair arm, as if he were ready at any moment to rise and pursue another sinner. How much did the painter, knowing the dread methods of the Inquisition, speculate on the character and psychology of his sitter at a meeting of such different philosophies of Christianity? What did he feel as he outlined so clearly the apostolic ring which so many had kissed, on the hand that with a wave could start the fire under the stake, what did he feel as he placed his signature like a calling card at the potentate's feet? Recent Spanish writers have remarked that the portrayal is unflattering; one calls it a *prodigiosa caricatura.*[102]

Painters and their sitters often struck up rapport, such as that between Titian and Charles V. One wonders what the various ecclesiastics talked of with the stranger, the *Griego,* who, in his mid-thirties when he came to Toledo, must have spoken Spanish with a heavy foreign accent. Did they know that he had a number of prohibited books in his library? Were they interested in a world of which they knew little? Was the Greek painter cautious, with his wisdom and sense of self-preservation, not to incriminate himself?

With the third cardinal, Juan Pardo de Tavera, no dialogue was possible. He died in 1545, before Greco's arrival in Toledo. It is recorded that this cardinal, also a Grand Inquisitor of Toledo, spent vast sums of money on churchly buildings. His main beneficence was perhaps a new hospital which was dedicated to St. John the Baptist in the first half of the sixteenth century. As Toledo was already crowded, the new establishment was erected outside the fortification walls. Its relatively simple façade (*Pl. 53C*) with the quiet, slender portal encloses a large classical patio. In the archives of the administration (*Pl. 53A*) folios are preserved which show that Arabic numerals were in use there when cumbersome Roman numerals were customary elsewhere—another survival from the centuries of Moorish occupation.

Cardinal Tavera had lived in ostentatious pomp and unusual luxury, yet in some ascetic gesture, or pose that he lacked human vanity, he refused to be portrayed, though surrounded by painters and sculptors. After his death the hospital he had endowed wanted a memorial of him, and commissioned El Greco to paint a portrait, furnishing the cardinal's death mask for the resemblance. Most of El Greco's paintings were of biblical characters, whose physiognomy Byzantine tradition had long established. He had depicted Count Orgaz who died in the fourteenth century. But it was a different task to achieve a portrait of a near contemporary which older residents of the city might judge for its likeness. El Greco had to visualize the face with opened eyes. But he made the skin ashen, the cheeks hollow, and gave the eyes the gaze of a ghost (*Pl. 57B*).

Historians report among the extravagances of Tavera that in his retinue he always kept forty pages, descendants of the noblest families of Spain. Whatever large staff had surrounded the Grand Inquisitor—princelings, priests, peons—they served him no longer. That dominating, domineering figure in scarlet silk was the equal of any mortal before the God whose powers he had arrogated to himself while on earth. The civil war that caused so much devastation wrought particular havoc in Toledo, and the Tavera portrait was badly damaged. Perhaps some descendant of a maltreated peon—as if paying back an old debt—pushed his knife into the canvas, gouging the head. By now the painting has been restored, covered with a mercifully thick layer of varnish, and hangs on the wall in the same building for which it was originally ordered. The face stares stiffly out on the visitor today—just as pallid and like a death mask as before—keeping the insult of modern times to itself.

A. Istanbul. Ruins of the Fortifications

B. Kariye Cami

PLATE 1

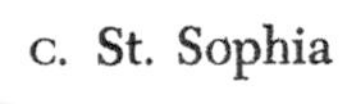

C. St. Sophia

A. Near Aswan, Egypt. Ruins of Coptic Monastery

B. Cappadocia, Turkey. Ruined Church at Til Keuy. 6th

PLATE 2

C. Damascus, Syria. Omayad Mosque, formerly Byzantine Church. Early 5th C.

D. Syria. Church of St. Simeon the Stylite. Early 7th C.

A. Turkish Armenia. Church at Achthamar. 10th C.
PLATE 3

B. Detail of Frescoed Interior

C. Story of Jonah. South Wall

A. Turkish Armenia. Cathedral at Ani.
End of 10th C.

PLATE 4

B. Cairo, Egypt. East Pit of Nilometer.
A.D. 861-2

C. Ramla, Israel. Cistern with Pointed Arches.
A.D. 789

A. Syria. Crusader Castle, Krak des Chevaliers. 12th C.

PLATE 5

B. Passageway

A. Mt. Athos, Greece. Monastery of Vatopedi

PLATE 6

B. Vatopedi. Refectory

A. Mt. Athos, Greece. Courtyard of Vatopedi

B. Pyrgos. Medieval Tower

PLATE 7

C. Vatopedi. Church Interior

A. Mt. Athos. Greece. Monastery of Simopetra

PLATE 8

B. Monastery of Panteleimon

A. Mt. Athos, Greece. Lavra. Passageway to Church

PLATE 9

B. Christ the Judge. Mural. Dochiariou. Mid-16th C.

C. Monastery of Grigoriou

A. Mt. Athos, Greece. Monastery of Iviron
PLATE 10

B. Dionysiou. View into the Aegean Sea

C and D. Refectory Murals. Dionysiou. 16th C.

A. Death of St. Athanasius.
Mural. Lavra, Mt. Athos. 16th C.

PLATE 11

B. Death of St. Ephraim.
Mural. Dochiariou. Mid-16th C.

C. Death of St. Ephraim.
Mural. Siatista, Greece. 1611

A. Mistra. Greece. General View

PLATE 12

C. Church of Peribleptos. Exterior

B. Apse Mural. Peribleptos. Mid-14th C.

Mistra, Greece. Church of Peribleptos. Interior. Mid-14th C.

PLATE 13

A. Kastoria, Greece.
View of Lake

PLATE 14

B. Church of Anargyri. 10–11th C.

C. Church of Mavriotissa. Entrance with Murals

A. Kastoria, Greece.
Church of Mavriotissa

PLATE 15

B. Detail of Mural, The Last Judgment. Late 12th C.

C. Detail of Mural,
The Dormition of the Virgin.
15th C?

D. Detail of Mosaic. Torcello, Italy. Early 13th C.

A. Rila, Bulgaria.
Monk Retouching Murals

PLATE 16

B. General View of Monastery

C. Courtyard

D. Main Church. Interior

A. The Last Judgment. Repainted Mural. Rila, Bulgaria

PLATE 17

B. Sucevita, Rumania. Painted Apse

D. The Ladder to Heaven. Mural

C. Monastery and Church

A. Sopocani, Yugoslavia. Church Exterior

PLATE 18

B. Saintly Witnesses. Mural

A. Dormition of the Virgin. Mural. Sopocani. Mid-13th C.

PLATE 19

B. Saintly Witnesses. Mural

A. Pec, Yugoslavia. Warrior Saints

PLATE 20

B. Studenica. Convent and Chapel

C. Pec. Triple Church

A. Gracanica, Yugoslavia. Church Exterior

PLATE 21

B. Mileseva. Church Exterior

C. Angel at the Tomb. Mural. Mileseva. 13th C.

A. Ohrid, Yugoslavia. Church of S. Jovan Kaneo

PLATE 22

B. The Ascension. Mural. Anargyri, Kastoria, Greece. 11th C.

C. The Ascension. Mural. St. Sophia, Ohrid. Before 1056

D. Detail from Dormition of the Virgin. Sopocani. Mid-13th C.

A. Adoring Angel. Mural. St. Sophia, Ohrid, Yugoslavia. 11th C.

PLATE 23

C. Detail of Apse. Anargyri, Kastoria, Greece. 11th C.

B. Standing Angel. Mural. Kurbinovo. Mid-12th C.

B. Mt. Athos, Greece. Monastery of Iviron

A. Manasija, Yugoslavia

PLATE 24

C. Manasija. Monastery Complex

A. Pippo Spano, by A. del Castagno.
Florence. Mid-15th C.

PLATE 25

B. Two Warrior Saints. Mural.
Manasija, Yugoslavia. Early 15th C.

C. St. Mercurius. Mural. Karyes,
Mt. Athos, Greece. 15th C.

A. Heraklion (Candia), Crete. The Fortifications in Late 19th Century

PLATE 26

B. Harbor View with Mt. Ida

A. Clan Chapel near Rethymnon, Crete

PLATE 27

B. Gortyna. Ruins of St. Titus Basilica, ca. 4th C.

A. Detail of Iconostasis. Old Metropolitan Church. Heraklion, Crete

PLATE 28

B. Iconostasis. St. Matthew. Heraklion

C. Life of St. Haralambos. Icon. Heraklion

A. Kritsa, Crete. Church of The Dormition

PLATE 29

B. Detail of Ascension. Mural. Kritsa. 14th C?

A. Potamies, Crete. Monastery Church of Gouvernotissa

B. Two Church Fathers. Mural. Gouvernotissa. Early 17th C.

PLATE 30

C. Cretan Landscape in the Myron Valley

A. The Miracle of the Loaves and Fishes, by Paleopapas. Gonia, Crete. 1643

B. SS. Anne and Joachim in the Temple. Mural. Drakona. 14th C?

PLATE 31

C. Gonia. Monastery

A. Sfakion, Crete. Chapel of the Holy Apostles

PLATE 32

C. Komitades. Shrine of St. John

B. Komitades. Painted Interior of Shrine. 1313

A. SS. George, Demetrios, and Michael. Mural. Platanias, Crete

B. Messenger of God. Mural. Athens. 11th C?

PLATE 33

C. St. Michael. Mural. Formis, Italy. Late 11th C.

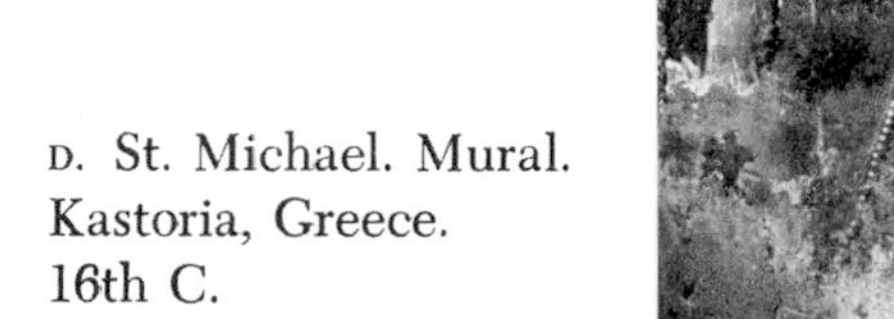

D. St. Michael. Mural.
Kastoria, Greece.
16th C.

A. Corfu, Greece. Convent of Vlacherna and Ponticonissi Island

PLATE 34

B. Dubrovnik, Yugoslavia. Rector's Palace and Mint

A. Dubrovnik, Yugoslavia. City Walls

PLATE 35

B. Split in the 18th Century. Engraving

C. Split. Inner Court of Diocletian's Palace

A. Porec, Yugoslavia. Basilica. Entrance

B. Venice. St. Mark. Detail of Interior

PLATE 36

C. Porec. Basilica. Interior. 6th C.

D. Ravenna. S. Apollinare in Classe. Interior. 6th C.

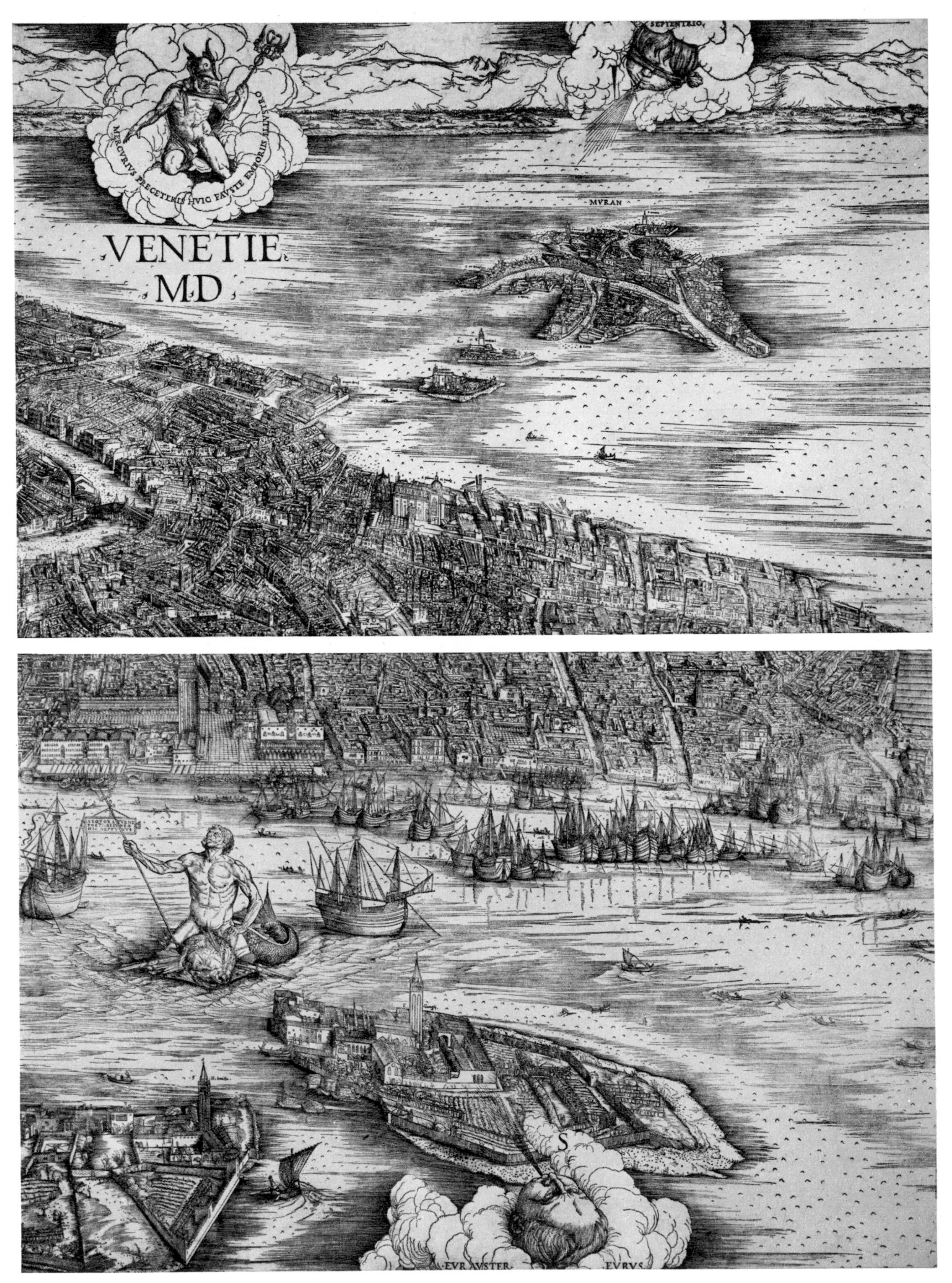

Bird's-Eye View of Venice, by Jacopo de Barbari. Woodcut. 1500

PLATE 37

A. Venice. Riva degli Schiavoni and The Arsenal

PLATE 38

B. Rialto Bridge

A. Venice. St. Mark

PLATE 39

B. View from a Painting by Titian. 1566

Venice. St. Mark. Interior

PLATE 40

A. La Pala d'Oro. Altar Screen. St. Mark, Venice. 11–12th C.

PLATE 41

B. Christ in Majesty. Detail of Pala d'Oro. Late 11th C.

C. Byzantine Chalice.
Treasury of St. Mark. 10th C.

A. Venice. House of Titian

B. House of Tintoretto

C. S. Pietro di Castello, former Seat of Cardinal

A. Torcello. Basilica and Santa Fosca. 9–11th C.

C. Basilica. Nave

B. The Last Judgment. Mosaic. Basilica. Early 13th C.

A. Venice. San Giorgio dei Greci

PLATE 44

B. St. John the Baptist Proclaims the Redeemer. Icon. San Giorgio dei Greci. 17th C.

A. Gabriel Seviros, First Bishop of the Greek Community, Venice. Late 16th C.

PLATE 45

B. San Giorgio dei Greci. Interior

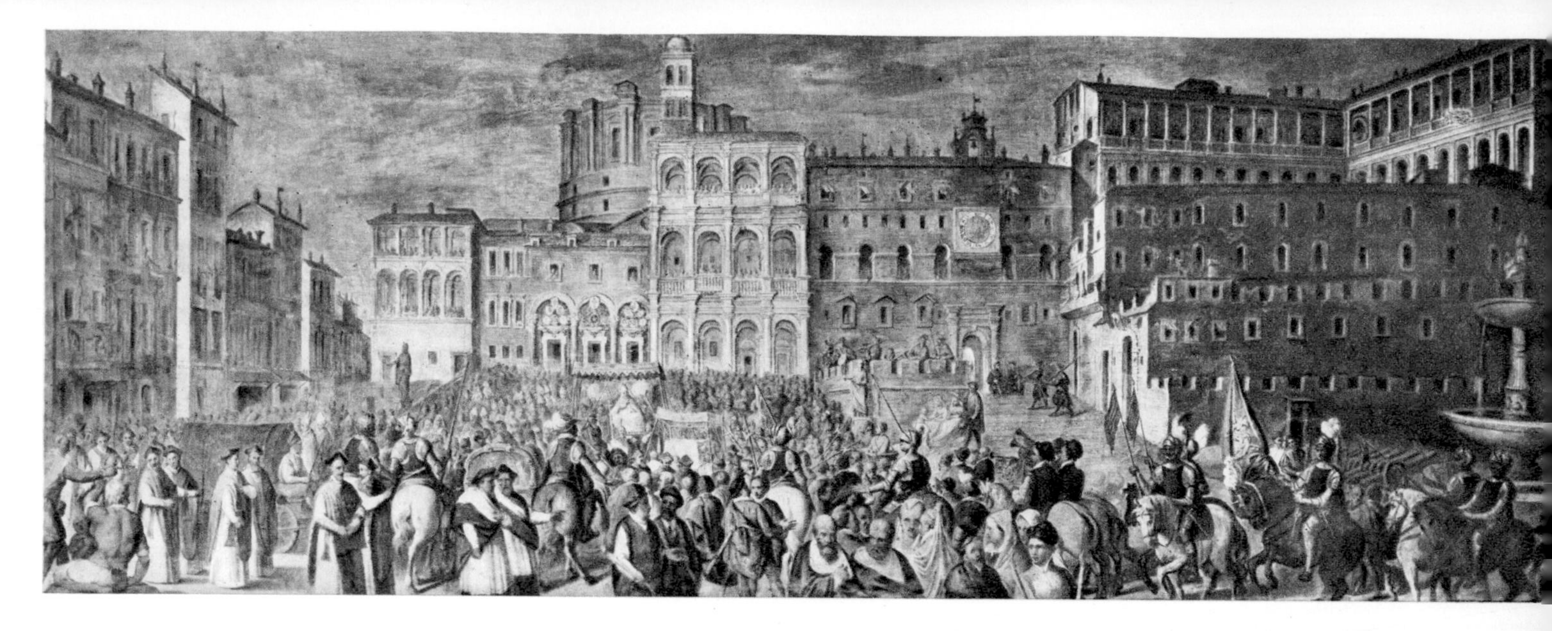

A. Rome. St. Peter's Square in 1580. Detail of Fresco. Vatican

PLATE 46

B. Piazza del Popolo in Early 17th Century

C. Piazza di Spagna in 17th Century

A. Grottaferrata. The Greek Abbey

PLATE 47

B. The Abbey in Early 19th Century. Engraving

C. Church Interior

A. Bust of Philip II of Spain, by Leone Leoni

PLATE 48

B. Escorial. General View

A. Escorial. Monastery Church

PLATE 49

B. Monastery Church. Interior

A. Toledo. View towards Cathedral

B. Alcántara Bridge

A. Toledo. Cathedral

B. Cathedral. Choir

PLATE 51

A. St. John the Baptist.
Woodcarving by A. Berruguete.
Cathedral, Toledo

PLATE 52

B. Cathedral. Main Altar

C. Cathedral. Chapel of Santiago with Tombs

A. Toledo. Tavera Hospital. Archive

PLATE 53

B. Tomb of Henry VII and His Queen, by Torrigiani. Westminster Abbey, London

C. Tavera Hospital. Main Portal

A. Toledo. Cristo de la Luz

PLATE 54

B. Puerta del Sol

C. Sinagoga del Transito

A. Thessaloniki, Greece. St. Catherine

B. Toledo. Santiago del Arabal

PLATE 55

C. Cristo de la Luz. Interior

"Casa del Greco"
PLATE 56

·V·

THE GREEK DIASPORA

Even before the fall of Constantinople, Greek scholars journeyed westward, enlivening interest in the Hellenic culture. Whether natives of Anatolia, Syria, Macedonia, or the heartland of Greece, they were all reared in the climate of Byzantine civilization, and identified themselves with it. Manuel Chrysoloras, a native of Constantinople, for instance, went to Venice as early as 1394 to solicit aid against the Turks, though with little success, and a few years later was called to Florence as a professor of Greek. In Venice, Padua, Milan, and Rome, centers were being formed to study Greek culture. A pupil of Chrysoloras was among the first of many Italians to travel to Constantinople for the purpose of collecting Greek manuscripts.[13] The great Renaissance princes of Italy, whose ancestors vaunted their horses, their falcons, their knights, began to vie with one another for the possession of some exquisite volume for their growing libraries and for the copying of a rare manuscript.

As Sultan Mohammed closed in on Constantinople, the inhabitants fled in masses toward the West. The city that the Turkish army entered was a shadow of the once magnificent capital; its population is estimated to have been no more than a hundred thousand. Although the customary atrocities were committed—which were routine in that period and survive on the largest scale to the present day—the conqueror put a stop to them before the destruction came near to that wrought by the valiant Christian warriors of the Fourth Crusade. Resolved to make his capital great and beautiful once more, the sultan decreed that repairs begin; municipal bazaars, baths, inns, and kitchens for the poor were constructed; and gardens with fountains were laid out to revive the brilliance for which the city had been famous. Although a number of Christian churches were transformed into mosques, the new buildings were nothing to be ashamed of, for the Ottoman Turks looked back on an old tradition of imposing buildings crowned with gilded domes. As a statesman, Mohammed showed imagination and sagacity. He invested the incumbent Orthodox patriarch with civil authority over all Christians in his realm, and assured them of religious freedom. Besides the Turks, whose influx was natural for administrative, religious, military, and commercial purposes, Mohammed permitted to settle in his capital Jews who had become wanderers, expelled from a number of West European lands. Armenians, Syrians, and especially Greeks from Asia Minor were encouraged; craftsmen, artists, and scholars were made welcome. Mohammed, himself a poet, desired his capital to be not only a fortress but a center of learning and culture.

Unfortunately, neither his successors nor various local caliphs shared his broad-mindedness. And the westward movement, already following an established route, carried more and more Greeks toward uncertain destinations. Some, however, remained in the Phanar section of Istanbul on the southern shore of the Golden Horn, where their descendants still are today; whoever has attended services in the patriarchal church there can see that more than five hundred years of strife and even a recent massacre have not broken the Greek spirit. Alexandria also continued as a great Greek center for centuries, and the graduates of its school filled important posts in many Greek-speaking communities.

Most of the Greek émigrés did not know in what place, with what foreign language spoken around them, they would close their eyes for the last time. Homeless, they carried with them their pride in a thousand years of civilization. They received sympathy, homage was offered to their scholarship, and many of them achieved high positions. In various Western cities at the end of the fifteenth century, medals were coined in honor of distinguished Greek scholars. Their conduct was that of balanced members of the society which surrounded them.

The Greeks called their dispersal *diaspora.* The word appears in the Greek translation of the Bible in connection with the scattering of the Jews after captivity in Babylon. It signifies not only a scattering but the scattering of the seed. Thus it was used again to denote the setting forth of Christianized Jews in the Apostolic Age. Applied to the dispersion of the Greeks, it carries the definite implication that they also had a mission. Wherever they lived, the majority kept up their traditions. At the same time they showed an open mind toward the intellectual achievements of the West. Their numbers were a guarantee against absorption. Nostalgia for the lost homeland gave them cohesion. Their religious and social life fed on tradition and memories. Further, correspondence with relatives, in other cities of the West or in Turkish-occupied lands, made for solidarity. Their mutual experiences as refugees or émigrés soldered them together into a unity which was a main factor in keeping them from melting into their surroundings. The fact that for centuries such Greek colonies lived as separate bodies, whether in Italy or in the Balkan States, explains the unparalleled homogeneity.

Besides the Greek colony in Venice, already discussed, a number of ports on the eastern shore of Italy had large Greek Orthodox communities. Greeks had migrated there long before the tenth century; the contribution of their broad cultural background to the development of medieval Italy is a factor that is seldom given proper emphasis.[13] From the port of Brindisi, the Ionian Islands could easily be visited by a short trip across the Adriatic, and thus communication with the Greek world could be kept up. Bari, the residence of the Byzantine governor of Apulia in the ninth century, together with Ancona, established refugee churches. Reggio Calabria had numerous Greek colonists and a magnificent basilica in Byzantine style. Its college enjoyed all privileges, and its *protopapa,* or chief priest, exercised jurisdiction over his own religious community. On the west side of the Italian peninsula, the ports of Livorno (Leghorn), Pisa, and Genoa had large Greek populations, whence further migration was possible into Western Europe. Even the island of Corsica, an Ottoman province in the second half of the sixteenth century, had its Greeks, and Malta still keeps up its Orthodox church.

The kingdoms of Naples and Sicily, later known as the Two Sicilies, present a somewhat different situation. According to many, this area has as eloquent remnants of classical Greece as Greece itself—in Paestum, Taormina, Siracusa, Agrigento. Some families have continued from the original Greek colonies of Magna Grecia who first brought the Romans into contact with Greek culture. Others descend from the Byzantine colonies of the sixth century and later, while some came at the time of iconoclasm. During the Turkish wars in the fifteenth century a group of Albanians of Orthodox faith settled near Palermo, and their descendants still keep up ancient traditions in dress and dialect. After the fall of Constantinople, over two hundred thousand more Greeks came to these regions as time passed. Their Greek origin survives in village and family names; in certain mountain areas a Greek dialect is still being spoken, mixed with Italian words. Having come under Spanish authority, and especially through the efforts of Pope Gregory XIII, most of this Greek population became Uniate. The role of the Abbey of Grottaferrata and of the seminary and church of St. Athanasius in Rome have already been mentioned.

Greek names are notably difficult to write as well as to pronounce, and many found on documents and in records in Europe are unidentifiable. A number of artists and craftsmen in Italy received the appellative of Greco, the Greek. In the first half of the sixteenth century a Vettore Greco and a Domenico dalle Greche were active in Venice, the latter working in the studio of Titian. A Giovanni Greco is recorded at Cividale, northern Italy, at that time, and an Antonius Basilakas was helper to Tintoretto and Veronese for years. A Michele Greco was engraver and painter in Rome toward the end of the sixteenth century, and a Paolo Greco was the teacher of Salvatore Rosa in Naples. In the same city a painter, Jenaro Greco, was active in the second half of the seventeenth century. About the same time a chess expert in Italy, Joaquin Greco, brought out a book on his subject. Vasari mentions an engraver of medals whose name was Italianized to Alessandro Cesari but who was generally known as Il Greco. Gaetano Greco, a Greek composer born in Naples in the second half of the seventeenth century, was a pupil of Alessandro Scarlatti and a teacher of Giovanni Pergolesi. How many families in New York even today show Greek descent is evidenced in the Manhattan telephone book, which contains nearly a hundred entries under Greco or Grieco.

Those who came from the West into Greece as administrators of the Latin occupation became impregnated with Greek culture—the family Acciaioli, for instance, whose head was a Duke of Athens. Though the family returned to Italy about eighty years before the fall of Constantinople, it evidently kept up its pride in the Greek language and culture. Donato Acciaioli, born in Florence, translated Aristotle and Plutarch with the cooperation of his Greek tutor Argyropoulos. Another scion, Zenobio, a Dominican in Florence, translated Hebrew and Greek works (lives of the saints) into Latin. For a time he was librarian in the Vatican. The family palace, standing near Florence on the road to Siena, is known as Monte Gufone. A few decades ago it was acquired by Sir George Sitwell, father of the talented literary trio, who restored not only the building but also the surrounding gardens. During World War II its storm-battered walls housed the masterpieces from the Uffizi and Pitti galleries, as well as other irreplaceable art collections.

In a number of Western countries, Orthodox communities existed under considerable restriction. Their churches had to be built in courtyards, off and away from streets where important traffic flowed; towers and domes, if permitted at all, had to be kept so low as to remain inconspicuous; no bells were allowed. Nevertheless, intellectually, a congenial atmosphere existed for the Greeks in many places, through the flourishing spirit of the Renaissance. The Venetian Republic, especially after the loss of Crete, applied a less heavy hand toward her Greek Orthodox subjects. They were permitted to practice their religion, they retained their rights, and status was given their priests. As early as 1582 the Venetian Senate made protective rulings that applied especially to the Dalmatian cities of Cattaro, Sebenico, and Zara, as many

Greek mercenary soldiers with their families resided there, some retired from, and some still active in, the service of the republic.

Both Trieste and Pola on the Istrian Peninsula, which once belonged to Venice, had large Greek colonies, living witnesses to the steadfastness of a suppressed people. At the time of Napoleon, Trieste alone counted over 1,200 Greek Orthodox residents, who sustained seventeen priests, many of them from Mount Athos, and kept up close connections with the Greek patriarch in Constantinople. The city offered a foothold also to Orthodox Serbian refugees. In Pola a colony was founded before 1580, mainly by people from Crete, especially Candia, but also from Cyprus and Apulia. That the widely scattered Greeks still feel close ties to the Orthodox world is shown by the fact, already mentioned, that during the War of Independence in 1821 the icons from the monastery of Gonia in Crete were sent for safety to Trieste and, during World War II, were safeguarded in Pola.

Of the Orthodox that moved toward the West, the earliest came mainly to appeal for help against the Turks. Later came the intellectuals, then the merchants and craftsmen and the little people, many of whom already had connections there through family or friends. Since Russia was converted to Christendom from Byzantium, it was natural that a number of the highest ecclesiastics, nobility, and artistic elite should be drawn to that vast territory, where, among their coreligionists, they contributed greatly to the religious and intellectual life. One of the finest Byzantine painters, known as Theophanes the Greek, is regarded as having set the standard of Russia's religious painting in the late fourteenth century. Within the next hundred years Russia had absorbed various outside influences, regional characteristics became more and more marked, and a national school made its appearance.

On the northern limits of Turkish-occupied Europe, the lands belonging to the Hungarian and Austrian crowns became hosts to many thousands of refugees. In the principality of Transylvania, in eastern Hungary, a bastion of Protestantism since earliest times, unusual tolerance existed. A refugee scholar, Jacobos Palaeologos, was for years the head of the Unitarian College in Kolozsvár (today Cluj in Romania). In the early seventeenth century, the Cretan Stavrinos, also a refugee in Transylvania, wrote an epic poem in Greek on the valiant Moldavian prince who erected splendid churches and monasteries in his principality (see *Pl. 17B* and *C*). More than 150 Hungarian place names either prove to be of Greek derivation or carry the adjective "Greek" as prefix. In a number of instances, Greeks and refugee Serbians worshiped in the same building until they were able to build their own churches.

The success of the Greek refugees can be mainly explained in that they worked in brotherly partnership. Through their wide-flung connections they had the advantage of exchanging correspondence, information, and trade that cut across borders. In Hungary alone, more than twenty-five commercial companies existed who maintained commercial relations with West and East, since they had the confidence equally of Christian and of Moslem authorities. During the entire period that the Danubian plain was occupied by the Turks, Greek merchants traveled from Moslem-controlled areas into the Habsburg domain and farther west. They were known as skillful and reliable businessmen. Though scattered over many parts of the globe, the Greeks were conscious of belonging to a great nation, and cherished the hope of return to their ancestral lands.

As Greek scholarship rose in the West, it diminished in Turkish-occupied territories with the increasing exodus. But as the prosperity of the refugees grew, they did not forget relatives living under Turkish occupation. In the seventeenth century the well-established Greek colonies, notably in Venice, took the initiative, subscribed money, and sent teachers back. Powerful Greek schools were kept up by such contributions in Siatista, Kozány, and Moshopolis, all in Macedonia, and Istanbul, Jassy, Bucharest, Athens, Chios, Smyrna, Thessaloniki, and Kastoria, among many others. Over twenty-five Greek schools of high scholarly standing were supported by the colonists residing in Hungary. Greek books were printed in a number of cities in the Habsburg domain and sent as far as the shores of the Black Sea and even beyond, while Greek presses in Hungary in the seventeenth and eighteenth centuries produced more than a hundred titles. For a time both Vienna and Venice published Greek newspapers.

The stream of Orthodox refugees dwindles when followed into Western Europe, and the tight cohesion of the group loosens. Their progress can be traced only haphazardly, mostly as individual careers to be found in the records of the universities, libraries, in commercial contracts, or even police registers. Generally in the Germanic lands, where Protestantism was strong, the Orthodox émigrés encountered few handicaps.[39] France, after the fall of Constantinople, took Greek refugees into the army as officers as well as common soldiers—probably mainly as technicians. Records show some Greeks in the University of Paris, others in commerce. Around 1470, Louis XI invited Greek weavers to Tours when he founded the silk industry there, as they were very skillful in the craft. Charles VII gave pensions to a number of Greeks, which are documented in the ledgers of the *gendarmerie du roi.* One of the pensioners was George Palaeologos, nephew of the Byzantine emperor who fell in the defense of Constantinople.

A typical career was that of Joannis, or Janus Lascaris (ca. 1445–1535), who after the conquest of the capital was taken as a child to the Peloponnesus and thence to Crete. He later appears at the court of the Medici in Florence. A protégé of the great Bessarion, Lascaris was instrumental in the purchase for the Medici library of more than two hundred Greek manuscripts from the sultan in Istanbul. At the downfall of the Medici, during the invasion of Charles VIII of France, Lascaris followed the French king to Paris, where he lectured in Greek. Returning to Venice as an emissary of the French king, he was called by the incumbent pope, a Medici, to take charge of the Greek college which was planned for Rome, and he founded a Greek printing press in that city. Meanwhile Francis I of France invited a group of Greek scholars to organize, catalogue, and study the contents of the library at Fontainebleau. The catalogue, finished in 1552 by Constantin Palaeokapa, lists 546 Greek manuscripts. The keeper of this library, under Francis I and three subsequent kings, was the Cretan Angelos Vergitzes, known in France as Ange Vergece, an expert copyist who bore the title of Grec du Roi. He later designed a famous letter type. His Cretan-born son, Nicolas, spent his entire life in France and was curator of the library at Fontainebleau.[38]

Instrumental in bringing the "new learning" to England, specifically Oxford, was the English physician and humanist Thomas Linacre (1460–1524), best known as the teacher of Erasmus and personal physician to Henry VIII. Having accompanied the ambassador of Henry VII to Italy in his younger years, he took the degree of doctor of medicine at the University of Padua. He made friends with a number of Greek refugee scholars and is said to have been among the first Englishmen to study Greek in Italy. Among Greeks who were active in England were John Serbopulos, employed as a regular copyist of Greek manuscripts in the abbey at Reading, and Demetrios Cantacuzene, who held the same post in London. The distinguished scholar Andronicos Callistos, born in Thessaloniki, was called to the University of Paris from Italy and thence to London.

The Byzantine libraries of classical works were the largest and most complete in Christendom, and without the meticulous work of the Byzantine copyists probably much of our classical heritage would have been lost. The monastery of St. John the Evangelist on the island of Patmos once owned six hundred manuscripts of the greatest biblical importance. Many found their way to the West during the centuries. Similarly, the various monasteries at Mount Athos served as fountainheads of historical and religious authority. Though the vandalism of the Fourth Crusade and the Turkish conquest destroyed many precious works that had been brought together in Constantinople, innumerable volumes remained. Quantities of these were sold to buyers from the West, principally Italian, when the Turks occupied the city. Refugee families sold their books to contribute to their livelihood. As late as the seventeenth century, Byzantine manuscripts still lay about Istanbul, and the sultan honored the ambassador from Spain with a valuable selection.[13]

In Europe, only a few years before Constantinople fell, Johann Gutenberg had brought out the first printed Bible (1436 or 1437) produced from movable type. And the printed page served the spread of Greek culture in the Renaissance at an accelerated pace. Tedious lettering with a quill pen was no longer the only means of distributing the thoughts of distinguished philosophers in a wider circle. The printed and bound book was easier to handle, and chapters could be scanned in a short time. Ideas which up to then had been concentrated on scarce handwritten pages could provide new stimulus with the new technique, in new areas. The first Greek book was issued in 1476 by the press of Constantin Lascaris—probably the elder brother of Joannis Lascaris just discussed—in Milan, where he acted as tutor in Greek to the daughter of the Sforza duke. Well known among later Greek scholars in the West is Leon Alatris, or Alatres, Latinized Allatius and Italianized Alacci, who was born on the island of Chios in 1586. Noted for his remarkable memory, he was translator and commentator of numerous Greek authors, editor in chief in Rome and Paris. Allatius became librarian of Cardinal Barberini in Rome and later held the same position in the Vatican.

In the first two decades of the sixteenth century, Greek books were printed outside Italy in Erfurt, Wittenberg, Tübingen, Strasbourg, Leipzig, Basel, Vienna, Nürnberg, Augsburg, and Cologne. In 1513 the first Greek printed books appeared in Antwerp and Louvain; in 1517 in Paris; Cambridge, England, followed in 1521; Cracow, Poland, in 1529; and London in 1543.

As for Spain, in 1499 Cardinal Jiménez, Archbishop of Toledo and founder of the university in Alcalá de Henares, invited Demetrios Dukas, a Cretan, a member of the Academy of Aldus Manutius in Venice, to come to Alcalá and establish a printing shop for Greek books. The first imprint of his Spanish shop in 1514 was the tale of Hero and Leander. The same year Jiménez brought out the first polyglot Bible, with Hebrew, Chaldean, Greek, and Latin texts. Another Cretan, known only as Andreas of Crete, was numbered among the first professors at the university. In Salamanca, the university's Plateresque façade, built in the mid-sixteenth century, has a medallion of Ferdinand and Isabella in the center, with an "homage" inscribed on the frame—not in Spanish, but in Greek. That Greeks were settled in Spain in larger groups than is realized today can be seen in the fact that a village called Griegos still exists with a population of about five hundred, in the municipality of Teruel in Catalonia, a region internationally known for its remarkable Byzantine-influenced Romanesque murals.

Data, often stumbled upon, reveals wandering Greeks, educated or skilled in crafts, turning up at an early date and in most unexpected places. Greek artists appear in Spain before El Greco. In 1563 a Pedro el Greco is recorded as painter and poet active in Barcelona; he decorated an organ case in Tarragona. Somewhat later a Nicolas Greco appears in Segovia as painter and *pirotécnico,* having personally installed a fireworks display there with "serpents and other animals of fire." He constructed and painted also a gigantic funerary monument at Segovia for the memorial services of Philip II.[90] From a manuscript copied in Spain at William H. Prescott's expense for *The Conquest of Peru,* it transpires that Pizarro's commander of artillery on that spectacular expedition was a Pedro de Candia, apparently a man of many-sided talents, useful in such an enterprise. "Greek fire" was by no means the loftiest achievement of Byzantium, but sailors and soldiers feared it as an early version of the flame-thrower, and a number of Greek military technicians seemed to have possessed the secret of its manufacture. Pedro was one of fourteen who declared themselves willing to push on for Peru in ships that had been constructed in Panama. On one occasion he went ashore as spokesman, in full dress with polished armor and weapons. Later he supervised the casting of canon in Cuzco, high in the Peruvian Andes, with a number of "Levantines" (as Prescott calls them) who were well acquainted with such manufacture. They produced also firearms, cuirasses, and helmets, in which silver was mingled with copper, of such excellent quality that "they might vie with those from Milan." It would appear that Pedro de Candia was in the New World from 1524 to 1542 when he was killed by another Spanish conquistador in a factional war. In South America, at the end of the sixteenth century, are found in documents artists and artisans with such names as Juan Griego, Jacome Griego, and Juan de Candia, and in Mexico a painter by the name of Marcos Griego is recorded.

A Cardinal of Burgos, Diego Hurtado de Mendoza (1503–1575), was Charles V's Spanish ambassador in Italy for twenty years, residing mainly in Venice. He was very much interested in Greek literature, had a number of scholars scouting in Italy for Greek manuscripts, and spent much money to have manuscripts copied from the Bessarion collection in Venice. In the Ambrosiana Library of Milan is a catalogue, written in longhand, listing the Greek books which were copied for this cardinal. In Rome, also, he employed a number of Greek copyists, who acted as calligraphers as well, some of them from the island of Corfu, others from the Greek mainland. Mendoza even sent a Greek scholar back to Thessaly and to some of the monasteries of Mount Athos, to seek out and buy important Greek works for him. This cardinal also took part in the Council of Trent. He had never been a favorite of Philip II and was finally banished from the court to Granada, where he spent his last years in literary pursuits. After his death, just about the time that El Greco arrived in Spain, his entire collection of books was sent to the Escorial Library—not an unusual manner of increasing royal treasure.

The books in the Escorial Library were catalogued soon after the building was finished. The first list mentions thirty-five Greek manuscripts. It is interesting to note that the Byzantine medieval epic poem *Digenes Akritas* came to light in the Escorial collection.[46] Some forty Greek calligraphers were active in producing copies for the library, according to a list that contains not only the names of each copyist but also the copies that were made by his hand for the Spanish monarch. Few of these men were from the Greek mainland; most were from the scattered island empire of the Hellenistic world. Notable was Jacobos Episkopoulos, a calligrapher who came from Germany and found employment at the Escorial. Other Greeks established themselves as dealers in such manuscripts.

The first chief cataloguer of the Greek collection at the Escorial was Nicolaos Turrianos, with the title from Philip II of Copyist to the King. He was also a miniature painter.[96] The Spaniards, with the standard practice of European countries, simplified his name for their own usage, and from 1587 on he is often mentioned in documents as Nicolas de la Torre. He, however, always signs his Greek name in Greek characters and adds in cursive script *kres,* the Cretan—indeed, in the same manner in which El Greco generally signed his paintings. As we have seen, the pride of Cretans in their origin is variously preserved in signatures: a Byzantine hagiographer who supplied an icon of the Virgin and Child for a church in Cairo dated the work 1630 and signed it Angelos Kres; in Otranto, a large Greek settlement in southern Italy, the master of a busy studio of Cretan painters always signed beside his name the Latin phrase *Grecus Candiotus pinxit.*

Many foreigners must have resided in Toledo, as long as the court of Philip II was there with its diplomats and attendant retinue. The fact that the cardinal prince primate also lived in that city brought in others from distant lands. Among Toledo's industries silk weaving was famous, and it is probable that Greek craftsmen were employed there, as was the case when the French king established his factory in Tours.

If someone lived a quiet, simple life, it may be nearly impossible to find a trace of him beyond eventual vital statistics. Archives, even when complete, are necessarily limited to records of birth, marriage, death, eventual contracts, suits, or criminal records. Among the intellectuals, at least one Greek is recorded as established in Toledo at the time that El Greco first set foot there. This was Antonio Calosynas, also a Cretan, who achieved a certain fame as physician and author. Some of his poems were written in honor of Santa Leocadia upon the return of her remains to Toledo, her birthplace. For the same occasion, El Greco was commissioned to erect triumphal arches, of which more will be said later.

By the last quarter of the sixteenth century, and on into the seventeenth, another evergrowing group can be traced: Greeks and other nationals from the Turkish-occupied Levant and the Balkans came to Spain—as to various other European lands—to plead for funds with which to ransom relatives and friends from Turkish captivity. They presented their appeals to the archbishops of Burgos, Zaragoza, Seville, Granada; but they centered on Toledo because, besides being the seat of highest religious authority, it housed large establishments of the Trinitarian and Mercedarian orders which were formed expressly to help redeem prisoners of the Moslems. Miguel de Cervantes Saavedra, the author of *Don Quixote,* was ransomed from slavery in Algiers through the mediation of two Trinitarian monks (1580). Unfortunately the archives of neither order survive, and thus the full picture of their activities in the redemption of captives will never be known. By lucky chance a record of refugees who presented petitions in Toledo in the years 1602–1608 was found in an extant register of the royal notary.[104] As they were all foreign names, nearly all are distorted. Among others are listed:

Yanoda Bayboda [Voyvoda], prince of Moldavia [today Romania], to ransom his wife and children.

Martheros, archbishop from "Acta Mar," Greater Armenia, for the ransom of various clerics of his diocese. [This is Achthamar, which is discussed here under *Pl. 4A.*]

Dionisio Paleologo, bishop from the Ionian island of Ithaca.

Angelo Castro, bishop of Lepanto [Navpaktos].

Friar Niquiforo [Nicephorus?] of the Order of St. Basil [all Orthodox monks were Basilian] from the convent of Our Lady of Charity, province of Lepanto, asking alms to rebuild and decorate his monastery destroyed by the Turks in taking that land.

Estacio [Anastasius?] Iconomo and Jorge his son, from the city of Arta, province of Lepanto [a city in Epirus].

Jeronimo Cocunari, another bishop.
Estaphano [?] Jamarto, cleric from the Peloponnesus, to ransom his son and kindred.
Friar Sabba of the Order of St. Basil, from the convent of Santa María de la Iberia, Macedonia, to ransom six brother monks and the treasures of his monastery. [This is the monastery Iviron on Mount Athos (see *Pls. 10A* and *24B*), one of the earliest foundations there.]
Jorge Cocunari, governor and native of the island of Spiro [Skyros in the Aegean], endeavoring to liberate his wife and four children.
Constantino, a sea captain, to liberate one child and some sailors.
Jorge de Atenas [Athens], to ransom six captives who are prisoners.
Tomasso Trechello from Nicosia, Cyprus, seeking ransom for his wife and son.
Miguel Zuqui and his son Demetrios, for his wife and children.

Further documents cast a little light on several of these figures. In one, the bishops Paleologo and Castro named above give the power of attorney to Zuqui to collect whatever alms the archbishop may grant to them; the paper is witnessed by Trechello.

As a resident of Toledo and a personage of some reputation, El Greco came in early contact with various Greek refugees, and his name is connected with some of the persons on this list. He and his son Jorge Manuel testify that they know the Athos monk Sabba and that his claims are true (1603). El Greco is named as executor in the last will of Estacio Iconomo who had fallen gravely ill (1605). El Greco's servant-helper, the Italian Francisco Preboste, is witness to the withdrawal of the power of attorney from Cocunari the same year.

Trechello of Cyprus—whose name in Greek is Tsetselos—appears to have been an old friend of Manousos Theotokopoulos, a member of El Greco's household who is generally accepted as the painter's older brother. Ill unto death at the end of the year 1603, the Cypriote handed down minute instructions to Manousos how to deliver the ransom for his dearest ones if and when it should be received. Manousos himself was old and probably in poor health—he died late the following year. At any rate, he could not carry out his friend's last wishes. The licenses authorizing the collection of alms fell past due without being used. Manousos then applied for information about renewing them, using as witnesses Jorge Manuel and F. Preboste. Shortly afterward he presented a new appeal in favor of those distant compatriots. Jorge Manuel and Luis Tristán, a pupil of El Greco, witnessed this application, in which Manousos' signature reveals his debilitated condition.

The above-mentioned enumeration of refugees constitutes a fragmentary record of only six years. Neither before 1602 nor after 1608 is information available, a situation that is noted by the few who had access to the historical archive even before the civil war, as "most singular." El Greco was resident in Toledo for thirty-seven years. At the same rate, the refugees with whom he came in contact might reach nearly a hundred. The name of Dr. Calosynas was already mentioned here, and it is recorded that in 1582 El Greco acted as interpreter before the Inquisition for a compatriot named Michele Rizo Carcandil. Two other Greek refugees, Constantin Phocas and Dr. Demetrios Paramoulis, witnessed his signature of the power of attorney he gave his son a few days before he died in 1614. It cannot even be guessed how many more refugees came and went in Toledo before El Greco arrived and after he died. By chance, documentary proof was found in eastern Andalusia that, as late as the eighteenth century, Greeks from Moslem-occupied countries were still going about collecting ransom money.

The lack of a comprehensive catalogue, still more an index, in most libraries and archives in Spain makes thorough research of many matters nearly impossible, including the role of Greeks in the country. The civil war not only destroyed many municipal and institutional archives but, as aftermath, often produced frustrating furtiveness among the officials, in trying to cover up these losses.

While the life history of today's refugee, if he achieves distinction, most likely will become the subject of newspaper and magazine articles, if not a book, such publicity was nonexistent in previous centuries. Later chroniclers wrote all too often from hearsay and anecdote, and are unreliable.

One reason for the spottiness of published biographical information from the sixteenth to the nineteenth centuries stems from the scarcity of paper. When Europe began the production of rag paper, it was an expensive process. By the seventeenth century the need was so great that the population was encouraged to wear clothing made of linen, so that the discarded rags could be used in the manufacture of paper. War is a major factor in the destruction of assembled archival material. During the Napoleonic campaign, great losses occurred in the archives of both the church and the chapter house of San Giorgio dei Greci in Venice. Toledo also suffered under the Napoleonic invasion, and the recent civil war brought especially savage destruction. When order was restored, the financial situation of the country was at a low ebb. There was a shortage of everything, including paper. But good paper can be produced by reprocessing old material, especially old rag paper, a custom practiced in many countries. Paper collections were undertaken in Spain several times in the last decades. The eager collector, often spurred by a premium offered, found a treasure-trove in the archives of past centuries. Many of these were no longer in their original locations but had been deposited in attics, basements, and in unguarded warehouses, if not in barns. From there to the pulp mills, the way was short and simple.

Individual ignorance and carelessness were responsible for much loss. Franz Schubert left an opera, *Claudine von Villa Bella,* the only extant score of which was an autograph, kept in the cupboard of a friend after the composer's death; Acts Two and Three were used piecemeal by the servants of the old man, to kindle fires.[4] Further, it has been found that old documents and pages of books were sacrificed to strengthen the binding of newer books, by gluing together layer upon layer, over which the end papers were then pasted. In one case, parts of a twelfth century Greek liturgical text, a Georgian manuscript, a tenth century and an eleventh century Greek text, a work in Arabic, and a Hebrew manuscript were all found pasted together.[48]

Still another important reason for the disappearance of archival material has not received consideration. Since the invention of gunpowder, fireworks became increasingly popular. By the seventeenth century, the display of splendid fireworks became a standard part in the celebration of victories, royal marriages or births, and other joyful occasions. Pyrotechnical effects were combined with scenic and dramatic shows. Nürnberg was the center for northern Europe, and in Italy each large city had its local craftsmen. A Bolognese pyrotechnician was brought to Paris by Louis XV, and the success of the Italian's layout at Versailles made fireworks quasi-obligatory at any self-respecting court. Essential to fireworks, whether fixed on a wooden structure or projected as rockets, were a paper cap and a paper case. For these, a reliable and durable paper was needed. The casings had to remain intact while the fireworks went off, and, especially in the case of the rocket, had to last until the powder mixture had been consumed, and only then disintegrate in the air. The high-quality rag paper of the old archives was ideally suited to the needs of the pyrotechnicians. By the eighteenth century, archival and similar material, such as musical manuscripts, had grown to vast proportions. Openly or clandestinely, such paper was pilfered for the fireworks maker. Fascicles referring to foreigners, such as the Greeks in Spain, or written in a foreign tongue, such as the records in San Giorgio dei Greci in Venice, seemed of little interest, and expendable. The old paper provided for the spectator momentary brilliance, but its destruction over the years has plunged into darkness social and biographical data of inestimable value.

No information is extant as to the religious life of the Orthodox or the Uniates in Spain. It should be remembered that, since they came from an area that has practiced Christianity from earliest times and from a faith that was looked on by the Roman Church as schismatic but not heretical, a different kind of suspicion was directed toward them than toward Protestants, Moslems, and Jews. The rites of the Uniates which were encouraged by the Vatican do not differ much from those of the Orthodox. But seemingly not even the Uniate Church was ever established in Spain, though the practice of the ancient Mozarabic Rite was permitted. The intransigence of Spain toward any other faith is manifest when we realize that only in the second half of the nineteenth century, and upon the strongest pressure from the czarist court, was an Orthodox chapel permitted to function in Madrid, even though it was intended only for the service of the Russian Embassy. Recently, when the United States established Air Force bases in Spain, an effort was made to force a ruling by which American military personnel of all faiths would have to have the sacraments of baptism, marriage, and burial administered exclusively by a Roman Catholic priest.

Blown by all winds, washed by all waters, barked at by all dogs, the refugees of the Greek diaspora had developed a strong sense of diplomacy, avoiding committing themselves when it was not absolutely necessary. Cognizant of the ruthlessness of the ecclesiastic authorities in Spain, the refugees doubtless kept to themselves and did everything that a mature philosophy and their experience as travelers dictated not to provoke enmity or even evoke attention. While their names occur in various documents, their activities, their entrances and exits go almost unilluminated. Those who remained in Spain apparently adjusted to their surroundings. Those who settled in countries where the Orthodox Rite was permitted or who went back to the biblical lands of Greece returned to the bosom of their mother church.

·VI·

SIXTEENTH CENTURY ÉMIGRÉ

With the arrival and departure of Greek refugees and others in transit in Toledo, El Greco must have been well informed about conditions in Crete. The ring of Turkish conquest was steadily tightening around the island empire of the Venetian Republic. Venetian overlords drove the local population mercilessly, not only to subdue their rebellious spirit but also to force the maximum assistance in the fortification and defense of the island which also served as a main naval base. Natives could at any time be drafted for the digging of trenches and the construction of fortifications. In 1562 the Cretan men pressed into service in Venetian galleys began a revolt in Rethymnon harbor, to which the population added strength in an insurrection that lasted for nine years. In this period the population fell off alarmingly. Cretans continued to migrate from the island, often even preferring Istanbul to their native land.

Under the prevailing conditions, it is small wonder that El Greco was not eager to return. Nor were his successes in Italy apparently enough to satisfy him. He could not become a leading painter among the many masters whose background and manner of painting were so different from his own. He may have felt even more restless in the atmosphere of Rome—at once pagan and Baroque and so alien to his Christian ideals as he had learned them in Crete.

Besides, the Turks were at the very gates of Italy. The island of Malta, so close to the Italian mainland, was raided as early as 1472, and many inhabitants were carried into captivity. African Arabs ravaged it in 1551, and the great siege came in 1565. Although the Turks were driven off after four months of fighting, Malta was the subject of vicious subsequent attacks. Two faces of a harassed Venice must have been all too clear to Greek refugees—the one, fully sovereign in the council of other great powers and liberal toward the residents of her capital, the other severe in the administration of her colonies.

For many Greeks, Spain represented the most unyielding bulwark against the Moslem power. Cortés, the conqueror of Mexico, accompanied the Emperor Charles V in a Spanish campaign against the Turks. John of Austria, half-brother to Philip II, the hero of Lepanto, is said to have cherished the ambition to liberate the Hellenic lands and rule over them. Spain also sometimes combined forces with the Papal States in trying to stem the overbearing attitude of Venice, and sometimes used Greek scouts to foment disorder among the Venetian mercenary troops, who comprised many of the Orthodox faith.[103]

While he was in Italy, El Greco could consider going back to Candia or staying in the Byzantine area. But once in Spain, in his mid-thirties, with a household established, he must have known that another move was impractical. For a contemplative person such as El Greco was, the landlocked city of Toledo, with its reduced tempo, its many-faceted art, and highly intellectual atmosphere, might well have appeared attractive—especially after Philip II had declined to employ him further in the Escorial. Pressed as Toledo was within the ring of its fortifying walls, the city's artistic opportunities were limited—the chance to set up a new retable, to construct a chapel, or decorate some new structure beyond the city walls. His stature was larger there than in Madrid or at the Escorial, where favored artists congregated in great numbers and spun their intrigues.

Since the first monographs on El Greco were written, two world wars and subsequent upheaval have made multitudes homeless. The early years of the twentieth century saw first the wane of Turkish power on the European continent and, after World War I, the disintegration of three other large empires—Russia, Austria-Hungary, and Germany. In all these, various nationalities were living one beside another, differentiated by language, religion, and custom but held together by a centralized government. When these frames fell apart, forced and voluntary movement of masses began. Bolshevism, fascism, falangism, and nazism persecuted millions. By the time Hitler became the master of the European continent, the migration had grown into the hundreds of thousands. In Turkey, Kemal Ataturk forcibly evacuated a considerable Greek population from his country. In India, when the Hindu and Mohammedan areas were divided, large-scale forced migrations took place. The struggle going on in Asia and Africa shows what emotions are loosed in the movement of peoples of different race and religion. Today, when émigrés, refugees, and exiles are living in nearly all lands, the psychology of the uprooted has become familiar.

Some echo of what an infant hears in the parental house will always remain, whatever change occurs in its domicile; and the nation lives in its language. This writer spoke Spanish in Athens and Thessaloniki with descendants of Sephardic Jews expelled from Spain in the sixteenth century. Many grandchildren of the White Russians who left Russia in 1916 or later still speak their ancestral tongue. Walking by a Chinese laundry or restaurant in the United States, few of us realize that we are passing an alien island. The wife of a French refugee archaeologist who occupied a highly paid position in this country told this writer, "I speak English here only at the market." The Czech historian, a Hitler refugee, on leaving with his wife a party at his American benefactor's, with the hostess still standing in the door, will turn to Czech in mid-sentence before the elevator has closed upon them. When Thomas Mann reached the United States and was asked whether settling in California, so far from his native land, would influence his writing, his answer was, "Where my desk is, there is Germany. . . ." Igor Stravinsky has lived for many years on the Pacific coast, but few would list him as an American composer. During the war a German refugee in La Paz, Bolivia, urged us to buy prewar photographs of her native Dresden, bitterly deploring the bombing of the city. When I countered that London, Coventry, Amsterdam, and Belgrade also had been blasted, her answer was, "*Aber* they are not German cities!"

In the Greek, nationalism is fused with an inspired religious conviction. He is by temperament voluble, adventurous, and intransigent. He will sometimes admire the logic in an aphorism more than cold fact. His loyalty to the family clan is strong. Many a brother in the United States will not marry until he has supplied a dowry for his unmarried sisters in the "old country."

A Greek businessman who has made good in the United States will build a park, donate a hospital, a school, in his native village, as physical proof of his loyalty to his Greekdom. In Tarpon Springs, home port of sponge fishermen of Greek origin in Florida, there is a large Orthodox church and, on the beach, a sign warning against deep water—written only in Greek. After the last war a Greek friend of ours was assigned as ambassador to Holland. When, some years later in Athens, we asked him how he had liked his post, his answer was: "The ambassadorship was all right—but it was so tiresome to have to travel back and forth to Rotterdam. There are no Greeks in The Hague."

El Greco never failed to emphasize his Cretan birth—which to him meant the supreme among the superior. In his youth, Crete stood at a high cultural level. Candia especially had become a refuge and repository of Hellenic culture. Cretan murals and icons carried on the Byzantine tradition and embodied a profound spiritual content. Cretan romancers, poets, and dramatists had begun a new literary epoch. This enlightened spirit went into the forming of his character.

El Greco was thirty-six years old when the first document calls him a resident of Toledo. He must have had a certain nimbus of the much-traveled and experienced person about him, and to his Spanish contemporaries, few of whom by order of Philip II were permitted to travel abroad, he must have presented a fascinating personality. Greek was fashionable as a mark of highest culture throughout Europe. His library contained a splendid choice of books, among them the great authors of the Golden Age of Greece in the original. He must have been sought out by ecclesiastics and intellectuals of the city, many of whose portraits he painted. Francisco Pacheco, Spanish painter and arbiter of Spanish iconography for the Counter Reformation, who describes a visit with El Greco in 1611, reveals him to have placed philosophy over art, and records that he had written on art and philosophy. But the manuscript, which was most probably in Greek, was soon lost, unintelligible to those who handled his property.

No record survives of his contribution to the intellectual life of Toledo during the thirty-seven years of his residence there. Toledo had a university, though it was on a smaller scale than those of Alcalá and Salamanca. Theology, law, medicine, the arts, and Greek were taught—all subject to censorship of the church. Toledo also had several "literary academies." Here one should not think of nineteenth century institutions, with many rows of chairs set in a bleak assembly hall. The academies of Toledo met in the rooms of a vicar of the cathedral, the apartment of a count, a country mansion—known in Toledan vernacular as *el cigarral* for the crickets that sang in its garden.

The great Spanish poet and playwright Lope Félix de Vega Carpio, called Lope de Vega (1562–1635), lived in Toledo for some time during El Greco's residence there, as did Miguel de Cervantes Saavedra (1547–1616). There is no mention of El Greco in the writings of those two giants of Spanish literature or in the reports about them, although they are known to have had mutual friends. Nor have any of El Greco's portraits been identified as representing them. Cervantes, guest at a rustic Toledan inn at the edge of the city, was perhaps the most traveled of El Greco's contemporaries in Toledo, participant of the battle of Lepanto which cost him his left arm, fighter against the African pirates, and enslaved in Algiers for five years. But he wrote in the vernacular, and his scene was genuinely Spanish. El Greco, who had brought with himself the standards of an elevated classical world, may have found little in common with this realist of Shakespearean caliber and earthiness. Similarly Lope de Vega, although he boasted a command of the classical poetic forms, wrote his famous comedies in a manner to satisfy popular taste. While preparing for ordination as a priest (which took place in due time), Lope de Vega lived with a graceful comedienne in *concubinato y adulterio consentido.* It has been said that El Greco was theological-minded and ascetic; that the Toledan society was refined, of aristocratic temperament, and devout; and that nowhere else could El Greco have been understood, in a Europe which was "Protestant and paganized." However, it is difficult to reconcile such assertions with the fact that El Greco also lived in concubinage, acknowledging the son of this relationship only a week before he died.

Although El Greco was the only Greek whose name is lastingly connected with the history of art in Spain, the list is long of foreign artists and architects, especially Flemish and Italian, who lent their talents to Spain before she achieved a fully articulate national school. More Italian artists than Spaniards took part in the construction and decoration of the Escorial. Salvador de Madariaga, although an émigré for a quarter of a century, still lives in the climate of *el milagro español,* and writes that "Spain is the only part of the world in which the art of painting has been continuously cultivated since the prehistoric cave-dwelling days. . . . Painting as the soul's endeavor to capture and retain movement is a characteristically Spanish art." [84]

The lines that constitute the imaginary portrait of El Greco are blurred by overemphasis of his Spanish characteristics. Some Spanish writers have put up so much national bunting around him as almost to obscure his figure. Up to the threshold of our present century, El Greco was mentioned—when his name came up at all—as a foreigner, a Greek. In a catalogue of the Prado, dated as late as 1910, he is classified as a painter of the "Italian School." [107] Now, since his cult has begun, he is being presented as a Spanish painter, and his Cretan birth and formidable Byzantine heritage are hurried over.

A painter's life may be an open book, like Tintoretto's, who was born, was active, and died in Venice. The long distance El Greco traveled before he became known as a painter in Spain, and the lack of revealing personal data even in Toledo, leave much of his life and personality enigmatic.

Nothing is known about the woman who bore El Greco a son in 1578 except her name. El Greco gives it when, in 1614, the week before he died, he assigns the power of attorney to Jorge Manuel as his son and that of Jerónima de las Cuevas. No document has come to light to prove that he married her, nor has a registration of the birth or the baptism of the child been found, although Jorge Manuel's own two marriages are registered. Titian, on the other hand, married his consort, when she fell very ill, and legalized his grown children. It is probable that Jorge Manuel's mother was no longer in the household at the time of the painter's death, since she is mentioned only *ad passim,* while provision is made for a servant, María Gómez, who was with the family for twenty years.

Jorge Manuel was, like his father, painter, sculptor, and architect, and he worked with his father most probably from early youth. But he lacked the talent of the older man and the cosmopolitan and eclectic background. From 1597, at the age of nineteen—just about the age that his father is believed to have been when he arrived in Venice—Jorge Manuel assumed considerable authority in the business of the atelier.[108] His name occurs in documents chiefly as architect and sculptor, the designer of a number of retables. He died in 1631.

Jorge Manuel is a mellifluent name in Spanish; in Greek it carries considerable significance. St. George is one of the principal saints of Greek Orthodoxy, patron of the Greek nation, and one of the fourteen Holy Helpers. In the Greek royal family there is always at least one George. In Byzantine and later Russian art, the figure of St. George on a white charger, fighting the dragon, is one of the most popular subjects, whether on the walls of a medieval church or on an icon. The Greek church in Venice is dedicated to him. Jorge Manuel may also have been named for his uncle. Emmanuel is another favorite Greek name. Manos is the diminutive especially favored in Crete—and Manousos, a superdiminutive. This was the name of El Greco's older brother who came to Toledo and lived with him, possibly for more than a decade.

In recent research in the Greek archives in Venice, the name Manousos Theotokopoulos appears in two petitions to the Venetian Senate and in the replies of that august body. In the year 1572, the year after the battle of Lepanto, four Cretans, Spanopoulo of Sfakion, and Bassurati, Casavello, and Manusso (as he is spelled there) Theotokopoulos of Candia, offer their services as privateers to the Republic of Venice to harass the Turks, requesting the grant of galleys armed with artillery and sundry other weapons, for which they will pay, and submitting a rate at which they will divide with the republic the prisoners taken for ransom. They advance a bond in guarantee of the deal. In the subsequent consultation, Manusso and his companions are recommended as valorous and experienced in this profession, from whom "useful and fruitful service" can be expected. Thereupon the authorities of the Venetian arsenal are ordered to deliver four galleys well equipped, and the price of the prisoners is set at fifteen to twenty ducats apiece. The men are warned to keep outside the Venetian Bay and not to molest any Christian property unless especially instructed to do so. In reply, the privateers beg to be relieved of the responsibility of repairing their own ships (for, in efficiency, the great Venetian arsenal was above all competition), and in compensation they offer to deliver not a quarter but a half of their prisoners to the Signoria, to which the authorities agree.[66]

This might be the same Manousos Theotokopoulos who is named in the records of the Greek community in Venice in 1588 as a candidate for the Council of Forty which presided over the Greek colony there. He failed of election. Three years later the records show he again submitted his name and again failed.

A third instance in which the name appears is in the Cretan archives in Venice. This concerns a Manousos Theotokopoulos who was tax collector for the republic in the city of Candia from 1566 to 1583. It was not uncommon that such a fiscal agent, who obliged himself to pay a certain yearly sum to the authorities for the tax monopoly over a given territory, failed to meet his obligations. Manousos handled around sixty thousand ducats in the seventeen years and ended with a deficit of some six thousand. The sale of his property brought only half the amount, and he went to prison in default of the rest. Within an old fortification wall, today in the heart of Heraklion (Candia), a vaulted, windowless chamber—a section of the casemate—can be seen, which served the Venetian administration as prison for debtors and similar offenders. According to the documents, Manousos soon fell ill and was granted house arrest. After four years of such custody, in 1588 he petitioned the republic for twenty years of grace in which to raise the lacking sum, and seven months later he was accorded twelve years under condition of "worthy guarantees." [66]

Jorge Manuel indicates in a document that the Toledan Manousos, brother of El Greco, was born in 1529 or 1530. This would make him in his early forties when he proposed to undertake the strenuous and daring role of privateer—if that be our Manousos. If it be the defaulting tax collector, he would have been about sixty years old when he was released from Venetian custody in Candia. Considering the highly unsettled situation on his native island, there would have been little chance for him to raise the money there. It would have been attractive to the aging man to join his younger brother who was established in Spain. Then if his efforts to collect the money were unsuccessful, he would be entirely outside the jurisdiction of the Venetian Republic and still could enjoy his last years in a family circle among other Greek émigrés.

As previously mentioned, the name of Manousos occurrs also in the archives of Toledo in connection with the collection of alms to ransom the family of a refugee from Cyprus. He transfers the licenses late in October of 1604, because he is old and infirm. Two months later, in the register of the church of Santo Tomé is an entry that "Manuel griego" died, having received the sacrament.

Francisco Preboste, an Italian painter, trusted assistant and household servant, is recorded as living also in El Greco's home, together with Manousos and Jorge Manuel. In some contracts, Preboste was authorized to finish a project in case of the master's death. The famous art embroiderer Pedro de Mesa received a shipment of pictures on canvas and other objects from a "Dominico Griego" in May of 1597, sent by Preboste, for sale at the Seville art market. Seemingly an accounting was delayed, because somewhat later a Juan Agustín Ansaldo, native of Genoa who was living in Seville at the time, received a power of attorney signed by El Greco and Preboste, to take over those pictures which had not yet been sold and get the cash for the objects already disposed of. The transaction is not only revealing of Preboste's role in the administration of El Greco's affairs but also of the routine of the atelier. Like typical émigrés, the Cretan and the Italian did not seek out a Spaniard but another foreigner as a person of confidence. In 1604 Preboste gives his age as fifty. His name appears in a number of documents between 1576 and 1607. Luis Tristán, a Spanish pupil of El Greco's, seems to have been active in the atelier from 1603, at least until 1607.

One wonders what languages were spoken in the household of El Greco. Preboste commanded Italian best, and Jorge Manuel, born in Toledo, most probably spoke only Spanish fluently. The Cretan master preferred his native tongue. It has been said that he fell into Greek when anyone present spoke it and that he cursed in Greek; he probably counted and prayed in Greek. In one's twenties, as El Greco was when he lived in Venice, one does not easily change the habits formed in childhood, especially those involving his inner life. The Spaniards who spoke Greek with El Greco sought occasion to practice the language, and their conversations were probably of academic interest, high-flown and often remote in subject. From the behavior of present-day émigrés and refugees, analyzing and weighing their adopted land, we can surmise what El Greco discussed with his compatriots in their vernacular, practically a secret tongue in Toledo, when they sat in his house with the shutters closed for the night—what they praised, what they disparaged, how they devised plans for various eventualities and for mutual help. And when the actual matters had been discussed, how reminiscences of the homeland revived their spirit! The word "nostalgia" comes from the Greek *nóstos,* the return journey home, and *algos,* pain.

El Greco had several altercations about the payments due for his paintings. This alone was not unusual. Payments were very often delayed and reduced from what the artist claimed or even had definitely contracted for. Such giants as Michelangelo and Titian were notably involved in collecting their due. The latter wrote a number of letters to Charles V and Philip II to urge them to send him the price of paintings already in their hands. Artists in all periods were concerned to have a steady income instead of the fluctuating sums that occasionally fell to them for their work. Tintoretto requested from the Venetian Senate that an annuity of about a hundred ducats—part of the returns from a brokership in the Fondaco de' Tedeschi—be assigned to him as payment for his vast canvas of the Battle of Lepanto.[70] It is illuminating of El Greco's character that he—as a foreigner—had the moral conviction and the courage to take his claims to the law court and fight for his rights, in one instance appealing to the king, in another threatening to take the matter as high as the Vatican.

In view of the experiences of various foreign and even Spanish artists before the Inquisition, El Greco's first lawsuit is revealing of his intransigence, on the occasion when he came the closest to a brush with the Holy Office. In 1579 he delivered his painting of the Disrobing of Christ for the Cathedral of Toledo (see *Pl. 58B.*) As was the custom, experts were appointed by both parties to set a value on the painting. They, as well as an arbiter later called in to settle the dispute, agreed on a price the cathedral authorities felt was excessive. At this point the church officials brought in theological objections to the composition: other heads had been placed higher than that of Christ in the arrangement; the three Marys were put in the left foreground close to the figure of Christ, when in the Scripture "they stood afar off." El Greco was summoned to the mayor of Toledo ostensibly to argue the price of the painting, but the case soon turned to the uncommon grouping in the biblical scene. This was the first time that he had stood before authorities in a foreign country who were keeping a wary eye on new-come aliens, and he showed amazing acumen. He said that he was unfamiliar with the Castilian tongue and asked for an interpreter. (He had lived two or three years in the country.) He requested a transcript of the proceedings. When he was asked why he had come to Toledo, he said he was not obliged to answer the query. Although he was instructed to change some details of the composition, the fact remains that it was finally accepted as originally painted. Further, the composition was seemingly so well liked that around seventeen versions of the subject were executed, some the work of his atelier.

In the case of the Burial of Count Orgaz (see *Pl. 68A*), the two experts who examined the finished painting put a higher evaluation on it than the price originally agreed to. The church officials contested the change, and the intractable painter appealed from authority to authority, threatening to turn to the pope himself. When the quarrel began to take on exaggerated proportions, El Greco was persuaded to accept the original terms if paid within a short time (1588).

Another suit developed from the painting of St. Martin and the Beggar in which an expert was brought in from Madrid to assess the value of the work. And El Greco finally received the amount he had originally asked.

At the turn of the century, El Greco contracted to execute an entire retable, even to the gilding of the woodwork, for the chapel of the Hospital de la Caridad at Illescas. The town of Illescas had considerable importance at that time. Halfway between Toledo and Madrid, it served as an overnight station for travelers. As seldom as the king went in those years to the old Castilian capital, nevertheless a massive and sumptuous *casa real* was maintained for him at Illescas—which has become a sorry sight today. In litigation over his payment, El Greco again opposed powerful antagonists, and again, when outside authorities were called in, they vindicated him.

While El Greco's unusual and in some ways rebellious character is illuminated in the foregoing cases, the most significant was his behavior in a matter also identified with the Illescas retable, that resulted in a unique victory for the painter. At the time of Philip II, it was the custom in Castile to exact a tax of 10 per cent on every item which was sold in any business—a forerunner of our modern sales tax—and this was applicable to every product, whether a piece of art, a strip of velvet, a chair, or the eggs and salad in the market place. Each time an article changed hands, the 10 per cent was again collected. This was so much resented that the communities arranged with the finance authorities to pay a lump sum annually, which in 1581 brought in, for Castile alone, a quarter of a million gold ducats. Nevertheless Spain was already bankrupt. It should be recalled that the nobility and the clergy were tax free in those days. The privilege of these groups was one cause of the many upheavals in the history of feudal Europe, which lived on an authoritarian basis. In certain lands, up to the revolutions of 1848, the nobleman and the priest did not even pay the few pennies required for a ferryboat passage or for the toll at a bridge. Thus the entire burden of taxpaying fell on the "lower classes."

When El Greco was called in 1600 to work at Illescas, the local tax collector came to him also for his due. The Cretan protested, and refused to pay. He declared that he did not wish to sell his paintings but that as long as the tax suit remained undecided he would pawn them to the particular party, keeping his rights of ownership. For, the sales tax being levied only on what was sold, if the paintings were merely loaned no tax would be due.[86] He carried the suit up to the Consejo de Hacienda in Madrid which decided in his favor. The actual documents of this litigation have not been found, but his successful arguments and the decision in his favor before the tribunal are repeatedly cited in the claims of artists after him. Aside from the monetary loss which such a tax involved, the artist felt it degrading to be classed with the merchant and the peasant.

Besides various suits concerning his paintings, El Greco appeared before the tribunal of the Inquisition in Toledo (1582) as an interpreter for a Michele Rizo Carcandil, a tailor from Athens, who was accused of following Moslem customs. It was at this hearing when, according to rule, the interpreter or the witness had to give his personal data, that he made the deposition that he was a native of the city of Candia. Lately, on the basis of a publication by a Greek writer, a small village near the Cretan capital has been proposed as El Greco's birthplace. However, since more than once the painter declared himself "*natural de la ciudad de Candia,*" there is no reason why his statement should not be accepted. Also in connection with an appearance in court on a later occasion, the year of his birth was established as 1541.

The name Domenikos Theotokopoulos is preserved on El Greco's canvases, where always, up to the last instance, he signed in Greek characters. In the documents concerning him, the name is simplified and Hispanized. Although Manuel Cossío has done more to give El Greco his due than any other single person, he also fell into the standard practice. In his pioneering monograph, he brings the signature in Greek, in which even those not familiar with the Greek alphabet can see that both names end in *os,* and translates them as Domingo Teotocópulo. Cossío says that in his book he will call the painter Dominico Theotocopuli, as El Greco signed when he used Latin characters. But Latin characters were employed by the Cretan only when signing contracts and other business papers—ephemeral occasions for him, compared to his artistic works. Cossío lists a number of misspellings and distortions to demonstrate the trouble the amanuenses had with the strange Greek name. As he suggests, the simplified spelling was adopted to help the scribes who, able to write only in Spanish, could better grasp an Italianate name, such as Cellini, Bellini, Robusti. Foreign names are very often changed when they present the slightest contrariness to the character of the tongue; in the English-speaking world, the name of the former rulers of the Holy Roman Empire is generally spelled Hapsburg, although it is correctly Habsburg, derived from the original seat of the family, Habichtsburg. So careless were the church authorities that in the church register of Toledo, the brothers Manousos and Domenikos Theotokopoulos go down merely as Manuel and Dominico griego.

El Greco's last signature appears on the power of attorney given to his son a week before he died. The document is very often called a "testament," which has given rise to misunderstanding. In it, Jorge Manuel, as his universal heir, is given power to make and execute his father's last will. The introduction proceeds in formal phrasing: ". . . stretched upon my bed, ill with the infirmity which it has pleased the Lord our God to give me, being of sound mind and normal understanding, holding, believing, and confessing as I do, I believe and confess all that which believes and confesses the Holy Mother Church of Rome and in the Mystery of the Most Holy Trinity, in which faith and belief I declare to live and to die as a good, faithful, and Catholic Christian . . ."—obviously a standard formula set down mechanically by a scribe. The stricken man himself had so little strength that his signature is weak and incomplete, a trailing scrawl. The document is witnessed, not by any of his distinguished Spanish friends, but by two Greek émigrés (named in the chapter on the Greek Diaspora). Seven days later the following laconic entry appears in the church register: "Dominico griego died without making a will after receiving the sacraments."

Upon these two documents—the opening phrases of the power of attorney and the words of the church register—the often-repeated claim is based that El Greco was a believing, practicing Roman Catholic. Yet, in view of what has already been said of the psychology of the Greeks of the diaspora, the conventional phraseology written by alien hands offers no real proof. Having lived several decades in the strictly controlled religious atmosphere of Toledo, El Greco would have complied at least externally with general custom. His living depended largely upon his connections with the ecclesiastics, with a number of whom he stood in friendship. Anyone who has seen the last sacrament administered to a semiconscious person or at a fatal accident can judge the validity of the standard entry in the church register, written by someone who did not even trouble to spell out the dying man's name. If the Cretan wanted a Christian burial at all, he had no alternative but to conform to the only existing church in Spain. And there would have been no reason for him to refuse the sacrament, a consolation to any Christian.

If El Greco had had the physical and mental agility and the will to formulate a testament in his own words, the text would have revealed a mind nourished on Aristotle and the Greek classical tradition. His contemporaries repeatedly praise his high thinking and outstanding intellect. He must have known, being beyond the seventies, that death could not be far off. In his last years he had empowered his son to assume more and more responsibility. In 1612 Jorge Manuel had acquired a vault in the monastery church of Santo Domingo el Antiguo as a burial place for his father and himself. Yet El Greco never made a will. Perhaps, philosophically, he did not want to influence events after he was gone, but preferred to let the customs of the country take their course.

He died a stranger, an émigré in Toledo. For those who stood about El Greco's deathbed, he must have been a lonely figure.

In early April the ground is still cold around Toledo, and from the autumn plowing only small tufts of green show on the earth. Few spring flowers have opened their heads reluctantly and the storks are just beginning to return from the warmer climate of Africa. The water of the Tagus is greenish, rushing and chill. The alleys of the city get little sunshine to warm them.

Much of the dank air of winter still lingers there in morning and evening, and the stone houses are cold and cheerless. On April 7, 1614, El Greco died and was buried in the vault that had been acquired two years earlier.

It was customary at that time to eulogize departed personalities. But in vain did the poet, Luis de Góngora, proclaim "his name which loud-voiced heralds might declare in tourney-field of Fame. . . ." In vain did Fray Hortensio de Paravicino assert that the silent grave could not deprive the world of his fame. . . . By the time these elegies for the dead painter were published, El Greco's tomb was already obliterated. Less than four years had elapsed after his father's death, when the monastery asked Jorge Manuel to remove the bones from the vault which had been purchased "for always and forever." [105] Some suggest that the church planned a reconstruction of the building, in a city which was bursting with churches. That year (1618) Jorge Manuel was working as architect on the church of San Torcuato, and in lieu of payment he was permitted to construct a tomb for himself and family, where he then transferred his father's remains. When San Torcuato was later demolished, there was no marking left to immortalize the name Theotokopoulos. The son of Jorge Manuel took orders with the Augustinians in 1622 as Fray Gabriel de los Morales, using his mother's name, and trace of other kin is lost. Recent excavations in the places where El Greco's remains or where eventually a grave marker might have lain have turned up only scattered, unidentifiable bones.

·VII·
A LIBRARY

With the power of attorney given to his son Jorge Manuel, an inventory of El Greco's estate was made four days after his death. Published early in the present century, the diligent investigations in the archives of Toledo by Francisco de Borja de San Román provide many illuminating clues to the life of the painter. The furnishings of his rooms appear sparse and plain and do not confirm any suggestion of the "lavish living" implied in earlier reports. At the time of his death El Greco owned four shirts and one spare suit—a contrast to Michelangelo's legacy, which enumerated twenty-six shirts and elegant clothing. While Michelangelo left also eight thousand gold ducats in a walnut strongbox, El Greco had only debts when he died. Illness may have reduced his income and his estate. When Pacheco visited him in 1611, it was Jorge Manuel who showed the distinguished guest around the house, the studio, and the stockroom, and it has been suggested that even then El Greco was not able to do much work. It is also probable that the Cretan gave financial help to refugees coming through Toledo, taxing his resources. Some 144 paintings are mentioned in various stages of completion. No exact measurements are given. Such designations as "very small," "small," "large," make difficult the positive identification of canvases that were later so widely dispersed.

Usually a painter is judged from the quality of his work and his artistic activity as far as records are extant. In El Greco's case, the contents of his library are very significant in the forming of an imaginary portrait. Only forty-four individual titles can be constructed from the hastily written list, said to be in the handwriting of Jorge Manuel. Of these, twenty-seven are Greek works and seventeen Italian. Jorge Manuel only approximated the titles of the Greek books and recorded even the Italian ones without care, although they could have been copied from the title pages. His spelling is colloquial Spanish. After the list of individual titles, he enters: "other fifty Italian books," "other seventeen books of Romance," "nineteen books on architecture," totaling 130 works, of which eighty-six are unidentified. A second inventory was made in 1621, when Jorge Manuel married for the second time. Seven years had passed since the death of El Greco, and much had happened to the original collection. Here the son lists only thirty works by title, many of them on architecture (which was his specialty). Then he adds the laconic, "twenty books in Greek and Italian." The total here is only fifty, considerably less than half of those listed in the first inventory. It is highly probable that Jorge Manuel spoke only Spanish and that most books in other languages were expendable for him.

Nowhere in the history of art can one find an artist with a library even approximating El Greco's in linguistic and thematic variety. Titian collected not only gold but honors, and throughout his long life he remained a prince among the painters of his epoch, a status doubtless fully satisfying to him. Local wits and resident writers, such as Aretino, were his constant company, and many distinguished visitors brought a lively exchange of thought and information to his house. But Titian himself seems to have been rather a listener, amused and entertained by all the mental fireworks which went on around him. Peter Paul Rubens (1577–1640) was an excellent Latin scholar at the age of ten, and his paintings show his familiarity with mythology and the Bible. In the midst of artistic activities he became engaged in diplomacy also, and acted as go-between for the Netherlands and Spain; he negotiated agreements between Spain and England, and handled diplomatic tasks involving the houses of Austria, Poland, and France. His writings show a person of rare tact and skill—rather a man of action than of philosophy.

Book printing was a new art in El Greco's time. Many works, as they began to achieve a wider distribution, were put on the Index of prohibited books, either that issued by the pope or imposed by the Spanish ecclesiastical authorities. Most of the Greek books in El Greco's possession were probably printed in northern Italy, especially Venice, and much of his library must have been acquired there where censorship was lenient.

The bibliophiles and connoisseurs of Toledo must have browsed with delight among El Greco's books. The range of his interests gives proof of the inquisitiveness and the broad horizons of his typically Greek mind. Many of the Spanish and Italian works might have been for his professional use. Volumes on architecture, geometry, and perspective are enumerated in the second inventory, together with books on history, arithmetic, geography, descriptions of Roman antiquities and cities, and religious history. No mention is made of books of popular or light character.

Not one Spanish work is specifically named, nor is a Spanish group listed in the first inventory. It has been suggested that some Spanish works may have been among the "seventeen books of Romance." The efforts of the Spanish writers of El Greco's day to make malleable their own language must have had little appeal to one who was the product of the Hellenic classic tradition. The Greeks had become masters of rhetoric when the other European nations were not even formed. The perceptive twist of a phrase, the crisp succinctness of an aphorism was an old art when most of Europe was still illiterate. Even Latin was for many Greeks a language of barbarians. Nor does Jorge Manuel mention specifically any books in Latin in the first inventory. The few works by noted Latin authors named in the second inventory could all be had in Italian translations by El Greco's time.

El Greco could well have learned Italian when still in Candia. The general administration of the island was strongly Italianized, and it may be supposed that, particularly in the cities, many Cretans were bilingual. Besides the Greek books which make up the backbone of his library, El Greco apparently also bought in Venice the works of contemporary writers on romantic themes, as well as early Italian poets such as Petrarch.

Francesco Petrarca (1304–1374) stands among the first true Renaissance figures. He collected coins, manuscripts, and delved into Greek and Latin classical poets, addressing epistles to Seneca and Cicero as if they were his contemporaries. Though his knowledge of classical Greek was probably negligible, he was a friend of a Greek scholar known as Leontius Pilatus to whom he was introduced by Boccaccio. His long epic poem *Africa* was written in Latin, but the more famous sonnets and other lyrics were in the Italian vernacular of the day. Though some of the works of Petrarch, a cleric, came on the Index, this did not restrain the Republic of Venice from accepting his library as a bequest.

The work by Lodovico Ariosto (1474–1533) mentioned in the inventory was most probably *Orlando Furioso,* the complete edition of which appeared in print at Ferrara in 1532. Orlando, better known to us as Roland, was one of Charlemagne's knights who executed a valiant rear-guard stand against Basque border tribesmen in 778. The incident was developed into a heroic legend by the French *trouvères;* the Basques became Saracens, and the adventures of the protagonists were colored with many details. The story always fascinated the Italians—Dante meets Orlando in his Paradise, Ariosto's epic made him a living figure in Italian literature, and to this day the exploits of Orlando are the theme of the great Sicilian puppet folk plays. They occupied also the fantasy of the Cretans and have a place in their folklore. Cervantes' *Don Quixote* was the satirical commentary of a veteran of actual warfare on the "cops and robbers" games to which such ancient tales had degenerated.

The poet Bernardo Tasso (1493–1569), father of the more famous Torquato Tasso, was born in Venice. His long and complicated romantic poem entitled *Amadigi* is listed as "Camadji" by Jorge Manuel. Printed in Venice in 1560, this book was a current favorite of the literati when the young Cretan arrived in the lagoon city.

An Italian work of much later date, noted in the inventory as "Relación unibersal de botero," is the *Relazioni universali,* by Giovanni Botero, which was published in five parts between 1591 and 1593. By that time El Greco was already well established in Spain, and that he should select such a work is still greater proof of his always wakeful intellect. Botero was Jesuit-educated, became a member of the order, and then left it. With his encyclopedic mind, he was the first European to assemble statistics by inquiry and observation, in market places, at the city gates, and other appropriate points. He developed the theory that a nation's wealth lies, not in its silver and gold, but in its agriculture and industrial production. His work is a treatise of universal political geography—what today would be called geopolitics—remarkably accurate for the time. It contains a description of all countries of the known world and of all known political systems, as well as information concerning all religious beliefs, especially the Christian denominations, even including remarks on the diffusion of Christianity in the New World. In the last section of the work, Botero brings his statements up to date and adds a discussion of the importance of climate in the development of various civilizations, an idea which at that time was just short of revolutionary.

Other contemporary Italian works in the library include a book by one "Ju° franc . . . co milanese"; also, "Camilo agripa"—that is, Camillo Agrippa Milanese's *Trattado di scientia d'arme con un dialogo di Filosofia,* Rome, 1553. This is illustrated with a series of nudes in fighting pose using various weapons. The plates were engraved by Marcantonio Raimondi, probably after designs by Michelangelo, who was a friend of the author. It has been pointed out that Raimondi's engravings, among others, influenced certain compositions by El Greco. Indeed, it was general custom for painters to study woodcuts and engravings when contemplating a new composition—especially in the absence of intensive action studies, such as are practiced today.

While the Italian books in themselves point to an unusual intellect, El Greco is mirrored in truest proportions by his choice of Greek books, corroborating Pacheco's statement that he put philosophy above art. Certain of the twenty-seven works will be discussed in detail because they illuminate something of El Greco's personality. It is easily possible that Jorge Manuel's inventory does not cover his father's entire Greek library. Printed and illustrated works were collector's items in those years, and especial value was placed on early printed Greek volumes. El Greco may have presented some valuable tome to one or another of his Toledo friends, as he also seems to have received some. When he was ill and the income of his house was low, certain rarities may have been sold for cash.

The question may arise as to how it was possible that this painter who, according to some writers on art, came to Venice as a very young and inexperienced boy had such command of the Greek tongue that Greek classical authors made up the core of his library. Even if we admit, for the sake of theory, that El Greco arrived in Venice about 1560—a matter that will be taken up later in more detail—he was then nineteen or twenty years old, and no "empty slate." In the Byzantine world, as we have seen, higher education was not the privilege of the feudal class or a monopoly of the church. The Orthodox youth of any poor family, if talented and industrious, could attain a thorough education, in the democratic tradition of ancient Greece. Manuscripts were rare and highly venerated. But with broader access to printed books possible just around El Greco's time, it was no longer necessary to learn everything by repetition and rote. It is clear that El Greco could read both ancient and modern Greek and write Greek fluently.

It has been suggested that after Rome, he returned to Venice and that he visited a number of Italian towns; some writers would have him go back to Crete, and even spend some time at Mount Athos. These are all possibilities. But the years up to his arrival in Spain are, with the exception of the Clovio letter dated 1570, entirely undocumented, and inferences as to his activities during that time are based on pure speculation. However, his twenty-seven books in Greek are fact. The unique choice of the works reveals the positive side of him.

The authors are discussed here generally in chronological order, and titles appear also as Jorge Manuel wrote them in the inventory. The list should begin with the earliest poet of Greece, that legendary Homer whose name is associated with the two great epics the Iliad and the Odyssey. In the latter, Crete is described in some detail. Homer tells that the men from Knossos of the Great Walls, Phaestus, and Rhytion (Rethymnon) lived in fine cities and were valiant spearmen; that for nine years King Minos ruled in Knossos and enjoyed the friendship of almighty Zeus. . . . The king's daughter Ariadne, mistress of the Labyrinth, for nearly three thousand years has stimulated the fancy of poets and writers of romance and librettos. El Greco may even have known some of the sites described in Homer, for landmarks still stood in the mid-sixteenth century which the occupations of the Turks and of other enemies have since rendered unrecognizable. The first printed edition of Homer was brought out in Florence by the Greek printer Demetrius Chalcondylas in 1488. Soon the Aldine Press in Venice issued other printings—in 1504, 1517, and later. When the young Cretan came to the lagoon city, he had quite a choice of editions.

Similarly from the sunrise of Greek literature come the fables of Aesop, which might be called the forerunners of all parables and apologues up to George Orwell in our present day. Aesop, who is said to have been a slave, lived about the sixth century before Christ on the island of Samos in the Aegean. It is becoming more and more evident that his tales were not written down in classical times but recited from generation to generation, thus keeping their living rhythm, their warmth and directness of experience. The significance and broad practice of this "oral tradition" which preserved and kept vital so much of ancient legend and tales, parallel to written literature, is only now being realized. Especially in the many lands where schooling is sporadic, this is the chief medium of folk expression, fortunately in some places still available for recording. So popular was Aesop through the ages that three hundred years later, Lysippus, sculptor to Alexander the Great, made a statue of him for the Athenians. In the first century before Christ, Plutarch had him appear as a guest in his *Symposium of the Seven Sages*. The collection of Aesop's tales was translated into Syrian, as well as into Arabic, and it seems that from one of those Near Eastern tongues they were translated into Greek about the time of the Renaissance. Before any Greek printed version appeared, a selection of some hundred fables was published in Latin in Rome in 1476.

The only one of the great Greek writers of tragedy listed in the inventory of El Greco's library is Euripides (ca. 484–407 B.C.), who greatly influenced subsequent Greek authors. He was noted for his unorthodoxy of thought and his elaborate but lucid style. Works of Euripides were first printed in Florence in 1469 by the Greek Joannis Lascaris already referred to in the chapter on the Greek Diaspora. Aldus Manutius in Venice published them in 1503. By the mid-sixteenth century the most popular plays were widely distributed. El Greco's preference is notable, for Euripides is the least "religious" and the most progressive among the great Greek dramatists of the Classical Age.

A considerably different orientation and interest are manifest in the book listed in the inventory as "ypocrates." Hippocrates (ca. 460–377 B.C.), a Greek physician, was the first in the Western world to attempt a general and systematic treatment of the problems of medicine. A group of medical works, since known as the Hippocratic Collection, began to circulate in the ancient world around 300 B.C. It sets the goal of physicians to the present day, recommending ability, grace, speed, painlessness of treatment, readiness, and elegance. This work, with a number of other Greek scientific treatises, seems to have come into Europe by way of Sicily, and was popular in El Greco's time.

The great historian Xenophon was born about 430 B.C. in Athens, when that city was still the center of Greek culture. Besides philosophical essays and literary portraits, he wrote a chronicle of the Persian-Greek War, in which he had fought as a general in the Greek Army. Xenophon praises his men as not only conscious of their common nationality but also imbued with strong local patriotism and a fierce feeling of each man's right as an individual. He describes a skirmish in which his Cretan soldiers, with clever maneuvering and a display of their widely feared archery, brought the participants of the expedition safely back to camp. Later, looking back on his life, he realized that the unification of all Greeks should be striven for but that the old ideal of democracy combined with imperialism was impracticable.

Not long ago (1939), in the National Library of Madrid, a volume of Xenophon printed in Florence was found, inscribed as coming to El Greco from the library of his friend Antonio de Covarrubias, a Latin and Greek scholar, canon of the cathedral of Toledo from 1580. This might be the work mentioned in the first inventory. It seems that Jorge Manuel sold the volume to Tamayo de Vargas, a Toledan scholar of the seventeenth century, and it was he who made the notation. Remarkable is that in it he calls El Greco "the Apelles of our time." Apelles was perhaps the most celebrated painter of antiquity, court painter to Alexander the Great. Thus the inscription contained a graceful allusion to El Greco's lifelong interest in that bygone hero.

The Attic orator Isocrates (436–338 B.C.), whose works were also represented in El Greco's library, headed a school that rivaled that of Plato and drew pupils from all the Greek-speaking world, from Sicily to the Black Sea. Isocrates also advocated the unification of Greece through concerted attack on Asia, but he foresaw that a lasting conquest would be achieved rather through the diffusion of Greek culture than through occupation. An outstanding rhetorician, he set a distinguished standard of prose which inspired even Cicero. The Renaissance sought out Isocrates' works with zeal, and for a competent modern edition libraries of Milan, Florence, Venice, Urbino, and the Vatican had to be consulted.

El Greco owned Aristotle's *Physics* and *Politics*. Born in 384 B.C., the great philosopher worked for years at the side of Plato. His writings on logic and scientific method are fundamental to all subsequent efforts in these fields. Among the great Aristotelian commentators were Arabs, notably the twelfth century philosopher ibn-Rushd (Averroës), who lived in Córdoba, Spain, whence the Aristotelian tradition passed into Christian Europe. When, in the following century, the Latins captured Constantinople, Roman Catholic clergy set themselves to learn Greek, so as to translate the manuscripts found in Byzantine libraries. Thomas Aquinas (1225–1274) essayed a synthesis of Aristotelian philosophy and Christian belief, which was at first regarded with suspicion but finally acclaimed by the Roman Church. While the Italian Renaissance derived a great impetus from Neoplatonism, by the time El Greco grew into manhood Aristotle was the leading philosopher. At his height, he represents the invincible logic and the insatiable curiosity of the Greek mind—a type of personality not too far removed from that of El Greco himself.

The logic of El Greco's thinking is evidenced in the fact that he owned also the commentaries of Joannes Philoponus on Aristotle. This Greek philosopher lived in Alexandria in the late fifth and early sixth century of our era and was cognizant of, if not actually involved with, the Christian Copts there. Among his surviving writings are discussions of Aristotle's *Physica* and *De anima*—the latter of which appears in Jorge Manuel's inventory as "filipono en los libros de anima."

Contemporary with Aristotle is Demosthenes (ca. 384–322 B.C.), one of the great orators of all times. He exhorted his fellow countrymen to preserve the patriotic spirit which had once made Athens great; he admonished judges to practice tolerance, the statesmen to be guided in all policies by a higher concept of the general interest. The Aldine Press in Venice published the works of Demosthenes in 1504, and El Greco had opportunity to buy subsequent editions also. One visualizes him reading the passages against brute force and graft and the pleas for tolerance, in Toledo—where public offices and ecclesiastical posts were purchasable and the inquisitor's lackeys darted through the dark after new victims.[87]

Not only with Philoponus did El Greco's interest follow the Hellenistic spirit into the Christian era. Plutarch, Greek biographer and author, lived at the end of the first century. Having been trained at Athens in philosophy, he traveled much and in Rome he lectured in Greek on philosophy. His chief fame comes from his *Parallel Lives*, called "bite di Plutarco" in the inventory. In this work he pairs a Greek personality with a Roman, whether warrior, statesman, orator, or legislator (among them, for instance, Julius Caesar is placed beside Alexander the Great, to the benefit of the latter). The inventory records also the "filosofia moral di Plutarco"—sixty essays on various subjects, enhanced by excerpts from Greek poems that are lost in the original. The essays treat "how a flatterer may be distinguished from a friend," "how a young man should listen to poetry," "on the education of children." There is also a study "on exile," illuminated with plentiful quotations.

The book cited in the inventory as "Josefo de belo Judaico" denotes *The Jewish War* by Joseph ben Matthias, a Jewish historian of the first century of our era, later known as Flavius Josephus. He was also for a time a military commander. Involved in various religious and military conflicts, he saved himself from the soldiers of Vespasian at the last moment, by prophesying that their leader would become emperor. Since this came to pass, Josephus was returned to favor and accompanied the Romans to Alexandria and thence to Rome, where he was made a Roman citizen and received an estate in Judea. Josephus' work was written in Aramaic, the language in which the Gospel was first recorded, and was soon translated into a distinguished literary Greek. In it he describes the main events as they occurred and makes various forecasts, some of which came true. He shows a vast knowledge of classic history, of the exploits of Alexander, of the past of the Jews, and of the geography of Asia Minor. His book illuminates not only the contemporary situation in Galilee and Egypt but also the relationship of the various sections of Jewish population to one another, as well as their standing in the empire, shedding light on many entries of the New Testament. The sect of the Essenes, never mentioned in the New Testament, is fully described by him, with a detailed report of their rites. This is especially relevant today, when interest is increasingly concentrated on the sect through the discovery of the Dead Sea Scrolls. Josephus' writings are considered so accurate that modern archaeologists are using them in work on the ruins of ancient Caesarea in Palestine. The Greek translation of Flavius Josephus was first printed in Protestant Basel in 1544 and later in Geneva in 1611. It is most probable that the first edition was in El Greco's possession. As the complete work comprises over 150,000 words, the early volumes were a condensation with many abbreviations. Josephus' tome was also among the few books in Rembrandt's library, showing that it was widely distributed, although in Spain its importation was restricted.

Mentioned in the inventory as "ariani de belo alexandri" is a work by Arrian, also known as Flavius Arrianus, a Greek historian and philosopher, who was born in Nicomedia in Asia Minor, near Constantinople, at the end of the first century. Having studied among pagan philosophers, Arrian found in their teachings much of the early Christian spirit. In a century when the Greek language was no longer at the highest level, he uses a polished style based on classical authors. Arrian's handbook on moral philosophy was adopted for Christian use by St. Nilus of Constantinople in the fifth century and was regarded in the Middle Ages as a guide to monastic life. His most important surviving work is his *Life of Alexander the Great,* which first appeared in print in 1522. This is the book El Greco owned. It begins with the origins of the hero's career, and recounts his conquests in Europe and Asia by land and by sea.

Alexander the Great had a broad concept of the world and clarified ideals of administration. For many centuries, deep into our modern age, it was thought that Western civilization owed more to him than to any other single man. This was the hero of El Greco. His achievements are perhaps best and most fully documented in Arrian's book.

El Greco showed interest in a Latin author who treated his favorite figure—Quintus Curtius Rufus, who lived in the mid-first century. His work *De rebus gestis Alexandri Magni,* listed as "quinto curzio de fati alexandro" under Italian books in the inventory, was popular until recent research proved it not entirely reliable.

With the work of the Roman historian Cornelius Tacitus (ca. 55–120), El Greco followed the incorporation of the Greek world into the Roman Empire. The record of those centuries of transition and decline furnish melancholy reading. The dramas of the Golden Age were replaced by bloody spectacles in the circus. In art, statues became larger and larger, the features portrayed coarser and coarser—as if size could make up for quality. Tacitus was an academic republican and could only see the darkest side of the imperialism through which he lived. His annals are actually concerned with ethics rather than with politics. The work, most probably an Italian translation, is listed only in the second inventory, as "Cornelio tazito."

In the library we find Greek authors also from the second and third centuries of our era.

Lucian, a Greek sophist and satirist, mocked at Christianity. He was born in Syria and traveled widely in his native Asia Minor, in Macedonia, Greece, and Italy, and as far as Gaul. He wrote much literary criticism (a model essay on "how history should be written"), as well as romances and satirical dialogues. Lucian narrates the abduction of Europa to Crete. Indeed, many classical authors wrote at considerable length about the island.

The third century Heliodoros, also born in Syria, a student of Homer and Euripides, is represented with his *Aethiopica,* possibly the best as well as the oldest of the Greek romances that have come down to us. The first manuscript copy of this work was found when the Turks overran Hungary in 1526 and sacked the famous library of the Hungarian Renaissance king Matthias Corvinus in the royal palace at Buda(Pest). Printed in Basel in 1534, the romance came into immediate vogue, influencing such authors through the years as Torquato Tasso, Cervantes, and Racine.

A new facet of El Greco's psychology is revealed in the item "arte midoro," which stands for the work of Artemidorus Daldianus, a soothsayer and collector of dreams, active in the mid-second century. His *Interpretation of Dreams* in four books affords valuable insight into ancient superstitions. El Greco's copy is in Greek of which the first edition appeared in Venice in 1518. Numerous Italian translations followed.

From the formative period of Christianity comes the work listed as "Boecio seberino." Anicius Manlius Severinus Boethius (ca. 480–524), philosopher and statesman, was a Roman consul at the time of Theodoric the Ostrogoth. He was Orthodox, as opposed to the Arian ruler. Accused of treason, Boethius was imprisoned, and during his incarceration he wrote his famous work *De consolatione philosophiae* (On the Consolation of Philosophy), in which he contemplates man's free will and God's foreknowledge, concluding that they are not incompatible. Boethius planned to follow with translations of the works of Aristotle and Plato and to reconcile their philosophies. But he was put to death before he could conclude the project.

A work from a much later period, listed also among the Italian books, is *Ten Dialogues on the Reading and Writing of History,* whose author is generally given as Francesco Patrizzi, also as Patrizio and Franciscus Patritius (1529–1597). Patrizzi was born Franjo Petric on the Dalmatian island of Cherso, a stronghold of Slavic culture. To make a career, like El Greco, Patrizzi left his home and, through the patronage of the Bishop of Cyprus, who was himself a refugee, came to Venice where books of his were published in 1560 and 1571. This is the period during a part of which at least El Greco lived in Venice; and it is possible that Patrizzi and the young Cretan became acquainted. Both foreigners to the Italian cultural climate and at home in the Byzantine civilization, they could really engage in dialogue. In spite of the general preference for Aristotle's philosophy in that epoch, Patrizzi was a strong Neoplatonist, insisting that Aristotle's thought was incompatible with Christianity. In 1593, in distant Hamburg, a volume of his was printed which contains essays on the philosophy of Zoroaster and the Chaldean oracles, among other subjects. The Slav philosopher must have been a stimulating conversational partner.

Jorge Manuel lists the Old and New Testaments in Greek, in five volumes, as part of his father's library. Erasmus published the first New Testament in Greek in 1516. Two years later the Aldine Press in Venice brought out a large folio edition of the complete Bible in Greek (see *Pl. 110C*). Soon, in Strasbourg (1526), then a Protestant city, another edition of the complete Bible came out, bound in five volumes, reissued in Basel in 1529. El Greco must have owned one or the other of these issues, as no other five-volume Bibles are recorded in this period. They are in a handy octavo size; the text is fluently set, and precise and easy to read. As more and more printed editions of the Bible appeared in Europe, this book also became subject to scrutiny by the Inquisition. Certain marginal notes of a Latin translation by Michael Servetus which appeared in Lyons in 1542 caused the editor to be put to death at the stake (1553). A French translation published in Antwerp in 1530, although issued under a grant of Charles V and with ecclesiastical approval, was put on the Index for its marginal notes; its translator had died meanwhile.

It is noteworthy that of the twenty-seven entries of Greek books named in Jorge Manuel's first inventory, only eight are religious works, all belonging to the Orthodox world.

Justin Martyr was born in Palestine around 100. He was converted to Christianity when about thirty years old and began to preach the Word while still wearing the cloak of the wandering teacher of philosophy. He recognized classical Greek thought as a preparation for Christianity and was among the first who endeavored to reconcile the two different philosophies. Justin describes the rites of the church of the second century, the ceremonies of Baptism and the Eucharist. From his works it becomes evident that at that time there was no fixed collection of apostolic writings.

The homilies and orations of Basil the Great are listed. He was Bishop of Caesarea in the fourth century—that impressive province of Herod the Great described by Josephus. Basil studied the practices of the hermits of Syria and Egypt and laid down the first rules of monasticism, declaring community life to be spiritually superior to that of isolation. Basilian monasticism spread from Greece to Italy, Russia, and the Balkans, and strongly influenced Benedict in founding his order in the West. The chief collections of Greek manuscripts in Western Europe, such as those of Bessarion in Venice and a great number of those in the Vatican, come from the plundering of Italian Basilian houses.

What Jorge Manuel wrote down as "oraziones de S. Juo grisostomo" refers to the *Orations* of St. John Chrysostom, "the golden-mouthed," the most famous of the Greek Church fathers (345–407). Born in Antioch and influenced by the Syrian school, he was uncompromising in expressing his convictions, elevating the ascetic and laying stress on the Scripture. As early as the fifth century he was cited by Greeks and Latins equally as a church authority. Both he and Basil are noted for the elegance of their Greek style.

Another interesting item is the work called by Jorge Manuel "constituziones de los SS. Apostoles." This is a collection of canon law which originated in Greek in fourth or fifth century Syria. Besides giving ancient practices of the church, it contains rules on Christian morals, and the sequence of feasts and fasts. The compilation was later falsely attributed to Clement of the first century—one of the Roman Catholic Church fathers—to give it authority in the West.

The incomplete recording of one Greek book, listed merely as "S. dionisio," makes its identity uncertain. Another, however, is named as "S. dionisio de Celesti yerarquia," that is, *Concerning the Celestial Hierarchy* by the Pseudo-Dionysius the Areopagite. It may be assumed, therefore, that the first is the companion volume which treats of the ecclesiastical hierarchy. The true Dionysius the Areopagite lived in the first century in Athens and was converted by St. Paul. His name, however, was confused with a fifth or sixth century Greek author in Palestine, in whose writings Oriental, Jewish, and Hellenic thought are intermingled with Christian. This author is now called the Pseudo-Dionysius the Areopagite. The Celestial Hierarchy consists of the ranks of the Heavenly Host, while the Ecclesiastical Hierarchy comprises the counterpart of this system on earth, within the Christian Church. Here it should be remembered that the art of early Christianity, indeed long past the schism, was based entirely on the iconography established in the Eastern countries of the Mediterranean. The works of Dionysius—which include *Concerning Divine Names* and a treatise on mystic theology—strongly influenced literature and art in Western Europe throughout the Middle Ages. El Greco's thorough familiarity with the celestial and ecclesiastical hierarchies is evidenced in the only three large group compositions which chance put in his way: The Martyrdom of St. Mauritius, the Adoration of the Holy Name, and The Burial of Count Orgaz (see *Pls. 64B, 66B,* and *68A*), as will be discussed in detail in connection with the paintings themselves. Dionysius was long held in high honor. An icon entitled "S. Dionigi Areopagita" is in the Scuola dei Greci in Venice, signed by Canghelarios in Athens, 1729.

As already mentioned, the Council of Trent (1545–1563) was urged by Charles V to clarify the various religious disputes and to reform ecclesiastical abuses. Through the passive resistance of the papacy, that longest of church conventions never accomplished all objectives. However, it produced the reform of ecclesiastical discipline, a profession of faith, a new decree of the catechism, a list of prohibited books. In addition, rulings concerning the arts were laid down, such as the prohibition of the symbolic representation of the Trinity with three heads or as three human figures exactly alike and of the portrayal of women saints in sensuous dishevelment or in the nude. A few years after the end of the council, certain decisions were printed in book form. It is known that French, Dutch, and German translations appeared before the end of the century, and seemingly El Greco owned a Greek copy, as "sinodo tridentino" is listed under his Greek books.

El Greco was no haphazard reader. He selected his books with deliberation for their particular subject matter. There is logic in the build-up of his library, and a continuity of thought. The name of Alexander the Great weaves in and out of the list. Aristotle was a tutor of the young prince; Demosthenes, a contemporary. Plutarch presents his figure with sympathy in his *Parallel Lives.* Arrian wrote his biography in Greek, and Quintus Curtius Rufus, in Latin. A number of authors in the collection manifest an interest in coordinating the philosophy of classical Greece with that of Christianity.

The library does not show one book by a Western church father, such as Augustine, Jerome, Gregory, Ambrose, or by such saints as Benedict, Dominic, Thomas Aquinas. There is not one "mystic" writer named in El Greco's inventory—in that sense of mysticism which was romanticized later in the West and explained into the works of various painters. The belief that man may attain an immediate or direct knowledge of God through contemplation and love alone, without the process of reason, is out of keeping with El Greco's character. Not only would his Greek rational philosophy keep him far from the mystic figures, but it should not be forgotten that they were looked upon as suspect by the Inquisition—a fact today not taken into consideration.

The émigré or refugee of the twentieth century turns to the books in his mother tongue for fullest relaxation and stimulus. When we discussed the art of America before Columbus, a most recent chapter in the history of art, with a refugee writer, not two minutes passed before the German quoted Goethe—though in his time no one gave a thought to the aesthetic evaluation of the civilization of Maya and Inca. In clinging to books of his native land, the émigré makes a declaration of cultural belonging which is independent of country or century. The old saying "Show me your books and I will know who you are" applies also to El Greco. His Greek books must have been a tonic for his soul. They were reminders of Hellenic greatness not only to his Greek visitors but also to the Spaniards who came to his house. They were, for the émigré of his time also, instruments of equilibrium.

•VIII•

ENIGMATIC PAINTER

Venetian, Roman, and North European painters of the period made increasing use of themes outside the religious world. El Greco, like many of his contemporaries, owned prints which at that time circulated widely in Europe and brought the achievements in art of one country to the cognizance of another. Yet the vast majority of his paintings is religious, and only once did he reach for a Greek mythological theme, the Laocoön. This is remarkable, because in his library there were many books treating legendary, mythological, and historical matter which would have furnished adequate stimulus for secular compositions.

El Greco never submitted entirely to Western concepts of painting. Although his work apparently fulfilled the demands of the market in Spain, he retained many practices of the hagiographer. He had in his house small-scale duplicates that gave his repertory of paintings and may have served as a catalogue of stock merchandise from which choice could be made. El Greco had nothing of the vanity of the Western painter when it came to repetitions. Six repetitions by himself or his studio are recorded of the Baptism of Christ, and St. Martin and the Beggar, eight of the Adoration of the Shepherds, and the Mount of Olives, and seventeen of the Disrobing of Christ. His representation of St. Francis in Ecstasy, a widely sought-after subject of his atelier, according to some sources was repeated over eighty times. A few themes went through considerable changes across his entire artistic activity, as will be discussed later in detail.

It is not so much the total impression of El Greco's painting as characteristic details that recall his heritage, growing more pronounced with his artistic isolation in Toledo. For this reason, his work constitutes a category for itself in Western painting. In his most Venetian paintings he is not fully Venetian, and in paintings in which he gives the Spanish "atmosphere" convincingly he achieves it with means which were distinctly his own. His inability or unwillingness to conform with his contemporaries places him outside the traditional development of schools of painting. This is one of the reasons why the appreciation of his work coincides with the acceptance of Impressionism—a style by no means exclusive to France. When, about the end of the nineteenth century, composition and coloring were freed from academic traditions, the mode of El Greco could start.

A subject seldom encountered in painting at the time of El Greco is The Disrobing of Christ (El Espolio), although it is one of the fourteen Stations of the Cross. A relatively late example is a panel by Fra Angelico from the early fifteenth century. However, the concept survives considerably later in Flemish and German prints. El Greco's painting (*Pl. 58B*), commissioned in 1577, was to be placed in the section of the sacristy of the Toledan cathedral known as the Vestuario, where the priest assumes the robe symbolic of Christ on earth. Although the work was highly praised, an acrimonious litigation arose in 1579 over payment of the agreed price. In an effort to deprecate the work, it was protested that other heads had been placed higher than Christ's and that the presence of the three women in the left foreground was not according to Scripture. In the end, however, the composition remained unchanged, and no less than seventeen replicas and studio copies exist. In some of these, the shape has been changed to horizontal and the four figures in the foreground have been left out—or eventually cut off—greatly altering the effectiveness of the composition.

In this large painting, nearly six feet high, there is little effect of foreshortening, and, in spite of the brilliant highlights, shadows are absent—both characteristic of El Greco's art. The composition is built up from the lowest part toward the center and above. Christ's figure, as in all Byzantine representations, is the largest and is presented in full length. Although the other figures form a tense circle around him, the work has the static quality of a vision, which is also Byzantine. At first sight, the figure of Christ in the incandescent red of his garment—the royal "purple" of the highest Byzantine ruler—is so overpowering that the sense of the action dawns only later.

For his compositions El Greco blended impressions gathered from various sources. The mingling of Byzantine elements with those of Western painting gives his art its unique character. As a result, some of his compositions contain—whether deliberately or not—reminiscences, even definite borrowings. The Disrobing bears a relationship to the Byzantine representation of the Betrayal or the Kiss of Judas. In a page of a Byzantine Greek manuscript executed in the early twelfth century (*Pl. 58A*), some of the same tension can be found, the wreath of menacing heads, the reaching arms, the threatening lances, and the crowding to such a degree that most of the bodies except Christ's are not visible. Even the flame-like plumes and the dramatic light in the background of the painting remind one of the torches in the manuscript. As if to contradict the criticisms of the theological experts of Toledo, in the manuscript also several rows of heads appear above the head of Christ. This manuscript was presented to Louis XV of France by the French ambassador to the Porte, Istanbul, in the mid-eighteenth century. The text is taken from Jesus' farewell to the apostles at the Last Supper, and reads: "From the Gospel of John: He said to his disciples, Now is the Son of man glorified and God is glorified in him."

Representations of the Disrobing of Christ occur in the murals of Mount Athos and survive also at Zemen, Bulgaria.[34] But the subject of the Betrayal of Christ was more popular. In a late rendition by Theodoros Poulakis (*Pl. 58C*), a seventeenth century Byzantine icon with Western overtones, parallel details can be observed, such as the soldier in armor at the left, the stooping figure in the lower right. In all cases, Christ is presented in full length, with even the forward-thrust foot showing.

As to the three women in the foreground of El Greco's painting, they are similar to various groups of mourners that can be found in Macedonian wall paintings and in Late Byzantine panels (*Pl. 59A* and *B*). The three women at the foot of the Cross have a precedent in Byzantine art that goes back to the eleventh century.[57] Both in the Dormition of the Virgin and in the Crucifixion, shown here, groups of mourning women are placed in the foreground. That this arrangement is based on biblical text might be one explanation that the three Marys in El Greco's painting were finally accepted. The heavy drapery around the Virgin's head, the contrast of light and dark, the "speaking" hands, the sorrowful expression emphasized by the deep shadows about the eyes (especially clear in *Pl. 59C*) all stem from the same tradition.

Another subject of El Greco's which is rarely encountered in the painting of the Western world in the second half of the sixteenth century is Christ in the act of benediction. After the Council of Trent, renewed emphasis was put on the cult of Mary. For the Orthodox Christian also, Mary was important, not only as the Mother of God but as the embodiment of His Church on earth. The cult of Mary goes back to the earliest centuries of Christianity in Syria and the Near East with their hermits. But when she dies she does not ascend bodily; Christ receives her soul in the form of a newborn infant, and angels descend from heaven to carry it upward (see *Pl. 15C*). In the Byzantine world, which had no statues in its churches, Mary is sometimes represented in overpowering dimensions that fill an apse or cover a large section of the walls (see *Pl. 12B*), but her Child remains, even as an infant, the King.

El Greco painted the Virgin in various aspects. He had seen in Venice healthy peasant women serving as models for Titian's Madonnas; Tintoretto and the Bassanos brought the figure of the Virgin among their nervously vibrating compositions heavy with people. But El Greco's concept shows his own individuality. She always has an amazingly small head; the elongated body is clothed in heavy garments; the figure is coloristically always touching, some would say sentimental, as the Spaniard wished to have it.

But in his Christ in Benediction (*Pl. 60B*) there is no sweetness or novelistic ambience. This is the Pantocrator of Byzantium, the all-seeing and all-understanding judge. This Christ goes back to the godhead who filled the highest place of the Byzantine dome or apse (see *Pl. 9B*).

The Orthodox representation of Christ is based on a vision which appeared to King Abgarnus of Edessa in Asia Minor, healing him miraculously from a serious illness. Legend has it that the artist was stricken blind while painting the vision from the king's description, and upon recovery found the picture finished. This early type has been followed ever since in Byzantine art, as the actual earthly aspect of Christ—hair parted, a mild and joyous expression, brilliant, piercing eyes.

El Greco's Christ in Benediction is nearer to its forerunners and contemporaries of the Byzantine school of painting than any other subject he ever painted. An early and a late icon (*Pls. 60A* and *61B*), a late mural from Crete (*Pl. 60C*), and an early one from Macedonia (*Pl. 61A*) show the influences that were absorbed by him. Not only the pose of the body and the gesture of the hands show Orthodox tradition, but also details such as the angled line of the shirt, the cap of thick hair, the heavy fall of the cloak over the left shoulder, the high lights in the drapery, the strong illumination of the forehead and the wide cheekbones bringing out the depth of His gaze. The long straight nose with its curled nostrils is Byzantine convention, as is also the skillful painting of the eyes that seem to look at one from any angle but also through and beyond one. Obvious similarities can be found in an icon that we discovered in a monastery in western Crete (*Pl. 61B*), the painter of which may have been a contemporary of El Greco.

The pose of the upraised hand in benediction is derived from the ancient language of gesture in classical art. The Greek benediction, in which the third finger joins the thumb so as to form a circle, is a hieratic form.

Little explanation is needed to bring out the differences between the five paintings discussed and that of Raphael (*Pl. 61C*).

Derived from the Greek word meaning "fiftieth," the Pentecost is an important feast in the Jewish as well as in the Christian religion. In Old Testament times it fell fifty days after the Passover, about the time the harvest was finished in Palestine, and it is known in the Bible as the Feast of the Weeks, or the Feast of the First Fruit. Its religious observance commemorated the delivery of the Law to Moses on Mount Sinai. On this feast day, fifty days after Christ was crucified, the Holy Spirit descended upon the apostles as "they were all with one accord in one place." In early centuries converts were baptized on this day, and from the white garments they wore then comes the English name Whitsunday.

The representation of the Pentecost has gone through considerable evolution. Reproduced here (*Pl. 62A*) is an illustration in the Rabula Gospels, the earliest and most celebrated Syrian codex, now preserved in the Laurentian Library in Florence. It was written and illuminated by the monk Rabula in A.D. 586, in the monastery of St. John at Zagba in Mesopotamia. The recording of name, date, and place in the manuscript is unique in its time. In the illustration the Virgin Mary, embodying Christ's Church on earth, stands in the center flanked by the apostles, all touched by tongues of fire.

Mention has already been made here of the immense influence which Syrian iconography exerted on the early Christian, Byzantine, and finally Western art. The holocausts that have visited Asia Minor through the centuries have wiped out much important artistic evidence. However, enough survives to serve as convincing clues to those who give it their attention.

In most medieval representations of the Pentecost Mary is notably absent (see *Pl. 112A*). In that period emphasis was placed on the apostolic succession, and this interpretation survives in the Orthodox world today. Later, the Western world included her figure once more in a more humanized interpretation of the scene, together with "the women" spoken of in Acts 1:14, and even sometimes with other brethren besides the twelve apostles.

The Pentecost as painted by El Greco (*Pl. 62B*) shows some Orthodox characteristics. The arched ceiling which in the Rabula Gospel indicates "the upper room" is present. Here also the heads of the figures, with tongues of flame above them, form nearly a straight line placed high on the canvas. Although presenting a different scene, the Byzantine icon from Mount Athos (*Pl. 62C*) shows relationship in the tenseness of the gesticulating figures, the central position of the Virgin, the even line of the heads, and the flame-like shape of the trees.

In comparing Titian's painting of the Pentecost (*Pl. 63A*) it should be repeated that Titian's iconography was not strictly Western; the great Venetian master often went to the Basilica of San Marco in Venice to study the composition in the Byzantine mosaics. In Titian's case, the Italian art historians call the process "inspired by . . .", "borrowed from . . . ." When El Greco does the same, it is plagiarism.

In Titian's Pentecost the arch is built into a solid architectural structure and, with the background, takes up more than half the canvas. The feeling of height of "the upper room" is clearly indicated by El Greco through steps and the suggestion of a platform. The important figures occupy the upper third of the canvas, while Titian has placed his in the lower part of the painting. The empty upper space is filled with a strong fan-like ray, as against the modest light of El Greco's around the Dove.

El Greco includes with Mary another woman, who is reminiscent of the white-veiled mourner of the Disrobing. What makes his painting individual is the presence, second from the right, of the only figure looking out of the picture—a distinguished elderly man with a pointed beard. This is thought to be a portrait of El Greco himself. The explanation might be sought in the Scriptures (Acts 2:5–11), when, after the descent of the Holy Spirit, devout men of every nation came together to bear witness to the miracle. And were amazed that ". . . Parthians and Medes . . . dwellers in Mesopotamia . . . and Egypt . . . Lybia, and strangers of Rome . . . Cretes and Arabians, we do hear them speak in our tongues the wonderful works of God." El Greco's inclusion of himself could have two explanations: he indeed could discourse in several tongues, and above all, he was a "Crete." A precedent can be found in Dürer's woodcut of the Pentecost (*Pl. 63B*), in which three witnesses or observers sit on a bench in the background.

The version by Guido Reni (*Pl. 63C*), nearly contemporary with El Greco, which now hangs in the Vatican, shows inspiration replaced by sentimentality.

The painting, appearing in a catalogue of the mid-nineteenth century as "The Dream of Philip II," and later renamed by Cossío "The Glory of Philip II," is now given the title The Adoration of the Holy Name of Jesus (*Pl. 64B*). It has been suggested that El Greco executed this painting as a bid for the royal patronage of Philip II, who was then building and decorating the Escorial. Another, smaller version exists, some twenty-one by fourteen inches, painted in tempera on wood panel with considerably less detail.

The composition falls into three sections. In the upper part the angelic host forms a wreath about the monogram of Jesus' name. On the left, in the background, the multitude of the blessed kneel in prayer. In the lower right corner yawn the jaws of Hell slavering with bodies of the damned, and the middle ground shows more of the wicked being thrust into the lake of fire. A group of potentates, warriors, and others kneel in the foreground, among whom the black-robed figure of Philip II is easily recognized. His companions have been identified as Pope Pius V (shown in full face) and the doge Luigi Mocenigo (with his back to the onlooker) who with the King of Spain formed the Holy League. The warriors then might represent the generals at Lepanto—who were John of Austria for Spain, Marcantonio Colonna for the Vatican, and Sebastiano Veniero for Venice. This central group finds a prototype in the commemorative and allegorical paintings so magnificently executed for various occasions in Venice. Veronese painted an allegory of Lepanto for the Ducal Palace and Tintoretto a commemorative canvas for a chapel in SS. Giovanni e Paolo.[94]

While this interpretation of the group in El Greco's painting as the members of the Holy League seems acceptable, the work in its entirety contains a much more complex symbolism; the other sections have little relevance to a naval victory. Actually, the theme is the Last Judgment, which the Orthodox call the Second Coming of Christ. It has been pointed out that Philip II liked fantastic and supernatural compositions, such as those by Hieronymus Bosch, Martin de Vos, and others, a number of whom depicted the Last Judgment. But the iconography of the Second Coming of Christ long occupied Orthodox imagination. Its main episodes were described in the fourth century by Ephraim the Syrian and, in the ninth, were combined in pictures as an admonition, in the educational program of the church. They are set down in Denys of Fourna's *Painter's Manual* (see *Pls. 15B* and *43B*). On the refectory wall of the Lavra monastery at Mount Athos (*Pl. 65B*), the depiction of the gates of Hell as the open jaws of a monster appears somewhat later but is fully a part of the Orthodox representation. The position of the monster and his vertical pointed snout are almost exactly like those in El Greco's composition. In Bulgaria, at the monastery at Rila (see *Pl. 17A*), we see the same idea. Here it should be mentioned that the monster does not appear in Last Judgments either by Hieronymus Bosch or Martin de Vos, or in the earlier depictions by Fra Angelico. A panel in the Byzantine Museum of Athens shows the devil with a great hook raking in the damned from the river of fire. Independent depictions of various punishments accorded to the damned cover the walls of many rural churches in Crete; Gerola reported nearly fifty such instances in murals of the fourteenth and fifteenth centuries. In El Greco's painting, through the archway beyond the lake of fire, two gibbets are visible with hanging figures, while others fall into the flames.

Despite the small size of El Greco's work, the Byzantine manner of separating different scenes is striking. The various groups—the potentates, the company of the saved, and of the damned—are enclosed in lozenge-shaped compartments (compare *Pl. 65C*). El Greco arranges his figures of the blessed to denote masses, so that only those in the front row can be distinguished, and the heads finally recede into a series of semicircles (compare *Pl. 65A*).

Although it has been suggested that the painting glorifies the Spanish king, the focus actually is on the celestial vision, which occupies a full half of the composition. With a touch of what might be called surrealistic technique today, El Greco separates the heavens from the earthly landscape. Mature angels, larger than the rulers' figures in the foreground, with powerful heavy wings, circle around the monogram IHS surmounted by the Cross and blazing in celestial radiance. El Greco's angelic host has much in common with the Byzantine *Hetimasia,* or Preparation of the Throne for the Second Coming, as it is depicted in the church of St. Demetrios in Mistra (*Pl. 64A*). The contemporary Cretan Damaskinos painted a related group in the scene of the Burning Bush in which God the Father delivers the tablets of the Ten Commandments (*Pls. 64C* and *112B*). In both cases the angels are rampant; their corpulent bodies, their solid wings and freely moving legs, as they encircle the heavenly light, are basic elements of Byzantine painting. They are the angels to which El Greco's are related.

In the earliest Orthodox symbolism of the apocalypse in Nicaea and elsewhere, the Throne was depicted with a scroll upon it ("the Word") and the monogram of Jesus above it, signifying His elevation to the right hand of God as final judge. As St. Peter said, "for there is none other name under heaven given among men, whereby we must be saved" (Acts 4:12). The scroll was later—with the invention of binding—replaced by a book with seven seals. In some instances the Throne is indicated by a cross with the Book at its foot (see *Pl. 15B*).

From the radiant letters IHS originates the latest caption under which the painting is known. To quote Matthew 24:30, "Then shall appear the sign of the Son of man in heaven . . ." and Paul's Epistle to the Philippians 2:9 and 10, "that at the name of Jesus every knee should bow . . . ." Those three letters IHS constitute the monogram in Greek—iota, eta, sigma—of Jesus: IHSUS or IHCUC (the letters S and C being variant forms in the Greek alphabet). A line above the central character is the Greek sign of contraction or abbreviation, and a cross is formed if the first stroke of the h is lengthened, so as to strike through the line. Long after the Orthodox and Roman rites had separated, the Jesuits sought a Latin interpretation of the Monogram, which by that time was too broadly applied to be neglected. With a twist, the letters were declared to stand for "Jesus Hominum Salvator," Jesus Savior of Mankind, with a special interpretation for the Spanish: "Jesus Hijo Sacro," Jesus Divine Son. The IHS is also sometimes read as "In hoc signo (vinces)"—the sign which Western interpreters say appeared to Constantine. This explanation is especially fallacious. Constantine was Balkan-born and educated in the Eastern court. The supernatural admonition "By this (sign) conquer" was evinced to him in Greek, and the "sign" itself was the Greek monogram of Christos—the Chi Rho which subsequently he adopted for his personal device.

The complex symbolisms of El Greco's painting reveal the profound and philosophically acute iconographic knowledge of the painter. Although this composition was never executed on the large scale to which it is eminently suited, it may have been instrumental in gaining the painter the one royal commission of his life, The Martyrdom of St. Mauritius for the Escorial.

Sometimes the wrong title clings to a picture stubbornly. When, after World War II, the Night Watch of Rembrandt was thoroughly cleaned, it was established that it commemorates a gathering in bright daylight of a company of civic guards, and has nothing to do with either night or watch. Nevertheless it is still referred to under its former title. What title El Greco gave to his painting is not known; no mention of such a composition can be found in his inventory and no archival material is extant which could shed light upon it.

Among the very few large canvases with many figures which El Greco had occasion to execute, The Martyrdom of St. Mauritius and the Theban Legion (*Pl. 66B*) is revealing of his talent for monumental composition. It was planned to fill the center section of an altar in the church of the Escorial.

Mauritius was commander of a Roman legion recruited in Egypt in the late third century. Marched across the Alps to reinforce the army of Maximinian in the suppression of a revolt in Gaul, they were commanded to take part in public sacrifices near Geneva and in the persecution of Christians. But, as many of them were already converts to the same faith, they refused. In punishment, the troop was twice decimated and finally exterminated.

In El Greco's depiction, Mauritius in the center discourses with his saintly comrades. The soldiers wear the leather shirts of the Roman army of the second or third century. All figures but one are barefoot. Mauritius has a large jeweled clasp on his mantle, a traditional sign of rank. The drape of the cloak, the clasp, and some details of his kilt-like uniform show similarity with an eleventh century soapstone carving of St. George from Mount Athos (*Pl. 66C*). Still more striking are the similarity of stance and the gesture of hands and arms. The costume, with its unusual revealing of the navel, appears in the drawing of a statue of a Byzantine emperor in the heyday of Constantinople (*Pl. 66A*). In contrast, two spectators with portrait-clear heads but without bodies or feet appear behind Mauritius—one accoutered in greaved armor and fine narrow white ruff of the sixteenth century.

Toward the left in the painting we see the second scene of the legend. Mauritius stands beside the decapitated nude body of one of his soldiers, his arms stretched outward and downward in a gesture of compassion. His standard-bearer remains at his side, and again a Spanish knight looks on. Beyond this scene is a third in which the legion is driven to execution (*Pl. 67B*). The bodies are only sketched and the numbers suggested with receding semicircles for the heads. But there is considerable movement in all of the groups, as well as an amazing lack of the stereotype. The contrast between the meek and the mighty could not be brought out more clearly than by the figures of the warriors on horseback at the left, resplendent in full sixteenth century armor.

The heavens, opening, reveal angels ensconced on a shelving cloud, playing celestial music. A lute, a recorder, and a viol make up an exquisite contemporary trio. The angelic singer who seems also to be beating time holds an antiphonary on which the musical notation is clearly marked—a touch of the miniature painter. Farther to the right, angels poising on broad wings wave long palms, the symbol of martyrdom, and hold high the martyrs' crowns of victory.

El Greco began the painting in 1579 or early 1580. That he did not deliver it for almost four years bears out Pacheco's report of his methods of working, that he returned to a picture again and again, putting in new touches and high lights. The Spanish master adds: "that is what I call painting to stay poor. . . ." Rising to the challenge of a royal commission, El Greco has freed himself of a number of tight Byzantine formulas. The painting exhibits his unusual sense of coloring, as well as his command of the technique of painting in oil.

A relatively broad section of the foreground is without figures, displaying a finely executed still life. The red lilies symbolize the martyrdom of the innocent. The cut-down young tree might refer to the sacrifice of young lives, and also suggests the passage in Job 14: "there is hope of a tree if it be cut down, that it will sprout again . . . ."

In the right corner, a serpent holds in its mouth a slip of paper bearing the Greek signature of the painter: "Domenikos Theotokopoulos made me." One Spanish writer explains the snake as the spirit of the earth or the earth force,[95] while another suggests that it was painted to symbolize the envy and malice which engulfed the Cretan as a foreigner and abetted the king's lack of enthusiasm for the painting.[102] But for one so widely read as El Greco and with such profound philosophical bent it appears to have a more pertinent symbolism. In ancient lore the serpent is said to flee in terror from a man who quickly discards his clothing, as Satan flees from those who free themselves from sin; and even more relevant: as the serpent exposes his whole body to his enemies, so also must the Christian not hesitate to endure affliction for the sake of the Lord.[15] The nakedness of the soldiers, which is said to have displeased Philip, thus gives significance to the presence of the serpent. That El Greco puts the label with his signature into its mouth calls to mind the fact that the ancients associated subtlety and wisdom also with the reptile. The Greek god of medicine Asklepios is represented with the caduceus, a staff with serpents coiled around it, which the medical branch of the United States Army today wears as its insignia.

El Greco's painting was never put in the place for which it was intended. Instead, the Spanish monarch had a rendition of the same subject by Romulo Cincinnato placed on the altar (*Pl. 67A*). His painting is pedestrian, and since it was executed later than El Greco's, some might see in it a certain influence from the disparaged canvas. Cincinnato, one of the numerous Italian hack painters around the Escorial, was born in Florence, studied in Rome, and came to Spain about 1567 on the recommendation of the Spanish ambassador.[93] Today his name is remembered only in connection with this incident, a conclusive demonstration of the conventional taste of the monarch.

Another Italian, Veronese, in his scene Christ and the Centurion (*Pl. 67C*), shows how a Venetian master dressed his Roman soldiers, with what skill he arranged his groups and suggested perspective. The two Italians, hack and master, have nevertheless much more in common with each other than with El Greco.

To many, The Burial of Count Orgaz (*Pl. 68A*) is El Greco's masterpiece, the painting in which his rich and varied faculties come to fullest expression. Gonzalo Ruiz de Toledo, Lord of Orgaz, a town belonging to the province of Toledo, died in the first quarter of the fourteenth century. His descendants later received the title of count, which is now applied to him also.[111]

A devout and generous personage, he rebuilt and "dowered" the church of Santo Tomé about 1300, and also ceded property to reestablish the Augustinian monastery, leaving instructions that the church be called San Esteban for Stephen, the first martyr. Upon completion of the monastery complex, his body was transferred there from Santo Tomé, and the assembled company witnessed the appearance of the saints Stephen and Augustine who lifted the body and placed it in the tomb. Though it was felt that the miracle should be worthily commemorated, it took some 150 years to have this done. Early in 1586 El Greco was commissioned to paint the scene, and it was specified that the canvas be in place by Christmas—perhaps in the knowledge that the master was a slow worker. While it is most probably a coincidence that a Cretan received the commission, it should not be left unmentioned, as one more echo from the Byzantine past, that the lordly family was related to the Palaeologues, the last dynasty of the Byzantine Empire.

A ceremonially solemn and pious muteness characterizes the dark wall of the personages who witness the scene. Color draws the eye to the resplendent vestments of the celebrants in the foreground. There is a Byzantine reminiscence in the way in which the two saints clasp the body of the count. An example can be seen in a mural of the Entombment of Christ, assigned to the Cretan school in the monastery of Dochiariou, Mount Athos (*Pl. 69A*). The even line-up of the group of mourners in an unbroken row has also Byzantine antecedents, apparent in scenes of the deaths of Athanasius and Ephraim (see *Pls. 11A* and *B*).

As previous authors have pointed out, the composition of El Greco's canvas was influenced by the established formula for depicting the Dormition of the Virgin (see *Pls. 15C, 19A,* and *69B*), in which her soul, as a newborn infant, is held in the arms of Christ and angels descend to receive it.[10] This representation disappears from Western art as Mary is given more and more importance. However, medieval reliefs and paintings show it, even in Spain. In Toledo, in the treasury of the cathedral, there is a Byzantine soapstone plaque where this form is clearly visible (*Pl. 112A*). The Prado has among its treasures an Annunciation by Fra Angelico in which one panel of the predella, or base, pictures the same scene (*Pl. 68B*). This is in contrast to the Assumption in the Roman Catholic Church, in which Christ is not present and the Virgin ascends full grown. In The Burial of Count Orgaz, El Greco depicts the soul of the dead count as a newborn infant—still more like a translucent ectoplasm—which is carried upward in the arms of an angel through the one opening in the clouds. The representation in connection with a mortal stands alone in the entire history of Western painting.

El Greco reveals a familiarity with the ranks of the hierarchies as established by Dionysius the Areopagite whose works in Greek he had in his library. The ecclesiastical hierarchy is present in the lower group: bishops, presbyters, deacons ("hierarchs, light-bearers, servitors"), monks, the initiate laity, and "catechumens"—the last represented by the boy in the foreground.

It is known that the Council of Trent found the representation of the celestial choirs too much of a residue of the backward Middle Ages. Although it was not forbidden, it nevertheless occurs seldom in Western art after the Counter Reformation.[11] In his depiction of Heaven, El Greco does not cling to the categorical. Nevertheless he indicates the various ranks by a separation into oval compartments which is reminiscent of the cloud boats in which the apostles were summoned for the Dormition (see *Pl. 19A*). His clouds have the solidity of starched woven material. Uppermost in the center we see Christ, draped in white folds, Mary and the Baptist at His feet as supplicants for the soul—a Byzantine concept. Toward the right, beyond the figure of John the Baptist and quite close to the company of the apostles, a typical Habsburg head is portrayed. It has been suggested that this represents Philip II. But it is very doubtful that El Greco, with his thorough knowledge of iconography, would have placed a living mortal —even the King of Spain—among the heavenly choirs. Rather, it might be Philip's father, the Emperor Charles V, who died in 1558 and whose magnificence was still vivid in memory.

It is generally accepted that the small boy next to St. Stephen is Jorge Manuel, El Greco's son, at the age of eight. From his pocket, a white kerchief emerges, on which the Greek text reads "Domenikos Theotokopoulos I made it," and the date, added in Greek, is not the year when the painting was contracted or when it was delivered but 1578, the year when the child was born. The flash of wit in this instance was seemingly suffered in that generally humorless society.

While the men gesticulate with amazement toward the miracle, the child, looking straight at the spectator, points not—as so often stated—at the center of action, but directly into the white and gold rose framed within a circle which is embroidered on Stephen's dalmatic (*Pl. 70B*). This detail, important for its symbolism, has until now been strangely overlooked. The two monks in black and gray at the left seem grouped with the boy, pondering his gesture. And Stephen looks down upon him.

The circle, being without beginning or end, is the symbol of eternity. The rose has been popular through the ages, and variously applied. As an ancient symbol of love it denotes (especially enclosed in the esoteric circle) Divine Love, hence also Christian Faith. The white rose symbolizes the messianic promise of salvation.[15] The white rose also stands for innocence, that is, virtue, blamelessness, purity of heart—hence the frequent application to the Virgin Mary. In his *Divine Comedy,* Dante brings the vision of Paradise as a great white rose made up of saints and angels.

It is possible that for the erudite Cretan the rose had still more definite association. The cathedral of Toledo owns one of the largest Byzantine soapstone carvings in existence, previously mentioned, with reliefs of the Twelve Feasts of the Church, dating from the twelfth century (*Pl. 112A*). In two of the scenes, the Annunciation and the Baptism, the Holy Ghost descends on a beam of light, not as a dove, but in the form of a rose (*Pl. 70A*). If El Greco knew the carving, he understood it as few others in Toledo. The implication of the rose in this painting then would be that, like Stephen—who was the first to be confirmed under the apostles and also the first to give his life for the Christian faith—Orgaz too was vouchsafed the gifts of the Holy Spirit.

How different El Greco's scene is from a typical Spanish concept can be seen when it is compared with The Burial of St. Bonaventure by Zurbarán (*Pl. 69C*). In the latter canvas the onlookers are statue-like in placement and lighting, without the vibration of El Greco's work. In The Burial of Count Orgaz, tension is achieved by drawing the earthly participants into one shallow plane in the foreground. Both burial scenes have a Spanish quality, but the atmosphere is quite dissimilar.

The Council of Trent decreed that Christ rose out of a closed tomb.[11] El Greco painted The Resurrection in his earliest years in Spain in a rather Italianate version. The soldiers are dressed traditionally and the tomb is clearly depicted. In a version from his older age, the Byzantine echoes have become stronger (*Pl. 71A*). There is nothing which might suggest a tomb. The background is without depth. Whatever sense of perspective is given comes from the bold foreshortening of the agitated figures and the fact that the tallest is placed in the foreground.

The soldiers are no longer traditionally uniformed—the impression is of nudity—and their gestures are terror-stricken.

This later version, of which some four replicas are extant, has strong affinities with the Orthodox rendition of the Transfiguration, as illustrated here from a manuscript executed in early fourteenth century for a member of the Palaeologue family (*Pl. 71B*). Moses and Elijah have no place in El Greco's painting, but the floating quality of the figure of Christ and the apocalyptically tumbling witnesses are related. Against the opaque curtain of the backdrop, El Greco has painted what can be recognized as a similar circular aureole of yellowish golden light, reminiscent of the gilded backgrounds of miniatures and icons. Even a diamond and a square radiation are superimposed—the last brought out by the lines of Christ's raised arm and the fluttering drapery.

The Byzantine depiction of the Transfiguration is one of the most traditional. It occurs with little change in the mosaic in the church of the Twelve Apostles in Thessaloniki, in murals in the Mount Athos monasteries of Chilandari, Pantokratoros, St. Paul (*Pl. 71C*), in the rural chapels of Kastoria, as well as in many icons. In Russia, too, derived from the famous fifteenth century icon of Andrei Rublev, the Christ in blazing aureole and the tumbling figures have become stock elements of this scene.

In Tintoretto's canvas (*Pl. 71D*) the landscape has not only perspective but shows vegetation. The tomb is an important and solid element in the composition. The soldiers are conventionally clothed, and the two in the foreground make up passive bystanders, posed as in a *tableau vivant*. Tintoretto's Christ leaps as if propelled out of the tomb, while El Greco's figure floats upward, calm, weightless.

El Greco approached the subject of The Agony in the Garden of Gethsemane relatively late in his lifetime. Reproduced here is the representation strongest in Byzantine echoes (*Pl. 73A*).

After celebrating the Passover, Jesus went with His disciples to the Mount of Olives as was His wont, and taking Peter, John, and James to one side, prayed that this cup might be removed from Him. Though He bade the apostles to watch and pray with Him, they fell asleep. Thrice He offered the prayer and thrice awoke His friends; the last time, Judas and the soldiers approached.

El Greco's depiction of the scene brings the figure of Christ in dominating size and position illuminated by a heavenly ray. Behind Him, framing and isolating His figure as in a mandorla, rises what might be a rock—but the rock of a stage setting, slanting upright like a cresting wave. A massive angel with powerful wings holds the cup. The sleeping apostles are visible in an oval grotto. Peter leans his head on his right arm while his left encircles it in an unusual and uncomfortable gesture; James in the center bows forward, while John, with his head pillowed on his arm, lies stretched at full length.

In the distance, right, a group of soldiers with lances and torchbearers advances, with one long-robed figure in the lead. The "garden" is suggested only in shorthand by a few twigs and leaves. In the foreground a truncated tree calls to mind the Baptist's admonition that on the Last Day every tree which brings not forth good fruit shall be hewn down and cast into the fire. Beyond the angel, apocalyptic clouds are translucent with light. To the right, in a turbulent sky, a veiled full moon is floating, making in total effect as unrealistic and ominous a landscape as might have been dreamed by a surrealist.

There is an unusually strong sense of perspective in El Greco's painting, although it is achieved without the geometric devices of contemporary Western masters. El Greco had the remarkable faculty of bringing out perspective with color. Here the angel appears to be farther in the foreground than the figure of Christ—indeed, quite outside the frame. While in the reproduction the position is perceptible through the fact that the robe overlaps the tree, in the original the full effect is achieved by the coloring.

In Tintoretto's painting of the same scene (*Pl. 73B*) the angel flies in from the right, offering the cup without the gesture of obeisance and "comfort" shown in El Greco's painting. The scene lacks the eerie moonscape of El Greco. The three apostles are posed more naturally, amid massive vegetation. In the left background, the approaching soldiers are outlined by torchlight. El Greco and his atelier made seven or eight renditions of the subject, with slight variations; but the pose of the three apostles is always the same.

In the Byzantine representation of the Agony in the Garden, the text of St. Luke is usually followed and all the apostles appear. The sleeping group is placed also in a grotto-like oval in the twelfth century mosaic in the cathedral of Monreale, Sicily (*Pl. 72A*). The uncomfortable, unrealistic poses in many Byzantine renditions are strikingly similar to El Greco's—the sharply bent arms, the central figure of James with forward-bowed foreshortened head, and the beardless John stretched at full length. In the two fourteenth century versions shown here, the murals at Mount Athos and the Yugoslav-Macedonian monastery of S. Andreas (*Pl. 72C* and *B*), the huddled, crowded effect is also preserved and the stupor tellingly portrayed. Although El Greco includes only three figures, for which there is ample space, the crowding is retained.

The hills in the Byzantine landscape—arid truncated cones with slanting step-like ledges—are taken from the actual tells, the barren, rocky mounds which can be seen by the hundreds in the Near East.[5] El Greco's landscape with its sharp, rigid outlines, from which any attempt at realism is absent, shows derivation from Byzantine antecedents. Indeed, Western painting, before it achieved roundness and three-dimensional realism, drew from the same early conventionalization (*Pl. 73C*). These hard and scaled surfaces in stereotype repetition make up the traditional composite landscape of Late Byzantine art, as shown in *Pl. 96*. El Greco's settings with their unreal elements, sometimes abstracted, sometimes stylized, bear a distinct relation to this landscape.

El Greco painted The Healing of the Blind Man several times, but all renditions are works of his youth. In the scene illustrated (*Pl. 74A*) his preoccupation with perspective is evident in the converging lines of the pavement, in the rather arbitrarily placed steps, in the introduction of groups of diminishing size, and in the line of the arcades ending in a vaulted ruin. This last detail has been identified as taken from a book by Serlio on architecture, a copy of which El Greco had in his library.[112]

Of the many figures in the scene, the group on the left is dominated by a young man, naked to the waist, who points into the corner. One wonders if there was once an inscription on the lintel beyond his finger. In the group at the right, a wise old man nearest the miracle indicates amazement. The painting does not yet speak the particular subjective idiom of El Greco. Most of the persons depicted are more or less stock figures; note the repetitions in the stance. Even the gesticulations of the hands could have been executed by one of the many adept painters who supplied the Venetian market, profiting from prints of the masters. It might be worth mention that this canvas once belonged to the Farnese family and was catalogued in the seventeenth century as the work of Veronese.[114] In all three known repetitions of El Greco's Christ Healing the Blind, the general arrangement is the same and the figure of Christ remains unchanged, suggesting that the paintings do not fall far from one another in time.

Of especial interest for us is the figure of Christ, which shows a relationship to the Creto-Venetian tradition. As sympathetic as the delineation is, it is also a stock figure but one from another artistic ensemble. In the gallery of San Giorgio dei Greci in Venice, there is an icon of the Risen Christ with the two Marys (*Pl. 74C*) which remains recognizably Byzantine, though it displays concessions to the Western taste. In this painting the benign pose of Christ's figure, the folds of the drapery, the line of the shirt around the neck, and the throw of the mantle over the left arm call the El Greco to mind. The stance has an unyielding quality which is traditional. The Christ in a panel by Michele Damaskinos (*Pl. 74B*), today in the Metropolitan Church of Heraklion (Candia), is even closer to El Greco's figure; and the figure of Mary is composed in similar relation to Him as that of the blind man. In both icons a series of other scenes is included in the background. This also is in the Byzantine tradition already seen in El Greco's The Martyrdom of St. Mauritius.

In The Cleansing of the Temple a development can be observed, from the early hesitant compositions to those painted in El Greco's very late Toledan years. The figure of Christ goes through a metamorphosis, although preserving the Creto-Venetian character which it had also in the first essay. In a relatively similar architectural arrangement to the previous subject, Christ is again placed in the center of the composition (*Pl. 74D*). On the left there is again a young man naked to the waist, but instead of pointing, he bends his arm as if protecting himself from blows. At the right again, closer to the action, are wise men who are more onlookers than participants. The intention to demonstrate a command of perspective is again evident. The artist has set himself a more complicated problem and has resolved it successfully. The palace with its balcony (left center) is so Venetian that it could stand on the Canal Grande. In the lower right corner, four heads are inserted with no connection whatsoever with the action. These have been tentatively identified as Titian, Michelangelo, Clovio, and Raphael. It has also been repeatedly suggested that the younger man may be a self-portrait.

In this composition the figure of Christ has about the same dimensions as the other figures and the gentle pose is changed into a militantly active one. Christ grasps a whip, and in the crowd a radius is left open as if to give space for the swing of it. To be remarked in the early version are also the nudity, the hair-dos of the women, Venetian in style and set forth in elaborate detail, the babies, or *putti*, in Venetian tradition, worthy indeed of a "disciple of Titian."

In the later versions of this same theme (*Pl. 75B*)—as when an orchestra has repeated a musical composition for a long time—a smoothness in the ensemble is noticeable. Absent are a number of details. The cherubic babies are no more to be seen nor are the anecdotal touches which mellowed the atmosphere. The buildings are subordinated, less defined and more distant. The pavement has a uniform pattern. Between the columns, in a number of versions, two reliefs with symbolic meaning are presented: on the left, the expulsion of Adam and Eve from the garden, on the right, Abraham about to sacrifice his son. This manner of placing small reliefs into an architectural frame to elucidate the main theme was a favorite device of Bellini and Titian.

Instead of the step in the foreground a new element is introduced—the upturned table of the money-changers which serves a similar purpose in the design. This is a harking back to earlier prototypes, as exemplified in the twelfth century mosaic at Monreale, Sicily (*Pl. 75C*). There is also another parallel: the figure of Christ is accentuated by the curve of an arch.

In this last version of El Greco's, Christ has grown in size and vehemence. This is an avenging Christ who establishes order, whom nobody dares to counteract. As in Byzantine art in general, He stands drawn in full; not the slightest detail is permitted to obliterate any part of the dominating figure.

This emphasis of the main protagonist is especially clear in a mural in the side chapel of Kariye Cami, in Istanbul, just recently cleared of obscuring whitewash. Here Christ in Limbo is represented, the Byzantine concept of the Resurrection known as *Anastasis* in Greek (*Pl. 75A*). He stands astride the blasted gates of Hell. Death himself lies manacled underfoot, and locks, hinges, and bolts are scattered about. The triple mandorla inclines to the left, subtly following the movement of His figure. Three tones of blue came to light upon cleaning, and stars were uncovered, applied in gold leaf.[50] With forceful authority Christ lifts Adam and Eve out of the Kingdom of Death. The physical effort is at once perceivable, but still more powerful is the spiritual communication. The appearance is kindred in more than one way to El Greco's Saviour.

El Greco has come far, on one hand, from the Creto-Venetian hagiographers and also, on the other, from the models of the Venetian school, as is evident from the Bassano painting of the Cleansing of the Temple (*Pl. 75D*). Here the figure of Christ is no larger than the others, and, enveloped by the crowd around Him, does not command attention. The group with the Jewish High Priest takes the emphasis, standing high above His head on the landing of the temple, with strong illumination falling upon it, and weakens the point of the work.

Few events of the Bible have the idyllic grace of the angel's annunciation to Mary. The scene is usually presented as one of truly angelic serenity. It was extremely popular in sixteenth century Venice, with the madonneri and their Greek equivalents, the hagiographers. An example from the Scuola di San Giorgio dei Greci, believed to be from the end of the sixteenth century, is reproduced on *Pl. 76C*. The Virgin kneels at a prayer desk at the right of the canvas. Her canopied bed is visible, as often shown in early manuscripts and prints. Beyond the terrace a landscape stretches with houses and a campanile. The checkered floor and somewhat uncertainly designed steps reveal an attempt at handling perspective. The archangel carries a branch of lilies. God the Father with the orb is to be seen as He dispatches the Dove. This part of the painting is in a cloud—always a good device for presenting transcendental appearances.

Many similarities can be observed in the Veronese rendition of the Annunciation (*Pl. 76B*), most probably painted not much earlier, and eagerly copied by the "popular" painters. The pose of the archangel, the Virgin's arms crossed in humility, the placement of the landscape, and many other details are like. In the differences in execution and coloring, the wide range of quality becomes clear in the contemporaneous art production of this one city.

The Annunciation belongs to the few subjects which inspired El Greco across the years. Several paintings executed in Italy have been credited to him, then again declared doubtful. One such, shown on *Pl. 77A*, once hung in the State Gallery in Vienna but was lost during World War II. Here the column and the heavy drapery only suggest the bedchamber. A more successful perspective is displayed through the arcade, with a more elegantly patterned floor.

The Dove enters on an unobtrusive ray of light, and the angel occupies only a small area of the painting, floating in on heavy wings. As generally in the West, the second wing is suggested by a view of its curving edge over the far shoulder.

The next example (*Pl. 77C*) is attributed to a follower of Titian. Mary kneels now at the left. The bed again is clearly visible, topped by a large pillow with silken high lights. Genre touches are introduced, in the cat, the chest, the workbasket. The handling of the drapery is skillful, the perspective no longer obtrusive. The checkerboard pattern of the pavement guides the eye to the symbolic "closed garden" in the background.

In all of the Annunciations which El Greco painted, Mary is placed at the left. In the first example here reproduced (*Pl. 77B*), she kneels on a platform and there is no suggestion of a bedchamber. The checkered pattern of the floor extends down a long vista to a gate that suggests again the closed garden. To the right of the Venetian-style balcony, reminiscent of that in the Cleansing of the Temple, a miniature fountain appears—the "fountain of living waters" is another attribute of the Virgin. The romping *putti* tend to distract the eye from the Dove. Gabriel carries no lily but hails Mary with upraised hand. The curve of the right wing, in the Western manner, is outlined beyond the shoulder.

A mural dated 1547 in the church of the Holy Apostles at Kastoria, Macedonia (*Pl. 76A*), demonstrates the contrast between the Byzantine Greek and the Venetian, even the Creto-Venetian concept of the subject. Here Mary stands before a throne-like seat provided with the imperial cushion. She holds a distaff in her left hand; the thread runs across her raised right hand between thumb and forefinger. The bright wings of the archangel are spread to show entire, one on each side. From a rainbow-rimmed circle the Dove descends, wearing a tiny triradiant halo and emanating a ray of light from its beak. The architectural background is painted in the Byzantine manner, and a number of other details hark back to miniatures and mosaics.

El Greco in a later version of the Annunciation (*Pl. 78A*) has discarded the elements of architectural perspective. A workbasket is set at the Virgin's feet, and Gabriel carries a lily stalk. His outspread tinted wings that fill the upper third of the canvas are related in their strong decorative power to Byzantine prototypes, such as the mural at Mount Athos (*Pl. 78B*), where, indeed, a variety of positions of wings can be seen. In a crystal vase, prominent in the right foreground, is a branch of the Burning Bush. The Lord announced to Moses out of a burning bush that he had been chosen to free Israel. In Orthodox iconography the symbolism was applied to Mary, as the instrument of God in the redemption of mankind. Panels showing her with the divine Infant in the midst of the bush, "burning but not consumed," hang in the gallery of San Giorgio dei Greci in Venice. A notable example is in the Metropolitan Church of Heraklion (Candia) (*Pl. 112B*), signed by Michele Damaskinos. The icon presents parallels between the Old and New Testaments, with an explanatory text above each scene. The Virgin and Child sit in the center, in a mandorla formed by the Burning Bush. Above her, God the Father delivers the Ten Commandments, while at the right the children of Israel are seen worshiping the Golden Calf, and in the opposite background the Betrayal of Christ is depicted. If El Greco had instruction in painting before he left Crete, it was probably in the monastery of St. Catherine in Candia. This monastery was dedicated to the cult of Catherine of Alexandria whose bones were deposited in the mother house at Mount Sinai, the site of Moses' vision. Thus El Greco's familiarity with this dual symbolism of the Old and New Testaments is fully explained.

In a similar canvas of the same subject by El Greco (*Pl. 78C*), clustered cherub heads edge a great triangle of light surrounding the Dove. Again Mary's left hand lies on the book and her right is raised in a gesture of listening or acceptance. Here, the angel's arms are folded across the breast in reverence and the lily is placed in a vase. El Greco's typical "backdrop" closes off the scene. When the canvas was restored, the entire right wing seems to have been painted out. A suggestion of the outline can be discovered if this picture is compared with the painting reproduced below it.

In an example apparently painted late in El Greco's lifetime (*Pl. 79B* and *C*), Mary is turned toward the angel, away from her prayer desk, and stands with extended arms and open hands in the typical Orthodox *theomeni,* or *orans,* position of prayer—a considerable metamorphosis from the master's Italianate period. A perfect illustration of the *theomeni* pose can be seen in the lunette above the door at the Torcello basilica (see *Pl. 43B*). Over her head, not a lacy mantilla-like veil but her mantle is draped. Both gesture and costume echo the Byzantine past, as can be seen in the mural at Mistra (*Pl. 79A*). There is lettering on the embroidered strip laid across her workbasket, defaced by repeated "restorations." It has been suggested that this is El Greco's signature in Greek. But it could be rather the Greek words *O Kheretismos,* the Annunciation, as it was the custom to label the scene in early mosaics. The angel stands firmly upon the cloud, with heavy Byzantine legs and feet. His right wing is turned forward and downward, in a manner reminiscent of the Kastoria mural shown in *Pl. 76A,* counterbalancing Mary's pose. The backdrop is enlivened by the blaze of light emanating from the Dove, and in the spray of flowers in the background the red and gold flames of the Burning Bush are indisputably recognizable.

The angelic choir which El Greco pictures in various compositions comes here to splendid climax. A recorder, virginals, a lute, a harp and a viol—note the medieval position of holding the bow—make up a charmingly balanced ensemble. One of the angels holds the book of music and seems to conduct; again the pages of the antiphonary are painted with the explicitness of the miniaturist. A brightly colored fan of wings crowns the scene. It is recorded that musicians played when El Greco dined. Some felt this to be ostentation, but the artist and philosopher was evidently also a connoisseur of music. A long musical tradition was part of his Cretan heritage. The eighth century Metropolitan of Gortyna, Andreas of Crete, is said to be the initiator of the musical canon (the nomenclature is derived from the Greek). There is a "Cretan" manner of Byzantine chant, which passed through Corfu and Zante along the Dalmatian coast and as far as Hungary. Crete led in the reform and codification of Orthodox Church music. Further, it should be recalled that the music at San Giorgio dei Greci was recommended to all visitors to Venice as especially rich and unusually varied.

El Greco's imagination created his own peculiar stage on which his religious scenes were set. Toward the end of his life, he eliminated all but the essential from his compositions. At the height of his performance, he cannot be confused with anyone else.

Of the several meals in which Christ participated, the Feast in the House of Simon and the Last Supper were favorite subjects of Renaissance and Baroque painters. The arrangement of the figures and the solution of the perspective offered a challenge to every master. Many Creto-Venetian painters, following the Italian example, placed the participants of these scenes at a long refectory table across the foreground, as is illustrated in a work by one of the anonymous painters in the gallery of San Giorgio dei Greci (*Pl. 80B*).

Although there is no record that El Greco ever painted a Last Supper, in his Feast in the

House of Simon (*Pl. 81C*) he uses certain traditional elements of that representation. The room is small and narrow. The background has strong architectural features and, through its flatness, harks back to mosaics and enamels where realistic perspective was not yet an ambition of the artist. Note the similarity of grouping in his Pentecost (see *Pl. 62B*). Kinship with a mural of the Last Supper from a monastery at Meteora, Greece, can be seen (*Pl. 80D*) in the architectural setting, the arrangement of the persons, the round table with its scattering of dishes. The Last Supper by the Cretan-born Damaskinos (*Pl. 80C*), in the Metropolitan Church in Heraklion (Candia), also contains parallels, but it is nearer to the anonymous panel in San Giorgio dei Greci and to Western taste than to the work which El Greco painted in Toledo. The two Creto-Venetian examples show a tendency to expand in space and place the participants of the meal comfortably. In El Greco's version, there is a drawing-together which is in the ancient Byzantine spirit. This is well illustrated at the center of an onyx paten representing the Last Supper, an exquisite jewel of enamelwork said to date from tenth century Constantinople (*Pl. 80A*). There, as in the Meteora mural, and in El Greco's painting, the heads are composed to form a circle. The Knights of the Holy Grail sit at a round table. The circle, as the symbol of eternity and perfect unity, is also the basis for the halo.

In Western paintings of the Feast in the House of Simon (scripturally it was merely a supper), the woman, usually interpreted as the Magdalene, anoints Christ's feet and dries them with her hair, following Luke 7:38, as is illustrated here by a relatively early Spanish painter (*Pl. 81B*), Pedro Berruguete (d. 1503), and by Tintoretto (*Pl. 81A*) a century later. El Greco has again selected a moment, if less dramatic, of deeper spiritual significance, drawing his text from Mark 14: "There came a woman having an alabaster box of ointment of spikenard, very precious; and she brake the box, and poured it on His head." Some were indignant at the waste, but Jesus said, "Let her alone . . . she hath wrought a good work . . . she is come aforehand to anoint my body to the burying." This episode is emphasized in the Orthodox Church as a prelude to the Passion.

In the Byzantine depiction of the lamentation over the body of Christ (*threnos* in Greek), the setting is usually the foot of the Cross. Mary appears in close unity with her dead Son, even though often surrounded by a number of other mourners. Early examples are preserved in Greek and Serbian Macedonia (*Pl. 82B* and *A*). The paintings in the Anargyri church of Kastoria are dated in the last decade of the eleventh century. According to an inscription on the narthex, the church of St. Panteleimon at Nerezi was decorated by order of Alexius Comnenus in 1164. Both murals apparently go back to the same prototype. Both project considerable drama. Mary is weighed down by the lifeless figure in her lap. She presses her cheek upon His with a vehemence full of poignancy. Her right hand can be seen supporting His head, while with her left arm she gathers the body to her. In the Kastoria example the gesture is clear and natural; in the Nerezi mural, Christ's left arm was redrawn in restoration and pulled awkwardly over hers.

The spirit of the scene and many details are the same in a Cretan icon painted several hundred years later (*Pl. 82D*), although here Mary sits at Christ's head. The prone figure of her Son determined the narrow rectangular shape of the composition, forcing the attendant figures into attitudes of prostration (see also *Pl. 28A*). The sorrowful bearing of the group as a whole augments the emotional effect of the central scene like the chorus of a Greek tragedy. The upraised arms of the woman on the left have the impact on the onlooker of the sound of a shriek. This manner of representation survived the Turkish centuries, and a panel of it exists in a private collection in Athens, signed "hand of Efstathios Mavroyiannis, June 30, 1823."

In a Creto-Venetian icon of the sixteenth century (*Pl. 82C*), the dead Christ lies weightless in the lap of His Mother as she sits in solitude at the foot of the Cross.[58] The style of her garments and their elaborate folds, as well as the gold background, are in Byzantine tradition. The anatomy of Christ's body is highly conventionalized, as are the craggy rocks on the landscape. The monogram of Jesus Christ is inscribed in Greek above His head.

Another panel from about the same period, today in Athens, shows many similarities (*Pl. 83A*). Mary's eyes have the triangles of deep mourning already seen. The background again is gold, with the identical Greek lettering. Although her garments show Western influence, the high lights and the whole pose keep the tradition. In these last two panels also, Mary enfolds her dead Son on her lap, her right hand, with the fingers clearly delineated, holding His head, while the left reaches across the body under His left arm.

El Greco combined the traditional and the sophistication of the sixteenth century with his individual talent in his rendition of The Lamentation (*Pl. 83C*). Mary's relationship to her Son is still the closed, inner circle. It is evident that nothing in the world exists for her except her sorrow. Her carriage, the poise of her head, even the shadowed eyes are taken from the Orthodox representation. Her fine right hand and fingers, painted with the usual mastery and expressiveness of the Cretan, hold the head, and the left arm reaches across the sagging body, under the left arm of Christ, exactly as in the Byzantine examples. The scene is laid, traditionally, at the foot of the Cross, as seldom in contemporary Western painting. One concession is made —the right hand of Christ rests on the ground, achieving a broader and more immediate rhythm in the composition. The delineation of the sagging body shows the same hand which painted that of Count Orgaz and numerous Crucifixions (see *Pls. 68A, 100, 101*).

The mourning figures of Mary Magdalene and Joseph of Arimathea are only auxiliaries to the personal drama so subjectively and movingly portrayed. If they are removed (*Pl. 83B*), the relationship of El Greco's composition to the Byzantine prototypes is more powerfully revealed. El Greco's Marys never wear the wimple of a nun.

Many Western painters have rendered the Pietà. Bassano's contemporary composition (*Pl. 83D*) demonstrates how far the Cretan stood from the fully Western spirit. Bassano's figures are loosely arranged as against the tight participation of all of El Greco's. In the Venetian we miss the tense physical and emotional relationship of Mother and Son; her hands hang limp and her eyes are closed in a swoon. While effectively grouped and well painted, the picture is without the warmth which permeates El Greco's canvas.

In early Italian paintings, Mary is crowned by God the Father alone. Later, with the growing Mariology, the Trinity came to participate in the act. El Greco painted The Coronation of the Virgin several times, in an oblong, sometimes oval form (*Pl. 85B*), showing Christ and God the Father holding the crown and the poised Dove also seeming to share in its support. God the Father is enveloped in the spacious white chiton of the antique Greek world, which loses itself downward into clouds, with a great mantle draped loosely back to free the arms. The sweeping folds of the garments and the surging clouds give buoyancy to the composition, and the arrangement in the oval with its marked foreshortening achieves a sense of unfathomable space. Both the Father and the Son hold a rod in their left hands, symbol of the final authority of justice. That "He shall rule with a rod of iron" is several times mentioned in the Bible.

The rod of chastisement is seldom represented so late in Western art. But an interesting holdover was observed by this writer at the Good Friday ceremonies in St. Peter in Rome, when a file of penitents, after depositing their offerings at a barrier, knelt before an aged priest enthroned upon a dais and received a tap from his long rod, in token of justice administered and forgiveness attained.

The rod, the white robe, and draped mantle are appurtenant to God the Father in the Orthodox representation of the Holy Liturgy (*Pl. 84A*). The phrase derives from the Greek, meaning "public service," and denotes the order of celebration and administration of the Eucharist. There are a number of liturgical groups in the Christian world, including the Syrian, Egyptian, Persian (Nestorian), Mozarabic. They were developed in the first centuries of Christianity, independent from the Byzantine and the Roman rites, and even today their sovereignty covers a larger territory and more believers than is generally known in the Western world. In this esoteric rendition—which is never portrayed in the West—God the Father is seen sitting in a position similar to that in El Greco's painting, with the fold of cloak across the shoulder and His long beard flowing over the white garment. His right hand is raised in the Orthodox gesture of blessing, His left hand holds the rod. Christ at His right in the robes of an Orthodox priest is celebrating the Mass before the ranks of the celestial hierarchy who frame the scene.

In the depiction of the Baptism of Christ, Italian painters since earliest times generally showed Jesus standing in the shallow water of the river Jordan, His head slightly bowed, and John the Baptist to the right in the picture, with a shell in his hand. A clear and poetic landscape formed the background, often containing reminiscences of the region where the painter was active (*Pl. 84C*). A work by a Spanish master, Juan de Juanes (1523–1579), who was popular when El Greco arrived in Spain, typifies the didactic interpretation of this scene in the spirit of the Counter Reformation (*Pl. 85C*). Jesus bends deep to show respect, His hands crossed on His breast in humility, as decreed by the Council of Trent. A thin reed cross in the hand of the Baptist emphasizes his identity. The river is expertly painted, showing a long perspective that leaves space for luminous sky, in which the Dove appears. Heaven is separated by large cumulus clouds, from which the figure of God the Father emerges, dressed in dark fitted garments, both hands outstretched. Since at the Baptism the divinity of Jesus was affirmed, the event had great significance for the theologians. And the Spanish painter has put the four doctors of the Latin Church into the picture—Gregory as pope, Augustine and Ambrose as bishops, and Jerome wearing ecclesiastical robes, all carrying the volumes of their theological dissertations. The kneeling priest at the left, with open book, might be the donor of the picture or the founder of the order that commissioned it. The five ecclesiastical figures outnumber—and outweigh—the transcendental ones. Unwittingly the painter has demonstrated that, in that period, it was all too often not the hierarchy who served the Church, but the reverse.

The Orthodox baptism even today is performed by full immersion. In Byzantine mosaics and paintings, Christ often stands up to His shoulders in the river. The Baptist is always placed on the left of the picture, his face raised to Heaven, whence issued the Dove and the Voice, and three or more ministering angels are grouped on the opposite shore (*Pl. 84D*). The name of Manuel Panselinos is associated with the murals in the Protaton church at Karyes, Mount Athos, but his activities in time and place are far from clarified. Some writers would place him at the beginning of the fourteenth century; others, more than two centuries later. The fact that he is mentioned first in a seventeenth century text, without exact dates, keeps him still in the realm of conjecture.

While the same arrangement is retained in the triptych assigned to El Greco's youth (*Pl. 84B*), in The Baptism of Christ painted in Toledo he followed Western practice as to the placement of the various figures (*Pl. 85A*). Here the river Jordan is no more than a pool. Christ stands on the shore, one knee resting on a rock, and bends His head only slightly; His attitude is one of prayer. John stands erect—no melodramatic gesture of obeisance. An angel between them helps hold up the swirling mantle, that takes on the shape of a mandorla. Again there is no attempt to suggest a surrounding landscape. The canvas has the spaceless perspective of El Greco's biblical scenes.

As so often, the celestial takes up a good half of the canvas. God the Father sits in the same white chiton that we have seen in the Coronation, His hand raised in benediction—a figure strongly reminiscent of the Holy Liturgy.

When the painting was transferred to the Prado Gallery, the margins on which El Greco is said customarily to have wiped his brushes were left exposed, showing strips of variegated color that often prove confusing to the spectator. This space was originally intended to be covered by the heavy architectural frame of the altar for which the picture was planned, so that the composition itself would not be encroached upon. As with nearly all large paintings of El Greco which were taken out of the massive and ornate retables for which they were composed, the effect is impeded. When they are hung at a different level than was intended, and placed on a wall, often uncongenial, or in some aseptic museum room, much of the painter's calculations of lighting, the adjustment of perspective, and the subtle harmony with the original frame are lost.

Closely related to the Karyes mural (see *Pl. 84D*) is the mosaic of the Baptism in St. Mark at Venice (*Pl. 86A*). The angled high lights and rugged outlines in the mosaic make for a striking design. Note the ax at the foot of the tree so clearly represented behind John. It is one of the Baptist's important appurtenances in Orthodox iconography, signifying his warning of the Last Judgment: "Now also the axe is laid unto the root of the trees: every tree therefore which bringeth not forth good fruit is hewn down, and cast into the fire" (Luke 3:9). The ax can be seen in a late icon in Venice (*Pl. 44B*) and also in El Greco's Baptism (*Pl. 85A*), between the Baptist's knee and the angel, although partly obscured by ununderstanding restoration. The cut tree appears also in *Pls. 66B* and *73A*, further proof of the philosophical depth of El Greco's symbolism.

John the Baptist, Prodromos or Forerunner, lanky and tall in his rough garment of camel's skin, is a fascinating figure. Both his parents came of priestly families, and as a lad he retired into the desert for contemplation. He is represented in art sometimes as a youth, even a child (see *Pl. 73C*), sometimes as a mature man. In the wilderness he experienced a revelation and began to preach the baptism of repentance. John denounced Herod, King of the Jews, who for a time was reluctant to act against him because of his great following. But at a birthday feast, Herod's stepdaughter Salome danced so ravishingly that the king promised her the fulfillment of any wish. At the instigation of her mother, Salome demanded the head of John, already prisoner of the king. Salome, balancing John's head in a platter on her own head in real oriental fashion, was depicted in numerous Byzantine mosaics and paintings.

The Orthodox representation of John the Baptist can be recognized in a large panel which has been transferred from an older location to the modern iconostasis of the Metropolitan's church at Kastoria, Greece (*Pl. 86B*). Jesus called him ". . . much more than a prophet. This is he of whom it is written, Behold, I send my messenger . . . which shall prepare thy way" (Luke 7:26). And as a messenger of the Lord he is an archangel and wears wings. The landscape is strongly conventionalized. At the foot of the saint in a platter lies his own head, in accord with the transcendental interpretation of his mission. In the icon, the whites and blues touched with red stand brilliant against the gold of the background.

The intellectual radiation of El Greco's St. John the Baptist (*Pl. 86C*), the gaunt height, the forlorn gaze of the deeply shadowed eyes, the gesture of the elongated fingers, all are closely related to the Byzantine model, as are also the unkempt curly hair, scrawny neck and prominent ears, the bony feet and conventionalized stance. Where the clouds part and an opening is formed, one might even imagine the shape of wings.

Portrayed by Titian, there stands a healthy, handsome, and reassuring figure (*Pl. 86D*). He shows nothing of the emaciation resulting from privations in the desert or of the exaltation of the Forerunner, of whom Flavius Josephus wrote: "His face was like a savage's . . . he wore animal hair on those parts of his body not covered by his own. He called on the Jews to claim their freedom . . . with an earnest exhortation to abandon their evil ways." For a Spanish example of the Baptist, see also *Pl. 52A*.

An art dealer who emigrated to England describes an episode from his childhood in a Russian village at the end of the nineteenth century. An itinerant painter persuaded his grandfather—a learned person with a long white beard, intelligent forehead, and lively eyes—to sit for a free portrait. Some years later, wandering about the fairground, the boy saw his grandfather's likeness on several icons which were laid out in a booth. Through priestly garb and other paraphernalia a composite picture had been achieved. It seems that in the Orthodox world the process was not unusual of revivifying a saintly figure by building it up from elements taken from life, while satisfying tradition also. The familiar features of more prominent saints were carried across the centuries by the Byzantine painter (as demonstrated here in *Pls. 86* and *88*) while for other figures, stock models sufficed.

El Greco also kept in his mental storehouse the salient characteristics of certain important saints; in other instances he seemingly applied the composite method. His Saint Jerome as cardinal, several times repeated, has always the same elongated head accented by a long beard (*Pl. 87D*). His hands rest on a book, symbol of his learning, as the translator of the Bible into Latin Vulgate. The head, rising from the stiff folds of his cardinal's garb, has little connection with the shoulders. The expression is vigorous and uncompromising, giving character to an otherwise conventional representation. Compare the pose and the robe in the portrait of Cardinal Tavera, see *Pl. 57B*. Both are striking and masterly works, even though permeated by an inscrutable, chilling atmosphere.

A detail of a mosaic of St. Gregory (*Pl. 87A*) from the mid-twelfth century, in the Cappella Palatina, Palermo, Sicily, has similar features. The thin straight nose, the balding forehead, the prominent ears, the beard jutting out at the sides and parted in the middle, the hollow cheeks, anatomically false but pictorially expressive—all show a relationship despite the restraint of the line in the mosaic as against the dexterous brushwork on the canvas. Ears are made prominent in Byzantine iconography, not in an attempt at realism but as a symbol that they had heard "the Word."[40]

In an icon of St. Basil (*Pl. 87B*) with its shining gold background we see another relative. It hangs today in the gallery of San Giorgio dei Greci in Venice, and is signed by Emmanuel Zane, also a Cretan, and dated 1656. Here the saint sits enthroned like a Byzantine emperor, the imperial cushion visible at the side.

In our survey of Macedonian mural painting, at the outskirts of the town of Kastoria we came to a rural shrine dedicated to the little known St. Nicholas of Traianou, standing in a neglected courtyard. We were all tired from clambering over the hilly countryside in hot weather all day long. But wooden shutters were quickly lifted off and we found ourselves among a series of life-sized saintly "witnesses" that lined the walls, lighted by the late afternoon sun. The mural was evidently the work of an itinerant painter. He could not have been well paid in early seventeenth century, when this territory had been for more than two centuries in Turkish hands. But the great tradition still held, and in places inspiration rose above workaday craftsmanship. For some the figure of St. Stelianos (*Pl. 87C*) might be less an Orthodox saint than an imaginary portrait of Zoroaster. The calligraphy of the mantle shows a swift, decisively working brush. Again the garments are depicted in the flat Byzantine manner, the gaze is directed at the onlooker, and the head seems to float above the collar with little anatomical connection.

Four different saints are grouped here, ranging in time from the mid-twelfth century to the late seventeenth, in provenience from Crete, Macedonia, Sicily, and Spain, depicted in mosaic, panel, mural, and canvas. What they have in common can be less defined in words than perceived by the eye.

St. Paul, Apostle to the Gentiles, who died around 67, was the first great Christian missionary and theologian. Born and bred a strict Jew, he was active in the persecution of early Christians and "consented to" the stoning of Stephen, the first martyr. Miraculously converted, he transferred his zeal to the cause of Christianity. It was Paul who distinguished clearly between the tenets of Judaism and the Gospel of Christ and who presented Christianity as the universal religion, not merely a Jewish sect. He was born in Tarsus in Cilicia (in present-day Turkey). Greek ideas abound in Paul's philosophy, and it is now accepted that he came to these through his familiarity with the Judaeo-Greek literature.

For a Greek and especially for a Cretan, such as was El Greco, the life and philosophy of Paul had many points of contact. Paul's activities in Thessaloniki and on the Greek mainland are recorded in his epistles; he traveled in the Near East and also westward into other Mediterranean countries. When El Greco portrays SS. Peter and Paul, the former is represented as a sturdy graybeard with no sharply drawn features, but Paul's are unmistakably marked, individual, portrait-like (*Pl. 89A*). Paul takes up most of the space, the books are before him, and he is the one who points to the Word (though the hand is badly redrawn), looking straight at the onlooker with a gesture as if expounding the text.

Another depiction (*Pl. 89B*), which El Greco painted several times, is still more significant. Not only are the drapery and hands characteristic, but the face also, in all examples, reveals the somewhat emaciated, intellectually keen, and spiritually ardent personality of the Apostle. Here Paul stands alone, the sword of his martyrdom in his right hand, and in the left the familiar device of El Greco—a slip of paper. In this case it is folded into a letter inscribed in cursive Greek script: "It was written to Titus, ordained the first bishop of the church of the Cretians, . . ." the words at the end of the Epistle to Titus. In Gortyna (Gortys), less than thirty miles south of Candia, are the ruins of the basilica on the site where Titus held services as the first bishop of Crete (see *Pl. 27B*). During an insurrection of the Cretans in 1363, the Venetian administration was driven off the island for three years, and Cretan public officials took over. The primacy of the Greek Orthodox Church was reaffirmed and, in place of the flag of St. Mark, which symbolized the Venetian overlords, the flag of St. Titus, original protector of the island, was raised. [54]

El Greco's figure of St. Paul is the image of Byzantine tradition. In the library of the monastery of Vatopedi at Mount Athos, a fragment of a mural with Peter and Paul is preserved (*Pl. 88B*), originally painted for the refectory. Some date it in the fourteenth century, some at the end of the twelfth. From a mosaic of the life of Paul in the twelfth century Cappella Palatina in Palermo, Sicily (*Pl. 88A*), we see him, blinded by the vision of the Lord on the road to Damascus, as he is led into the city. The long head and balding forehead, the black hair, hooked nose, and prominent ears are by now familiar from other examples. Paul is again recognizably portrayed in the mural of the Dormition of the Virgin in the Monastery of Mavriotissa at Kastoria, Greece, which is believed to date from the fifteenth century (see *Pl. 15C*). The detail reproduced here (*Pl. 88D*) shows him bending over the foot of Mary's bier. His features are unmistakable, as we follow his representations in mosaic, wall paintings, on icons and on canvas.

In a more or less contemporary painting by Ribera (*Pl. 88C*), we find the romantic, coloristic approach of a free artistic imagination, upon which the tradition of the saint's physical appearance has not been ingrained.

The Orthodox world does not have many women saints. Among them, a conspicuous role was given to St. Catherine of Alexandria, who died a martyr's death in 310. According to the legend, she preached against the worship of false gods, incurring the wrath of the emperor. Although fifty scholars disputed with her, she defended her position successfully and thus was made the patroness of philosophers. The emperor ordered her broken on the wheel, but the wheel itself was shattered by her touch. Finally she was beheaded, and her body was borne by angels to Mount Sinai. The importance to the Byzantine world of the monastery of Mount Sinai dedicated to St. Catherine was discussed in the first chapter. At El Greco's time, Cretan communities were still paying dues toward the support of the mother house. A well-to-do church and monastery dedicated to the saint was maintained in Candia, with a notable school of painting, whence icons and large panels were exported as far as Russia. In the West, five other Catherines were later elevated to sainthood—all of them of European origin, four Italian—so that the Alexandrian saint was somewhat eclipsed. Her attributes are a section of the spiked wheel and a sword in hand, the two instruments of her martyrdom. An open book symbolizes her wisdom, and sometimes a crowned head lies at her feet, representing the pagan emperor.[77]

El Greco's representation of St. Catherine of Alexandria has brought what was essential to identify her (*Pl. 91B*). She wears a many-pointed crown, as royal princess, and holds the sword and the palm of martyrdom. Only a small section of the spiked wheel is visible. Titian's St. Catherine (*Pl. 90A*), in contrast, is a Venetian lady, elegantly attired. She kneels on a fragment of the wheel, and the sword is laid against it. The scene is arranged in a spacious Renaissance hall with a Venetian landscape beyond the colonnade. A heavy silk curtain adds to the display of sumptuousness. On the base of the crucifix, perhaps a sarcophagus, is a relief of the Entombment. Such reliefs, in amplification of a subject, were favorite devices of Titian and his master Bellini; El Greco uses them in various versions of his Cleansing of the Temple (see *Pl. 75B*) and achieves somewhat the same purpose with the embroidered scenes on the saints' robes in The Burial of Count Orgaz (see *Pl. 68A*)—a clear influence from the Venetian.

In the depiction of St. Catherine by a Spanish contemporary, Sánchez Coello (*Pl. 90B*), her expression is that of a girl scout doing a noble deed. The sword, the palm of martyrdom, and the crown are there. Her dress is a strictly tailored all-covering costume of contemporary fashion. Under her feet lies the prostrate emperor. In the background, soldiers fall thunderstruck as two gigantic wheels burst asunder on touching her naked body. The Italian Enea Talpino, called Il Salmeggia, another contemporary, was not so prudish as his Spanish colleague and brought the nude saint into the foreground (*Pl. 90C*). These closely parallel representations of the saint's martyrdom can be traced to a painting by Giulio Romano reworked by Rubens.[64]

The cult of St. Catherine of Alexandria remained popular in the Orthodox world up to our day. The visitor in Heraklion (Candia) will find in the church of St. Matthew a number of panels transferred from defunct monasteries and churches and ranging from early strongly Orthodox "portraits" to nineteenth century sentimentalizations and souvenir prints for pilgrims. One of the finest and oldest of the panels (*Pl. 91A*) is said to have belonged to the monastery of St. Catherine of Sinai in Candia and to have been removed from it at the time of the Turkish conquest. The Cretan Catherine has imperial eagles embroidered in gold on her mantle and wears the many-pointed crown to show her royal descent. Note the large eyes, pensive tilt of the head, the long, nervous hands. The icon, which might date from late fifteenth century, is painted on fine canvas over wood upon which a thick gesso base was applied. But it shows signs of tampering. The Rococo touches in the upper corners and some of the text might be later additions. The cheap modern gray of the frame is out of keeping with the high degree of craftsmanship on the mantle. On close examination, it is obvious that the ermine edging of the cloak was put on later with quite another paint; the gold of the older design shines through underneath. The crucifix extending into the margin of the painting is an alien touch and might also have been introduced later.

Not only does El Greco show familiarity with Byzantine models in certain compositions but his manner of delineation also is based on a long Orthodox tradition. The Egyptians who, being near the Holy Land, became early converts to Christianity were known as Copts, derived from the Greek word for Egyptian. Coptic art, which flourished until the fourteenth century in Egypt, and included notable book illuminations, had antecedents that extended into the time of the Pharaohs; it shows strong Hellenistic influence also. The ancient custom of embalming the dead survived into the Christian centuries. Usually a portrait of the deceased was placed on top of the mummy bundle. Such panels were executed posthumously by a painter who often had not seen the subject, and thus they show stereotyped treatment.

In *Pls.* 92 and 93, portraits by El Greco are grouped with mummy panels from the second century, in one case a Byzantine glass painting from the fourth. The point of the comparison lies in the conventions of portrayal—the full face, the large luminous eyes with high lights, the shaded lids, the long straight nose with curling nostrils and the manner of connecting it with the eyebrow, the calligraphic flourish of the lips, the prominent ears, and a number of details which individual observation will add. A head of Fray Hortensio Félix Paravicino is paired with a second century panel (*Pl. 92B* and *A*). The illustration below (*D*) shows Jorge Manuel, the painter's son, as he appears in The Burial of Count Orgaz, beside him a boy's head from a mummy pack (*C*). El Greco has painted a decorative text on the kerchief of his son, with his signature and the year of the boy's birth (see also *Pl. 70B*). The boy in the Coptic panel wears a tunic decorated with lettering giving his age, parentage, and provenience. This embellishment of textiles with text was seen also in El Greco's Annunciation (see *Pl. 79C*).

On *Pl. 93A* a small portrait known as The Lady with Flower is paired with a mummy panel of the second century (*B*). Although the latter was mishandled, and the damage detracts from the expressive face, similarities can again be observed. A family portrait on glass of Byzantine workmanship dating from the fourth century, set into a reliquary cross (*Pl. 93D*), shows three figures, apparently mother, daughter, and son. It is remarkable to what degree it resembles the Coptic panels—although it was painted two centuries later—and also, to a certain extent, some of El Greco's heads (*Pl. 93C*).

One would think that portraits in mosaic would be affected by the limitations of the medium, resulting in a certain stiffness and coldness. Despite technical differences that can be discerned in the two, the saints in mosaic—one from eleventh century Thessaloniki (*Pl. 94A*) and the other from the mid-twelfth century Palermo (*Pl. 94C*)—show that profound characterization was possible. Between them (*B*) is reproduced a canvas thought to be El Greco's portrait, as suggested by an entry in the second inventory: *"retrato de mi padre."* Even with allowance for probable restorations, the characteristic shaping of the skull, the lines around the mouth, the formation of eyebrows and eyelids, the narrow nose, the unrealistic modeling of the cheeks, and the emphasis on the ears are recognizable here also.

The artist of those days was apparently at home in various media. It is now believed that the cartoons for the mosaics in Kariye Cami, notable for their superior quality and dating from the early fourteenth century, were designed by the same hand that painted the magnificent murals there (see *Pl. 75A*). The tradition of the mosaic maker was handed on to mural and icon painters. No claim is made that El Greco knew the parallels presented here. But he was a product of the same tradition, which was ingrained in him more deeply than the restless and eclectic West can fathom.

The hagiographer painted the Twelve Feasts of the Church as often as required. He also repeated Mother and Child, Christ in Benediction, Christ Crucified, and the Descent into Hell, to take their places on the iconostasis or in a home. Deviation from the established formula of the representation would have been resented and refused. It might be said that few changes in iconography are noticeable until prints began to circulate, starting new fashions.

Not only the representation of a subject was fixed by tradition: the place of the painting in the church where it was to be displayed and its relationship to the other subjects were also decreed. In the church of Anargyri, Kastoria, a thick layer of plaster crumbled from a pilaster, revealing an earlier mural of St. Nicholas (*Pl. 95C*). Both inscriptions remain to dispel any doubt as to the saint's identity. Compare the mural with the mosaic above (*Pl. 94C*).

El Greco and his studio painted St. Francis in various poses again and again—according to one source, more than a hundred times. If a prospective client preferred the picture of St. Francis receiving the Stigmata (*Pl. 95A*) to St. Francis in Meditation, shown to him in El Greco's stockroom of models, the painter's studio would furnish it as selected. It meant earning a living by satisfying a customer. A page of an authoritative book on El Greco (*Pl. 95B*) shows eleven surviving examples of the same rendition. Even insignificant details are identical. It is the mark of the hagiographer that the image retained its vigor and spontaneity.

St. Francis was one of the very few later saints whom the Cretans venerated. Pacheco praises El Greco for his appealing portrayal, saying that his representation conformed best to how history describes the saint. Practically all canvases of this subject carry a label with El Greco's signature in Greek; where it is not visible, it was most probably covered by some "restorer," or the paint was so flaked that it disappeared when the canvas was relined. The signing of these repetitions gave them augmented value.

The lines of the aureole and certain shapes in the Byzantine landscape were used to set off one scene from another. The Nativity as represented in a twelfth century mosaic in Palermo (*Pl. 96B*) shows Mary resting on light-colored material in a grotto, the edge of which forms a third, lighter-colored frame, suggesting a triple mandorla. (In the Holy Land a cave served as stable.) A depiction of the same subject—not in mosaic or from a royal city but in a mural in a small town in Yugoslav Macedonia—shows again the aureole and the holy grotto as standard devices to separate and emphasize (*Pl. 96A*).

An illuminated manuscript at Mount Athos portrays St. John the Evangelist Dictating the Gospel to Prochorus, his amanuensis (*Pl. 96C*). Here the disciple (who, with Stephen, was one of the first deacons to be consecrated) is framed against the hillside, while the Evangelist stands free against the open sky. In an icon of the same subject in San Giorgio dei Greci, Venice (*Pl. 97B*), both are enclosed in a grotto. A basket with rolls of parchment hangs on the wall. Prochorus has just inscribed in Greek the first words of The Gospel According to St. John. The scroll, apparently laid out to dry, seems to contain phrases from the Revelation. The icon, painted on panel covered with canvas, is dated 1602 and signed Emmanuel Lambardos, who is known to have assisted in decorating the church of San Giorgio dei Greci. The Cretan Lambardos obviously kept to his native tradition, although he had ample opportunity to study the finest of Venetian style. Although in the four centuries intervening, the scene went through many changes, the spiritual content is preserved. In both manuscript and icon, John turns his head away from his amanuensis and toward the divine Hand which seems to be guiding him.

Two other applications of the grotto are reproduced here (*Pl. 97A*) from the exterior murals at Siatista, Macedonia (see also *Pl. 11C*). At the left, Anthony the Abbott discourses with the hermit Paul of Thebes. Note the raven carrying food, as to the prophet Elijah. Anthony, a hermit of upper Egypt in early fourth century, was one of the first to gather fellow anchorites into loose communities, forerunners of monastic life. He visited and comforted the ancient hermit and, returning later (right), he found him dead, mourned by wild animals. The mural as a medium, whether executed on a wet wall (fresco) or a dry surface (secco), gives the painter greater freedom than the exacting mosaic or the icon with its limited size. Further, the mural painter, working fast, had to adapt his scheme to varying and larger surfaces, and took liberties, especially in details. Here the grotto has a stalactite-like framing; but the dark opening still serves to set off the protagonists. The rigidity of the tradition is loosened, but the distance to naturalism is still great. Vegetation is used to liven the background and fill space, but it is still highly conventionalized. The mural, dated 1611, was executed by an itinerant painter schooled at Mount Athos; it is monotone in coloring and rather "bookish" in effect.

The aureole is often suggested by El Greco in light or shadow or in the outline of a rock, such as frames the figure of Christ on the Mount of Olives (see *Pl. 73A*). Grottoes and compartments of light and clouds are part of the composition in The Adoration of the Holy Name and The Burial of Count Orgaz (see *Pls. 64B* and *68A*). The grotto shape is also present in El Greco's St. Francis in Ecstacy (*Pl. 97C*), formed by the characteristic clouds that are lined with an eerie light and swirl across the background.[44] In places the clouds enveloping the saint appear even farther in the forefront than the figure itself, giving still more the effect of a grotto. Another relationship with the Macedonian mural can be detected in the wavy, uneven framing of the protagonist.

The Trinity, also called The Throne of Mercy, is among the few subjects that El Greco appears to have rendered only once (*Pl. 98B*). It was commissioned in the first years of his residence in Spain. The crucified Christ lies in the lap of the Father, as above them hovers the Dove. The sagging line of the lifeless body is strongly reminiscent of that in The Lamentation (see *Pl. 83C*). Stalwart angels frame the composition into a well-knit unit. This is one of the earliest instances in which El Greco essays to bring a figure (the archangel with back turned, on the left) far into the foreground by means of sheer color. An anonymous Spanish painter's work from the mid-sixteenth century (*Pl. 98C*) uses the same elements with a few more angels, some carrying symbols of the Passion.

The representation of the Throne of Mercy appears to be a Western invention, and Dürer's handling of the theme in a woodcut set the model for subsequent painters (*Pl. 98A*). It is most probable that El Greco had one of Dürer's widely popular prints in his collection. At any rate there are many similarities in his work. But in one detail, which has not been previously remarked upon, the Cretan does not follow the German master. His God the Father does not wear the papal tiara, prominent in both the Dürer prototype and the Spanish painting.

The word "tiara" is derived from the Greek, designating a tall peaked Persian cap which, when worn by kings, was encircled with a crown. The papal tiara with its triple crowns, symbolizing the Trinity and the three estates of the Kingdom of God, did not reach its present form until the early fourteenth century.[7] It is believed that the Van Eyck brothers of the early fifteenth century were among the first to apply it to the figure of God the Father, and the well-known woodcut of Dürer disseminated the representation. Luis Tristán, one of the very few Spaniards who is known to have worked in the studio of El Greco, painted a Throne of Mercy obviously influenced by that of his master (*Pl. 98D*). His God the Father is bareheaded; his triangular halo is drawn with a single line.

In El Greco's painting, however, God the Father, recalling Jehovah of the Old Testament, wears the headgear of a Jewish high priest. No other instance, contemporary or later, is known to this author. Blue and gold and white ("fine linen") predominate in the coloring of the garments, as prescribed for the robes of Aaron, the first high priest of the Jews, in Exodus 28. That El Greco well knew what he was painting is proven by his unfinished work The Marriage of the Virgin (*Pl. 99A*), executed at the very end of his life, in which the Jewish high priest officiates in exactly the same headgear. This type of headgear, ancestor to the bishop's miter, appears all through Renaissance and Baroque times in the painting of scenes laid in the Jewish Temple, such as the Presentation, the Circumcision, the Purification. It is found in the works of Tintoretto, Veronese, Lorenzo Lotto, Palma Vecchio, Federigo Barocci—to mention only some who lived in El Greco's time. In Ribera's St. Simeon with the Christ Child (*Pl. 99B*), the headdress pictured is absolutely traditional, even to the gold band inscribed in Hebrew. It occurs frequently also in paintings by the Bassano family (see *Pl. 75D*) whose work was often confused with El Greco's, and appears in a canvas (*Pl. 99C*) once ascribed to the Cretan but now thought to be by Francesco Montemezzano, active at the end of the sixteenth century, who combined popular manners in his compositions.

El Greco in his Throne of Mercy has created a painting which was apparently satisfactory to the Western eye, although he was never to repeat it. But deeply interested, as is evidenced by his library, in the spiritual sources of Christianity, he demonstratively took a position for the ancient biblical tradition when he could have remained on neutral ground. Nor did he place the doge's *corno*, the Spanish crown, and the papal tiara on the ground to identify the three protagonists in his Adoration of the Holy Name (*Pl. 64B*), as Tintoretto and others did in similar commemorative scenes.

In painting the Crucifixion, El Greco never emphasized the drama, the historical pageantry of the scene. In a few cases, Mary and the youthful John stand together or on either side of the Cross; donors are seldom included. The body of the Crucified is sometimes straight, sometimes slightly twisted. Whether He looks down with half-open eyes or heavenward, He is the Living Christ, symbol in Byzantine tradition of the conscious sacrifice.[23] The inscription at the top of the Cross, "Jesus of Nazareth the King of the Jews," is always given in Hebrew, Greek and Latin, as both Luke and John record. Flavius Josephus mentions the trilingual practice in Palestine. This label in three languages in precise and articulate script is one of the sure signs of El Greco's hand.

Of the sixteen or so renditions of the Crucifixion by El Greco or his studio, some ten or eleven have only a small-scale landscape beyond the Cross. Even before Dürer, landscape for its own sake was executed by Flemish and Italian painters. These were successful attempts at realistic recording. In a number of works by Venetian masters, notably portraits, through a window or beyond a balcony a vista opens onto the Veneto mainland. El Greco's landscapes carry his characteristic stamp. He uses them at the foot of a Crucifix and as a base out of which rise his tall, slender saints; a few canvases of anomalous purpose are extant, without central figures. It is interesting to observe how El Greco manipulated the various details.

Titian is known to have delivered a canvas of Christ Crucified to Philip II, which is in the monastery of the Escorial. Recently, a small portable panel of the subject was discovered in the rooms of the Spanish monarch, encased in a leather binding of Persian style fashionable in Venice in the sixteenth century.[98] An engraving of it, signed by Giulio Bonasone, identifies the painting as the work of Titian. This is dated 1563, coinciding with El Greco's alleged Venetian stay. He easily could have acquired a copy, thus having a prototype for later work. It is known that when the great Venetian master left his studio, his pupils immediately started to copy what work of his lay about.

In Titian's canvas (*Pl. 100B*) the mound of Golgotha is visible, and the skull which gave the place its name lies at the foot of the Cross. The body of Jesus hangs lifeless, with drooping head. The inscription is in Latin only: INRI. In the background (left) the company of Roman soldiers can be seen withdrawing along a winding road toward a castle on the bluff, followed by two riders—on a light and a dark horse—bearing a standard. A single footsoldier brings up the rear. To the right, the women depart toward a city impressive with turreted towers, a large domed structure, and outlying fortifications.

El Greco's Crucifix similarly occupies the entire height of his canvases. In one case (*Pl. 100A*) the Virgin and John stand together on the left. Two riders with a standard can be seen on the winding road (right), preceded by a man on a galloping horse and followed by two gesticulating figures on foot. The city in the distance is characterized by a tall spire and fortress-like walls.

There are no large attendant figures in another representation (*Pl. 100C*), and the landscape with towers and several domed buildings spreads across the canvas. The three riders with their standard are placed at the right. El Greco's fine calligraphy records the inscription in three languages.

In a canvas reproduced on *Pl. 101C,* the pose of Christ is the same and the landscape has similar elements, although somewhat differently grouped. The city with spires and dome is far in the distance, though clear. The grove of trees takes a more prominent place.

In another rendition (*Pl. 101A*) Christ's figure is unchanged, but as background a composite picture of Toledo appears. The spire has the vertical accents of the city's Gothic cathedral, and the craggy, rearing walls suggest the Alcázar. The standard bearers, on their light and dark horses, and other miniature figures are included. The buildings break off abruptly at the cross, and at the right we see the Alcántara Bridge with a long low barracks-like structure beside it. Still another rendition (*Pl. 101B*) presents the figure of Christ in a different pose, but the landscape is practically the same, with still more small figures.

A distinguished scholar, with profound knowledge of El Greco's work, has suggested that the dome so prominent in these landscape details might be the dome of the Mozarabic chapel of the cathedral at Toledo.[110] The chapel was under construction for several decades, and Jorge Manuel worked on it; it was finished after El Greco's death. Often when an addition to a building is contemplated, a drawing is available before the work itself is concluded. Since the dome was a family project, it could have been included in a painting before it really appeared on the skyline. On the other hand, the cupola in the painting is much larger in its proportions, more like the dome in Titian's landscape than like that of the Mozarabic chapel, as a recent photograph shows (see *Pl. 50A*). Further, the three-language inscriptions are all in the elegant, mature, flowing script of the father, quite different from the less expert hand of the son.

When El Greco's panorama in the Plan of Toledo (*Pl. 103B*) is compared with an engraving of the city made about 1630 and a very recent photograph (*Pl. 102*), it is clear that he could be topographically accurate when he wished. The painting was executed for the new Tavera Hospital which lies outside the city gate, the Puerta de Visagra. Jorge Manuel drew the admirable plan in the foreground and wrote the accompanying text, which explains that the hospital was brought forward in the picture and turned to face the onlooker, as otherwise part of the city view would have been blocked.

Toledo is again presented with recognizable fidelity in El Greco's Laocoön (*Pl. 103A*)—the only mythological subject essayed by the painter. While the church spires are omitted from a view intended to represent prehistoric Troy, such topographical details as the double-headed eagle on the Puerta de Visagra in the center are distinct.

Notable features of the Toledo skyline appear on the canvas known as The View of Toledo (*Pl. 104A*), sometimes called "Toledo in Storm" because of its dramatic sky, although any of the skies of the crucifixions and even those in the panorama and the Laocoön are scarcely less dramatic. A writer on art has declared most recently that The View of Toledo is neither a romantic landscape nor a panorama, neither Toledo in Storm nor Toledo in Thunderstorm—but Toledo in Heat Lightning; it stands for the physiognomy of Heaven and Earth; it is symbolic of Eternity and also of the cosmos; it is, finally, an apocalyptic, chiliastic manifestation.[101] If the reader turns to *Pl. 107B,* he can see that El Greco's sky even on a canvas of a few inches' span has identical tonalities of light and dark.

In his View of Toledo, the painter has exaggerated the height of the hill, pulled together certain elements of the topography, redistributed and emphasized others. The Alcántara Bridge is clearly recognizable, and the Castillo de San Servando on the hill above it, which El Greco included in only a few instances. On the summit rises the Alcázar, the royal palace. The prominent spire was identified as that of the cathedral, though the actual position of the two buildings is reversed. Curiously, this View of Toledo shows less than half of the city. At the end of the Alcázar the panorama stops abruptly. The descending curve of the skyline toward the right, so clearly continued in The Laocoön and the city plan, is cut off. The progression of lozenge-shaped elements, so characteristic in El Greco's work, is arrested. Tiny figures are sprinkled about in the water and on the banks—even a rider, near the great rock in the river bed. Above the embankment-supported shore at the right, parts of a trough-like wooden structure are visible.

Practically the same landscape, even to the water trough, appears in the painting of St. Joseph and the Christ Child, although cut into two parts by the figures (*Pl. 104B*). The full painting is reproduced on *Pl. 112F*. The detail reveals the ragged and patched state to which some of El Greco's canvases were allowed to deteriorate.

In the landscape detail from St. Martin and the Beggar (*Pl. 106B*), nothing of the houses of Toledo is seen. But the bridge of Alcántara and the castle of San Servando can be identified. The contraption under the left forefoot of the white horse, a wheel outlined with white high lights and attached to a trough-like sluice, makes the canvas a record of especial interest. This may be an allusion to the apparatus built in 1568 to carry the water of the Tagus up to the city on the height. It was the work of Giovanni Turriano (born in Cremona in 1501, died in Toledo 1575) who is known in Spain as Juanelo de la Torre. He was a watchmaker, architect, and mechanical engineer, a companion of Charles V in his retirement at Yuste; for this monarch, with his lively intellect, also had an interest in clocks and other mechanical devices. Turriano was a celebrated personality in Spain in his time. A bust of him survives and also a commemorative medal struck in his honor. Various poets of the epoch lauded his many talents. His water-lifting apparatus was installed near the Alcántara Bridge. Cervantes and other contemporary writers mention it as a rare attraction of Toledo. And El Greco apparently found it a picturesque and characteristic addition to the riverscape, for he included it in several of his paintings with the bridge. (See also *Pl. 104B,* right.) It was not until a century later that in France Louis XIV had something similar constructed, when he had another pleasure palace erected, at Marly near the Seine. A Belgian engineer, Arnold Deville, was called in to solve the mechanical problem of supplying water for the play of fountains. Today, when credit is so often reluctantly given to a foreigner, it is worth mentioning that the work was done in Spain by an Italian, in France by a Belgian.

Turriano's apparatus, however, was costly and inefficient and it was replaced by a sturdier one. The same artist who sketched a panorama of the city, already seen, left an engraving in which the bridge and castle are featured (*Pl. 105A*). Beyond the bridge a building at the river level can be seen, connected with another on the hill by a construction with five roofs like the pleats of an accordion. This was the second apparatus designed to lift the water of the Tagus for use in the city.

Details of Toledo's landscape are rearranged to fill the left background of El Greco's painting of St. James the Great (*Pl. 107A*). The spire with a small dome before it is here placed at the right of the Alcázar. On the opposite side of the saint is a glade, the tree trunks delineated by characteristic wavering curves. Buildings are seen only in the very distant background in the painting of St. Andrew (*Pl. 107C*), without any details which would make them clearly identifiable in the mild landscape. In both paintings the flap-like hang of the clothing is identical, as is the highly Byzantine stance.

Two lonely trees appear on the crest of El Greco's hill. Nowhere are they so marked as in a small landscape, only 14 inches high by 6⅜ wide (*Pl. 107B*). El Greco's brush stroke is by now familiar, as are the lozenge shapes, the strong contrast of light and dark which he worked into his skies, with little bearing on actual weather. These are evidently standard props in his landscapes, which, with other details, he repeated again and again, with the unconcern of the hagiographer who was not striving to produce an "original" composition for each occasion.

Most of El Greco's views of Toledo deviate strongly from the photographic reality. He selected elements of the scene, inserting and interchanging details in the interest of the total effect. These observations apply also to his View of Toledo, with its dramatization into the vertical, in which the landscape is not subordinated to a larger figural composition. Here the same lack of focus can be observed as in the secondary scenes. His brush stroke in the treatment of a landscape is the same, whether for a large or for a small canvas, whether for a landscape alone or as background at the foot of the Cross or behind a saintly figure. When a detail from the View of Toledo is compared with one from a Crucifixion (*Pl. 105B* and *C*), the similar approach to landscape as such becomes evident. Not too different is the impressionistic manner in which Titian rendered a panorama of Venice in an allegorical composition (*Pl. 39B*), also as an auxiliary detail.

The View of Toledo was discovered by Manuel Cossío in the dark corridor of the apartment of two old ladies in Madrid who were related to various high ecclesiastics and in whose family the portrait of the Grand Inquisitor came down (see *Pl. 57C*). Cossío called their attention to the authorship of the smaller painting, and made the first photograph for his monograph. The picture is of unusual size and shape and is painted very thinly on a loosely woven canvas. One wonders whether it was not executed for some temporary construction, eventually in combination with another, complementary landscape. Various canvases, elegantly framed, are hanging nowadays in distinguished collections, of which few spectators know that they are not complete paintings but fragments—representative and expressive enough, nevertheless, to justify their placement on the walls.

For the visits of royalty to their cities, the professions erected triumphal arches, vying with one another in the splendor of their execution. When Philip II visited Lisbon, arches are recorded from the silversmiths, merchants, candlemakers, jewelers, money-changers, tailors, painters, and some religious guilds. The Flemings and the Italians, even the German and English residents of Lisbon, were represented with arches.[113]

Two instances are recorded in which El Greco and his studio executed temporary constructions and furnished the decorations. The first was in 1587 when the bones of St. Leocadia were returned to Toledo. Up to the mid-seventeenth century (1643) comparatively few saints received formal canonization from Rome; the approval of the local bishop was considered sufficient. For this reason some saints are popular in one country who are practically unknown in another. Leocadia, born of a Toledan family, died a martyr's death in the third century. The return of her remains to her native city occasioned great solemnities. Philip II, King of Spain, and his family honored the Castilian town with their presence. The houses were hung with colorful rugs and tapestries, and the churches displayed their treasures. Some four years later a book was published describing the ceremonies in detail.[79] The procession entered the city by way of the Puerta de Visagra, accompanied by personages of high rank, singing motets in praise of the saint. A Doric monument stood within the gate and triumphal arches decorated the route of the procession. These constructions were built on solid wooden framework covered with thin boarding or similar material and then painted, often to imitate marble, silver, bronze. Architectural elements predominated, ornate portals, columns and pediments, obelisks and finials, interspersed with pictures and statues that were sometimes real, sometimes simulated in paint. Saints and allegorical subjects were presented, with various heraldic emblems. At the entrance of the cathedral stood a marvelous portico which alone had cost some seven thousand ducats. "After motets and praises and reverence" the body was carried inside, "and afterwards was great celebration in dancing and music."

The book, written by a Jesuit, contains nearly three hundred pages listing saints, royalty, ecclesiastical and secular potentates, and leaders of the procession. It details the decorations and even mentions that Greek inscriptions, as well as Latin and Spanish, were applied on some of the structures. In an addenda are included sonnets, epigrams, and other eulogies written for the occasion. But *not a single line* records the artists and craftsmen who created the pomp against which the elite could glitter.

The second occasion for which El Greco agreed to erect a temporary construction is recorded in a contract, signed by him and his son, to execute a catafalque for memorial services held in the Toledan cathedral in honor of Queen Margarita, the wife of Philip III, who died in 1611. It was specified that the catafalque, designed to stand in the crossing, was to be 110 Spanish feet high and fourteen feet wide, in carved and painted wood to simulate stone.[106] It contained allegorical statues, portraits of kings, coats of arms, amid an impressive architectural build-up of Ionic order, and was topped by a dome and lantern with an angel ten feet high holding the imperial crown. The memorial service in the cathedral of Toledo was set for the 19th of December, and the catafalque was dismantled by the 24th, so that the entire work was on display no longer than five days. As a consequence of an "incident of protocol" between the king and the municipality of Toledo, no one of the royal family came to take part in the ceremony.

In a sonnet eulogizing El Greco, Paravicino writes of the structure as if it were of marble. But it is generally accepted that it was made of wood and was mainly the work of Jorge Manuel. In this connection, it is revealing to point out that a late rendition of the Cleansing of the Temple from El Greco's studio (*Pl. 112G*) is the only one in which the engaging Venetian perspective is replaced by a tall architectural build-up, reminiscent of a catafalque, with an obelisk as finial. This is also the only late rendition of the subject in which the two symbolic reliefs are omitted.

In the second inventory of El Greco's estate, made by Jorge Manuel seven years after his father's death, there are certain entries: "Un lienzo grande blanco y negro de los arcos," also, "Un lienzo grande de los arcos fingido de bronce, de quando Sª Leocadia saliò del sepulcro"—that is, a large canvas in white and black for the arches, and a large canvas imitating bronze, of when St. Leocadia came forth from the tomb (and appeared to St. Ildefonso). Five other canvases "for the arches" are listed, as well as a "fable" or "legend" and a painted royal coat of arms which might well have served the same occasion. Thus, thirty-four years after the solemnities for Leocadia, and nearly a decade since his father's death, mementos of these ceremonies still lay around the studio.

There are six further entries in the inventory of 1621, listing *paises,* or landscapes, of which three are specified as "of Toledo." These paintings must have represented little value, either because of their execution or because of their condition. Two landscapes were given by Jorge Manuel to the Tavera Hospital, and when El Greco's Baptism of Christ there was restored, around 1660, the two landscapes were attached to the bottom of the large canvas and painted over "to represent the river." [106] In view of El Greco's apparent indifference to repetitions, and his recorded participation in the design and execution of triumphal arches and at least one catafalque, it would not seem impossible that some of the canvases of unusual shape or small size might have been intended as models for the atelier or have found their first application in temporary constructions. All such provisory structures had to be strongest at the base, which was the most exposed to pressure and the jostling of masses. The real decorative elements were placed above eye level to be visible to all. The bottom sections had to be kept open, so that the craftsmen in decorating the upper parts could climb inside on ladders or ramps; at the very end, these utilitarian parts were camouflaged with some artistic covering.

No drawing or print survives either of the arch or of the catafalque for which El Greco and his son contracted, but others from about the same period give an idea of the general design. The drafting was put in the hands of well-known artists. When Henry III, King of France, visited Venice in 1574, he was honored by triumphal arches designed by Palladio and painted by Tintoretto. Rubens designed a triumphal arch for a projected visit to the Netherlands of Philip IV, son of Philip III and the deceased Margarita mentioned above (*Pl. 109A*). After Philip's death, elaborate memorial services were held even in the far reaches of his colonial empire. A contemporary woodcut shows the catafalque erected in the cathedral of the Mexican capital (*Pl. 108A*). Note the paintings around the base. For the canonization in 1671 of Ferdinand III, thirteenth century King of Castile, who recaptured Seville from the Moslems, a festive monument was erected in the cathedral of that city. The engraving (*Pl. 108B*), with its imposing display of arts and crafts, probably presents an apotheosis rather than a record of actuality.

The custom of erecting triumphal arches goes back to antiquity and survives even into our present century. Such constructions were sometimes transformed later into permanent monuments. An impressive arch on Madison Square in New York to honor the home-coming troops of World War I has vanished (*Pl. 109C*), while the arch at Washington Square, also first made of perishable material, is now a solid masonry structure (*Pl. 109B*).

In the Greek classical world, vases were signed as early as the seventh century before Christ, the names always accompanied by words signifying "made" or "painted." Double signatures indicate that the potter and the painter were two different craftsmen:

"Ergotimos made me
Klitias painted me"

Excavations at the workshop of Phidias in the Peloponnesus uncovered a broken cup of the period (fifth century B.C.) meticulously incised "I belong to Phidias." From Attica alone, more than a hundred vase painters' and potters' names are known. Later, stamps were also used to a similar purpose on drinking cups, saucers, and bowls. Pottery with red figures on a black background and with black figures on a red ground most frequently carried the signatures of potters and painters, since these pieces were made also for export to Italy, to Sicily, and other parts of the Mediterranean world. Signatures are still frequent on the products of folk art—majolica, wood carving, embroidery. The epics, legends, and fables preserved by the oral tradition of repeated recitation end often with a rhyme or phrase known in Greece as the "seal," which indicates whence the tale was derived and gives the name and home of the singer with the prayer, "Remember him." As already mentioned, in the great cisterns of Constantinople, a number of which are still in use, many of the bricks bear a date of the fifth and sixth centuries of our era stamped upon them, and the upper stone courses show the monograms of Byzantine masons.

The practice of signing a work of art, taken up in the Renaissance, is a harking back to the classic, as well as the mark of a dawning individual self-consciousness, as is so often stated. In sixteenth century Venice, where the population was very art conscious, the great masters seldom signed a canvas commissioned in their own city. But when a work was ordered for export abroad, as so often in the case of Titian for his noble patrons, the signature lent the necessary authenticity. Some Western artists, such as the Italian Andrea Mantegna (1431–1506), occasionally signed in Greek to show their erudition, and in the classicizing style of the early nineteenth century certain painters and sculptors revived the custom.

Byzantine icon and mural painters were wont to place inscriptions, their signatures, and sometimes the date, on a painted label or cartouche at the base of their work. A small chapel in the region of Sfakion, Crete (see *Pl. 32B*), has the date and the painter's name recorded in this manner.

El Greco nearly always signed his work, placing his name on either the background or the landscape of a painting or conspicuously on a painted label. Besides the full name Domenikos Theotokopoulos, he usually added the Greek word *epoie*— "made" or "did"—the identical phrase found on the black-and-red vases of classical Greece. Frequently the word *kres* appears, the literary Greek term for "Cretan." Individually characteristic is the painted label which he places like a calling card at the foot of the Grand Inquisitor (see *Pl. 57C*). And still more subjective is the inscription with the phrase "I made it" and the child's birth date on the folded kerchief in The Burial of Count Orgaz (see *Pl. 70B*). The paper with Greek text addressed to Titus which he placed in the hand of his St. Paul is revealing of his spiritual loyalty (see *Pl. 89B*). The significance of the inscription on his crucifixions, without exception trilingual, has already been mentioned, as well as the unique instance in which the slip of paper with his full autogram is held up by the serpent (*Pl. 111E*). His signature of the Assumption of the Virgin, now in the Chicago Art Institute (*Pl. 110B*, bottom), reads, after his name, "he who has manifested it in [the year] 1577." A highly unconventional place for a signature is the forehead of the lion, upon which he inscribed his monogram, in the painting of the Virgin with Two Women Saints now in the National Gallery of Art, Washington, D. C. The lion as symbol of courage and character is well known.

No Western painter, to this writer's knowledge, has put his signature on the Cross itself, as did El Greco (*Pl. 111D*). This also might indicate a Byzantine custom. It is paralleled in a standard, preserved in Venice (*Pl. 111A* and *C*), which flew from the flagship of Francesco Morosini (1618–1694), one of the greatest naval commanders of his time. Having repeatedly proved victorious over the Turks, he was appointed to the defense of Crete, but after eighteen months of siege was forced to surrender to save the surviving inhabitants of the island. At the age of seventy he was elected doge. When five years later he again took command of the Venetian forces, the Turks, upon hearing that he had been called out against them, withdrew.

The standard, painted on canvas in bright colors with much gold and red, shows Christ on the Cross, and, kneeling beside it, a saint in bishop's robes decorated with crosses in the Orthodox manner. His hands are raised in the Greek *theomeni* attitude of prayer. The open book before him suggests that this is St. Mark the Evangelist, the protector of the republic. At the left, the winged lion representing Venice stands with one paw placed on the coat of arms of the Morosinis and the other grasping the Cross. Above him, seeming to rest on his wings, is a version of the Virgin and Child known in Italy as Madonna del Soccorso (Our Lady of Perpetual Help). This representation goes back into early Byzantine times when the original, a miraculous icon, was brought from Jerusalem to Constantinople.[28] Venerated there as one of the holiest treasures, the Hodegetria was copied again and again. In Carpaccio's Legend of St. Ursula, in a typical fifteenth century room, the same version of Virgin and Child hangs on the wall. It became popular in many parts of the West—indeed, as far as Bolivia, where in colored lithographs it still attracts worshipers. On each side of the Morosini standard, the busts of Orthodox and Roman Catholic saints form a vertical frame, in the manner of a Tree of Jesse—an iconographical device not often encountered so late in Western art. The Morosini standard, carrying the Hodegetria, the Greek crosses, and the various saints, is another proof of how long the Venetians clung to Byzantine tradition.

At the foot of the Cross, a damaged signature appears in Greek letters: *Bi . . . tor, B* and *V* being interchangeable in Greek, this might mean Victor. There was a priest and painter named Victor in the Venetian Greek colony, and in the collection of San Giorgio dei Greci there are several paintings signed and dated by him between 1651 and 1674, coinciding with Morosini's career. One panel represents the Tree of Jesse, which the painter seemingly favored; another, representing the Trinity, is framed with saints in a manner similar to that on the standard. When we pointed out the fragmentary Greek lettering on the Cross, the curator of the museum brushed it aside with complete indifference. As long as the Western world, and particularly Venetian scholars, whose past is steeped in the Byzantine, continue to underplay that tradition, the humanistic panorama of Western civilization will remain grossly incomplete.

Hagiographers at the time of El Greco often signed their works in Greek, prefixing their baptismal names with "creation," "poem," "hand." A number of paintings are extant with the signature in Greek, "hand [of] Domenikos." The name Domenikos is the Latinized form of Kyriakos; both comprise the word for God. By the sixteenth century the Venetian possessions were considerably Latinized, and baptismal names were made to conform more or less to the customs of the Venetian overlords—a general practice when the rulers' language differs from that of the natives. Damaskinos signed a Westernized name, with many others of his conationals—Michele, not Mihales. And there were a number of painters named Domenikos. But nowadays many such panels, produced over a wide time span, are assigned to El Greco, regardless of quality. Certain paintings signed "hand [of] Domenikos," such as the Veil of Veronica in Spain, are doubtless the work of his brush. But it cannot be emphasized strongly enough that a number of his early paintings carry his full name followed by the words *kres* (*Pl. 110B*), *epoie,* or both.

The Venetian hagiographers signed in majuscule, or capital letters. It appears that shortly before 1580, early in his stay in Spain, El Greco changed his signature from majuscule to cursive script, as shown in the middle example, where under his name is the Greek word for "made." From that time on, he signed exclusively in cursive. The third signature given on *Pl. 110B*, that of his Assumption of the Virgin, has already been discussed.

Through their very nature, the evenly blocked capitals can show little individuality. But El Greco's cursive, written with the brush as fluently as with a pen, reveals considerable personality, as modern graphologists testify.[108] In the framework of the cursive, he varies his signatures. Sometimes he uses the *X* character (*chi*) instead of the *K* (*kappa*), which are phonetically related in Greek. Sometimes he puts the article before his name so as to read "the Domenikos Theotokopoulos." When there is little space on the canvas, he divides his name or carries up letters above it. And he elides the *t* and the *o* in the third syllable of his last name. All of these practices are characteristic of the Greek scribes, proficient in writing, accustomed to working with long lines, who were employed as copyists all over Europe.

Greek characters, like the Chinese, have not changed much in the past two thousand years. A first century papyrus (*Pl. 110A*) shows two types of Greek script. In the longer upper section, which is executed in clear manuscript hand, certain letters are nearly identical with those which El Greco painted on his canvases some fifteen hundred years later; on the lower, shorter section of the papyrus can be seen the cursive—personal, and hard to decipher today. The fine writing which was practiced especially in Greek manuscripts of the ninth to twelfth centuries was revived in the fifteenth century by Greek scribes in the West who were engaged in copying the ancient texts. Late in that century, Aldus Manutius gathered Greek scholars and compositors around him in Venice. As mentioned in the chapter on Venice, he published Greek classics, from Aristotle to Xenophon. He used the lettering of Greek manuscripts as model for his type. The last page of text from an early printed Greek Bible (*Pl. 110C*, top) shows how the clear and elegant manuscript hand was adopted for printing. The final page (*Pl. 110C*, bottom) bears the colophon of the Aldine Press in Venice and the date 1518, and contains in both Latin and Greek a key to the sequence in which the sheets should be laid for the binder. After Aldus's death his brothers-in-law and later his son were active with the press, and the firm continued in Venice until 1585.

Up to El Greco's thirtieth year, few paintings of his of indisputable authenticity have been found. It is recorded that he set philosophy above painting as an art. All the examples of El Greco's handwriting show his familiarity with writing with the brush. His deft and expert application of majuscule and cursive and his habits of elision and separation are those of the copyist, the compositor, the proofreader. The thought occurs whether the young Candiote did not find employment, for a time at least, with one of the presses in Venice. Here it should be recalled that the librarian and calligrapher of Philip II in the Escorial, the Cretan Nicolaos Turrianos, signed his name in cursive, adding the word *kres*, in the same way as El Greco.

In our present day, when narrow professionalism is elevated to a sacrosanct position, it is difficult to imagine that talented people should earn a living in different fields of endeavor. Leonardo da Vinci and Michelangelo are well known as "polyhistors." Sebastiano del Piombo (1485–1547) was at first a musician, a solo player on the lute; then he turned to painting. Active in Venice and Rome, he was not forty when the Medici pope employed him as the sealer ("piombo") of the briefs of the apostolic chamber. Thereafter he spent little time with the arts. Pacheco mentioned El Greco among the few painters of Europe skilled in the humanities. His son, Jorge Manuel, lists in his inventory five manuscripts of his father—one of which was illustrated with sketches.

On looking at the signatures of El Greco's paintings, it should be taken into account how often restorers who did not know any Greek have "strengthened" the lines and letters. Even so, his signature shows strong consistency, direction, and a firm sense of the horizontal which reveals the experienced draftsman. These characteristics can be observed throughout his signatures in Spain, with the exception of a few on documents in the years when he was ill. It was customary at that time for a master to affix his signature to a work done under his supervision in his atelier, with some final touches by him.

Besides the cartouche-like white slips on which he liked to sign, El Greco painted subjects where text was required, such as on the phylacterium of the Nativity and the flag carried by the Lamb of God in representations of John the Baptist. It is highly doubtful whether on any occasion, El Greco included long Latin texts in his painting. An example from an Adoration of the Shepherds survives in which the ribbon carries a recognizable Greek text, although much worn (*Pl. 111B*). In most cases the paintings have gone through many hands, and the original Greek lettering, perhaps faded and flaked, most probably illegible to the restorer, was overpainted with bright, appropriate Latin texts.

The Byzantine, Venetian, and Spanish ingredients in El Greco's painting constitute a subtle and personal blend. Even in his nickname El Greco, the Greek, as has been pointed out, the article "El" is Spanish, while the "Greco" is Italian. Logically, he should be either Il Greco or El Griego. In his early works he was influenced by what he saw around him and what was in demand. Like the other hagiographers of his time, he could work in the Western manner. Later in Spain, exposed to other expressions, new demands, and a very different intellectual and artistic climate, his art went through another modulation. As a foreigner, he saw much in Spain from a different angle than the natives—this is perhaps the reason that his Spanish portraits make such a "Spanish" impression.

As his life circle passed the fifty-year mark, in 1591 or so, his artistic isolation becomes more evident in his painting. By that time Toledo's golden period was past, Philip II was aging, and the market for artistic products was elsewhere. As the man grows older, the experiences of his childhood and youth come into special focus, and El Greco was no exception. His retrospective process was sharpened and enlivened by the arrival of his brother and groups of refugees. He probably spoke much Greek in those years, and with words come the pictures of remembrance.

Clovio's letter, written in Rome in 1570, calls him a "discepolo" of Titian. This has been translated as "pupil," although the word can be interpreted as follower, student, admirer. The questionable translation comes most probably from Carl Justi, who also made the "giovane Candiotto" in the same letter, into "Jüngling," or "youth." Carl Justi, Swiss archaeologist and art historian (1832–1912), with his slavish admiration of Winckelmann's eighteenth century theories of classical values, was far from being the right person to understand El Greco. His volume on Velázquez, published for the first time in 1888, is full of disparagement of El Greco's art.[81] And indeed, although he visited Spain repeatedly between 1872 and 1886, according to his faithful and admiring biographer he had difficulty finding the "soul" of Spain.

"Giovane Candiotto" means, not "youth," but a young Candiote—and the twenty-nine-year-old Cretan would certainly count as young to Clovio, who was seventy-two and so infirm that his artistic activities were drastically reduced. But for nearly the past hundred years, the young Candiote has been treated all too often as a youth just emerging from boyhood, who arrives in Venice with little education and a doubtful knowledge of painting. Credit for the eminence he achieved goes to Venice and to Spain; and the intellectual climate of sixteenth century Crete, with its possibilities for the education of an intelligent, ambitious young man, has been overlooked. Based on Justi's assumptions, much-quoted writers claim that El Greco had to spend at least ten years in Venice to learn to paint. And since the Clovio letter is dated 1570, this would make him arrive about 1560, as a nineteen-year-old.

Even if we accept this hypothesis—which is entirely without evidence—we must realize that in those days a nineteen-year-old was quite mature. ~~Leonardo da Vinci was apprenticed~~ to ~~Michelangelo at fifteen~~. Raphael at seventeen was established as an independent artist. Veronese was at work at fourteen. Velázquez when eighteen passed his examination and was admitted to the guild of painters. And Dürer was not twenty when he produced some of his finest portraits; he is known to have been in the profession since he was fifteen. Gilbert Stuart, famous for his portraits of George Washington, began at fifteen; and a portrait by Picasso when he was only fourteen is a pride of its owner.

But we should review perhaps a still more complex art, that of musical composition. Mendelssohn finished a delightful string quartet when he was fourteen and composed music for *A Midsummer Night's Dream* at seventeen. Mozart at seventeen had brought forth one of his most graceful and beloved symphonies, the D major. A great many of Schubert's songs and other musical works of high quality were produced by the time he reached eighteen, and at nineteen he wrote his hauntingly melodious Fourth Symphony. El Greco's son was just past nineteen when he was named in a contract of considerable importance as a substitute to finish the work in case his father should become incapacitated.

Even before modern psychological studies on childhood, it was recognized that impressions of the formative years cannot be erased. A classical philosopher has said that what a man is at twelve or so he will be all through his life. Rouault, starting his career at fourteen with a master of stained-glass windows, throughout his life applied the technique of arranging small elements of color into a larger composition. Renoir was apprenticed to a porcelain painter, and in early years he also decorated screens and blinds; as a result, a swift brush stroke of great virtuosity characterizes his art. Franz Liszt left his native land at the age of eleven and lived a thoroughly cosmopolitan life, with a number of cities claiming him as resident. But many of his characteristic compositions are woven through with Hungarian folk melodies. Less known is his burning Hungarian patriotism which he carried sometimes into open insult at the Habsburg court. Cretan impressions and Greek psychology permeate the personality of El Greco.

Byzantine echoes in El Greco's art have been pointed out by writers and scholars ever since interest focused on the painter. But it is only within the last decades that many monuments of Byzantine art have become easier to approach and that modern photography is making the material available for study. Byzantine mosaics and murals of outstanding quality that have lain hidden under whitewash for centuries are only now being restored. And the vast scope and vigor of this art, which persisted for centuries even after the fall of Constantinople, is just now beginning to be revealed.

El Greco's stockroom, with samples of his repertory, and his calm multiplication of an identical subject on order are typical of the hagiographer. His frequent use of Orthodox sources in his representation, composition, and individual poses has been discussed here at length. His different interpretation of perspective is in the Byzantine tradition. The inscription on his crucifixes is always in three languages; and when he uses the Orthodox IHS for the name of Jesus, he places the stroke across the top to indicate abbreviation. Some Western painters, ostensibly using the three languages, actually transcribe the Latin words into Greek letters. As has been pointed out, in early versions of El Greco's Annunciation, the Virgin kneels before a prayer desk; in his last examples she has turned away and raises both arms in the Orthodox *theomeni* gesture. Other Byzantine characteristics in his work are the absence of middle ground, the low vanishing point, and a two-dimensional effect, often with tapestry-like interweaving of the figures. His architecture is schematized, toy-like, or like a design for a stage setting. It would seem that his almost austere iconography, based on early Christian traditions, was acceptable to the ecclesiastic authorities in Spain, as against the free interpretation and the pagan sensuousness they found objectionable in the art of the Late Renaissance and Baroque.

El Greco never painted the Spanish mystics such as St. Theresa of Avila, to whom certain writers like to connect him in inspiration—not even Loyola, whose influence was so powerful at that time. His Apostle James the Great, patron of Spain, always stands as in a Byzantine mosaic, and never rides a charger as Matamoros, Killer of the Moors, although this representation was popular in Castile since the end of the fifteenth century.[88] In his Adoration of the Holy Name, where the temporal rulers, the doge, the king, and the pope kneel together, he omits the headgears customary in Venetian commemorative paintings, which would emphasize their rank. In his Throne of Mercy, he places the headgear of the Jewish high priest on God the Father—a unique instance in Western painting.

He lived his private life without much conformity. He never married the woman whose natural son, Jorge Manuel, he acknowledged officially only on his deathbed. He is recorded as dying without making a will, and for the power of attorney drawn up at the end of his life he did not request as witnesses two of his distinguished Spanish friends, but two refugee nobodies—who were, however, Greek, and one, at least, a Cretan.

As already mentioned, Julio Clovio's letter of 1570 is the first document extant that concerns El Greco. Clovio was born Jure Glovic (Glovocic) in the Balkans, and, according to Vasari, was known as "the Macedonian" among his colleagues. A painting of his in the Pitti Gallery in Florence is signed "Julius Clovius Macedo faciebat." It is understandable that the young Cretan, arriving in Rome, which was teeming with Italian artists, should seek out one who was akin in language and religion. Apparently the émigré's psychology in the sixteenth century was not much different from that of the present day.

In a most autocratic country, El Greco, the "foreigner," did not hesitate to assert his rights as a free man. His refusal to accept less for his work than had been agreed upon led to repeated lawsuits. His intransigence in not giving more than his name, age, and birthplace before a judge—in one case, his statement that he is not obliged to tell why he came to Toledo—reveals his knowledge of his rights before the law. He threatened to appeal cases to the highest authorities, as far as the king and the pope for justice. His protest that artwork should not fall under a tax like food and clothing set a precedent for which future generations of painters were grateful.

No previous author has ever pointed out that, in his lawsuits and in all his appearances before authorities, he *never* mentions by any word an Italian master or any years in Italy, although it might have eased certain situations to present himself as a pupil of Titian. He was a

Greek, a Candiote, and to build himself up with a boast of Italy would have been out of character.

El Greco must also have been reticent about his Italian years among the intimate circle of his Spanish friends in Toledo, who seemingly regarded him as a worthy representative of Greek humanistic education. In the poems written about him, Italy is never mentioned. The sitters for portraits by El Greco in Spain were mainly persons of ecclesiastical status or civilian administration in Toledo. On the benevolence of the civil authorities depended the permits of Greek refugees to stay in the city, while the ecclesiastics could give a helping hand in acquiring ransom money for his compatriots. It appears that El Greco painted several portraits of Fray Hortensio Félix Paravicino y Arteaga, theologist and littérateur. Born in 1580, Paravicino was two years younger than El Greco's own son. A descendant of a noble Italian family, he may have looked with awe to the much-traveled and erudite Greek, who was fifty-nine years old when the young friar was only twenty. There is a record of a typographer Dionisio Paravicino, who printed the first book in Greek characters, a grammar, in Milan in 1476. Fray Hortensio became *provinical* or district superior of the Trinitarian order in Toledo, an order founded specifically for the ransoming of captives from the Moslems. He was famous in his circle as a flowery orator and a prolific poet.

In each of his four sonnets addressed to El Greco, Paravicino alludes to the painter in the first stanza as Greek. He pairs him with Prometheus, and with Apelles, court painter to Alexander the Great. In the last sonnet, written on the occasion of the painter's death, Paravicino calls him "El Griego de Toledo." This was published in a posthumous volume in 1641. The final lines read:

Creta le dió la vida y los pinceles
Toledo meyor patria donde empieça
á lograr con la muerte eternidades.

(Crete gave him life and the brushes/ Toledo [a] better homeland where he/ achieved with death immortality.) In certain editions a comma is placed after "Crete gave him life," and "the brushes" are thus referred to Toledo that gave him immortality. The anomaly will hardly be cleared up, unless the original is found; but it is now accepted that the comma was inserted later.[95]

Another funerary sonnet survives, by Luis de Góngora, a Spanish lyric poet of the time, in which El Greco is called (as often by Paravicino) a "wanderer," a "pilgrim," a Greek—to whom Iris gave the colors, Phoebus the light, and Morpheus the shadows.

The twenty-seven Greek books of El Greco's library enumerated in Jorge Manuel's first inventory reveal the basis of his philosophy and his unique character. In the second list the son lumps them all together as "twenty Greek and Italian books." By that time the collection was scattered. One volume, in which El Greco is again compared to Apelles, came to light after the civil war, a witness across the centuries that he was admired as a Greek. He may be called in Italian Domenico Theotocopuli, in Spanish Dominico Greco. But the signature on his paintings reiterates the name under which he sailed from Candia:

DOMENIKOS THEOTOKOPOULOS

POSTLUDE

Spanish writers of the seventeenth and eighteenth centuries discussing the painters of their land generally include El Greco. They mention without exception that he was a foreigner, a Greek; but since a considerable part of his life was spent in Spain and many of his works are there, they deem it fair to give him space in their list.

In the early nineteenth century, travel was by stagecoach, strenuous, sometimes even perilous. Nevertheless, a number of European travelers visited and reported on Spain. The books of Lady Holland and Théophile Gautier have already been mentioned here. Captain S. Cook saw much of the country in the years 1829–1832, and his observations on social customs and economic conditions would in themselves make his book worth while. His descriptions of art and architecture are amazingly perceptive. Of El Greco he writes that he is less known "than the great Italians and Flemings . . . his name, his common designation of Greco and the habit he used occasionally of signing his pictures at length in the Greek character with *kres* added, put his native country out of all doubt and it is certain that he must have studied both at Venice and in the South of Italy. . . . Unfortunately he adopted an unique and extraordinary tone of color which destroys all pleasure in examining the greater part of his work, but the most masterly freedom of design is always to be seen."

Captain Cook recalls with horror how in the Prado, then a royal collection, paintings were being "restored." "The worst part of this noble institution is a gang of restorers . . . every picture in the gallery seems destined to undergo their discipline and neither age nor school escape their merciless grasp. Their methods seem to injure the Venetian pictures more than any other, and the mode of disturbing the surface and then glazing and substituting varnishes of their own completely alters the appearance of them and would astonish the artists if they revisited the earth and saw their production." [76] Ruskin some twenty years later reports that in Venice canvases of the masters were laid out on the floor, stitched together, and overpainted with house painters' brushes dipped into vats of ordinary nondescript color. Captain Cook must have had very good recommendations to be admitted to special rooms where, as he describes, some of the finest paintings of Rubens, Titian, and other Italians were locked away from the public, "from a fastidious and mawkish delicacy," so that the morals of the *madrileños* should not be corrupted by the sight of the ripe female nudes. At that time the great Assumption of El Greco, contracted for a church in Toledo, was no longer in its original location but the property of the Spanish Infante—on its way to being sold to America later. It was not until 1906, when The Burial of Count Orgaz was arranged to be sold abroad, that the outcry, "sacrilege" and "profanation" was heard by the authorities, and they stopped the export.

Another foreign author who had a good inside view of Spanish art was Louis Viardot who married Paulina García of the family of world-famous Spanish singers and singing teachers. Viardot's appreciative remarks about El Greco, in books published in 1839 and 1855, prove that the Cretan painter was never completely forgotten.[92]

When the railroad nets were extended across Europe, around the mid-nineteenth century, they brought additional visitors. The Spanish government required a wider-gauge track than was uniformly accepted for the Continent. No through trains could run into the country. All freight had to be reloaded at the border, and all the passengers had to leave the coaches. Luggage was dragged over a distance, from where the French train came to a halt, to a large hall where Spanish customs officials in shakos burrowed into all valises. This manner of isolation, paralleled only in czarist Russia, meant also the suspicious examination of all persons and ideas that might have brought the clarifying air of a more liberal Europe into the country. Nevertheless a group of Spanish scholars, writers, and artists felt that now was the time to lift Spain out of its morass of clerical Bourbonism, to make their country, which had produced so much that was superlative in the arts, conscious of its heritage, and to raise its prestige abroad.

Edouard Manet, father of Impressionism, having copied Spanish canvases busily in the Louvre, went to Spain in 1865. Without his study of the colors of Velázquez, his palette never would have acquired its characteristic velvety modulated tone. The Swiss art historian Carl Justi, as already mentioned, was several times in Spain.

With the rising interest in Spanish painting, it was unavoidable that the Cretan painter, nearly unknown outside the country, should receive a share of attention. By 1885, Manuel Cossío had published in an encyclopedia a long essay on Spanish painting, in which El Greco was highly valued. Cossío was the first to present him without any pathological qualifications that declared him to have suffered from astigmatism or from manifold manias. Although in 1881 the director of the Prado had expressed himself as hanging those "absurd caricatures" only at the order of his superior, articles on El Greco were published in various countries of Europe, and in 1902 the first exhibition of his work took place in Madrid, followed by a second in 1909.

In 1908 the pioneer Manuel Cossío brought out the first monograph devoted to El Greco—two massive volumes in which much data and healthy observation were presented. In 1909 the first edition of August L. Mayer's *El Greco* appeared in Munich, and this scholar remained until his martyr's death a staunch and articulate publicist for the Cretan's art. In 1910 the Toledan historian San Román published, as the result of patient and arduous efforts, archival data referring to the life, work, and death of El Greco. Even today the documents exhumed by this thorough searcher contain nearly all the factual information on the painter, which later writers use again and again. In 1910 Julius Meier-Graefe issued his *Spanische Reise*—a Spanish journey undertaken to learn more about Velázquez that brought forth another enthusiastic revelation of El Greco. By that time essays about this unusual and unconventional painter had appeared in nearly all European languages.

The year 1912 saw the publication of Maurice Barrès's *Le Greco ou le secret du Tolède,* a catchy title perhaps, but a mere pamphlet compared with the pioneering volumes which had preceded it. Here we must return to Manuel Cossío's monograph published four years earlier.

At the end of the nineteenth century, the Spanish scholar received an inquiry from an English publisher whether he would be willing to write a book on Murillo for them. Cossío had no special interest in the project, but offered the publisher his manuscript on El Greco. Upon seeing the sizable work, the Englishman refused it. The manuscript then went to a Parisian publisher, where it encountered the same fate. Finally, after years of lost time, it was brought out with a subvention under the imprint of a stationery firm that also issued textbooks for schools in Madrid. The daughter of Manuel Cossío has told us personally that when Barrès's book reached him, they were at their summer place in the mountains of Galicia in northwestern Spain. The father called his daughter into the garden pavilion where he used to work, and showed her in the Frenchman's book entire passages translated from his own monograph with scarcely a word changed and with no credit given.

In spite of El Greco's meteoric rise in the first decade of our century, his fame was not yet general. As late as 1902, a monumental volume of the history of art came out; it contained nearly seven hundred pages, and was widely quoted and used as a textbook.[12] Although it had a comprehensive section on Spanish art and architecture, including painters from Morales and Ribalta to Cano and Goya, as well as an index with more than two thousand entries, El Greco's name is nowhere to be found. In a work on Spanish Baroque, published in 1908, the same year as Cossío's monumental monograph, and still regarded as up-to-date in many ways, the author makes the astonishing statement that, although Philip II ordered The Martyrdom of St. Mauritius from El Greco, and paid for it in full, the painting had been destroyed.[91]

On the other hand, many of El Greco's paintings by that time were distributed in different parts of the world: before 1911, Austria had two El Grecos, Italy had six, Germany seven, England and France thirteen each. Budapest alone possessed eleven, and New York, the same number. An additional five in Philadelphia, one in Boston, and one in Chicago bring the total for the United States to eighteen, a goodly number for a country continuously deprecated for her lack of "culture." Less than a decade later, his name had become a household word; and since art history pigeonholes every artist, he is declared a Byzantine, a Gothic, a Baroque, a Mannerist painter.

Many nineteenth century writers speak of the "energy" in El Greco's painting, the impetuosity, the "saber blades" of his high lights. They were unused to his palette which "moderns" now accept. El Greco's work comes close to the moderns in a number of practices which, with him, stem from the Byzantine tradition. His appeal to the present day lies in the fact that in his manifold talent he never had all those components that were considered necessary to a Western master up to the mid-nineteenth century. Thus he stands for the direction into which moderns "reacted" from academic conservatism. He may use stock figures, but each time they are welded into a close-knit whole. His work is vibrant but not diffuse, nervous but directed.

El Greco's talent did not stagnate. The very distance from his homeland and the foreignness of his Spanish surroundings gave him unusual strength. As have many émigrés in our own days, he found a radius of activity that he could not have achieved in his native land.

El Greco's style was purely his own, developed from his experiences in the three worlds in which he lived—Candia, Venice, and Toledo. Candia is no more. Even its name is changed. But Venice and Toledo retain much of the visage that El Greco knew. These two cities, in their picturesque ambience, have managed to preserve a spectacular amount of their intricate history. Venice was limited by the waters of the lagoon. Toledo was contained upon its hill within medieval walls, and grew bigger and more compact within itself. To wander their streets at leisure—strange, that in both cities a street is called *calle*—will open to the visitor revealing vistas of their uniqueness.

City maps are interesting reading matter. They sometimes tell what is not in the guidebooks. Looking over the map of Toledo, one sees streets named for a few artists and writers; the rest are given to politicos, generals, archbishops, and cardinals. There is no street named after the Marquès de la Vega Inclán whose enthusiasm created the Casa del Greco, or for Manuel Cossío who brought justice to the painter. Nor does one find the name of the Marquès San Román Borja whose search for archival data brought out nearly all that is known about the painter. A street is named after the Frenchman Maurice Barrès, who exchanged a promising literary career for questionable reactionary political activities. It is said that Spaniards incline to xenophobia, but it must be recalled that the worthy Spanish champions of El Greco were all liberals —a word in some circles equivalent to "outcast."

The neglect of "grateful posterity" does not lessen the city's attraction. Auto buses, motorbicycles, and private cars nowadays bring the visitor to Toledo. And on Sundays the city, like an overladen excursion boat, rocks with the mass of humanity. Young people in bright clothing chatter with the abandon of their age, noting the aggressive posters of the moving-picture theater, commenting on their fellow men. Some have lunch baskets in their hands, some cameras over their shoulders; one carries a blaring transistor radio and expects the admiration of the passers-by. Older people in dark clothing walk slowly, stop frequently, and are rather subdued in their speech. For them it is still a city evoking respect.

And there are also the tourists, herded by a guide whose main concern is not to lose any of them in the labyrinthal streets or among the milling crowds. The foreign tourist is in a hurry. In the one day he has to "check out" all the famous monuments, art pieces, and sites in his itinerary—and often has to be back early in Madrid to catch the evening plane. By the day after tomorrow his impressions of Toledo will already have begun to lose their shape and color, among the mesmerizing mass of other cities in other lands.

For the Spaniards there will be another Sunday. For them Toledo is not a fleeting interlude. It is three-dimensional reality with its inescapable consequences, an epic of history preserved in stone.

We last saw Toledo on a warm October Sunday, when we were invited to dine in a country house outside the city. We drove out early so as to visit once more our favorite sites. We sat on a bench before The Burial of Count Orgaz, now decently displayed and lighted—not, as when I saw it the first time, with an impatient sacristan holding a flickering candle before it for a few moments.

It is hopeless to try to form an opinion of this moving work from color prints. The foreground figures are dark and dense. The row of pallid faces makes a terminating line. The contrast between earth and heaven is forceful. From realistic details such as the elaborate vestments, the ruffs of the hidalgos, the translucent white of the priest's robe, the painter makes a smooth and convincing transition to the absolutely unreal. Below, black and gold predominate. As the eye moves upward, the heavens open—opaline, shimmering in evanescent tones, boundless in space.

We listened to the parrot-like recitation of the guides, as they herded their flocks in and out, taking sometimes less than ten minutes. The Spanish discourse sounded apropos and melodious, as against the monotone of foreign languages memorized and rattled off.

Time came for us to leave also. Crossing the Puente de San Martín, our car began to mount the barren hill, and soon the gate of the Cigarral los Dolores came into sight. It was in the midst of an olive grove, a good-sized building, once a retreat for religious personnel. Today, modernized with graceful feeling for tradition, it is the country seat of a distinguished historian who wrote most of his works there. The cells were enlarged into bedrooms, the refectory was transformed into a dining hall, and at the far end of the sprawling mansion were several rooms lined with shelves of books from bottom to top. Here was a piece of Toledo's past: the paintings in dark hues on the walls, an El Greco miniature among them, the statues showing the subdued polychrome through the patina of centuries, the rugs faded by age but displaying their elegant craft, and the silver gleaming in the complacence of Spanish Baroque. One wall of the nuns' reception room had been broken out to a tiled terrace, and the heavy iron grille that had separated the inmates from their visitors, by means of glass and a curtain was made into a friendly window.

The table was laid with flower-embroidered linen and cheerful Talavera ware. For the meal there were a savory clear soup, partridge from the nearby hills baked in wine, an endive salad decorated with a scattering of pomegranate seeds. Cream puffs with tempting fillings were served, and marzipan and candied apricots, recalling the Arabian past. Dappled jugs set about the table contained a pleasantly cool Valdepeñas.

Afterward we walked out onto the terrace. Beyond the evergreen of the olive grove, flanked by dusty yellow and red foliage, stood tenacious, timeless Toledo—translucent as a projected stage setting, unforgettable in masculine majesty.

CATALOGUE OF ILLUSTRATIONS

This listing contains various credits not included in the text or captions. When a museum or collection owns the piece and has also furnished the photograph, the name is given only once.

The National Geographic Society, Washington, with exceptional courtesy, permitted a selection from its world-famous archive to be used. With rare cooperation, the ENTE, Venice, D. Stanimirovitch, Paris, and Dr. Karl Eller, Munich, furnished choice photographs and much important information. George Cserna, photographer, New York, improved a number of negatives and prints.

The full titles of books referred to can be found in the Bibliography.

The following abbreviations are used:

D.S.: D. Stanimirovitch, Paris
EZK: Elisabeth Zulauf Kelemen
G.T.: Greek Tourist Office, Athens
K.E.: Dr. Karl Eller, Munich
NGS: The National Geographic Society
S.O.: Spanish Tourist Office
Y.C.: Yugoslav Information Center
Coll: Collection
Cy: Courtesy
Ph: Photograph

Plate
1 A) Viollet, Paris. B) EZK 1956. C) Ph Pferschy. Cy Hilton Hotel
2 A) and D) Viollet, Paris. B) Ecole des Hautes-Etudes, Paris. C) Cy Arab Inf. Center
3 D) Pemberton Pigott, London
4 A) after Strzygowski, *Asiens bildende Kunst* . . . B) and C) Cy Prof. K. A. C. Creswell
5 Cy Arab Inf. Center
6 A) M. O. Williams. NGS. B) Lykides, Thessaloniki
7 A) M. O. Williams. NGS. B) Cy G.T. C) Lykides, Thessaloniki
8 A) M. O. Williams. NGS. B) Cy K.E.
9 A) Lykides, Thessaloniki. B) after Millet, . . . *Athos.* C) Cy K.E.
10 A) M. O. Williams. NGS. B) Cy K.E. C) and D) Cy G.T.
11 A) and B) Cy K.E. C) EZK 1956
12 A) and B) EZK 1956. C) Hautes-Etudes, Paris
13 EZK 1956
14 EZK 1956
15 A) and C) EZK 1956. B) Cy Pelekanidis. D) Cy ENTE, Venice
16 A) Wm. Tobin 1930. NGS. B) and C) M. O. Williams 1932. NGS. D) after Filow, *Alt-bulgarische Kunst*
17 A) M. O. Williams 1932. NGS. B) Wm. Tobin 1930. NGS. C) after Iorga and Bals, *L'art Roumain.* D) after Henry, *Les Eglises Moldavia*
18 Cy D.S.
19 Cy D.S.
20 Cy D.S.
21 Cy D.S.
22 A) Cy Y.C. B) EZK 1956. C) and D) Cy D.S.
23 A) Cy Y.C. B) Cy D.S. C) EZK 1956
24 A) Cy D.S. B) M. O. Williams. NGS. C) Cy Y.C.
25 A) Anderson. B) Cy D.S. C) Cy K.E.
26 A) G. Maraghiannis, Heraklion. B) M. O. Williams 1928. NGS
27 A) EZK 1956. B) A. Matton

28 EZK 1956
29 EZK 1956
30 A) and B) EZK 1956. C) M. O. Williams 1928. NGS
31 EZK 1956
32 EZK 1956
33 A) after Gerola, *Monumenti . . .* B) Cy K.E. C) after Diehl, *Manuel d'art byzantin.* D) Cy Pelekanidis
34 Cy NGS
35 A) Cy NGS. B) after Adam, *Ruins of the Palace . . .* C) after Ivekovic, *Dalmatiens Architektur . . .*
36 A) and C) Alinari. B) Cy ENTE, Venice. D) Anderson
37 Cy Cleveland Museum of Art. J. H. Wade Fund
38 Cy ENTE, Venice
39 Cy ENTE, Venice
40 Cy ENTE, Venice
41 Cy ENTE, Venice
42 Cy ENTE, Venice
43 Cy ENTE, Venice
44 Cy ENTE, Venice
45 A) EZK 1954. B) EZK 1935
46 A) Mus. Vatican. B) and C) Anderson
47 A) and C) Anderson. B) EZK
48 A) Cy Kunsthistorisches Mus., Vienna. B) Cy S.O.
49 Cy S.O.
50 EZK 1959
51 A) Cy René Taylor. B) Cy S.O.
52 A) Mas. B) and C) Cy S.O.
53 A) and C) Cy S.O. B) Westminster Cathedral, London
54 A) and C) Cy S.O. B) Mas
55 A) EZK 1956. B) Cy S.O. C) Mas
56 Cy S.O.
57 A) Naples. Anderson. B) Toledo. Mas. C) New York. Metropolitan Mus. of Art. Bequest of Mrs. H. O. Havemeyer, 1929
58 A) Paris. Bibliothèque National. B) Toledo. Mas. C) Athens. Cy Statathos
59 A) Benaki Mus., Athens. EZK 1956. B) Athens. Cy Statathos. C) Istanbul. Dumbarton Oaks
60 A) Mt. Athos. Cy K.E. B) Toledo. Mas. C) Kritsá. EZK 1956
61 A) Verroia. EZK 1956. B) Crete. EZK 1956. C) Brescia. Alinari
62 A) Florence. Cy Warburg Inst., London. B) Madrid. Mas. C) Mt. Athos. Cy K.E.
63 A) Venice. Cy ENTE. B) after Dürer, *The Small Passion* (1509–1511). C) Rome. Vatican Gallery
64 A) Mistra. Hautes-Etudes, Paris. B) Escorial. Mas. C) Heraklion. G. Maraghiannis
65 A) Istanbul. EZK 1956. B) and C) Mt. Athos. Hautes-Etudes, Paris
66 A) Budapest. Nat. Lib. B) Escorial. Mas. C) Mt. Athos. Cy K.E.
67 A) and B) Escorial. Mas. C) Kansas City. Wm. R. Nelson Gall., Mary Atkins Mus. of Fine Arts
68 A) Toledo. Mas. B) Madrid. Prado
69 A) after Millet, . . . *Athos.* B) Turin. Alinari. C) Louvre, Paris. Giraudon
70 A) Toledo. Cy Victoria and Albert Mus. B) Toledo. Mas
71 A) Madrid. Mas. B) Bib. Nat., Paris. C) Mt. Athos. Hautes-Etudes. D) Venice. Alinari
72 A) Monreale. Alinari. B) Andrejas. Cy D.S. C) Mt. Athos. after Millet, . . . *Athos*
73 A) and C) London. Cy Trustees, National Gallery. B) Venice. Anderson
74 A) Parma. Alinari. B) Heraklion. G. Maraghiannis. C) Venice. EZK 1935. D) Minneapolis. Inst. of Arts. Dunwoody Fund 1924
75 A) Istanbul. Dumbarton Oaks. B) London. Cy Trustees, Nat. Gall. C) Monreale. Anderson. D) Cadiz. Mas
76 A) Lykides, Thessaloniki. B) Washington. Cy National Gallery of Art. Samuel H. Kress Coll. C) Scuola dei Greci, Venice. EZK 1935
77 A) Vienna. Cy Akad. der bild. Künste. B) Madrid. Mas. C) Cy Erica Tietze
78 A) Budapest. Cy Fine Arts Mus. B) after Millet, . . . *Athos.* C) Siguenza. Mas
79 A) Mistra. Cy K.E. B) and C) Lugano. Cy Galleria Thyssen
80 A) Brussels. Giraudon. B) Scuola dei Greci. EZK 1935. C) Heraklion. G. Maraghiannis. D) Meteora, Greece. Papadopoulos
81 A) Escorial. Anderson. B) Jerez de la Frontera. Mas. C) Cy Art Inst. of Chicago. J. Winterbotham Coll.

82 A) Nerezi, Yugoslavia. Cy Y.C. B) Kastoria, Greece. Cy Pelekanidis. C) Bologna. D) Heraklion. EZK 1956

83 A) Benaki Mus., Athens. EZK 1956. B) and C) Paris. Mas. D) Venice. Cy ENTE

84 A) Heraklion. G. Maraghiannis. B) Modena. Cy Galleria Estense. C) London. Cy Trustees, Nat. Gall. D) Mt. Athos. Cy K.E.

85 A) Madrid. B) Illescas. C) Valencia. All Mas

86 A) and D) Venice. Cy ENTE. B) Kastoria. EZK 1956. C) San Francisco. Cy M. H. de Young Memorial Mus.

87 A) Palermo. Anderson. B) Scuola dei Greci. EZK 1954. C) Kastoria. EZK 1956. D) New York. Cy Frick Collection

88 A) Palermo. Alinari. B) Mt. Athos. Cy K.E. C) Vitoria. Mas. D) Kastoria. EZK 1956

89 A) Stockholm. Cy Nat. Mus. B) St. Louis. Cy City Art Mus.

90 A) Boston. Cy Mus. of Fine Arts. B) Escorial. Mas. C) Rome. Anderson

91 A) Heraklion. EZK 1956. B) New York. Cy Metropolitan Mus. of Art. Gift of Mrs. Ralph J. Hines, 1954

92 A) Manchester. Cy University Mus. B) Boston. Cy Mus. of Fine Arts. C) New York. Cy Metropolitan Mus. of Art. Gift of Edward S. Harkness, 1917–1918. D) Toledo. Mas

93 A) Scotland. Mas. B) Paris. Giraudon. C) Madrid. Mas. D) Brescia. Alinari

94 A) Thessaloniki. Lykides. B) New York. Cy Metropolitan Mus. of Art. Joseph Pulitzer Beq. Fund. C) Palermo. Anderson

95 A) Cadiz. Mas. B) after A. L. Mayer, *El Greco*. C) Kastoria. EZK 1956

96 A) Decani. Cy D.S. B) Palermo. Alinari. C) Mt. Athos. Cy K.E.

97 A) Siatista. EZK 1956. B) Scuola dei Greci. EZK 1935. C) Dublin. Cy Nat. Gall. of Ireland

98 A) after Dürer (1511). B) Madrid. Prado. C) Barcelona. Cy Mus. de Arte de Cataluña. D) Seville. Mas

99 A) formerly Bucharest. Mas. B) Ickworth. Coll. Marq. of Bristol. C) Paris. Cy Mus. Jacquemart André

100 A) Philadelphia. Cy J. G. Johnson Coll. B) Escorial. Mas. C) Amsterdam. Cy Rijksmus.

101 A) Cincinnati. Cy Art Mus. B) and C) Moreno Archive, Madrid

102 A) after Meunier, *Vues en Espagne*. Cy New York Public Library. B) EZK 1959

103 A) Washington. Cy Nat. Gall. S. H. Kress Coll. B) Toledo. Mas

104 A) New York. Cy Metropolitan Mus. of Art. Beq. of Mrs. H. O. Havemeyer, 1929. B) Toledo. Mas

105 A) after Meunier, *Vues en Espagne*. B) Cincinnati. Cy Art Mus. C) New York. Cy Metropolitan Mus. of Art

106 A) Cincinnati. Cy Art Mus. B) Washington. Cy Nat. Gall. Widener Coll.

107 A) formerly Budapest. Cy Bilderarchiv Marburg. B) New York. J. Hirsch Estate. Cy T. Virzi. C) New York. Cy S. C. Clark Coll.

108 A) Mexico. B) Cy Hispanic Society of America

109 A) after Gevaerts, *Pompa introitus* . . . B) and C) New York. Brown Bros.

110 A) Cambridge. Cy University Lib. B) upper and middle: Washington. Cy Nat. Gall. Lower: Chicago. Cy Art Inst. C) Washington. Cy Lib. of Congress

111 A) and C) Venice. EZK 1954. B) Toledo. Mas. D) after Legendre-Hartman. E) Escorial. Mas

112 A) Toledo. Cy Victoria and Albert Mus. B) Heraklion. G. Maraghiannis. C) Istanbul. EZK 1956. D) formerly Budapest. Bilderarch. Marburg. E) New York. Cy S. C. Clark Coll. F) Toledo. Mas. G) Madrid. Mas. H) Athens. Cy Statathos Coll.

BIBLIOGRAPHY

The literature of some of the subjects, on which this book sometimes only touches, is so vast that it fills entire libraries. Much useful material was found in periodicals which have been discontinued. Further, old guidebooks and exhibition catalogues contain valuable information and have helped to give a fuller picture.

Here only a selection of titles can be offered. Even the subject of Byzantine influence in El Greco's art has been discussed by numerous authors. Books may have been omitted which are as important to the specialist as those included here, as no bibliography can claim to be all-encompassing.

For general reference use was made of the *Encyclopaedia Britannica,* the *Catholic Encyclopedia, Enciclopedia Italiana,* the Spanish *Enciclopedia universal ilustrada,* the Stauffacher *Illustrierte Welt-Kunstgeschichte,* Thieme-Becker's *Künstler Lexikon,* as well as specialized iconographical and theological works.

Books with an extensive bibliography are marked with an asterisk.* The numbers refer to source references in the text and works in which further information can be found.

GENERAL

Argyropoulos, P. A., "Les Grecs au service de l'empire ottoman" in *L'Hellénisme contemporain.* Athens, 1953

Atiyah, Edward, *The Arabs.* London, 1955

Bühler, Curt F., *The Fifteenth Century Book.* Philadelphia, 1960

Cartellieri, O., *Abt Suger von Saint Denis.* Berlin, 1898

[1] Ceccaroni, Agostino, *Piccola enciclopedia ecclesiastica.* Milan, 1953

[2] Clapham, Sir Alfred, and F. Saxl, "Lincoln Cathedral, the Eleventh Century West Front" in *The Archaeological Journal,* London, 1947

[3] Creswell, K. A. C., *Early Muslim Architecture,* 2 vols. London, 1932, 1940

——, *The Muslim Architecture of Egypt,* 2 vols. London, 1952, 1959

Davis, R. H. C., and Helmut Domke, *Romanesque Europe.* New York, 1960

Deschamps, Paul, *Recueil de textes relatifs à l'histoire de l'architecture et à la condition des architectes en France au moyen âge.* Paris, 1929

[4] Deutsch, Otto Erich, ed., *Schubert: Memoirs by His Friends.* New York, 1958

Diringer, David, *L'Alfabeto nella storia del civiltà.* Florence, 1937

——, *The Alphabet in the History of Civilization.* London, 1948

[5] ——, *The Illuminated Book.* New York, 1958

Du Colombier, Pierre, *Les Chantiers des cathédrales.* Paris, 1953

Dupont-Sommer, A., *The Dead Sea Scrolls.* Oxford, 1952

[6] Egli, Ernst, *Sinan, der Baumeister osmanischer Glanzzeit.* Zurich, 1954

Entz, Géza, *A középkori Magyarország müvészete.* Budapest, 1959

[7] Ferguson, George, *Signs and Symbols in Christian Art.* New York, 1954 *

Fossey, Charles M., *Notices sur les caractères étrangers anciens et modernes.* Paris, 1948

Frisch, Teresa G., "The Twelve Choir Statues of the Cathedral at Reims" in *The Art Bulletin,* 1960

Gerö, László, *Eger.* Budapest, 1954

Gimpel, Jean, *Les Bâtisseurs de cathédrales.* Paris, 1958

Grillmeier, Aloys, *Der Logos am Kreuz.* Munich, 1956

Grunebaum, G. E. von, *Islam.* Chicago, 1955

[8] Holt, Elizabeth Gilmore, ed., *Literary Sources of Art History.* Princeton, 1947

[9] Huime, Edward F., *The History, Principles, and Practice of Symbolism in Christian Art.* London, 1891

King, Georgiana Goddard, "Iconographical Notes on the Passion" in *The Art Bulletin,* 1934

Künstle, Karl *Ikonographie der christlichen Kunst,* 2 vols. Freiburg, 1926–1928

Laliberte, Norman, and Edward N. West, *The History of the Cross.* New York, 1960

[10] Lecoy de la Marche, A., ed., *Oeuvres complètes de Suger . . . annotées et publiées d'après les manuscrits pour la Société de l'Histoire de France.* Paris, 1867

Lethaby, W. R., *Medieval Art,* revised by D. Talbot Rice. London, 1950

Lloyd, Seton, *Early Anatolia.* London, 1956

Lowrie, Walter, *Art in the Early Church.* New York, 1947

[11] Mâle, Emile, *L'Art religieux après le Concile de Trent.* Paris, 1951

Matthews, George T., ed., *News and Rumor in Renaissance Europe* (The Fugger Newsletters). New York, 1959

Menzel, Wolfgang, *Christliche Symbolik,* 2 vols. Regensburg, 1854

Muñoz, Antonio, *Iconografia della Madonna.* Florence, 1905

Ripa, Cesare, *Iconologia.* Rome, 1593

[12] Rosenberg, Adolf, *Handbuch der Kunstgeschichte.* Leipzig, 1902

[13] Thompson, James Westfall, ed., *The Medieval Library.* Chicago, 1939

Villard de Honnecourt, kritische Gesamtausgabe, Hans R. Hahnloser, ed. Vienna, 1935

[14] ——, *The Sketch Book of,* Theodore Bowie, ed. New York, 1959

Vlachos, N., "La Relation des Grecs asservis avec l'état mussulman souverain," in *L'Hellénisme contemporain.* Athens, 1953

[15] Webber, F. R., *Church Symbolism.* Cleveland, 1938

Wright, S., O. A. Jäger, and J. Leroy, *Ethiopia.* UNESCO, 1961

BYZANTINE

[16] Adam, R., *Ruins of the Palace of the Emperor Diocletian.* London, 1764

Andrews, Kevin, *Castles of the Morea.* Princeton, 1953

Athens. Benaki Museum Catalogue (in Greek), A[ndré] Xyngopoulos, ed. 1936

——. Museum of Dionysios Loverdos Catalogue (in Greek), A. A. Papagiannópoulos-Palaios, ed. 1946

——. *Musée Byzantin d'Athènes, Guide du,* G. Sotiriou and Anne Hadjinicolaou, eds. 1955

Atiya, Aziz Suryal, *The Monastery of St. Catherine in Mount Sinai.* Cairo, 1950

[17] Aubert, M., "Existe-t-il une architecture cistercienne?" in *Cahiers de civilisation méd.,* Paris, 1958

[18] Baltrusaitis, Jurgis, *Le Problème de l'ogive et l'Armenie.* Paris, 1939

Baynes, N. H., and H. St. L. B. Moss, eds., *Byzantium.* Oxford, 1949

Beckwith, J. G., "Two Exhibitions of Byzantine Art" in *The Burlington Magazine,* 1958

——, *The Art of Constantinople.* London, 1961

Beza, Marcu, *Byzantine Art in Roumania.* London, 1940

Bihalji-Merin, Oto, *Fresken und Ikonen: Mittelalterliche Kunst in Serbien und Makedonien.* Munich, 1958

Bréhier, L., *L'Art chrétien: Son développement iconographique.* Paris, 1928

Brockhaus, H., *Die Kunst in den Athos-Klöstern.* Leipzig, 1891

Budde, Ludwig, *Göreme, Höhlenkirchen in Kappadokien.* Düsseldorf, 1959

Byron, Robert, *The Station. Athos: Treasures and Men.* London, 1949

[19] ——, and David Talbot Rice, *The Birth of Western Painting.* London, 1930 *

Cairo, Musée Copte. *Guide sommaire.* 1937

Cavarnos, Constantine, *Byzantine Sacred Art.* New York, 1957

[20] ——, *Anchored in God.* Athens, 1959

Chatzidakis, Manolis, "Contribution à l'étude de la peinture post-byzantine" in *L'Hellénisme contemporain.* Athens, 1953

[21] ——, "Rapports entre la peinture de la Macédoine et da la Crète au XIVe siècle" in *Essays for Ninth [Internat'l] Congress of Byz. Studies, Thessaloniki,* 1953. Athens, 1955

——, *Byzantine Monuments in Attica and Boeotia.* Athens, 1956

——, *Greece: Byzantine Mosaics.* New York, 1960

Choukas, M., *Black Angels of Athos.* London, 1936

[22] Curzon, Robert, Jr., *Visits to Monasteries in the Levant.* Ithaca, 1955

[23] Dalton, O. M., *Byzantine Art and Archaeology.* Oxford, 1911 *

Dawkins, R. M., *The Monks of Athos.* London, 1936

Demus, Otto, *The Mosaics of Norman Sicily.* New York, 1950 *

Denys of Fourna, *Painter's Manual. See* Didron, A. N.

Didron, A. N., ed., *Das Handbuch der Malerei vom Berge Athos.* Trier, 1855

[24] ——, and Paul Durand, *Manuel d'iconographie chrétienne grecque et latine.* Paris, 1845

[25] Diehl, Charles, *Les Villes d'art célèbres.* Paris, 1924

——, *History of the Byzantine Empire.* Princeton, 1925

[26] ——, *Manuel d'art byzantin,* 2 vols. Paris, 1925–1926

[27] ——, and Peter Charanis, *Byzantium, Greatness and Decline.* New Brunswick, 1957 *

Diez, Ernst, and Otto Demus, *Byzantine Mosaics in Greece, Hosios Lucas and Daphni.* Cambridge, Mass., 1960

Dölger, F., *Mönchsland Athos.* Munich, 1943

Eller, Karl, *Der heilige Berg Athos.* Munich, 1954

——, *Aufstieg zum Licht, Bilder aus der Ostkirche.* Gütersloh, 1955

[28] Felicetti-Liebenfels, Walter, *Geschichte der byzantinischen Ikonenmalerei.* Lausanne, 1956 *

Fichtner, Fritz, *Wandmalereien der Athos-Klöster.* Berlin, 1931

[29] Filow, Bogdan D., *Alt-bulgarische Kunst.* Berlin, 1935

Focillon, H., M. Aubert, E. Lambert, J. Baltrusaitis, and others, "Le Problème de l'ogive" in *Recherche,* Paris, 1939

Forlati, Ferdinando, and others, *Saint Sophia of Ochrida.* Paris, 1953

Gerhard, H. P., *Welt der Ikonen.* Recklinghausen, 1957

Glück, Heinrich, *Die christliche Kunst des Ostens.* Berlin, 1923

Grabar, André, *La Peinture religieuse en Bulgarie.* Paris, 1928

——, *Byzantine Painting.* Geneva, 1953

Hamilton, Edith, *The Echo of Greece.* New York, 1957

Hasluch, F. W., *Athos and Its Monasteries.* London, 1924

[30] Henry, Paul, *Les Eglises de la Moldavie du Nord,* 2 vols. Paris, 1930

Herzfeld, Ernst, *Die Malerei von Samarra.* Berlin, 1927

Hristov, H., G. Stojkov, and K. Mijatev, *The Rila Monastery.* Sofia, 1959

Ioannou, Andreas S., *Byzantine Frescoes of Euboea.* Athens, 1959

Iorga, Nicholas, and Georges Bals, *L'Art roumain.* Paris, 1922

Ivekovic, Cirillo M., *Dalmatiens Architektur und Plastik.* Vienna, 1927

Jerphanion, Guillaume de, *Les Eglises rupestres de Cappadoce.* Paris, 1923

Kádár, Zoltán, *Bizánci müvészet.* Budapest, 1959

Klausner, Joseph, *From Jesus to Paul.* New York, 1943

Kondakov, N., *Geschichte und Denkmäler des byzantinischen Emails.* Frankfurt, 1892

Liddell, Robert, *Byzantium and Istanbul.* London, 1956

Lindsay, Jack, *Byzantium into Europe.* London, 1952

[31] Loch, Sidney, *Athos—The Holy Mountain.* London, 1957

London. *Yugoslav Medieval Frescoes* (catalogue), Milan Kasanin, ed. Arts Council of Great Britain, 1953

Mamboury, Ernest, *Istanbul.* Istanbul, 1953 *

Martin, John R., "The Death of Ephraim in Byzantine and Early Italian Painting" in *The Art Bulletin,* 1951

[32] Mathern, J., "Villes mortes de Haute Syrie" in *Byzance avant l'Islam,* Paul Goubert, ed. Paris, 1951

Mathew, Gervase, *Byzantine Painting.* London, 1950

Millet, Gabriel, *Le Monastère de Daphni.* Paris, 1899
[33] ——, *Monuments byzantins de Mistra.* Paris, 1910
[34] ——, *Recherche sur l'iconographie de l'évangile.* Paris, 1916
——, *L'Ancien Art serbe.* Paris, 1919
[35] ——, *Monuments de l'Athos.* Paris, 1927
——, *La Peinture du moyen âge en Yougoslavie.* Paris, 1956
——, and D. Talbot Rice, *Byzantine Painting at Trebizond.* London, 1936
Millingen, A. van, *Byzantine Constantinople.* London, 1899
——, *Byzantine Churches in Constantinople.* London, 1912 *
Mirkovic, L., "Die Ikonen der griechischen Maler in Jugoslawien und in den serbischen Kirchen ausserhalb Jugoslawiens" in *Essays for Ninth [Internat'l] Congress of Byz. Studies, Thessaloniki, 1953.* Athens, 1955
Moravcsik, Gyula, *Byzantinoturcica,* 2 vols. Budapest, 1942–1943
[36] ——, *Bizánc és a magyarság.* Budapest, 1953
Muñoz, Antonio, *L'Art byzantin à l'exposition de Grottaferrata.* Rome, 1906
——, *I Quadri bizantini della Pinacoteca Vaticana.* Rome, 1928
Müntz, Eugen, "Les Artistes byzantins dans l'Europe latine du V° au XV° siècle" in *Revue de l'art chrétien,* 1893
Muratoff, Paul, *La Peinture byzantine.* Paris, 1928
[37] Nersessian, Sirarpie Der, *Armenia and the Byzantine Empire.* Cambridge, Mass., 1947
[38] Omont, H. A., *Catalogues des manuscrits grecs . . . à Fontainebleau.* Paris, 1929
[39] ——, *Catalogues des manuscrits grecs . . . de Suisse.* Paris, 1929
Orlandos, An., "L'Architecture religieuse en Grèce pendant la domination turque" in *L'Hellénisme contemporain.* Athens, 1953
[40] Ouspensky, Leonid, and Vladimir Lossky, *The Meaning of Icons.* Lausanne, 1952 *
Papparrigopoulos, K., *History of the Hellenic Nation* (in Greek). Athens, 1932
[41] Pelekanidis, Stylianos, "Kastoria," Vol. I of *Byzantine Wall-Paintings* (in Greek). Thessaloniki, 1953
Pelka, Otto, *Elfenbein.* Berlin, 1923
Petkovic, V. R., *La Peinture serbe du moyen âge,* 2 vols. Belgrade, 1930–1934
[42] Pope, Arthur Upham, "Iranian and Armenian Contributions to the Beginnings of Gothic Architecture" in *The Armenian Quarterly,* reprint, n.d.
Porcher, J., M.-L. Concasty, and Charles Astruc, *Byzance et la France médiévale.* Paris, 1958
[43] Prescott, H. F. M., *Once to Sinai.* New York, 1958
Procopiou, Angelo G., *La Peinture religieuse dans les îles ioniennes pendant le XVIIIe siècle.* Athens, 1939
Radojcic, Svetozar, *Les Maîtres de l'ancienne peinture serbe.* Belgrade, 1955
——, *Yugoslavia: Medieval Frescoes.* Paris, 1955
Rêau, Louis, *L'Art roumain.* Lausanne, 1946
Recklinghausen. *Ikonen Museum Recklinghausen* (catalogue), M. Winkler and H. P. Gerhard, eds. 1956
Rice, David Talbot, *The Beginnings of Russian Icon Painting.* London, 1938
[44] ——, *Byzantine Art.* London, 1954
——, *The Beginnings of Christian Art.* London, 1957 *
——, *The Great Palace of the Byzantine Emperor.* Edinburgh, 1959
[45] ——, *The Art of Byzantium.* New York, 1959
——, *See also* Byron, Robert
Rondot, Pierre, *Les Chrétiens d'Orient.* Paris, n.d.
Ross, Marvin C., *Early Christian and Byzantine Art.* Baltimore, 1947
——, "An Emperor's Gift: Notes on Byzantine Silver Jewelry, Middle Period" in *Journal of the Walters Art Gallery,* Baltimore, 1956–1957
——, "The Chalice of Sisinios, the Grand Logothete" in *Greek, Roman, and Byzantine Studies,* Cambridge, Mass., 1959
——, "A Coptic Marriage Lampstand in Bronze" in *The Nelson Gallery & Atkins Museum Bulletin,* 1959
Rothemund, H. J., *Ikonenkunst.* Munich, 1954
——, *Aethiopische Malerei.* Munich, 1956
Rott, Hans, *Kleinasiatische Denkmäler.* Leipzig, 1908
Roudakis, Elephte, *Greek Encyclopedic Dictionary.* Athens, 1928
Sas-Zaloziecky, Wladimir, *Die byzantinische Baukunst in den Balkanländern.* Munich, 1955

Schweinfurth, Philipp, *Geschichte der russischen Malerei.* The Hague, 1930

——, *Die byzantinische Form.* Berlin, 1943

——, *Byzantinische monumentale Wandmalerei.* Mainz, 1947

[46] Setton, K. M., "The Byzantine Background of the Italian Renaissance" in *The Proceedings of the American Philosophical Society,* 1956 *

Sherrard, Philip, *Athos, Berg des Schweigens.* Lausanne, 1959

[47] Sicilianos, Demetrios, *Hellenic Hagiographers After the Conquest, 1450–1800* (in Greek). Athens, 1935

[48] Smith, Morton, "Monasteries and Their Manuscripts" in *Archaeology,* 1960

Somogyi, Árpád, *Az Esztergomi bizánci sztaurothéka.* Budapest, 1959

Sotiriou, G. A., *Manuel d'art byzantin.* Athens, 1942

——, "Le Musée byzantin d'Athènes" in *France Grèce,* 1955

Spiteris, Tony, *L'Evolution de la peinture post-byzantine dans les îles ioniennes.* Athens, 1952

Stefanescu, I. D., *Peintures murales valaques.* Paris, 1928

——, *Iconographie de la Bible.* Paris, 1938

Stewart, Cecil, *Byzantine Legacy.* London, 1947

[49] ——, *Serbian Legacy.* London, 1959

Strzygowski, Joseph, *Kleinasien, ein Neuland der Kunstgeschichte.* Leipzig, 1903

——, *Orientalische Kunst in Dalmatien.* Vienna, 1911

——, *Die Baukunst der Armenier und Europa.* Vienna, 1918

——, *Asiens bildende Kunst in Stichproben.* Berlin, 1926

——, *Origin of Christian Church Art.* Oxford, 1929

Stylianou, A. and J., *Byzantine Cyprus.* Nicosia, 1948

Tafrali, O., *Monuments byzantins de Curtea de Arges.* Paris, 1932

[50] Underwood, Paul A., 1st, 2nd, and 3rd *Preliminary Report on the Restoration of the Frescoes in the Kariye Camii at Istanbul* (1952–1954, 1955, 1955–1956) in "Dumbarton Oaks Papers." Cambridge, Mass.

——, *Paleologan Narrative Style and an Italianate Fresco of the 15th C. in the Kariye Djami* (ded. to W. E. Suida) in "Studies in the History of Art." London, 1959

Vilnay, Zev, *Israel Guide.* Jerusalem, 1958

Webb, Geoffrey, *Architecture in Britain: The Middle Ages.* London, 1956

Wendt, C. Heinrich, *Rumänische Ikonenmalerei.* Eisenach, 1953

West, Edward, *Byzantine Religious Art.* New York, 1958

Wulff, Oskar, *Altchristliche und byzantinische Kunst.* Potsdam, 1924

Xyngopoulos, A[ndré], *Thessalonique et la peinture macédonienne.* Athens, 1955

CRETE

[51] Chatzidakis, Manolis, "Wall-Paintings in Crete" (in Greek) in *Kretika Chronika,* 1952

——, "La Peinture de Macédonie en Crète" in *Les Etudes byzantines à Thessalonique,* Thessaloniki, 1953

——, *Mystras* (in Greek). Athens, 1956

——, "The Painter Euphrosynos" (in Greek) in *Kretika Chronika,* 1956

Crete (album). Athens, 1948

Folnesics, Hans, *Studien zur Entwicklungsgeschichte der Architektur und Plastik des XV Jahrhunderts in Dalmatien.* Vienna, 1914

[52] Gerola, Giuseppe. *Monumenti veneti nell'isola di Creta,* 4 vols. Venice, 1905–1932

Heraklion. *The Historical Museum of Crete* (catalogue), Stylianos Alexiou, ed. 1954

[53] Hertzberg, Gustav Friedrich, *Geschichte Griechenlands seit dem Absterben des antiken Lebens bis zur Gegenwart.* Gotha, 1877

[54] Jegerlehner, J., "Der Aufstand der kandiotischen Ritterschaft gegen Venedig, 1363–1365" in *Byzantinische Zeitschrift,* 1903

[55] Kalokyris, Konstantinos D., "Byzantine Monuments of Crete" (in Greek) in *Kretika Chronika,* 1952

——, "La Peinture murale byzantine de l'île de Crète" in *Kretika Chronika,* 1954

[56] ——, *The Byzantine Wall-Paintings of Crete* (in Greek). Athens, 1957

Lassithiotakis, K., "The Church of the Presentation in Fodele" (in Greek) in *Kretika Chronika,* 1951

[57] Matton, Raymond, *La Crète au cours des siècles.* Athens, 1957 *

Mourellos, J. D., *La Crète à travers les siècles.* Heraklion, n.d.

Notopoulos, James A., "Modern Greek Heroic Poetry" (with brochure). Folkways Records, New York, 1959

Pashley, Robert, *Travels in Crete.* Cambridge, 1837

Prevelakis, Pandelis, *Chronique d'une cité.* Paris, 1960

Spanakis, S., ed., "Guard Regulations of the Kingdom of Crete, 1598" (in Greek) in *Kretika Chronika,* 1948

VENICE AND ITALY

Arata, G. U., *The Lake of Como.* Novara, 1950

Armellini, Mariano, *Le Chiese di Roma dal sec. IV al XIX.* Rome, 1942

Arslan, W., *I Bassano.* Milan, 1931

[58] Bettini, Sergio, *La Pittura di icone Cretese-Veneziana e i madonneri.* Padua, 1933

[59] ——, *Il Pittore Michele Damasceno e l'inizio del secundo periodo dell'arte Cretese-Veneziana.* Venice, 1935

——, *Mosaici antichi di San Marco a Venezia.* Bergamo, n.d.

Bonnard, Fourier, *Un Hôte du Palais Farnese, Don Giulio Clovio.* Rome, 1929

Bozzi, Brusin, and others, *Il Friuli.* Udine, 1951

Bradley, John W., *The Life and Works of Giorgio Giulio Clovio.* London, 1891

[60] Brentani, Luigi, *Antichi maestri d'arte e di scuola delle terre ticinesi.* Como, 1937

Brown, Horatio F., *Venice, an Historical Sketch.* London, 1898

[61] Buccola, Cosma, *Monumentale badia greca.* Grottaferrata, 1933

Chiesa, Francesco, *L'Opera dei nostri artisti fuori del Ticino.* Lugano, 1928

[62] Cornaro, Flaminio, *Notizie storiche delle chiese e monasteri di Venezia.* Padua, 1758

Creighton, Mandell, *History of the Papacy from the Great Schism to the Sack of Rome.* London, 1900

[63] Dartein, F. de, *Etude sur l'architecture lombarde et sur les origines de l'architecture romano-byzantine.* Paris, 1865–1882

Fortescue, Adrian, *The Uniate Eastern Churches: The Byzantine Rite in Italy, Sicily, Syria, and Egypt.* London, 1923

Frigerio, Federico, *Il Duomo di Como.* Como, 1950

Frothingham, A. L., "Byzantine Artists in Italy" in *American Journal of Archaeology,* 1894

Gerkan, A. von, "Die Forchung nach dem Grab Petri" in *Evangelisch-Lutherische Kirchen-Zeitung,* 1952

Gilles de la Tourette, F., *L'Orient et les peintres de Venise.* Paris, 1924

Graeve, Mary Ann, "The Stone of Unction in Caravaggio's Painting for the Chiesa Nuova" in *The Art Bulletin,* 1958

Gronau, Georg, *Titian.* New York, 1904

Grote, Ludwig, *Hier bin ich ein Herr: Dürer in Venedig.* Munich, 1956

Guarducci, Margherita, *The Tomb of St. Peter: New Discoveries . . . in the Vatican.* New York, 1960

Guinta, Francesco, *Bizantini e bizantismo nella Sicilia normanna.* Rome, 1950

Hare, Augustus J. C., *Florence and Venice.* London, 1908

Hodgkinson, Harry, *The Adriatic Sea.* New York, 1956

[64] Jaffé, Michael, "Rubens and Giulio Romano at Mantua" in *The Art Bulletin,* 1958

Kirschbaum, Engelbert, *The Tombs of St. Peter and St. Paul.* New York, 1959

Klauser, Th., "Die römische Petrustradition im Lichte der neuen Ausgrabungen unter der Petrus-Kirche" in *Arbeitsgemeinschaft . . . Nordrhein-Westfalen,* 1956

Leon, Harry J., "The Greek Inscriptions of the Jews in Rome" in *Greek, Roman, and Byzantine Studies,* Cambridge, Mass., 1959

[65] Marconi, Sandra, "La Raccolta di icone Veneto-Cretesi della communità Greco-Ortodossa di Venezia" in *Atte dell'Inst. Veneto di Scienze, Lettre ed Arti,* 1947–1948

Mazzotti, Giuseppe, *Le Ville venete.* Treviso, 1954

Meester, Placide de, *Le College pontifical grec de Rome.* Rome, 1910

[66] Mertzios, Konstantinos, "New Information About Cretans from the Archive of Venice (referring to Manousos Theotokopoulos)" (in Greek) in *Kretika Chronika,* 1948

Molmenti, Pompeo, *La Vie privée à Venise.* Venice, 1895

——, *La Storia di Venezia,* 3 vols. Venice, 1908–1911

Morey, Charles R., "Castelseprio and the Byzantine 'Renaissance'" in *The Art Bulletin,* 1952
Musolino, Giovanni, *Torcello.* Venice, 1953
Netzhammer, R., *Das griechische Kolleg in Rom.* Salzburg, 1905
[67] Okey, Thomas, *The Story of Venice.* London, 1914
Paoletti, Pietro, *L'Architectura e la scultura in Venezia.* Venice, 1893–1897
Pecchiai, Pio, *Roma nel Cinquecento* in "Inst. degli Studii Romani," 1923
Perkins, J. B. Ward, "The Shrine of St. Peter and Its Twelve Spiral Columns" in *Journal of Roman Studies,* 1952
[68] Picenardi, G. Sommi, *Del Gran priorato dell'ordine gerosolimitano in Venezia.* Venice, n.d.
[69] Ragg, Laura M., *Crises in Venetian History.* London, 1928
Rocchi, A., *La Badia di Grottaferrata.* Rome, 1904
——, and Cosma Buccola, *La Badia di Grottaferrata.* Milan, 1930
Rodotà, Pompilio, *Dell'Origine, progresso e stato presente del rito greca in Italia,* 3 vols. Rome, 1758–1763
Sakcinski, Ivan K., *Leben des G. Julius Clovio.* Agram, 1852
Seppelt, F. X., *Geschichte des Pabsttums.* Leipzig, 1936
Tassini, Giuseppe, *Alcuni palazzi ed antichi edificii di Venezia.* Venice, 1879
[70] Tietze, Hans, *Tintoretto: The Paintings and Drawings.* London, 1948
[71] ——, *Titian: The Paintings and Drawings.* London, 1950
——, and E. Tietze-Conrat, *The Drawings of the Venetian Painters in the 15th and 16th Centuries.* New York, 1944
Toesca, Pietro, *San Vitale di Ravenna: I Mosaici.* Milan, 1952
——, and F. Forlati, *Mosaics of St. Mark's.* New York, 1959
Toynbee, Jocelyn, "The Shrine of St. Peter and Its Setting" in *Journal of Roman Studies,* 1953
[72] ——, with J. B. Ward Perkins, *The Shrine of St. Peter and the Vatican Excavations.* London, 1956
Valente, Attilio, *La Riviera del Brenta.* Venice, 1951
[73] Veludo, Giovanni, *Sulla colonia greca orientale stabilità in Venezia.* Venice, 1847
——, miscellaneous Greek and Italian booklets and pamphlets. Venice, 1890
Venice. *Museo di dipinti sacri (bizantini e post-bizantini),* Sofia Antoniadis, ed. 1959
Vicenzoni, Guido, *Bassano e il Monte Grappa.* Milan, n.d.

TOLEDO AND SPAIN

[74] Bashkirtseff, Maria, *The Complete Journal of.* Chicago, 1913
Bordona, Jesús Domíniguez, *Proceso inquisitorial contra el escultor Estéban Jamete.* Madrid, 1933
Brenan, Gerald, *The Face of Spain.* New York, 1951
Calvert, Albert F., *Toledo.* London, 1907
[75] *Catálogo de las causas contra la fé . . . Toledo* (Archivo Histórico Nacional). Madrid, 1903
Cirac, Estopañan S., *Los Procesos de hechicerias en la inquisición.* Madrid, 1942
Collins, W. W., *Cathedral Cities of Spain.* New York, 1911
[76] Cook, Capt. S. S. (S. E. Widdrington), *Sketches in Spain during the Years 1829–32,* 2 vols. London, 1934
Ellis, Havelock, *The Soul of Spain.* Boston, n.d.
Evans, Grose, *Spanish Painting in the National Gallery of Art.* Washington, D.C., 1960
[77] Ferrando Roig, Juan, *Iconografía de los santos.* Barcelona, 1950
[78] Gautier, Théophile, *Un Voyage en Espagne.* Paris, 1840
——, *A Romantic in Spain.* New York, 1926
Graux, Charles, *Essai sur les origines du fonds grec de l'Escurial.* Paris, 1880
[79] Hernández, Padre Miguel, de la Compañía de Jesus, *Vida, Martyrio, y Translación de la gloriosa Virgen, y Martyr, Santa Leocadia* . . . Toledo, 1591
Hutton, Edward, *The Cities of Spain.* New York, 1906
[80] Iglesias, Fernando Figeroa, *Goya y la inquisición.* Madrid, 1929
[81] Justi, Carl, *Velázquez und sein Jahrhundert.* Zurich, 1933
Kerr, Alfred, *O Spanien!* Berlin, 1924

[82] Lady Holland (Elizabeth Vassall), *The Spanish Journal.* London, 1910
[83] Lea, Henry Charles, *History of the Inquisition in Spain,* 5 vols. New York, 1905–1908
Lozoya, J. C., marqués de, *Historia del arte hispanico,* 5 vols. Barcelona, 1931–1949
[84] Madariaga, Salvador de, "Spain and the West" in *The Pen in Exile,* P. Tabori, ed., London, 1954
Marañón, Gregorio, *Elogio y nostalgia de Toledo.* Madrid, 1958
——, *Antonio Pérez, der Staatssekretär Philipps II.* Wiesbaden, 1959
Mayer, August L., *Meisterwerke der Gemäldesammlung des Prado in Madrid.* Munich, 1922
Mélida, José Ramón, *Escorial.* Barcelona, n.d.
Menéndez y Pelayo, M., *Historia de los heterodoxos españoles.* Madrid, 1947
Meunier, Louis, *Vues en Espagne.* Paris, n.d.
Miller, E., *Catalogue des manuscrits grecs de la Bibliothèque de l'Escurial.* Paris, 1848
Morton, H. V., *A Stranger in Spain.* New York, 1955
[85] Oliviera Martins, J. P., *Historia de la civilización ibérica.* Buenos Aires, 1944
Pacheco, Francisco, *Arte de la pintura,* F. J. Sánchez Canton, ed., 2 vols. Madrid, 1956
[86] Palomino, Antonio, *El Museo pictórico,* 2 vols. Madrid, 1795–1797
[87] Parry, J. H., *The Sale of Public Office in the Spanish Indies Under the Habsburgs.* Berkeley and Los Angeles, 1953
Pinta Llorente, Miguel de la, *La Inquisición española y las problemas de la cultura y de la intolerancia.* Madrid, 1958
Pogolotti, Marcelo, *La Contrareforma y la pintura del siglo de oro español.* Havana, 1943
Ponz, Antonio (1725–1792), *Viaje de España* (Vol. V, 1776). 18 vols. Madrid, 1776–1794
Pritchett, V. S., *The Spanish Temper.* London, 1954
[88] Proske, Beatrice Gilman, *Castilian Sculpture, Gothic to Renaissance.* New York, 1951
[89] ——, *Pompeo Leoni.* New York, 1956
Ricketts, Charles S., *The Art of the Prado.* Boston, 1907
[90] Rodríguez Escorial, José L., "El Pintor Nicolás Greco, Pirotécnico" in *Instituto D. de Colmenares.* Segovia, 1949
[91] Schubert, Otto, *Geschichte des Barock in Spanien.* Esslingen, 1908
Sentenach y Cabañas, Narciso, *La Pintura en Madrid.* Madrid, 1907
Soehner, Halldor, "Die Geschichte der spanischen Malerei im Spiegel der Forschung" in *Zeitschrift für Kunstgeschichte,* 1956 *
Soria, Martin, "Some Flemish Sources of Baroque Painting in Spain" in *The Art Bulletin,* 1948
Toledo. *Carlos V y su ambiente,* catalogue. 1958
Tormo y Monzó, Elías, *Toledo, tesoro y museos.* Madrid, n.d.
Trapier, Elizabeth du Gué, *Ribera.* New York, 1952
Trens, Manuel, *El Arte en la Pasión de nuestro Señor.* Barcelona, 1945
——, *María, iconografía de la Virgen en el arte español.* Madrid, 1946
——, *La Eucaristía en el arte español.* Barcelona, 1952
Vázquez de Parga, L., "La Dormición de la Virgen en la catedral de Pamplona" in *Principe de Viana,* Pamplona, n.d.
Viardot, Louis, *Notices sur les principaux peintres d'Espagne.* Paris, 1839
[92] ——, *Les Musées d'Espagne.* Paris, 1855
Zarco Cuevas, Julián, *Pintors españoles en San Lorenzo el Real de el Escorial.* Madrid, 1931
[93] ——, *Pintores italianos en San Lorenzo el Real de el Escorial.* Madrid, 1932

EL GRECO

Alenda y Mira, Jenaro, *Relaciónes de solemnidades y fiestas publicas de España.* Madrid, 1903
Babelon, Jean, "Greco" in *Gazette des Beaux-Arts,* 1937
——, *El Greco.* Paris, 1946
Bachelin, L., *Tableaux anciens de la Galerie Charles Ier Roi de Roumainie.* Paris, 1898
Ballo, G., *El Greco.* Milan, 1952
Barrès, Maurice, *Greco ou le Secret de Tolède.* Paris, 1912
Bertaux, E., "Notes sur le Greco: Le Byzantinisme" in *Revue de l'art ancien et moderne,* Paris, 1913
Beryes, Ignacio de, *Doménicos Theotocópoulos, El Greco.* Barcelona, 1944

Bettini, Sergio, "Precisazioni sull'attività giovanile del Greco" in *Arte Veneta,* 1952

[94] Blunt, Anthony, "The Dream of Philip II" in *Journal of the Warburg Inst.,* London, 1939–1940

Bourgeois, Stephan, "El Greco" in *Byrdcliffe Afternoons,* Woodstock, N.Y., 1940

——, Introduction to *An Exhibition of Paintings by El Greco.* New York, 1941

Bronstein, Leo, *El Greco.* New York, 1950

Budapest. *Catalogue des tableaux anciens de la collection Marczel de Nemes, Budapest,* Roger Mile, ed. Paris, 1913

Byron, Robert, "Greco: The Epilogue to Byzantine Culture" in *The Burlington Magazine,* 1929

Camón Aznar, José, *Bizancio e Italia en el Greco.* Granada, 1944

[95] ——, *Dominico Greco,* 2 vols. Madrid, 1950 *

Chatzidakis, Manolis, "Domenikos Theotokopoulos and the Cretan Painting" (in Greek) in *Kretika Chronika,* 1950

Colman, P., *La dalle funéraire du sculpteur Thomas Tollet (1537–1621).* Brussels, 1959

[96] Cossío, Manuel, *El Greco,* 2 vols. Madrid, 1908 *

[97] ——, *Dominico Theotocopuli, El Greco* (notas de Natalia Cossío de Jiménez). Oxford, 1955

Doménech, Rafael, *La Casa del Greco.* Barcelona, n.d.

Embiricos, Alexandre, "Hellénisme du Greco" in *La Tribune de Genêve,* 1955

Escholier, Raymond, *Greco.* Paris, 1937

Espresati, Carlos, *La Casa del Greco.* Madrid, 1912

Fiocco, Giuseppe, "Del 'Greco' veneziano e di un suo ritratto di Ottavio Farnese" in *Arte Veneta,* 1951

[98] ——, "A Small Portable Panel by Titian for Philip II" in *The Burlington Magazine,* 1956

Gevaerts, Jean G. (Joannes Casparius Gevartius), *Pompa introitus honori serenissimi principis ferdinandi austriaci.* Antwerp, 1641

[99] Goldscheider, Ludwig, *El Greco.* London, 1938

Gómez de la Serna, R., *El Greco.* Madrid, n.d.

Gómez-Moreno, M., *El Greco, el entierro de Orgaz.* Barcelona, 1951

Guinard, P., "Barrès et le Greco" in *Revue Hebdomadaire,* 1924

——, *El Greco.* Lausanne, 1956

Hinks, Roger, *El Greco.* London, 1954

[100] Jiménez, Natalia Cossío de, *El Greco: Notes on His Birthplace, Education and Family.* Oxford, 1948

——, "Don Juan of Austria" in *Gazette des Beaux-Arts,* reprint, n.d.

Kehrer, Hugo, *Die Kunst des Greco.* Munich, 1914

——, *Greco als Gestalt des Manierismus.* Munich, 1939

[101] ——, *Greco in Toledo.* Stuttgart, 1960

Kyros, A. A., *Domenikos Theotokopoulos the Cretan* (in Greek). Athens, 1932. (Summarized by F. Rutter in *The Burlington Magazine,* 1932)

Lafond, Paul, "Domenikos Theotocopouli" in *Les Arts,* 1906

Lafuente, Enrique, "El Greco, Some Recent Discoveries" in *The Burlington Magazine,* 1945

Legendre, M., and A. Hartmann, *Domenikos Theotokopoulos, Called El Greco.* Paris, 1937

Madrid. *Catalógo ilustrado de la exposición de El Greco,* Salvador Viniegra, ed. 1902

[102] Marañón, Gregorio, *El Greco y Toledo.* Madrid, 1956 *

Mayer, August L., *El Greco.* Munich, 1911

——, "Los Quadros del Greco . . . de la colección Nemes Budapest" in *Museum,* Barcelona, 1911

———, *Dominico Theotocopuli El Greco.* Munich, 1926 *

———, "El Greco: An Oriental Artist" in *The Art Bulletin,* 1929

——,"Notes on El Greco" in *The Burlington Magazine,* 1939

Meier-Graefe, Julius, *Spanische Reise.* Berlin, 1910

Mélida, J. R., *El Arte antiguo y el Greco.* Madrid, 1915

Neumeyer, Alfred, *El Greco: Das Begräbnis des Grafen Orgaz.* Stuttgart, 1957

Pallucchini, Rodolfo, *Il Polittico del Greco della R. Galleria Estense.* Rome, 1937

——, "Some Early Works by El Greco" in *The Burlington Magazine,* 1948

——, "Opere giovanili firmate e datate del Greco" in *Arte Veneta,* 1952

Pantorba, Bernardino de, *El Greco.* Madrid, 1946

Pla Cargol, J., *El Greco y Toledo.* Madrid, 1943

Preston, Stuart, *El Greco.* New York, n.d.

Prévélakis, Pandelis, *El Greco in Rome* (in Greek). Athens, 1941

[103] ——, *Theotokopoulos* (in Greek). Athens, 1942 *

Procopiou, Angelo J., "El Greco and Cretan Painting" in *The Burlington Magazine,* 1952

Rice, David Talbot, "El Greco and Byzantium" in *The Burlington Magazine,* 1937

——, "Five Late Byzantine Panels and Greco's Views of Sinai" in *The Burlington Magazine,* 1947

Rousseau, Theodore, Jr., "El Greco's Vision of St. John" in *Bulletin of the Metropolitan Museum of Art,* New York, 1959

Rutter, Frank, *El Greco.* London, 1930

——, "The Early Life of El Greco" in *The Burlington Magazine,* 1932

Salas, Xavier de, "La Valoración del Greco por los románticos españoles y franceses" in *Archivo español de arte y arqueología,* 1940–1941

[104] San Román y Fernández, Francisco de Borja de, *El Greco en Toledo.* Madrid, 1910

[105] ——, *El Sepulcro de los Theotocopuli.* Madrid, 1912

[106] ——, "De la vida del Greco" in *Archivo español de arte y arqueología,* 1927

Schweinfurth, Philip, "Greco und die italokretische Schule" in *Byzantinische Zeitschrift,* 1929–1930

[107] Soehner, Halldor, "Der Stand der Greco Forschung" in *Zeitschrift für Kunstgeschichte,* 1956 *

[108] ——, "Greco in Spanien" (I, II, III) in *Münchner Jahrbuch der bildenen Kunst,* 1957–1959 *–1960

[109] Trapier, Elizabeth du Gué, *El Greco.* New York, 1925 *

[110] ——, "The Son of El Greco" in *Notes Hispanic,* New York, 1943

[111] ——, *El Greco: Early Years at Toledo (1576–1586).* New York, 1958

[112] ——, "El Greco in the Farnese Palace, Rome," in *Gazette des Beaux-Arts,* 1958

Vallentin, Antonina, *El Greco.* London, 1954

[113] *Viagem da . . . Magestade del Rey D. Filipe II ao Reyno de Portugal . . .* Madrid, 1622

Villar, Emilio, *El Greco en España.* Madrid, 1928

Waterhouse, Ellis, "El Greco's Italian Period" in *Art Studies,* Cambridge, Mass., 1930

Wethey, Harold E., *El Greco and His School.* Princeton, in press

[114] Willumsen, J.-F., *La Jeunesse du peintre El Greco.* Paris, 1927 *

Zervos, Christian, *Les Oeuvres du Greco en Espagne. Paris,* 1939

INDEX

(Titles of paintings and plate numbers are in italics.)

INDEX

INDEX

A. Julio Clovio

PLATE 57

Three Portraits by El Greco

C. Cardinal Fernando Niño de Guevara

B. Cardinal Juan Pardo de Tavera

A. The Betrayal of Christ.
Byzantine Mss. Early 12th C.

PLATE 58

B. The Disrobing of Christ,
by El Greco

C. The Betrayal, by Poulakis.

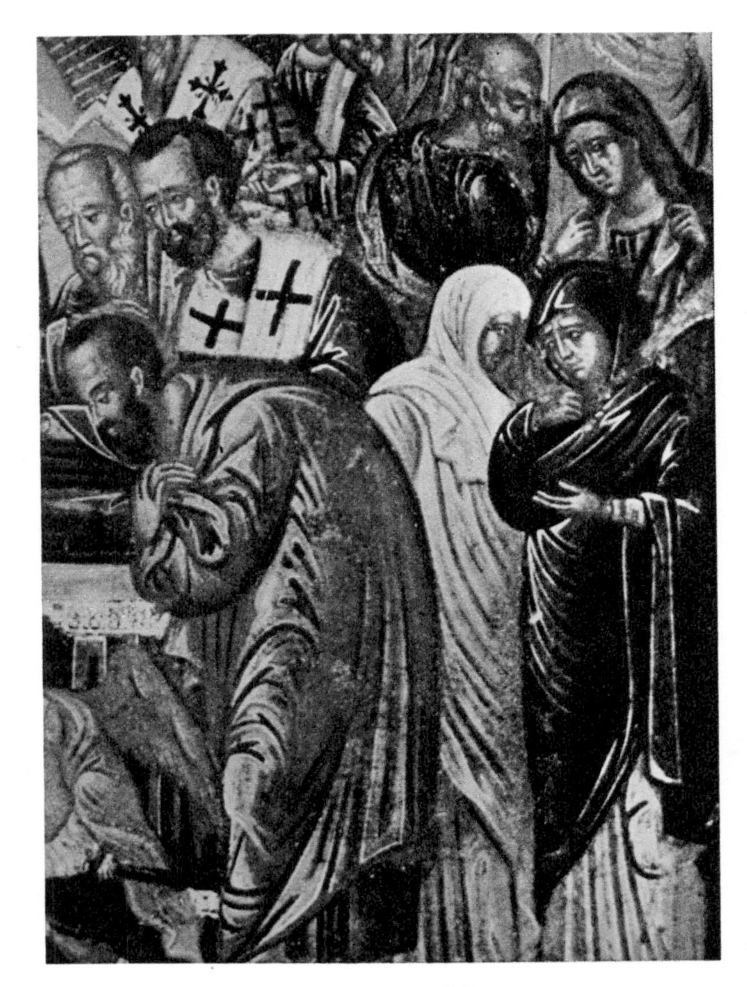

A. Mourning Women. Detail from
The Dormition of the Virgin. Icon. 17th C.

B. Mourning Women. Detail from The Crucifixion.
Icon. 17th C.

C. Figure of Eve. Detail, Mural.
Kariye Cami, Istanbul. 14th C.

PLATE 59

B. El Greco

A. Icon. Lavra, Mt. Athos. 14th C.

Christ in Benediction

C. Mural. Kritsa, Crete. 14th C?

A. Mural. Verria, Greece

PLATE 61

B. Icon, by Damaskinos? Crete. 16th C.

C. Raphael

Christ in Benediction

A. Page from the Rabula Gospels. Syria. 6th C.

PLATE 62

C. Detail from The Ascension. Icon. Lavra, Mt. Athos. Late 14th C?

The Pentecost

B. El Greco

A. Titian

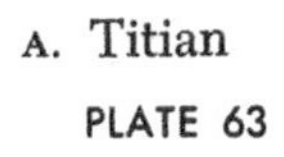

PLATE 63

B. Dürer. Woodcut

C. Guido Reni

The Pentecost

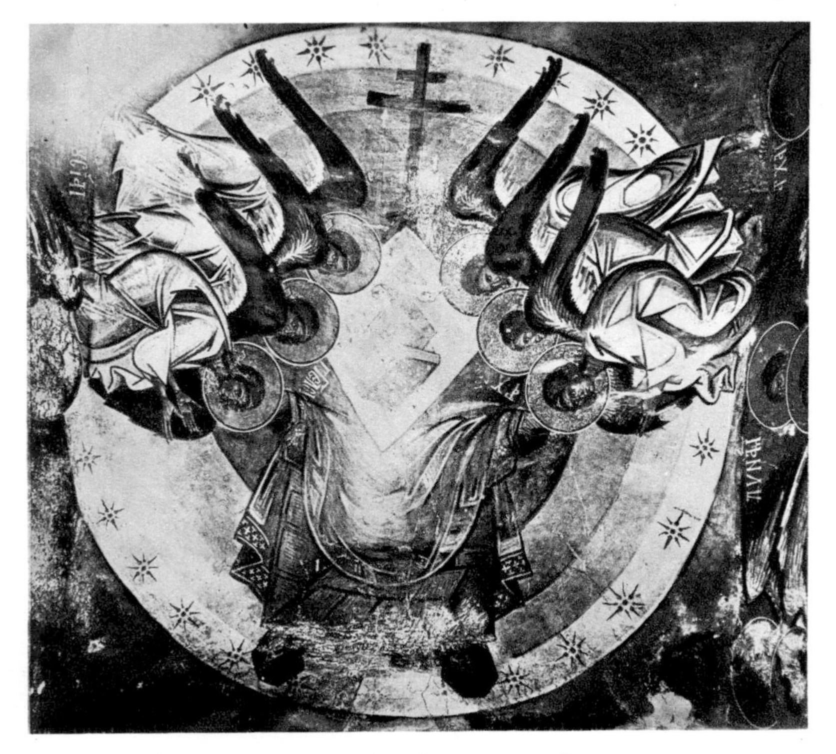

A. The Preparation of the Throne. Mural.
St. Demetrios, Mistra, Greece. Early 14th C.

PLATE 64

B. The Adoration of the Holy Name, by El Greco

C. Detail from The Burning Bush,
by Damaskinos. Icon. 16th C.

A. The Martyrdom of St. Haralambos. Detail. Icon. Istanbul. 1736

PLATE 65

B. The Last Judgment. Mural. Lavra, Mt. Athos. Early 16th C.

C. Detail from The Last Judgment. Mural. Lavra

A. Statue of a Byzantine Emperor. Drawing

PLATE 66

B. The Martyrdom of St. Mauritius, by El Greco

C. St. George. Soapstone Relief. Vatopedi, Mt. Athos.

B. El Greco. Detail

A. The Martyrdom of St. Mauritius, by Romulo Cincinnato

PLATE 67

C. Christ and the Centurion, by Veronese

A. The Burial of Count Orgaz, by El Greco

PLATE 68

B. The Dormition of the Virgin, by Fra Angelico. Detail

A. The Entombment of Christ. Mural. Dochiariou, Mt. Athos. Mid-16th C.

B. The Dormition of the Virgin, by Andreas Rizzo. 16th C.

PLATE 69

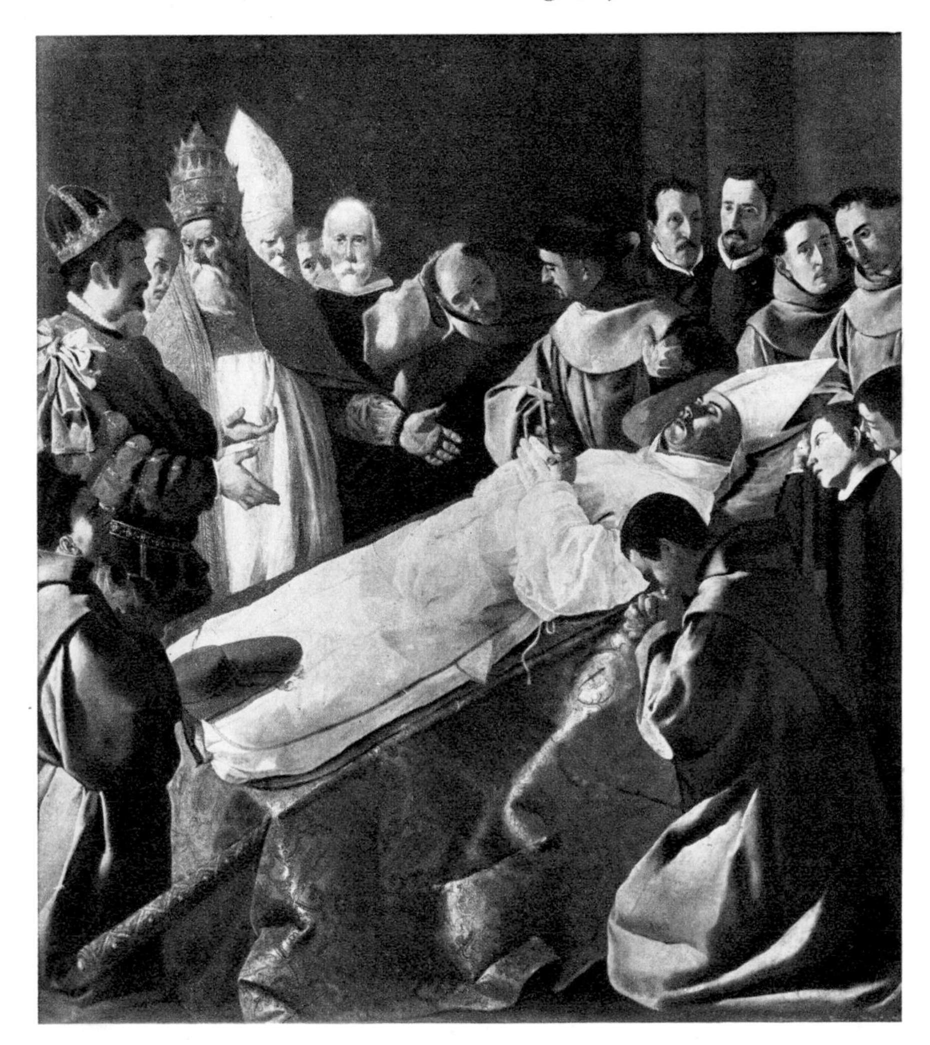

C. The Burial of St. Bonaventure, by Zurbaran

A. The Annunciation.
Byzantine Soapstone Relief.
Toledo. 12th C.

PLATE 70

B. Portrait of His Son,
by El Greco. Detail

A. The Resurrection,
by El Greco

PLATE 71

B. The Transfiguration.
Greek Mss. 14th C.

C. The Transfiguration. Mural.
St. Paul, Mt. Athos. Mid-16th C.

D. The Resurrection, by Tintoretto

A. Mosaic. Detail. Monreale. Late 12th C.

B. Mural. Detail. Andrejas, Yugoslavia. 14th C.

PLATE 72

The Agony in the Garden

C. Mural. Detail. Karyes, Mt. Athos. 14th C.

A. El Greco

PLATE 73

he Agony in the Garden

B. Tintoretto

C. St. John the Baptist entering the Desert, by Giovanni di Paolo. 15th C.

A. The Healing of the Blind, by El Greco

PLATE 74

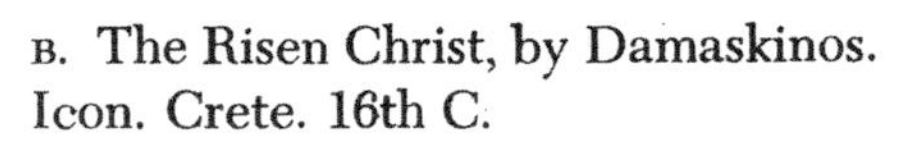

B. The Risen Christ, by Damaskinos. Icon. Crete. 16th C.

C. The Risen Christ, by E. Zane. Icon. Scuola dei Greci. Venice. 1686

D. The Cleansing of the Temple, by El Greco. Early Version

A. Christ in Limbo. Mural.
Kariye Cami, Istanbul. Early 14th C.

B. The Cleansing of the Temple, by El Greco. Late Version

PLATE 75

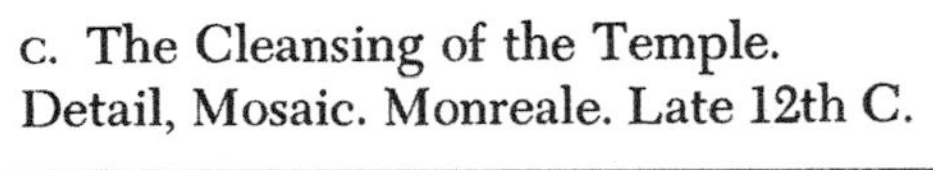

C. The Cleansing of the Temple.
Detail, Mosaic. Monreale. Late 12th C.

D. The Cleansing of the Temple, by Bassano. Detail

A. Mural. Apostolon, Kastoria, Greece. 1547

PLATE 76

C. Scuola dei Greci, Venice. Late 16th C.

B. Veronese

The Annunciation

A. Venetian School. Formerly assigned to El Greco

PLATE 77

C. Circle of Titian

B. El Greco. Early Version

The Annunciation

A. El Greco

PLATE 78

B. Angels. Detail from The Ladder to Heaven. Mural. Chilandari, Mt. Athos. 14th C.

C. El Greco

The Annunciation

A. Mother of God. Mural.
Pántanassa, Mistra, Greece.
Late 14th C.

PLATE 79

The Annunciation

C. Detail of Embroidery in B

B. El Greco. Late Version

A. Onyx Paten with Enamel Medallion. Byzantine. 9th C.

PLATE 80

B. Icon. Scuola dei Greci, Venice. Early 17th C?

The Last Supper

C. Damaskinos. Icon. Heraklion, Crete. 16th C.

D. Mural. Metamorphosis Monastery, Meteora, Greece. Late 15th C.

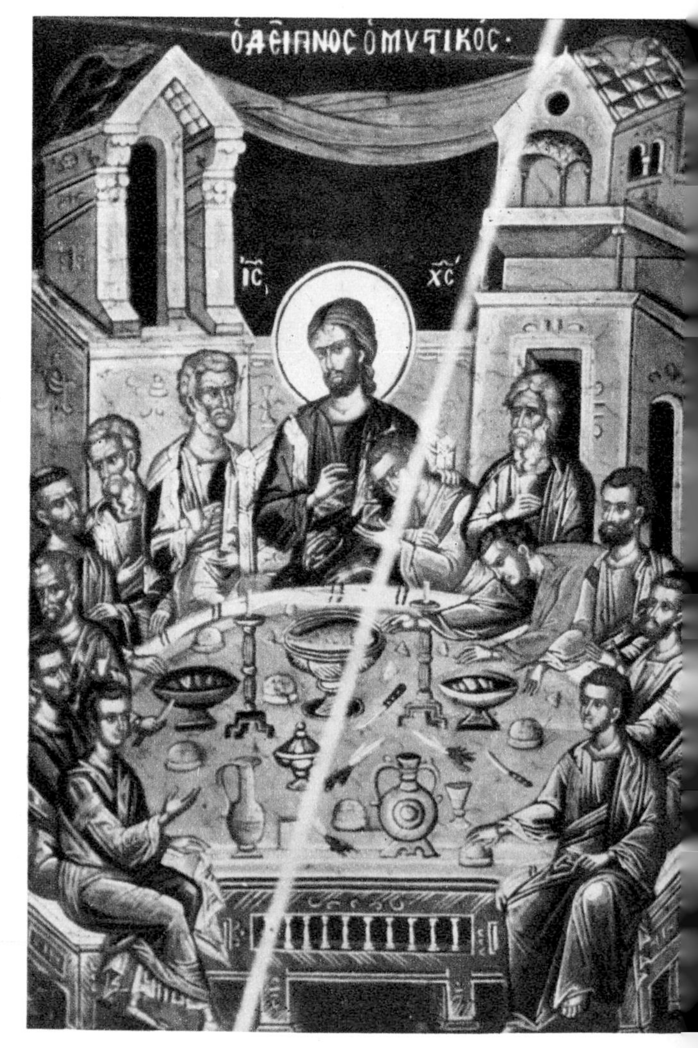

A. Tintoretto

PLATE 81

: Feast in the House of Simon

C. El Greco

B. Berruguete el Viejo

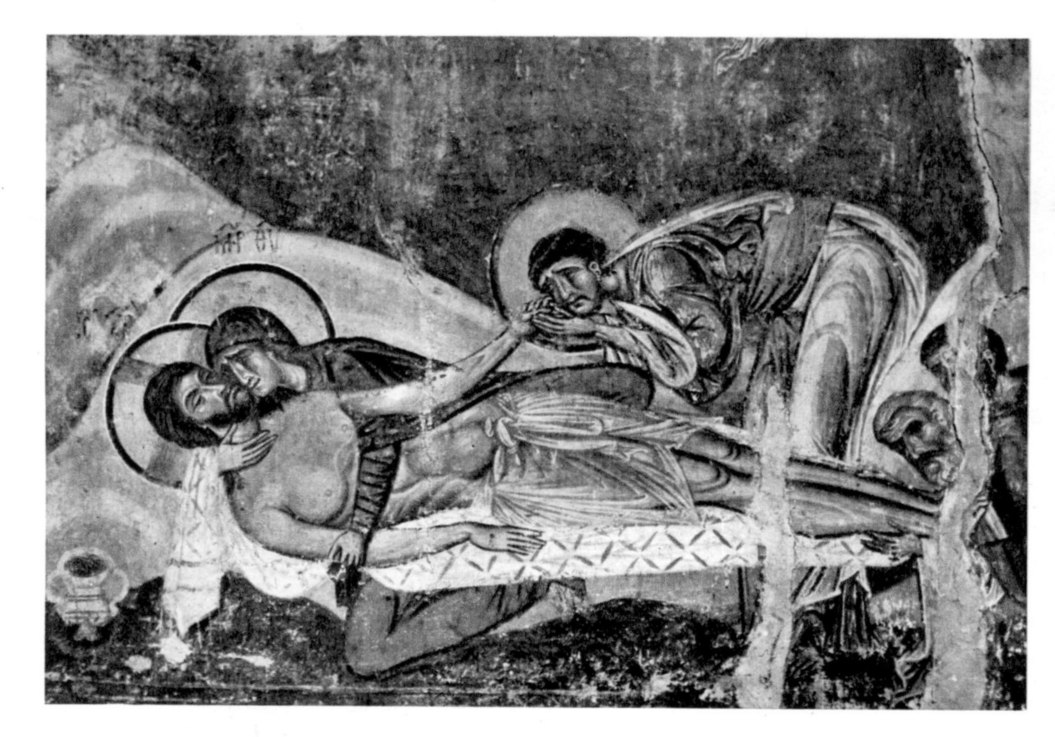

A. Mural. Nerezi, Yugoslavia. Mid-12th C.

B. Mural. Anargyri, Kastoria, Greece. 11th C.

PLATE 82

The Lamentation

C. Icon. Creto-Venetian. 16th C.

D. Icon. Heraklion, Crete. 17th C?

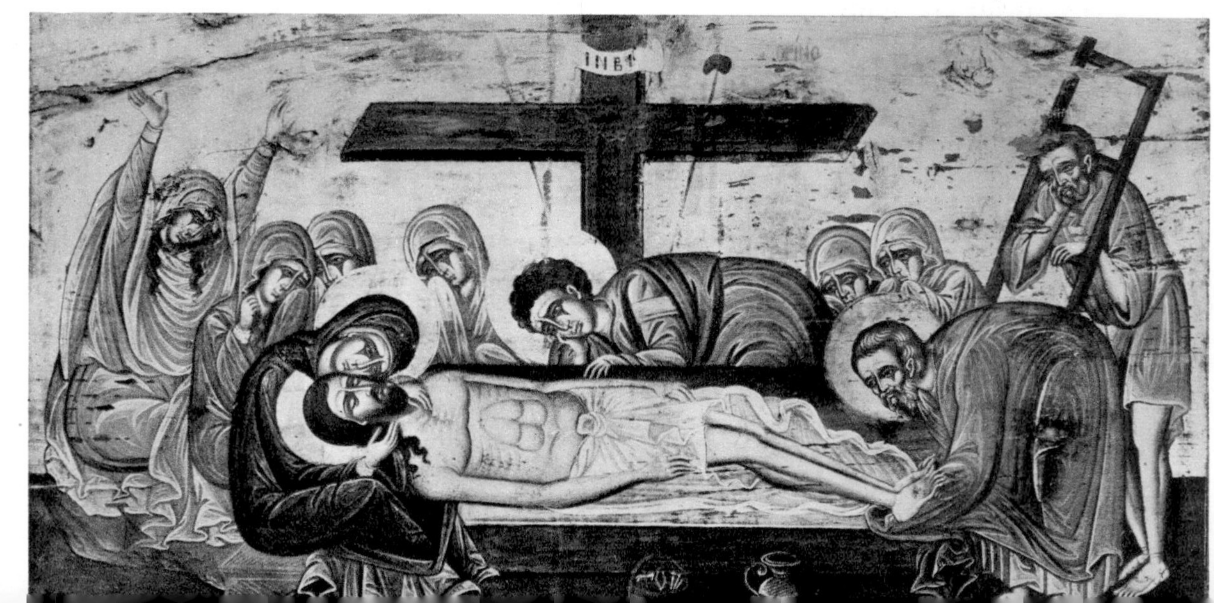

The Lamentation

A. Icon. Athens. 15th C?

PLATE 83

B. Main Figures from El Greco's Lamentation 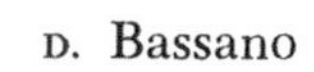

C. El Greco

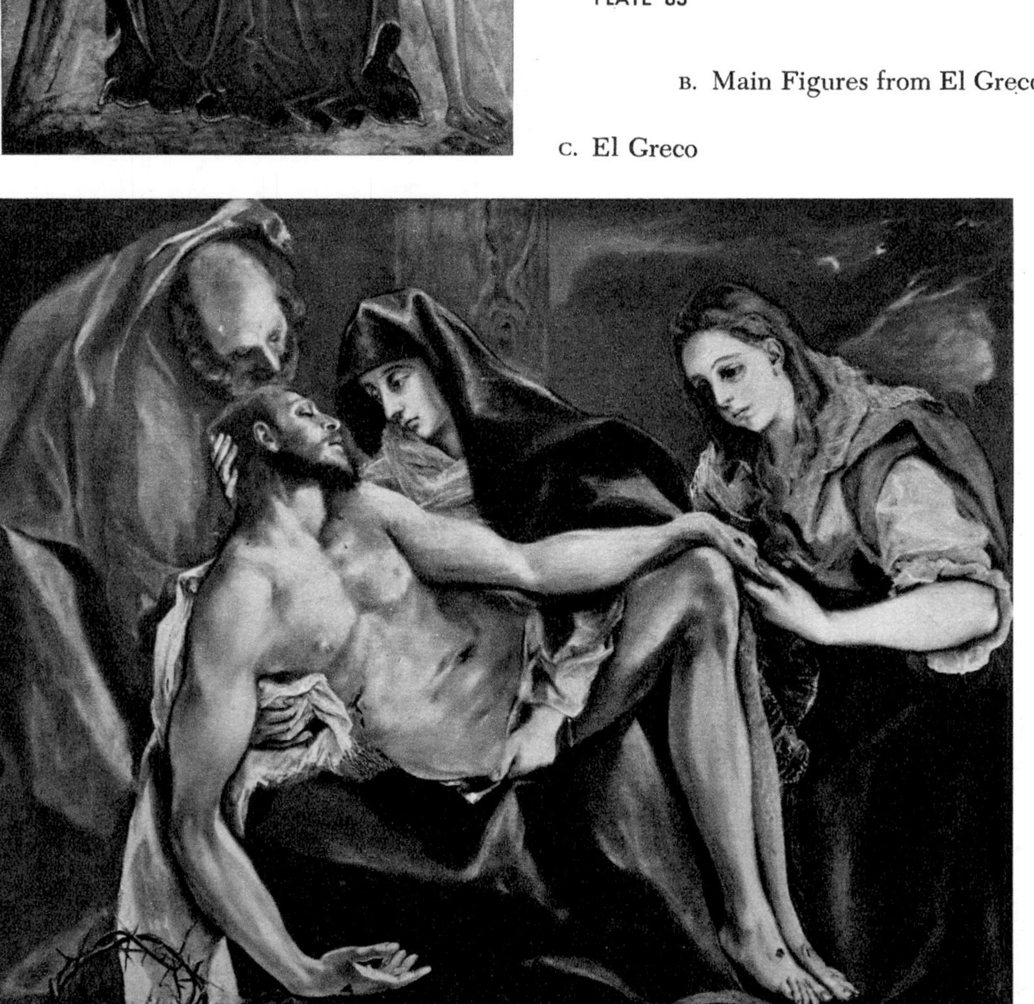

D. Bassano

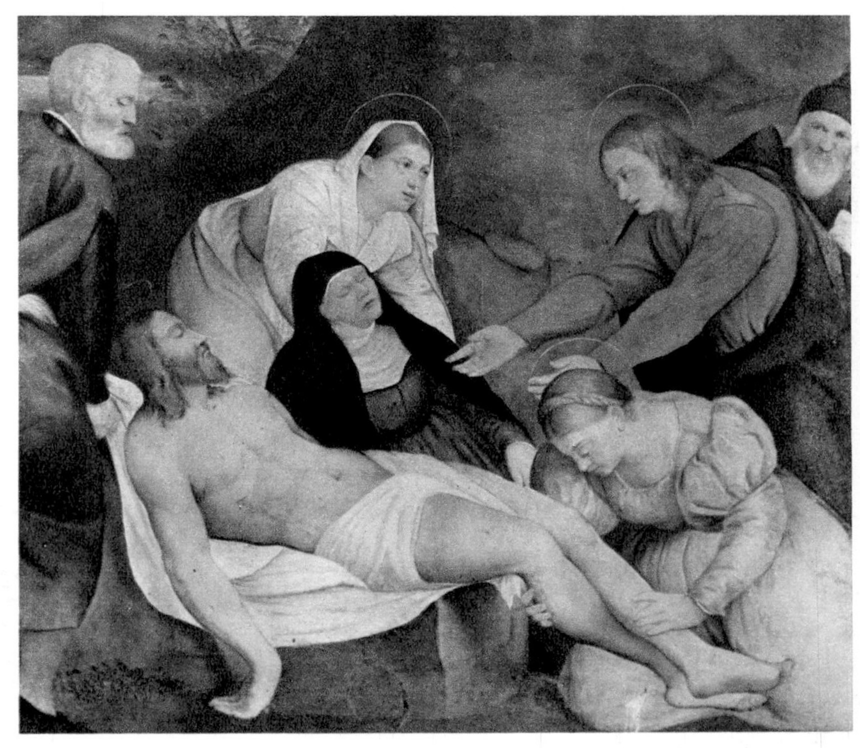

A. The Holy Liturgy, by Damaskinos. Detail, Icon. Heraklion, Crete. 16th C.

B. Right Wing of Triptych assigned to El Greco

PLATE 84

The Baptism of Christ

C. Piero della Francesca

D. Mural. Karyes, Mt. Athos. 16th C?

B. The Coronation of the Virgin, by El Greco

A. El Greco

PLATE 85

C. Juan de Juanes

A. The Baptism. Mosaic. St. Mark, Venice. 14th C.

B. Icon. Cathedral, Kastoria, Greece. 17th C?

PLATE 86

St. John the Baptist

C. El Greco

D. Titian

A. St. Gregory. Mosaic. Cappella Palatina, Palermo. Mid-12th C.

B. St. Basil, by E. Zane. Detail, Icon. 1656

PLATE 87

C. St. Stelianos. Mural. St. Nicholas Trianou, Kastoria, Greece. 17th C.

D. St. Jerome, by El Greco

A. Mosaic. Cappella Palatina, Palermo. Mid-12th C.

B. SS. Peter and Paul. Mural. Vatopedi, Mt. Athos. 14th C.

D. Detail from The Dormition. Mural. Mavriotissa, Kastoria, Greece. 15th C?

C. Ribera, Lo Spagnoletto

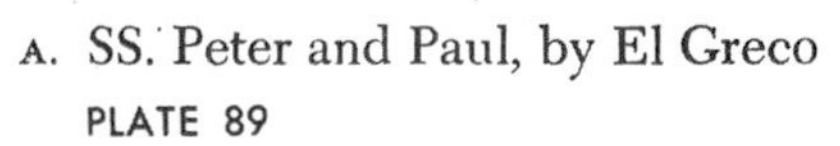

A. SS. Peter and Paul, by El Greco

B. St. Paul with Greek Letter to St. Titus, by El Greco

PLATE 89

A. Titian

PLATE 90

B. Sánchez Coello. 1581

C. Il Salmeggia. 1600

St. Catherine of Alexandria

A. Icon. Heraklion, Crete

PLATE 91

B. El Greco

St. Catherine of Alexandria

A. Portrait Panel. Egypt. 2nd C.

B. Fray Hortensio Felix Paravicino, by El Greco

PLATE 92

C. Portrait Panel. Egypt. 2nd C.

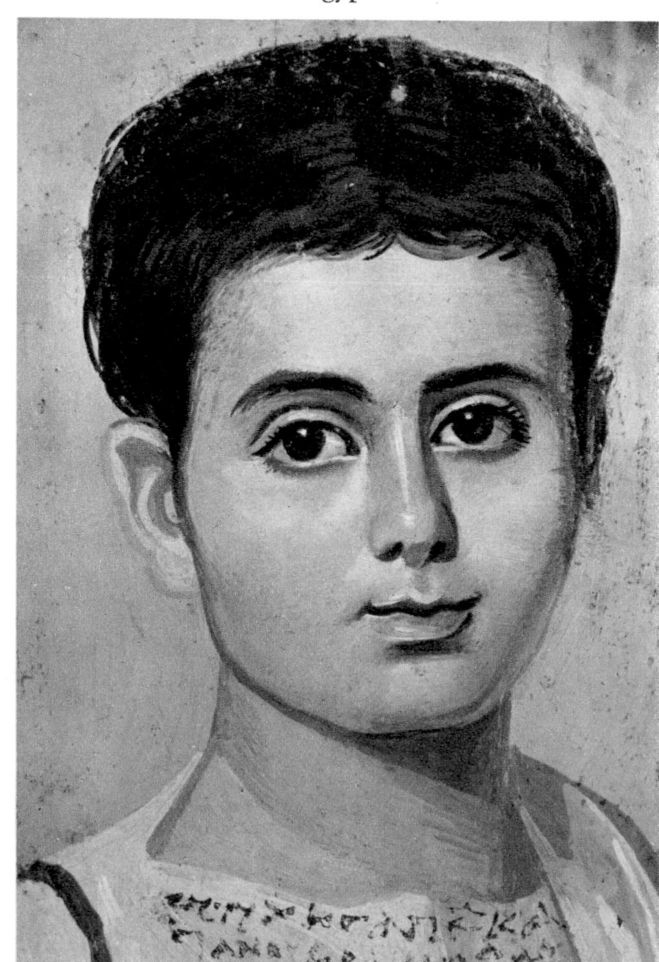

D. Head of Jorge Manuel, by El Greco

A. Portrait by El Greco

B. Portrait Panel. Egypt. 2nd C.

PLATE 93

C. The Virgin Mary, by El Greco

D. Family Portrait. Byzantine. 4th C.

A. Apostle. Mosaic. St. Sophia, Thessaloniki, Greece. 10–11th C.

B. Portrait, perhaps of the Artist, by El Greco

C. St. John Chrysostom. Mosaic. Cappella Palatina, Palermo. Mid-12th C.

A. St. Francis of Assisi, by El Greco

PLATE 95

B. St. Francis of Assisi, by El Greco.
Repetitions of the Same Theme.
A page from August L. Mayer's *El Greco*

C. St. Nicholas. Mural. Anargyri, Kastoria, Greece. Showing the Head of an Earlier and the Body of a Later Version

A. Nativity. Mural. Decani, Yugoslavia. 14th C.

PLATE 96

Backgrounds Derived from the Aureole and the Holy Grotto

B. Nativity. Mosaic. Martorana, Palermo. Mid-12th C.

C. St. John the Evangelist dictating the Gospel. Mss. Dionysiou, Mt. Athos. 13th C.

A. SS. Paul of Thebes and Anthony Abbot. Mural. Siatista, Greece. 1611

PLATE 97

ckgrounds Derived from the Aureole and the Holy Grotto

B. St. John dictating the Gospel, by Lambardo. Icon. Venice. 1602

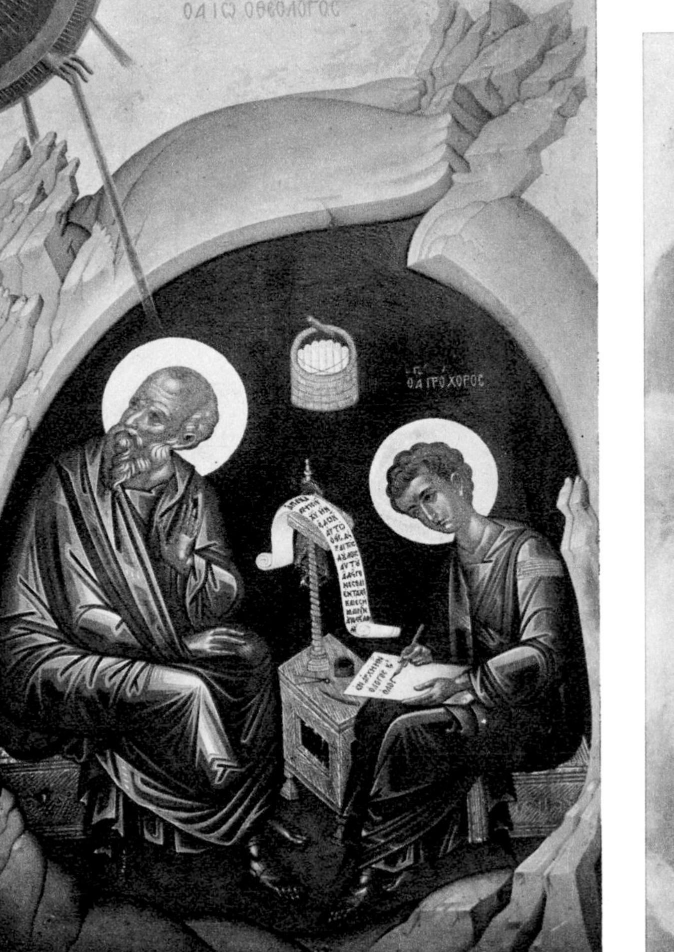

C. St. Francis in Ecstasy, by El Greco

A. Dürer. Woodcut

B. El Greco

PLATE 98

The Throne of Mercy

C. Catalan School. Panel. 16th C.

D. Luis Tristán

A. The Marriage of the Virgin, by El Greco

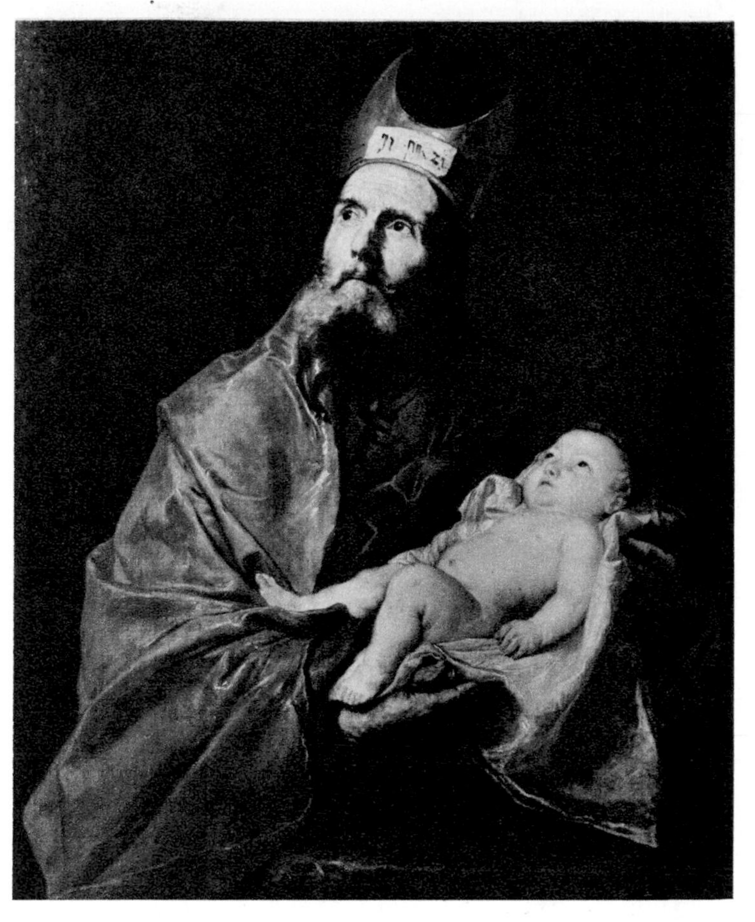

B. St. Simeon with the Christ Child, by Ribera

PLATE 99

C. The Presentation in the Temple, by Francesco Montemezzano. Formerly assigned to El Greco

A. El Greco. Philadelphia

PLATE 100

B. Titian

C. El Greco. Amsterdam

The Crucifixion

A. El Greco. Cincinnati

PLATE 101

B. El Greco. Formerly Bergamin Coll.

C. El Greco. Zuloaga Museum

A. Engraving by Louis Meunier. Mid-17th C.

PLATE 102

Panorama of Toledo

B. Recent Photograph

A. Landscape from Laocoon, by El Greco

PLATE 103

B. Plan of Toledo, by El Greco

A. View of Toledo, by El Greco

PLATE 104

B. Landscape from St. Joseph and the Christ Child, by El Greco

A. Toledo. Bridge and Royal Castle. Engraving by Louis Meunier. Mid-17th C.

PLATE 105

B. Landscape from Crucifixion by El Greco. Cincinnati

C. Detail from View of Toledo by El Greco

A. Crucifixion. Cincinnati

B. St. Martin and the Beggar. Washington, D.C.

PLATE 106

Landscape Details by El Greco

A. Landscape from St. James the Great by El Greco

PLATE 107

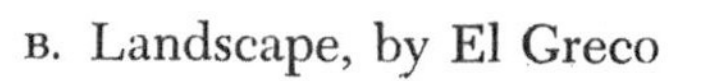

B. Landscape, by El Greco

C. Landscape from St. Andrew by El Greco

A. Design of Catafalque for Philip IV of Spain,
by Pedro Ramirez. Woodcut. Mexico. 1666

B. Design for Monument to St. Ferdinand,
by Valdes Leal. Etching. Seville. 1671

A. Design of Triumphal Arch to Philip IV of Spain, by Rubens. Engraving. Early 17th C.

PLATE 109

B. Washington Square. 1889

Temporary Triumphal Arches in New York

C. Madison Square. 1918

ΠΑΠΙΣΚΩΙ ΚΟΣΜ ΣΤΕ
ΤΗΣ ΠΟΛΕΩΣ ΚΑΙ ΣΤΡΑ
ΚΑΙ ΠΤΟΛΕΜ ΒΑΣΙΛΙΚΩ
ΚΑΙ ΤΟΙΣ ΓΡΑΦΟΥΣΙ ΤΟΝ ΝΟ
ΠΑΡΑ ΑΡΜΙΥΣΙΟΣ ΤΟΥ ΠΕ
ΣΙΡΙΟΣ ΤΟΥ ΠΕΤΟΣΙΡΙΟΣ Μ
ΤΡΟΣ ΔΙΔΥΜΗΣ ΤΗΣ ΑΙΟΛ
ΤΩΝ ΑΠΟ ΚΩΜΗΣ ΦΘΩ
ΤΗΣ ΠΡΟΣ ΑΠΗΛΙΩΤΗΝ
ΑΠΕΓΡΑΨΑΜΗΝ ΤΩΙ ΕΝ
ΤΩΤΙ ΙΒ L ΝΕΡΩΝΟ
ΚΛΑΥΔΙΟΥ ΚΑΙΣΑΡΟΣ
ΣΕΒΑΣΤΟΥ ΓΕΡΜΑΝΙΚΟ
ΑΥΤΟΚΡΑΤΟΡΟΣ ΠΕΡΙ ΤΗ
ΑΥΤΗΝ ΦΘΩΧΙΝ ΑΠΟ
ΝΗΣ ΩΝ ΕΧΩ ΘΡΕΜΜΑΤΩ
ΑΡΝΑΣ ΔΕΚΑΔΥΟ ΚΑΙ Ν
ΑΠΟΓΡΑΦΟΜΑΙ ΤΟ ΥΣ ΕΠ
ΓΟΝΟΤΑΣ ΕΙΣ ΤΗΝ ΕΝΕΣ
ΔΕΥΤΕΡΑΝ ΑΠΟΓΡΑΦΗΝ
ΓΟΝΗΣ ΤΩΝ ΑΥΤΩΝ ΘΡΕΜ
ΤΩΝ ΑΡΝΑΣ ΕΠΤΑ ΓΙΝΟΝ
ΑΡΝΕΣ ΕΠΤΑ ΚΑΙ ΟΜΝ
ΝΕΡΩΝΑ ΚΛΑΥΔΙΟΝ ΚΑΙΣΑ
ΣΕΒΑΣΤΟΝ ΓΕΡΜΑΝΙΚΟΝ
ΑΥΤΟΚΡΑΤΟΡΑ ΜΗ ΥΠΕΣΤ

A. Papyrus with Two Types of Greek Script. 1st C.

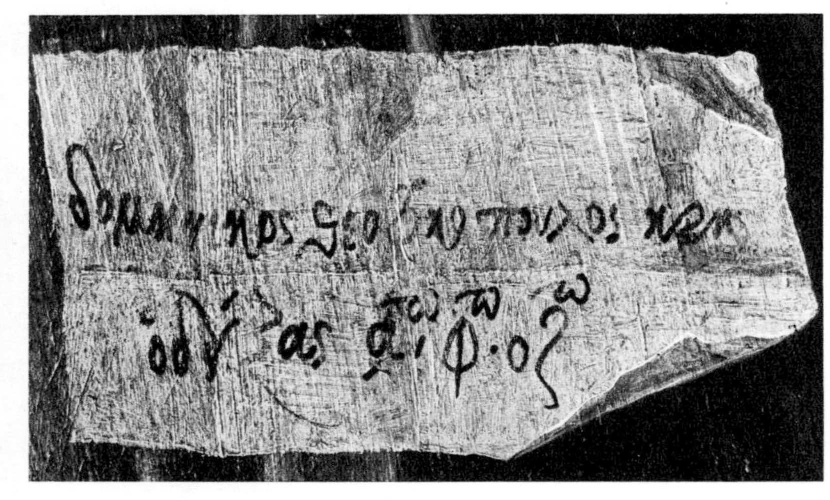

B. Three Signatures of El Greco

ΑΠΟΚΑΛΥΨΙΣ.

ρῶν τοὺς λόγους τῆς προφητείας τοῦ βιβλίου τούτου. Καὶ ἐγὼ Ἰωάννης ὁ βλέπων ταῦτα, καὶ ἀκούων. καὶ ὅτε ἤκουσα καὶ ἔβλεψα, ἔπεσα προσκυνῆ-
σαι ἔμπροσθεν τῶν ποδῶν τοῦ ἀγγέλου τοῦ δεικνύοντός
μοι ταῦτα, καὶ λέγει μοι, ὅρα μή. σύνδουλός σου
γάρ εἰμι, καὶ τῶν ἀδελφῶν σου προφητῶν, καὶ τῶν
τηρούντων τοὺς λόγους τοῦ βιβλίου τούτου. τῷ θεῷ
προσκύνησον. καὶ λέγει μοι, Μὴ σφραγίσῃς τοὺς λόγους τῆς προφητείας τοῦ βιβλίου τούτου. ὅτι ὁ και-
ρὸς ἐγγύς ἐστιν. Ὁ ἀδικῶν ἀδικησάτω ἔτι, καὶ ὁ ῥυ-
πῶν, ῥυπωσάτω ἔτι. καὶ ὁ δίκαιος δικαιωθήτω ἔ-
τι, καὶ ὁ ἅγιος ἁγιασθήτω ἔτι. καὶ ἰδοὺ ἔρχομαι
ταχὺ, καὶ ὁ μισθός μου μετ' ἐμοῦ, ἀποδοῦναι ἑκά-
στῳ, ὡς τὸ ἔργον αὐτοῦ ἔσται. Ἐγώ εἰμι τὸ α καὶ τὸ
ω, ἀρχὴ, καὶ τέλος ὁ πρῶτος, καὶ ἔσχατος. Μακά-
ριοι οἱ ποιοῦντες τὰς ἐντολὰς αὐτοῦ, ἵνα ἔσται ἡ ἐ-
ξουσία αὐτῶν ἐπὶ τὸ ξύλον τῆς ζωῆς. καὶ τοῖς πυλῶ-
σιν εἰσέλθωσιν εἰς τὴν πόλιν. Ἔξω δὲ οἱ κύνες καὶ οἱ
φαρμακοὶ, καὶ πόρνοι, καὶ οἱ φονεῖς, καὶ οἱ εἰδωλο-
λάτραι, καὶ πᾶς ὁ φιλῶν, καὶ ποιῶν ψεῦδος. Ἐγὼ
ἸΗΣΟΥΣ ἔπεμψα τὸν ἄγγελόν μου μαρτυρῆσαι
ὑμῖν ταῦτα ταῖς ἐκκλησίαις. ἐγώ εἰμι ῥίζα, καὶ τὸ
γένος τοῦ δαβὶδ, ὁ ἀστὴρ λαμπρὸς, καὶ ὀρθρινός. καὶ
τὸ πνεῦμα καὶ ἡ νύμφη, λέγουσιν, ἐλθέ. καὶ ὁ ἀκούων
εἰπάτω, ἐλθέ. καὶ ὁ διψῶν, ἐλθέτω. καὶ ὁ θέλων,
λαμβανέτω τὸ ὕδωρ ζωῆς δωρεάν. Συμμαρτυροῦ-
μαι γὰρ παντὶ ἀκούοντι τοὺς λόγους προφητείας τοῦ
βιβλίου τούτου. ἐάν τις ἐπιθῇ πρὸς ταῦτα, ἐπι-
θήσει ὁ θεὸς ἐπ' αὐτὸν τὰς πληγὰς τὰς γεγραμ-
μένας ἐν βιβλίῳ τούτῳ, καὶ ἐάν τις ἀφαιρῇ ἀπὸ τῶν
λόγων βίβλου τῆς προφητείας ταύτης. ἀφαιρή-
σει ὁ θεὸς τὸ μέρος αὐτοῦ ἀπὸ βίβλου ζωῆς, καὶ τῆς πό-
λεως ἁγίας, καὶ τῶν γεγραμμένων ἐν βιβλίῳ τούτῳ. λέγει ὁ μαρτυρῶν ταῦτα. ναὶ ἔρχομαι
ταχὺ, ἀμήν. Ναὶ, ἔρχου κύριε Ἰη-
σοῦ. ἡ χάρις τοῦ κυρίου ἡμῶν
ἸΗΣΟΥ ΧΡΙΣΤΟΥ
μετὰ πάντων ὑ-
μῶν. ἀμήν.

ΤΕΛΟΣ.

* aα bβ cγ dδ eε fζ gη hθ iι kκ lλ mμ nν oξ pο qπ rρ ſς tτ uυ xφ yχ zψ &ω aaαα bbββ ccγγ ddδδ eeεε ffζζ ggηη hhθθ iiιι kkκκ llλλ mmμμ nnνν ooξξ ppοο qqππ rrρρ ſſςς ttττ uuυυ xxφφ yyχχ zzψψ &&ωω aaaααα bbbβββ cccγγγ dddδδδ eeeεεε fffζζζ gggηηη hhhθθθ. Omnes ſunt quaterniones, præter * aaαα cccγγγ duerniones, uuυυ ternionem, & ddδδ rrρρ hhhθθθ quinterniones.

VENETIIS IN AEDIB.
ALDI ET ANDREAE
SOCERI. MD XVIII
MENSE FEBRVA
RIO.

C. Last Pages of Early Printed Greek Bible. Venice. 1518

A. Standard of the Doge Francesco Morosini. Venice. Late 17th C.

PLATE 111

B. Unretouched Greek Text, from The Adoration by El Greco

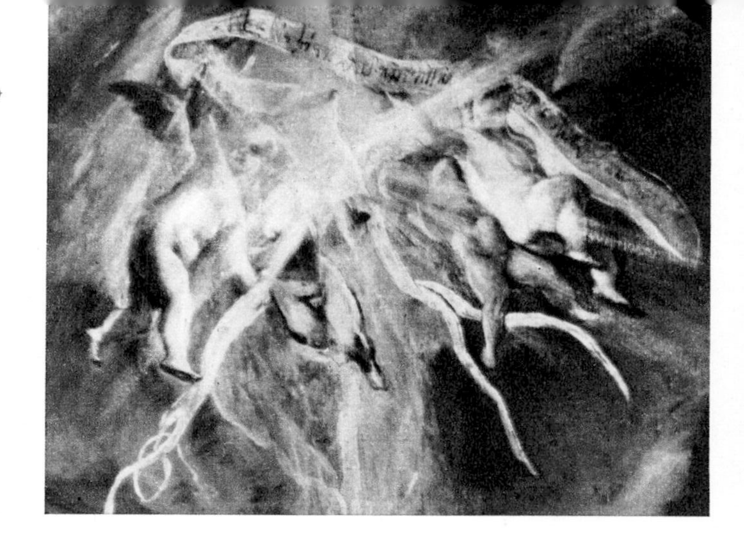

C. Signature in Greek on the Doge's Standard

D. El Greco's Signature, from Christ Bearing the Cross

E. Serpent holding El Greco's Signature, from the Martyrdom of St. Mauritius

A. The Twelve Feasts
(Pl. 70 A)

B. The Burning Bush
(Pl. 64 C)

C. St. Haralambos
(Pl. 65 A)

D. St. James the Great
(Pl. 107 A)

E. St. Andrew
(Pl. 107 C)

F. St. Joseph
(Pl. 104 B)

G. The Cleansing of the Temple
(Pl. 108)

H. The Crucifixion
(Pl. 59 B)

In the last decades Pál Kelemen, an outstanding authority on art, has devoted his energy to the art of the Western Hemisphere. His *Medieval American Art*, published in 1943, is now in its fourth edition. This magnificent study of the art of the Americas before Columbus filled a gap long felt by museums and scholars, and remains the definitive work in its field.

Subsequently *Baroque and Rococo in Latin America* appeared, based on five surveys in Latin America and repeated visits to the Iberian Peninsula. This volume reveals, as no other book, the dazzling and original developments that occurred in the transplanting of these styles to the New World.

Mr. Kelemen, long an American citizen, was born in Budapest and came to the United States in 1932 on what was planned as a short visit. He has published other works in various fields and contributed numerous articles to art magazines and scholarly reviews both in this country and abroad. He has lectured widely in the Old and New Worlds, at times in the service of the State Department.

The present volume is the result of many years of study and travel — notably visits to the monasteries of Mount Athos, a personal study of recently cleaned Byzantine wall paintings in Istanbul, and two weeks on the island of Crete, photographing murals and icons unknown outside their district.

His book constitutes a revisit to the various sites, recording observations of a subjective nature and offering historical parallels and pertinent episodes that enrich the background against which the artist moved. The result is a revealing character study of an enigmatic personality.

The MEDITERRANEAN WORLD of EL GRECO
at the end of the 16th century
Scale 0 300 Miles
0 500 Km.
by Erwin Raisz, 1961
TOLEDO
to Madrid
ROMAN RUINS
ALCAZAR
Pte de Alcantara
S. DOMINGO
REYES
S. TOME
Pta d. SOL
AYUNTAMIENTO
CATHEDRAL
Pte de S. Martin
CASA GRECO
REI DON PEDRO
R. Tagus
Ferry
Bay of Biscay
ATLANTIC OCEAN
FRANCE
Loire R.
Nantes
Tours
Orleans
Bordeaux
Toulouse
Lyon
Rhone R.
Marseilles
Rhine
THE EMPI
Turin
Como
Milan
Venezia
Venice
Po R.
Bologna
Genoa
Florence
Pisa
TUSCANY
Rome
Grottaferrata
CORSICA
to Genoa
SARDINIA
PYRENEES
Leon
Duero
Valladolid
Ebro
ARAGON
Zaragoza
CASTILE
Escorial
Madrid
Tagus R.
TOLEDO
CATALONIA
Barcelona
PORTUGAL
Lisbon
SPAIN
Valencia
BALEARES
Palma
ANDALUSIA
Seville
Granada
Cadiz
Strait of Gibraltar
MEDITERRAN
Algiers
Tunis
Oran (to Spain)
MOROCCO
BARBARY STATES
Monrea
ATHOS
Xerxes Canal
Akrotirion Pen.
Pyrgos
Wall
Chromitsa
Chilandari
Vatopedi
Pantokratoros
Stavronikita
Dochiariou
Xenophontos
Panteleimon
Xeropotamou
Karyes
Iviron
Daphne
Simopetra
Grigoriou
Dionysiou
Mt Athos
6670
Lavra
Karoulia
Kapsokalyvia
CRETE
50 Mi.
50 Km.
Gonia
Khania
Suida Bay
Rethymnon
CANDIA (Heraclion)
Potamies
Dracona
Mt Ida
Sfakion
Komitades
Platonias
Valsamonero
Kritsá
Lyna
15°
10°
5° W.
0°
5°
10°
50°
45°
40°
35°
30°